T.N. RAJARATTINAM PILLAI

T.N. RAJARATTINAM PILLAI

Charisma, Caste Rivalry and the Contested Past in South Indian Music

Terada Yoshitaka

SPEAKING TIGER BOOKS LLP
125A, Ground Floor, Shahpur Jat, near Asiad Village,
New Delhi 110049

First published by Speaking Tiger Books in association with the
Roja Muthiah Research Library, 2023

ISBN 978-93-5447-475-0
eISBN 978-93-5447-476-7

10 9 8 7 6 5 4 3 2 1

Contents

Foreword

NĀGASVARAM AND *TAVIL* are the ancient temple musical instruments in South India, generally indicated as *Periya Mēlam*. The word *'mēlam'* is a Sanskrit one, meaning 'joining' or 'assembly'. Generally, it indicates a troupe. *Nāgasvaram*, the wind instrument, has been in existence right from the early ages though with different names at various stages. In ancient Tamil works, it has been mentioned as *Peru Vangiyam*. *Vangiyam* means wind instrument, and *Peru Vangiyam* is *nāgasvaram*. There was (and still is) confusion as to the correct name of this aerophone, whether it is *nāgasvaram* or *nadasvaram* or *nayanam* and so on. The ancient works on music in Sanskrit clearly say that it is *nāgasvaram*. 'Nayanam' is a corrupt usage of the word *'nagachinnam'* found in some Tamil works. It is the main partner of the troupe. *Nāgasvaram* is the *marga darsi* (the one who shows the way) for raga elaboration in vocal and other instrumental music of the Carnatic system.

There were many greats in the field of *nāgasvaram* playing such as Keezhvelur 'Saveri' Kandasvami Pillai, Mannargudi Chinna Pakkiri Pillai, Tirumarugal Natesa Pillai and Tirucherai Muthukrishna Pillai and a few others. But since the beginning of the twentieth century, Tiruvavaduturai Rajarattinam Pillai has been hailed fittingly as another name for the *nāgasvaram* because he surpassed many of his contemporaries in handling the instrument.

As rightly pointed out by the author of this book, 'while scholarship does exist, it has never been allowed a status equal to that of Brahmans.' This is common and found even today in the case of vocalists and other instrumentalists. Generally, people accept what Brahmans say or write as true. For example, many have written and propagated that Sri Tyagaraja, one among the Trinity of Carnatic music, was born in Tiruvarur without any authentic evidence for the statement. My book on the birthplace of Sri Tyagaraja clearly denies this unauthentic statement by presenting evidence to prove that he was born in Tiruvaiyaru.

With regard to Rajarattinam Pillai, his father was Kuppusvami Pillai and his mother was Govindammal, who was not a devadasi. He was christened as Balasubramaniam at birth. Once, the great *nāgasvaram* maestro Mannargudi Chinna Pakkiri Pillai came to meet his colleague, Tirumarugal Natesa Pillai. He, on seeing the young child's eyes, suggested to Natesa Pillai that the boy should be named Rajarattinam and thus the name came to be used. TNR learnt music from Tirukkodikaval Krishna Iyer. For about five years he gave vocal recitals in duet with his sister, Dayalu Ammal, and for another two years with Tiruppamburam Svaminatha Pillai, who later became a great flutist. On the advice of the pontiff of the local *mutt*, he began to learn to play the *nāgasvaram*, with initial lessons from Markandam Pillai. Later, he became the disciple of Ammachatram Kannusvami Pillai, the great Tavil *vidvan*. Kannusvami Pillai was adept in playing the *nāgasvaram*, *jalatarangam* and *dholak*. He was a great composer too. TNR had never, not even once, told me that he learnt from Maratturai Vaidyanatha Iyer, who later came to be known as Konerirajapuram Vaidyanatha Iyer. On the other hand, Vaidyanatha Iyer had learnt music from the *nāgasvaram* *vidvan*, Konerirajapuram Vaidyalingam Pillai, a distant relative of Rajarattinam Pillai's.

Apart from the local *mutt*, TNR's first *nāgasvaram* recital was at llayanarvelur for the Kumbhabhishekam of the Sri Subramanya Swami temple, constructed by Saradambal, a devadasi and the first woman Harikatha artist. Here also, many Brahmans in their usual way, asserted that it was Sarasvati Bai who was the first woman Harikatha artist! Saradambal performed Harikatha during the wedding celebrations of Rajarattinam Pillai. Tumilan's statement that Rajarattinam Pillai played during the wedding of my own father, Needamangalam Minakshisundaram Pillai is not true, since my father's diaries clearly show that it was only Mannargudi Chinna Pakkiri Pillai and Vazhuvur Muthuveer Pillai (*tavil*) who did so.

For the Independence Day celebrations held in Delhi on 15 August 1947, Rajarattinam Pillai and a representative of the Tiruvavaduturai *mutt* were sent to Delhi by the pontiff of the *mutt*, and also my father, to accompany TNR. I was fortunate to be taken along with my father to witness him perform.

Every temple in Tamilnadu had its own traditional repertoire to be followed by every *nāgasvaram vidvan*, both for daily rituals and for the festival days. The *nāgasvaram* artist, after the Mallari, cannot play any raga for elaboration according to his wish because every temple has a certain specific tradition. The repertoire followed in the Tiruvarur temple is different from that of the other temples. In the Chidambaram Nataraja temple, there is a norm as to what raga should be played on what occasion. This is strictly followed even today. After Mallari, the raga specified for that day should be played throughout. Be it the *pallavi* or the *rakti*, should be only in that same raga. There is a strict rule that no composition, whatever it may be, should not be played throughout. Only when the deity reaches the eastern *gopura* (a large pyramidal tower over the entrance gate to a temple precinct) after its procession across the four streets, some selected composition may be played at the Tatti Sutru Mandapam. This must be strictly followed.

Band sets were used during marriage processions in the bygone days. Of course, the Nadamuni set was very popular and the main artist, Balaraman, was of an extremely high standard and the most sought after. Tanjavur Mahadeva Nattuvanar was the son of Sivanandam (one among the Tanjavur Quartet) and the father-in-law of Pandanallur Minakshisundaram Pillai. Mukhaveena was the supportive instrument in Bharatanatyam recitals in earlier days. When Mukhaveena players were not available to take part in Bharatanatyam recitals, Mahadeva Nattuvanar engaged Kodandi (Kodandaraman) of the famous Nani-Kodandi clarionet duo, who lived in Rani Vaikkal Lane, Tanjavur. By the way, the nattuvanar also learnt to play that instrument.

Madurai M.S. Ponnutayi was, no doubt, a highly talented *nāgasvaram* artist. But, the very first woman *Periya Mēḷam* troupe was that of Tanjavur Ramu Ammal. She was the main *nāgasvaram* player in that ensemble and Tanjavur Pakkiri Ammal and Tanjavur Kalyani played on the *tavil*. These *nāgasvaram* players were trained by Tanjavur A.K. Raju Naidu (paternal uncle of the clarionet maestro, A.K.C. Natarajan) and the *tavil* players were trained by Keezhvelur Ratnam Pillai, a resident of Tanjavur.

Tiruvavaduturai Rajarattinam Pillai, the greatest among the *nāgasvaram vidvans*, naturally had his own whims and fancies. He cropped his hair, draped shervanis and wore pants. He fought for equal treatment to *nāgasvaram* artists at par with the vocalists and the Brahman artists. He was the only artist to demand a platform to be arranged for his troupe to play. For a procession, he must be provided with a platform, that too, on a lorry. Leave aside all these, the important thing to remember is that he was able to play a raga for many hours, fully with imagination. Even when he repeated the same raga on the next day, it would be splendour anew with his extraordinary imagination.

Terada Yoshitaka, a Japanese scholar, has taken so many pains to collect information about *nāgasvaram* in general and highlighting the greatness of Tiruvavaduturai Rajarattinam Pillai, and share it with readers in this book. It is extremely strenuous to collect such a vast range of details about a *vidvan* and Terada has done it successfully. I would say this work is an encyclopaedia, which will be useful for future researchers as it is an outstanding history of two musical instruments. I heartily congratulate Terada for his endeavour.

Roja Muthiah Research Library, Chennai and Speaking Tiger Books, New Delhi have come forward to publish this rare and precious work and my hearty good wishes to them. I also suggest that they should bring out many more such worthy works.

Dr. B.M. Sundaram
Musicologist

A portrait photo of Rajarattinam Pillai taken during his performance tour to Malaysia (Photo courtesy: A. Sarangarajan).

Preface

THIS BOOK WOULD never have seen the light of day without the continuing encouragement of G. Sundar of the Roja Muthiah Research Library and his journalist colleague, Anitha Pottamkulam, who, to my good fortune, found some merit in my work on South Indian music and society. During my last visit to Chennai in January 2020, they came to meet me with a proposal to publish a book based on my dissertation, written almost three decades ago. While immensely flattered, I was a bit apprehensive at first about publishing such an outdated work, but discussing the possibility with them I was transported to the wondrous world of *Periya Mēḷam* musicians in which I had once been deeply immersed during my doctoral research from the mid-1980s through the early 1990s. The sights, sounds, smells and feel of the places I visited as well as the verve, humour, joys and frustration of the people I interacted with, all came rushing to life and gripped me. Brought back in time to my youthful days, I found it deeply satisfying to recapture the exhilaration of being in the field, discovering something new and challenging my limits every day, a feeling which had been dormant for long but never forgotten. By the time the meeting was over, I was completely sold on the idea of reliving my formative years, through preparing this book.

After finishing my dissertation in 1992 and writing several articles based on my doctoral research, I ventured into activities unrelated to India. These have consumed much of my time and energy since then. I have, however, continued to make a short visit almost every year to South India, to carry out smaller projects, but nothing substantial.

In preparing this work, I was fortunate to have the help of Kamini Mahadevan, whose scrupulous editing made it considerably more readable and consistent. Needless to say, all the remaining shortcomings are mine alone. On principle, I decided not to attempt any major structural revisions and only to correct the obvious mistakes, to make minor changes for better readability and to consolidate the list of references. I have occasionally added information and references which I came across after the original essays were written.

*

Apart from film music, the genre of instrumental music known as *Periya Mēlam*, featuring the double-reed aerophone (*nāgasvaram*) and the double-headed drum (*tavil*), is perhaps the most familiar and widely performed in South India. The importance of *Periya Mēlam* derives not only from its geographical spread, but also from the role it plays in the religious and social life of South Indian Hindus.

I was initiated to this music quite by chance, when I came across an LP recording of it at the University of Washington's Music Library in the early 1980s. I was captivated by the powerful and seemingly unstoppable sounds, its unusual rhythms and oscillations, and it piqued my curiosity: who plays and listens to this intense music and at what occasions? The record jacket had a brief note that emphasized its importance at temples and weddings, but my library search found virtually no information on the tradition beyond the liner notes. So I began my quest with a very simple question. Why has a musical tradition of religious and social importance in South India been neglected by Indian musicologists and non-Indian ethnomusicologists alike? This was not my primary concern while I was carrying out my research. On reflection, however, I believe that my dissertation was an attempt to understand this situation.

Early on in my fieldwork, I discovered both musicians and connoisseurs unanimously believed that the golden era of the *Periya Mēlam* tradition was already over and much of the traditional performance practice had been lost or was on the verge of disappearance. I decided then to reconstruct the older practice by interviewing senior musicians and through historic sound recordings and written accounts, in addition to documenting the current practice through participant observation. In the process of gathering information, I gradually realized that one particular *nāgasvaram* musician not only represented its past glory but was also instrumental for major changes during his lifetime: T.N. Rajarattinam Pillai (1898-1956). He was a highly charismatic musician whose impact has been pervasive and decisive among the practitioners and patrons of South Indian music, both during his lifetime and thereafter.

For my dissertation, I set two objectives. The first was to provide a detailed ethnographic account of *Periya Mēḷam*, which was lacking in the existing literature, viz., its instruments, the instrumentation of the ensemble, the performance contexts, and the practitioners of this tradition, besides some of the important changes which presumably occurred in the twentieth century. My second aim was to situate the diverse interpretations of T.N. Rajarattinam Pillai in the context of caste rivalry between Brahmans, *Isai Vēḷāḷars* and *Maruttuvars*. The Brahmans have been the most important patrons for *Periya Mēḷam* music, whereas most of the practitioners are from the non-Brahman *Isai Vēḷāḷar* and *Maruttuvar* communities. Through an analysis of the multiple interpretations of this charismatic musician, I also attempted to illuminate some aspects of caste-based power relations in South Indian music culture.

The recent history of South Indian music culture is characterized by the hegemony of the Brahman musicians and patrons, and in which non-Brahman musicians are effectively sidelined. The existing public discourses on South Indian music culture are advanced generally from a Brahman perspective, largely due to the Brahman monopoly of music scholarship and journalism. Given the historical importance of non-Brahman musicians, particularly of the *Isai Vēḷāḷar*, and their musical heritage, the increasing Brahman domination of music has created an atmosphere of ambivalence and conflict.

During my dissertation project, the number of people who extended their assistance to me is countless. When I arrived in Madras in March 1986, I had no contact with any *nāgasvaram* musicians. My academic advisor in India, T.S. Parthasarathy (then secretary at the Music Academy), placed me under the tutelage of Mambalam M.K.S. Palanisamy, a well-known musician in Madras, who played for all domestic rituals at the Parthasarathy's household. I took lessons from him for about eleven months. Although (and despite my objections) he insisted on coming to my place because of a lack of space and excessive distractions in his residence, housing many families, in Mambalam, in Madras, I had frequent opportunities to observe him and his ensemble perform at both temple and domestic rituals. Through Palanisamy, I met many of his relatives, accompanists, colleagues, and patrons. I also travelled with his ensemble outside of Madras.

Although I had planned to study with only one teacher throughout my stay in India, my discipleship with Palanisamy ended unexpectedly. The hospitalization of one of his sons as well as his tight performance schedule made it impossible for Palanisamy to continue teaching me. After consulting some connoisseurs of *nāgasvaram* music, I went to study with Tiruvarur S. Latchappa Pillai, because by that time I had interviewed him twice and I was impressed by his knowledge. I studied with him at his house for about five months, with lessons thrice a week.

Circumstances may have dictated the selection of my teachers, but studying with two teachers of distinct caste affiliations and ages turned out to be critical for formulating the main thesis in my dissertation. Palanisamy was in his early forties, and belonged to a *jāti* (caste group) whose primary occupation was barbering. He was attached to a temple in his neighbourhood and in good demand for domestic functions. Tiruvarur S. Latchappa Pillai, then in his late fifties, came from the jāti of musicians from Tanjavur district and had been teaching *nāgasvaram* at the Government College of Music since 1973. Latchappa's was a distinguished family of *nāgasvaram* musicians in Tiruvarur, considered the most important centre of the temple tradition of *nāgasvaram* playing. Because of Latchappa's solid reputation among musicians in Tanjavur district, for his personal integrity and excellence in teaching, my discipleship with him immensely facilitated my field research there. I made frequent trips to Tanjavur district throughout my stay in South India. The places I visited in this district include Kilvelur, Kumbakonam, Mayiladuthurai, Nagapattinam, Narasingampettai, Sikkal, Sirkazhi, Tandaracheri, Tanjavur, Tiruppungur, Tiruvaiyaru, Tiruvarur, Tiruvavadudurai, and Vaitheeswaran Koil (Map 3). I also visited places outside of Madras and Tanjavur district for conducting interviews and observing performances, including Chidambaram, Srirangam, Tiruchirappalli, Kanchipuram and Madurai in Tamil Nadu, Bangalore, Mangalore, Melkote, and Mysore in Karnataka, and Guruvayur, Trichur, and Trivandrum in Kerala (Map 1). Except for Guruvayur, Mangalore, Melkote, and Mysore, I visited all the places mentioned above on more than one occasion.

The observations and analyses in the book are based primarily upon the information I gathered from my own formal interviews and a variety of less formalized contacts with musicians and patrons. The list of primary individuals whom I consulted, with or without formal interviews, is provided in Appendix 1. Although painfully aware of my limited proficiency in Tamil, I decided to conduct most interviews by myself, without an interpreter, for fear that the caste and other affiliation of the interpreter would significantly alter the content of information given by the interviewees. Sometimes, those who accompanied me to the interviewees, if they were conversant in English, acted as casual interpreters whenever I needed help. In such cases, I tried to contact the same individuals later on when they were on their own.

With the permission of the interviewees, I recorded many of these formal interviews both to compensate for my limited language skills and to save time from writing everything down on the spot. I was aware of problems with recording interviews, such as the loss of candour and the distortion of information provided by the interviewee, but the decision to record interviews proved to be unexpectedly beneficial for this study. It provided a basis for sorting out the correlation between the types of information and the degree of the interviewees' desire for anonymity. A few interviewees flatly refused to have their interviews recorded, and others allowed it on the condition that the recording would be strictly for my use. The majority of interviewees graciously accepted the request, but in the course of the interview they would often asked me to turn off my tape recorder whenever the topic turned too sensitive. Yet others gave me additional, and often the most valuable information, after the interview. Nevertheless, due to the sensitive nature of topics raised in the interviews with the artists and other contacts, I have in many instances concealed the source of the information. I have done so not only when I was specifically requested not to reveal their identity, but also whenever I regarded its revelation as detrimental to the reputation or political standing of those who courageously shared their perceptions with me.

*

Even in producing a book as modest as this one, the number of people to whom I am indebted for their assistance and encouragement is overwhelming. During the course of my graduate studies, I was fortunate to get acquainted with many great scholars and individuals. Their presence has not only been a basis for my intellectual orientation, but also a source of inspiration and encouragement. First of all, my deepest gratitude is due to Daniel Neuman, my chief advisor, at the University of Washington. With his own ground-breaking work on *Hindustani* music culture, he not only inspired me to take up the subject for my dissertation, but guided me to overcome obstacles towards developing a mere idea into a study. I would also like to thank the members of my supervisory committee consisting of Lorraine Sakata, Ter Ellingson, Christopher Waterman, Barbara Lundquist, and Harold Schiffman, all of whom extended invaluable guidance when it was needed most.

Robert Garfias, who founded the ethnomusicology department at the University of Washington in 1962, impressed me with his encyclopaedic knowledge of the world's music cultures and sensibility toward local communities. Without his invitation to T. Brinda to teach in Seattle, my involvement in Indian culture may not have happened at all. At an early stage of my interest in Indian music, Douglas Knight patiently taught me how to appreciate the rhythmic principles in performance of South Indian music, which was crucial for my continued involvement in it. Kishibe Shigeo continuously encouraged me, although I was never his student in the strict sense of the term. He might have been moved to take interest in a Japanese student studying Indian music in North America, which was a rarity back then. His sincerity in scholarship and strict discipline were exemplary and a model to follow.

Many of my friends and colleagues have given me invaluable moral support during the dissertation project. For their constant friendship and support, I thank Usopay Cadar, Danongan Kalanduyan, Sakaba Junko, David Bilski, Kay Norton, Michael Monhart, R. Vasu, Rosario Perez, Michael Nixon, and Gayathri Kassebaum. I am particularly grateful to the last three, in addition to Kathryn Hansen, T. Sankaran, B.M. Sundaram, and Richard Wolf, for reading parts of the manuscript at different stages of completion, and offering invaluable suggestions. R. Vasu's generosity and patience in helping me with translations of Tamil manuscripts is also greatly appreciated.

While in India, I was fortunate to work with so many caring and competent persons. Above all, my gratitude belongs to the musicians who generously, and often courageously, shared their experiences and insights with me. I particularly thank my two *nāgasvaram* teachers, Mambalam M.K.S. Palanisamy and Tiruvarur S. Latchappa Pillai for their enormous patience and for sharing their life with me. The sustained contact with these two teachers, their extended families, and their accompanists has given me invaluable insights into the life of *Periya Mēḷam* musicians. Their dedication to music and warm hospitality were two sources of inspiration in continuing my fieldwork.

Without T. Brinda (Brindamma), I would never have ventured into South Indian music. It was my good fortune that she was a visiting artist at the University of Washington's Department of Ethnomusicology in 1977-8, when I joined as an undergraduate student. I took rudimentary lessons in vocal music, with great difficulty. I eventually learnt the *vīṇa* while I was doing my doctoral research in Tamil Nadu in 1986-7, although my frequent trips outside Madras made me less than a good student. I consider Brinda's occasional house concerts, at her one-storied house in Besant Nagar, as certainly the most extraordinary musical experiences of my life. Her son Sounder and his wife Jamuna, who lived with Brindamma, also need a special mention for their warm hospitality and timely advice. I would take the local bus from Tiruvanmiyur (then the southern end of Madras city), where I was staying, to Besant Nagar every other day to have a lesson with her in the morning. I still remember walking down the street to the nearby bus stop after the lesson, humming the song just learned that day, jubilant because of its sheer beauty.

Many scholars and connoisseurs of music also helped me in many different ways. T.S. Parthasarathy went well beyond his brief as my official academic advisor in India. His encouragement to my project and introduction to other individuals are acknowledged here with gratitude. T. Sankaran, formerly with All India Radio and Tamil Isai Sangam, and a cousin of my *guru*, T. Brinda, spent so much time, despite his failing health, in answering my questions and directing me to other individuals. B.M. Sundaram, a musicologist and the authority on *Periya Mēḷam* music, generously shared many years of his research with me, including a number of illuminating anecdotes and rare photographs of musicians. I will never forget an all-night discussion at his hideaway in Tanjavur. The perspectives of both Sankaran and Sundaram on caste issues in music culture reverberate throughout my studies.

I am extremely grateful for Sri Nagasvaravali, an organization to promote *Periya Mēḷam* music. N. Sivaramakrishnan and

Tanjavur Upendran, its co-founders along with B.M. Sundaram, kindly shared the membership list with names and contact addresses and personally introduced me to many musicians. Upendran, a noted *mridangam* player, also initiated me into music culture of a locale, outside of Madras, and accompanied me to meet a legendary *nagasvaram* musician, Chidambaram Radhakrishna Pillai.

L.S. Rajagopalan graciously shared his extensive knowledge on performing arts in Kerala, as well as translated the Malayalam manuscripts, and without M.K.K. Nayar's help I could not have acquired the permission to enter the Padmanabhaswamy Temple in Trivandrum (Tiruvananthapuram). L. Isaac and K. Malarvizhi kindly made their respective unpublished dissertations available to me. The passion and dedication of all the individuals mentioned above to music was extraordinary and a source of inspiration.

I also acknowledge Sampradaya, the research and archival organization in Madras, for making available to me previously recorded interviews and performances of *Periya Mēļam* musicians. It was a sheer delight to work with the officers there, Meera Rammohan, Parimala Rao, and A. Jayanthi, all of whom shared with me a keen interest in South Indian music. I also thank A. Sarangarajan, a filmmaker and a close associate of Sampradaya, for sharing his audiovisual documentation of *Periya Mēļam* music and other related genres.

My heartfelt thanks are due to K. Narayanan of the Government Arts College (Madras) for teaching me Tamil with humour and helping me translate Tamil manuscripts as well as providing a home-away-from-home during my 1988-9 research. Geeta Nayar of the United States-India Educational Foundation (USEFI) also extended assistance and friendship way beyond the call of duty.

While I was in India, several American scholars were also conducting doctoral fieldwork on topics related to performing arts in Tamil Nadu, including Matthew Harp Allen, David Nelson and Marcie Frishman. Although direct contact with them was minimal then, their subsequent work and the communications with them has inspired me greatly.

*

On the suggestions of Sundar and Kamini, I decided to include in the book three essays written after the dissertation. For the projects on which these essays are based, I am indebted to a new set of individuals in addition to those mentioned already, who contributed to my work greatly. S.V. Rajadurai (Mano) and V. Geetha deserve a special mention. Scholars of amazing intelligence and social commitment, they have been a great source of inspiration as well as joy. I thank them for stimulating conversations over the years, and Mano, in particular, for sharing his meticulously researched manuscript on *Tamil Isai*. I was introduced to Mano and Geetha by S. Ramakrishnan, the founder of Cre-A Publishers in Madras, who encouraged me over the years. The wide range and depth of his interests was astonishing and dinner at his place was always filled with delightful surprises and discoveries. Sadly, he passed away of Covid in November 2020.

Achuth Raman became my research assistant in 1998, when he was still a doctoral student at the University of Madras. He has assisted me in virtually all the projects that I have done since then. His skills are, indeed, admirable. Sharing the joy and agony of the demanding field trips with me, he has become a trusted friend and colleague. Among the many trips we made together, a visit to the former home of T.N. Rajarattinam Pillai in Tiruvavadudurai is unforgettable.

The project on nostalgia (Annexure 1) was a logical and natural extention of a theme upon which I merely touched in my dissertation. Inspired by a new set of readings on anthropology and cultural studies, I tried to foreground the importance of social memory in general and narrative strategies in particular when one studies South Indian music culture. An earlier version of the essay was presented at the Annual Conference of the Society for Ethnomusicology (SEM), held in Bellevue, Washington in the USA (1992).

The project on *Tamil Isai* (Annexure 2) was also an extension of my dissertation project. Rajarattinalm Pillai was widely recognized as a supporter of the *Tamil Isai* movement but I did not have enough understanding of the movement to contexualize his role, whether actual or symbolic, at the time of writing the dissertation. It was my privilege to interview committed scholars and cultural workers including V. Anaimuttu, N. Arunachalam, B. Balasubramanian, Theodore Baskaran, K. Kaliyappan, Pon. Kothandaraman, Madurai G.S. Mani, P. Muthukumarasamy, Nandini Ramani, Periyar Dasan, L.P.K. Ramanathan Chettiar, N. Ramanathan, Somasudara Desikar, Suguna Varadachary, V.P.K. Sundaram, and Tiruppanburam Shanmukasundaram. An earlier version of the essay on *Tamil Isai* was presented at the bi-annual World Conference of the International Council for Traditional Music (ICTM) in Hiroshima, Japan (1999) and at the Annual Conference of the Society for Ethnomusicology (SEM) in Toronto, Canada (2000). A special thanks is due to T. Viswanathan, who gave me detailed feedback on the paper, which was invaluable in revising it.

The project on the globalisation of South Indian music and dance (Annexure 3) called for multi-sited research. In the UK, T.L. Kothandapani and T.L. Sitalakshmi, the son and daughter of my *nāgasvaram guru* T.S. Latchappa Pillai, who had both migrated to the UK, introduced me to their circle of musicians and dancers in London. It was a joyous experience to work with my teacher's family members halfway across the globe. In Canada, Sudharshan Duraiyappah ushered me into an extremely active dance culture among Sri Lankan Tamils in the greater Toronto area in which he is an active participant. Interviews with Hari Krishnan, Srividya Natarajan and members of InDANCE group illuminated the interplay between artistic creativity and social change. Lata Pada and members of Sampradaya Dance Academy graciously allowed me to interview them and participate in their rehearsals and performances. Joanna de Souza and her students at Chhandam Dance Company granted me a spirited group interview. Neeharika Tummala, in particular, shared with me her on-the-ground experiences on the intergroup social dynamics within the diasporic South Indian community. In India, interviews with Cleveland, V.V. Sundaram and R. Sundar were crucial in my understanding of the global flow of South Indian music and dance.

In Japan, I have been a member of the Center for South Asian Studies (formerly Center for Contemporary India Area Studies) at the National Museum of Ethnology since 2010. I thank Mio Minoru, its director, and the members of the centre for their useful comments on my work. I also had a small study group on the globalisation of Indian music and dance in 2011-14. Sharing the research findings on the various networks of musicians of South Asian descent with Tamori Masakazu and Takemura Yoshiaki was highly beneficial for a comparative perspective on my own case study.

More recently, Gopalan Ravindran has been a source of inspiration with his committed social activism. He has repeatedly provided venues to share my work outside of India, with Indian audiences, which I wish to pursue more vigorously for inter-regional and inter-cultural communication. S. Subbiah has kindly kept me informed of latest social changes in India which I might miss otherwise. Finally, I thank Anna Morcom and Davesh Soneji for their timely invitation to participate in a webinar, *The Arduous Art: Caste, History and Politics of 'Classical' Dance and Music in South India* in January 2021. The public discussion on such a topic was unthinkable when I was doing research in the 1980s and 1990s, and it gave me great pleasure to be among a group of courageous performers and academics who are engaged in cultural work against the erasure of history, and for social justice. This event not only gave me a much-needed push to complete this book but also inspired me to envisage what I could engage in going forward.

*

My work on South Indian music has been generously funded by US and Japanese organizations. For my dissertation project and an essay on nostalgia (Annexure 1), I received the Junior Fellowship from the American Institute for Indian Studies (AIIS). Pappu Venugopala Rao, the director of its Southern Region and a noted musicologist, provided timely assistance. Shubha Chaudhuri, the director of the AIIS Archives and Research Center for Ethnomusicology (ARCE), provided many years of encouragement and friendship. Some of my field recordings were deposited at the archives. My project on *Tamiḻ Isai* (Annexure 2) was supported by the National Museum of Ethnology (Director-General's Leadership Grant), my home institution for many years (1996-2020), while research on the globalization of South Indian music and dance (Annexure 3) was made possible with two research grants from the Japan Society for the Promotion of Science (JSPS, #20520722 and #23401051) and another from the Center for Contemporary India Area Studies at the National Museum of Ethnology. I acknowledge their generous support with deep gratitude.

*

Time waits for no one. To my great regret, many individuals who extended me help have passed away. I can never thank them in person and show them my completed work, which I hope will contribute to a better understanding of the art forms they passionately cared about. I hereby acknowledge their generosity and kindness by listing their names: M.K.K. Nayar (1920-87), Kottur Rajarattinam Pillai (1932-87), Injikkudi Kandasami Pillai (1932-88), Tirucherai Kalyanasundaram Pillai (1918-89), Tanjavur Ramasami Pillai (1913-90), Tanjavur Upendran (1934-1991), A.V. Narayanappa (1912-94), Tirucherai T.V.S. Sivasubramanya Pillai (1927-94), Madurai M.P.N. Sethuraman (1928-2000), T. Sankaran (1906-2000), T. Viswanathan (1927-2002), V.P.K. Sundaram (1915-2003), Kishibe Shigeo (1912-2005), T.S. Parthasarathy (1912-2006), L.S. Rajagopalan (1922-2008), Madurai Ponnuthay (1929-2012), Periyar Dasan (1949-2013), N. Arunachalam (1940-2016), Kadri Gopalnath (1950-2019), P. Muthukumarasamy (1932-2019), Gayathri Kassebaum (1938-2020), S. Ramakrishnan (1947-2020), and V. Anaimuttu (1925-2021).

On a more personal note, my deepest gratitude is due to my late parents who gave me the necessary understanding, moral support and financial assistance. Looking back, my father Masao's independent style and my mother Makiko's *joie de vivre* have instilled in me an outlook of which I am immensely proud. My only regret is that I could not fulfil my mother's dream to visit India to see why it has become my second home.

The demise of one's gurus is devastating by all accounts but it is also a moment for utmost appreciation. I cannot find words to express my gratitude for my opportunities to study under them: T. Brinda (1912-96) and Tiruvarur S. Latchappa Pillai (1930-2013). Their music and their views on music became the very foundation of my work and my respect for them as musicians and individuals only grew as time passed. I dedicate this humble work to their memory.

ONE

Introduction

THIS STUDY IS an exploration of South Indian music culture through an analysis of one charismatic musician, Tiruvavadudurai N. Rajarattinam Pillai.[1] Born in 1898, Rajarattinam Pillai was a master of the *nāgasvaram* (double-reed aerophone). The rationale for selecting this particular individual musician for an analysis of South Indian music culture at large rests on his unique position in the matrix of complex relationships between the two important music traditions in South India: *Periya Mēḷam* and *Karnāṭak* music. *Periya Mēḷam* refers to a genre of instrumental music which accompanies temple and domestic rituals and festivities, and features *nāgasvaram* and *tavil* (accompanying drum), whereas *Karnāṭak* music is a tradition of 'classical' music performed most prominently in concert halls. Roughly put, these two traditions are based upon the same fundamental melodic (*rāgam*) and rhythmic (*tāḷam*) principles and share much of repertoire, yet they are separated from each other in the medium of performance and performance contexts.

The similarity of these two traditions derives from their historical connection. On one hand, *Periya Mēḷam* music was one of the three major sources from which *Karnāṭak* music developed (Seetha 1981; L'Armand and L'Armand 1983). The other sources were the tradition of devotional singing, which later evolved into court vocal music (Simon 1984) and *Ciṉṉa Mēḷam*, the tradition of temple dance and its accompaniment (Higgins 1973). *Periya Mēḷam* ('Big [drum] ensemble') and *Ciṉṉa Mēḷam* ('Small [drum] ensemble') were the two major musico-ritual traditions at temples until the latter was transformed into a concert-hall art form in the early decades of the twentieth century. The manner of extensive improvisation, and aspects of the complex rhythmic formula known as *kaṇakku* (calculation) are two major legacies of *Periya Mēḷam* music in *Karnāṭak* music today.

On the other hand, *Periya Mēḷam* musicians expanded their repertoire of compositions by learning from practitioners of *Karnāṭak* music as the emphasis of repertoire in *Periya Mēḷam* music shifted dramatically from extensive improvisation to compositions in the second half of the twentieth century. Many compositions which are identified as representative of *Karnāṭak* music, such as those by the famed three saint-composers of the early nineteenth century (Tyagaraja, 1767-1847, Muttusvami Diksitar, 1776-1835 and Syama Sastri, 1762-1827), figure prominently in the repertoire of *Periya Mēḷam* music today. Despite the interaction and consequent similarity between the two traditions, *Periya Mēḷam* music has kept a separate identity from *Karnāṭak* music, maintaining the original ritual settings as its primary performance context, instead of being completely absorbed into the latter.

Although *Periya Mēḷam* music is sometimes considered part of, or a specialized sphere of, *Karnāṭak* music due to mutually shared features, *Karnāṭak* music refers in this study to the classical music tradition, excepting *Periya Mēḷam* music. As many of the aspects of Rajarattinam Pillai's music and personality, which are spoken of with a rich variety of interpretation by musicians and patrons, are, in fact, those of fundamental importance in *Karnāṭak* music and *Periya Mēḷam* music alike, he may be regarded figuratively as a point of intersection of such aspects.

The purpose of the present study is threefold. First, I provide an ethnographic description of the contemporary *Periya Mēḷam* music, focusing upon its performance practice and major contexts as well as the *jāti* affiliation of its practitioners. Despite its acknowledged socio-cultural importance in South Indian culture and the growing interest and scholarship on *Karnāṭak* music in ethnomusicology, the tradition of *Periya Mēḷam* music has been neither fully recognized for its musical importance nor adequately studied. The present study is designed to address this lacuna, and to contribute to the increased understanding of the complex dynamics of South Indian music culture. Second, through the analysis of Rajarattinam Pillai as a symbol, I will document the multiple interpretations of South Indian classical music traditions. By revealing the discrepancies in perceptions, I point out how disproportionate and uncritical reliance on the dominant discourse has resulted in a monolithic and incomplete understanding of a music culture. Third, the present work can be perceived as a case study to illuminate the highly complex and sensitive issue of power relations and conflict between Brahman musicians/patrons and non-Brahman musicians. I argue that the ambivalent relationship between *Periya Mēḷam* musicians and Brahmans is a result of a multitude of factors, ranging from the urbanization and caste-based socio-political movements in South India to the mutual dependence between these two groups. In so doing, I wish to argue for the efficacy of investigating the discrepancy or 'gulf' between conflicting historical interpretations for a more comprehensive and nuanced analysis of the dynamics of music culture, and ultimately aim to propose an unexplored analytical model in the study of music culture in general (Ginzburg 1980: xiii-xxvi).

In contrast to the conventional history of Western classical music, the role of individual musicians or composers of exceptional merit has not been given much emphasis in ethnomusicological writings as a primary subject of inquiry.[2] Perhaps the most obvious reason for this lack of interest is that the identity of individuals in the past, be they composers or musicians, is unknown or unimportant in many music cultures investigated by ethnomusicologists. Yet, this neglect may also be partially attributed to an adverse reaction to the excessive reliance on individual achievements and the theory of genius in conventional Western music history, and partly due to the anthropological emphasis on cultures and societies in ethnomusicology.[3] Additionally, sensitive to the elitism manifest in conventional musicology, ethnomusicologists have been loyal to a conviction that they investigate the music of a people, hence to highlight individual achievements could be counterproductive. As a result, individual musicians and composers are, if discussed at all, typically treated as reflections of particular traditions, or prominent as embodiments of public musical sensibility.[4]

Does this general lack of attention to individual musicians mean that separate studies focusing on them have no legitimacy in ethnomusicological inquiry at all? Can we learn something significant about a music culture without succumbing to the elitist conception of the role of exceptional individuals in music culture? An answer to these questions may well rest on how effectively a study of individual musicians can be related to an analysis of the dynamics of a music culture as a whole.

If a wide range of the social constructs of a music culture are to be examined by analyzing an individual musician, not every individual can be a worthwhile subject due to an imminent danger of placing excessive emphasis on, thus over-interpreting, a particular person as a symbol for the sake of explanation. Instead, primary candidates for this type of inquiry are charismatic individuals who, as Geertz (1968: 54-7) suggests, embody or sum up the situation to which they belong. The rationale of selecting a charismatic individual rests on the fundamental assumption that a number of seemingly disparate factors of a culture are invested in the symbol of a particular charismatic individual in a highly condensed manner, and that the dynamics of the culture can be effectively investigated through the analysis of the individual.

Since the 1980s, a few new approaches have been advanced in the study of individuals in ethno-musicological writings. After producing works on the structure of music (1987), Stephen Slawek turned his attention to a cultural role played by his teacher Ravi Shankar (1991). In this, he examines Shankar's role as a mediator between the traditional music culture and modern cultural spheres. Charles Capwell, on the other hand, evaluates an important, but virtually forgotten, individual

(Sourindro Mohun Tagore) in the history of *Hindustani* (North Indian classical) music (1991). Drawing upon the concept of marginality by Robert Park (1928) and the socio-psychological work on colonialism by Ashis Nandy (1983), Capwell traces Tagore's vision of Indian music to the psychological complexity of the colonized. Kimi Coaldrake (1989) attempts to explain the rise and fall of the Japanese *Onna Gidayu* genre through the life of a charismatic musician, Ayanosuke, as its pivotal figure. Her analysis that Ayanosuke as an anomaly within the tradition could become a catalyst for a change and an innovator parallels the concern of this study (1989: 160).

In contrast to all of the works mentioned above which propose a new interpretation of the individual's role in the history of a respective tradition, my aim in this study is to examine different interpretations of a charismatic musician, or rather, how the nature and degree of the differences reflect the power relations among musicians and patrons. I ultimately argue that Rajarattinam Pillai's charisma sustains a dialectic relationship to both *Karnāṭak* music and *Periya Mēḷam* music to the extent that his charisma is simultaneously constituted by and emerges out of the conditions of these two traditions. Therefore, Rajarattinam Pillai as a symbol serves as a mirror which reflects both the socio-economic conditions surrounding South Indian music culture in general and the ambiguous and conflicting relationship between practitioners of these two musical traditions. The existence of and the interrelationship between incongruent perspectives of South Indian classical music tradition will form the basis for my discussion regarding the power relations between groups of musicians and patrons.

While I consider Rajarattinam Pillai to be the most fruitful subject of analysis for investigating the relationship between *Karnāṭak* music and *Periya Mēḷam* music traditions, he is by no means the only musician who deserves such treatment. In fact, numerous musicians and composers whose attributes (caste, gender, musical specialization, etc.) solicit multiple interpretations could be the potential candidates for analyzing power relations manifest in different layers of South Indian music culture. Several such individuals will be mentioned in the course of this study in conjunction with the analysis of Rajarattinam Pillai as a polysemic symbol.

Public discourse concerning South Indian music culture is generally advanced from a Brahman perspective. Although the Brahman perspective is in itself of prime importance because of the prominence of Brahmans in South Indian music culture, such a view appears to be biased due to the exclusion of the non-Brahman perspectives.[5] The Brahman orientation of public discourse may be partly a result of their domination of music scholarship and journalism, through which their view has been authenticated and their advantageous position justified,[6] and of what may be termed the dynamics of domination in which the perspectives of subordinate groups are excluded or left unarticulated at least in public domains of communication.

Foreign researchers have also been unable to escape from, and thus may have unwittingly reinforced, the Brahman perspective. Their inclination toward the Brahman perspective is ironic in the light of their professed neutrality based on the absence of innate sectarian affiliations which might significantly affect the orientations of native scholars.[7] The situation may be partly due to the greater accessibility of Brahman musicians and scholars and the literature reflecting their views, and partly because of the presumed difficulty in working with non-Brahman musicians. This difficulty is derived not so much from their marginal command of Western languages and alleged lack of sophistication in behaviour, which may be itself a case of imposed stereotype, as it is from their complex consciousness as political and economic subordinates to Brahmans which results in a lack of candor in publicly expressing conflicting views.

In addition, written history, which is the culmination of dominant public discourse and a domain dominated by Brahman scholarship, has been given a position of authenticity and authority, while oral history is neglected as being unreliable, or, worse, accused of being a groundless fabrication, unless it is recorded, and thus authenticated, by authoritative scholars.[8]

Existing literature, both native and foreign, on South Indian music history tends toward reconstruction of the chronology of events as true and authentic social facts and to establish causal relationships to explain how they happened as they did.[9] By framing written discourses as authoritative history, Brahmans have filtered the multiple interpretations which exist regarding South Indian music to establish the tradition that reinforces a sense of their identity in relation to others.

Yet, to equate written history with the Brahmans' perspective, and oral history with that of thenon-Brahmans is misleading. The power structure within the community of Brahman musicians and scholars often emphasizes a certain perspective in literature, therefore suppressing others. A division often expressed among Brahmans is the one between musicians and scholars, and a good number of musicians feel their views are not justly represented in the writings of music scholars. On the other hand, while non-Brahman scholarship does exist, it has never been allowed a status equal to that of Brahmans.[10]

My interest in the discourse of subordinate groups has been initiated by, and has a certain directional affinity with, social history, which emerged to challenge the so-called Rankean paradigm of the nineteenth century historiography with its primary, and often exclusive, interest in politico-economic aspects of the ruling classes of society (Braudel 1980; Fukui 1987). Although sharing the dissatisfaction with the absence of subordinate groups in existing literature, the premises of the present study differs from those of social history in two important ways. The first difference concerns the subject of analysis. While social history has focused its attention on the culture of ordinary people, the subject of the present study is not the masses of a society, but the particular subordinate groups of musicians within the musical system broadly defined as classical. The second difference concerns the purpose of investigation. Despite its original intention to treat a society at large holistically, social history often limits itself to descriptions of the masses, to the exclusion of the ruling class which had previously been the only subject for academic endeavor (Takimura 1988: 30-1). The chief emphasis of the present study, in contrast, lies in the interactive relationship between dominant and subordinate cultures, with a belief that studying one to the exclusion of the other will generate insufficient understanding of either. My aim in the present study is not to accumulate evidence to evaluate or judge the validity of each interpretation of Rajarattinam Pillai, but rather assess the reasons and nature of the difference in interpretation.

Although the immediate scope of the present study is limited to an analysis of one particular musician (Rajarattinam Pillai) as a symbol, the decision to focus on this subject was influenced, if not made, by my interest in the much larger issue of domination and conflict in South Indian music culture. The political and economic rivalry between Brahmans and non-Brahmans in South Indian society has been frequently investigated by historians.[11] One of the major issues concerns the interpretation of the theme of Brahman domination in South Indian society. Since what was perceived as Brahman dominance was the primary target of the non-Brahman movement, interpretations of the phenomenon have often been politically motivated. At least three different interpretations are discernible. The first is the view that the rise of Brahmans as the dominant group in South Indian society occurred gradually in the last several centuries (Visswanathan 1982). The second is that Brahmans were prominent throughout history, but became decisively dominant in the nineteenth century by means of their economic prosperity derived from their association with the British Raj (Subramaniam 1969). The third is the denial of the theme of Brahman dominance altogether. The protagonists of this view interpret the emergence of the theme as political propaganda put forth by power-seeking non-Brahmans and emphasize utopian harmony among different castes in the past (S. Sundararajan 1989).

The non-Brahman movement was triggered by the high-ranking and economically prominent non-Brahmans' dissatisfaction with the disproportionate presence in governmental positions and higher education of Brahmans.[12] Although it has been argued that an essentially economic conflict became highly politicized and disguised as a caste issue (Washbrook 1989), there is no denying that through various social and political movements, the division between Brahmans and non-Brahmans has been crystallized as the major social division in South India. This is particularly true in Madras and the Tanjavur district, the two areas on which the present study focuses, because the political conflict between Brahmans and non-Brahmans was seen most prominently in these two areas.[13]

Although the relationship between Brahmans and non-Brahmans in music culture cannot be separate from this larger and more encompassing social division, the former must not be seen as a mere extension or reflection of the latter. The uniqueness of the Brahman/non-Brahman relationship in music derives from its reversed numerical constitution: Brahmans comprise the majority of patrons of classical music traditions (both *Karnāṭak* music and *Periya Mēḷam* music) and the majority of *Karnāṭak* musicians, while they constitute only a fraction of the entire population. As I will explain later in detail, the primary source of Brahman/non-Brahman conflict in music derived from Brahmans' successful attempts to characterize the classical music tradition as having a wider validity, while it was nurtured both by Brahman and non-Brahman musicians for the maintenance of their identity.

If Brahmans have established, as I argue, hegemonic control over non-Brahman musicians, it has been achieved and maintained not through single, but multiple channels. Although closely related to each other, these channels as sites of contestation for hegemonic control may be divided into two large categories: public and private. The private domain includes individualized communications, such as gossip, rumors, and myths through private conversations and discipleship, whereas the public domain consists of a variety of institutions (music associations, universities, music schools, publications, mass media, etc.) as well as of publicly displayed rituals and functions. While the private domain is the main focus of this study, it is important to remember that analysis of the private domain is possible only in relation to the public domain, as James Scott (1990) examines with remarkable detail.[14]

A few words are in order concerning the key concepts used in this study. The concept of hegemony serves as a general orientation as to how the multiple interpretations of one particular musician can be related to the domination of Brahmans over non-Brahman musicians. In this study, I do not use the term hegemony as political rule or domination, as is commonly defined in political parlance. Instead, I follow the concept of cultural hegemony initiated by Antonio Gramsci, who established the theoretical foundation for analyzing the general relations between culture and power, and developed and crystallized by those influenced by Gramsci, most notably Raymond Williams and Stuart Hall.

Stuart Hall's definition of hegemony, summarizing Gramsci's fragmented writings, serves as a starting point.

> 'Hegemony' is in operation when the dominant class fractions not only dominate but *direct*—lead: when they not only possess the power to coerce but actively organize so as to command and win the consent of the subordinated classes to their continuing sway. (Hall 1977: 332; italics by author).

The novelty of the concept of hegemony lies in the recognition that 'winning the consent' of the subordinate class is indispensable in achieving hegemony. This perspective not only distances itself from the tendency in conventional Marxism to overemphasize economic factors, but it also commands a redefinition or widening of the meaning of ideology, since the manipulation of ideology is, for Gramsci and his followers, a means to 'win the consent.' Gramsci regarded ideology as 'the terrain on which men move, acquire consciousness of their position, struggle etc.' to establish hegemony (1971: 377; also Mouffe 1979: 185-6; Turton and Tanabe 1984: 5). An important notion related to this definition is that hegemony is conceptualized not as a system or structure, but as a process. Therefore, hegemony is never total or complete as a form of domination. It is, to quote Raymond Williams, 'continually to be renewed, recreated, defended and modified' as well as to be 'resisted, limited, altered, and challenged.' (1977: 112). These notions surrounding the concept of hegemony provide the basis for investigating the nature of domination and conflict in South Indian music through the analysis of the ways that an ideology is appropriated. I consider the issue of the multiple interpretations of Rajarattinam Pillai to be a potent case of ideological contestation, and therefore to be a subject beneficial for the understanding of power relations, an important aspect of South Indian music culture in general.

Seeing hegemony as a dynamic process allows one to understand the complexity and multifaceted nature of the relationship between dominant and subordinate cultures, and thus to discard the simplistic top-down model of domination. As Jackson Lears aptly describes, the line between these two resembles 'a permeable membrane' (1985: 574). While the dominant ideology persuasively and forcefully penetrates the consciousness of subordinate groups, the possibility of creating counter-hegemony always exists no matter how small that possibility might be. Moreover, the perspectives of the subordinate groups sometimes affect, or become part of, dominant ideology, though they are sanitized or attenuated, thus not imminently dangerous to the maintenance of the hegemony. The relationship between dominant and subordinate groups is constantly negotiated and redefined through discursive practice with each group trying to maintain or better its respective position. Furthermore, Gramsci has advanced a notion of 'contradictory consciousness' which refers to a complex mental state mixing accommodation and resistance among subordinate groups. It permits us to see how the members of subordinate groups may discursively participate in maintaining a symbolic universe, even if it serves to legitimate their being dominated (Gramsci 1971: 333).[15]

A vexing problem of a study on power relations in general derives from the penetration of dominant ideology into the consciousness of the subordinate. Since 'every language contains the elements of a conception of the world and a culture' (Gramsci 1971: 325), the available vocabulary and modes of expression themselves are imbued with dominant ideology. Given this decisiveness of the ideological penetration into subordinate consciousness, establishing a discursive practice totally independent of dominant ideology is impossible. In this sense, it is an inescapable irony that an ideology has to be decoded by means of a language which derives from it. Nevertheless, it is also true that a different set of vocabulary is sometimes maintained parallel to that associated with dominant ideology. In fact, the linguistic strategies employed to legitimize the dominant ideology serve as ideal analytical units for studying the nature of power relations and the limitations of dominant ideology.

The present study deals with the discursive analysis of Rajarattinam Pillai as a symbol.[16] The notion of discourse shifts our epistemological and methodological presupposition from a positivistic orientation to a semiotic one. Turning the focus of attention from evidence documenting the fact of what a musician actually did or accomplished to a representation of imagined fact which emphasizes ways in which a musician's presumed achievements and personality are interpreted and represented is one way to shift the lens through which an individual is examined. This shift opens a way to study a music culture by means of the analysis of a specific individual musician on the basis of the different interpretations surrounding him/her as a symbol. In other words, what is attended to is not the musical achievements and outwardly observable social implications of a charismatic individual as such, but the construction and usage of the discursive practice surrounding that individual.

Although Gramsci himself identified the role of language in reinforcing domination, thus anticipating Foucaultian emphasis on discursive practice (Lears 1985: 569), it was a

Marxist linguist-philosopher, V.N. Volosinov of the famed Bakhtin circle, who first analyzed in detail the inseparableness of ideology and symbol (sign in Volosinov).[17] For Volosinov, language use or discourse itself is 'the ideological phenomenon par excellence' and thus a locus of class and group conflict (1973: 13). Squarely criticizing the Sausurrean concept of language as 'absolute objectivism', he emphasized that utterance is wholly a product of social interaction, and therefore cannot be reduced to an autonomous individual self (Volosinov 1973: 45-63). An important implication of Volosinov's work is that language exists in, or constitutes, asymmetries of power, either in the form of patriarchal domination or economic dependency (Stam 1989: 8). Given the political nature inherent in language, the discourse on Rajarattinam Pillai as a symbol becomes a site of ideological contestation, where a multitude of social 'accents' are accorded to it.[18]

Investigating the multiple interpretations of a past musician by contemporary musicians and patrons, the present study deals not only with a discursive strategy of legitimation by means of symbol using, but also with the issue of representation of the past. For this purpose, the present study employs as a device for inquiry a notion of social memory, which can be defined as the entirety of socially constructed and structured knowledge of the past. The relevance of the analytical notion of social memory for this study lies in its ability to connect the use of the past with political practice. It directs our attention not to the past but to the past-present relation, and more specifically to the ways in which the past is used to account for, justify, understand, or criticize the present (McDonald 1986).

What is crucial, therefore, about the nature of the past is its inevitable ideological mediation. The content of what is presented as having really happened is determined, or even created, through the process of interpretation and representation, and, as Hobsbawm and Ranger (1983) so effectively demonstrate, it is never an unmediated reality. Therefore, we always need to ask, to quote Edmund Leach, 'in whose interest is it that the past should be presented to us in this way' (1990: 229).

Furthermore, according to Ana Maria Alonso (1988a: 34-5), discursive strategies are deployed by both oral and written histories to create 'effects of truth' or an illusion of unmediated reality, and to transform partiality into totality. It is important to remember that the conventional assumption described above underlies not merely a different methodology of doing historiography, but indicates a fundamental epistemological difference: it constitutes a kind of legitimation device through which a power relation is expressed and maintained. This is why certain historical representations achieve centrality whereas others are marginalized, excluded, or reworked (Popular Memory Group 1982: 207).

Social memory is produced not through dominant public discourses alone, as they are not monolithically installed nor everywhere believed, but is also constituted by subordinate discourses, regardless of how the former appears on the surface to be prominent.[19] Since, as in the case of non-Brahman musicians, the subordinate groups often have little access to, or are effectively excluded from dominant (public) discourse, even that concerning their own tradition, they are forced to depend on orally formulated social memory for their own historical vision. If the Brahman domination of music scholarship has been an important means to maintain the symbolic universe beneficial to them, non-Brahmans' competing interpretations of the past in oral and privately shared discourses can be read as a form of their resistance against Brahman dominance.[20] As Alonso characterizes it, social memory is 'a profoundly complex, active and ongoing process in which different interpretations of the past engage each other and struggle for dominance' (1988a: 51). If intimate and intricate connections exist between knowledge and power, social memory both reflects and affects the distribution and exercise of power, and is thus an important site of political conflict.[21] Given the crucial role of discursive practice in reinforcing cultural hegemony, the prominence of the Brahman discourse speaks eloquently to their domination of South Indian music culture.[22]

The discussion in succeeding chapters will proceed as follows, to facilitate the analysis of the ways in which Rajarattinam Pillai was placed at the pivotal position in South Indian music culture in the twentieth century. After a brief account of Rajarattinam Pillai's life in Chapter 2, I provide in Chapter 3 historical and morphological description relating to the instrument (*nāgasvaram*) in which Rajarattinam Pillai specialized and the ensemble in which it was found. An emphasis is placed on the aspects of the instrument and instrumentation which Rajarattinam Pillai is believed to have changed.

Chapter 4 is concerned with the delineation of the performance contexts for *Periya Mēḷam* music in which Rajarattinam Pillai performed and gained recognition. In the first section, I describe the temple rituals and festivals which constitute the original and most traditional contexts for *Periya Mēḷam* music, focusing upon its performance practice, repertoire exclusive to these contexts, and the nature of employment. Describing the discourse on the weakening performance tradition in these contexts, I try to demonstrate that such decline, which was manifested in drastic changes in repertoire, instrumentation, and hierarchy among *Periya Mēḷam* musicians, was closely related to the sociopolitical currents of the first half of the twentieth century. I analyze, in the following section, another set of traditional contexts, those surrounding domestic functions, which have become the primary source of income for *Periya Mēḷam* musicians. Rajarattinam Pillai made a fortune because of his immense popularity at such occasions and which provided the economic base for his allegedly lavish and even immoral lifestyle. In this section, I also discuss the increasing indifference among non-Brahmans in general to *Periya Mēḷam* music which has accelerated both the economic dependence on and artistic identification with Brahman patrons on the part of *Periya Mēḷam* musicians.

This enhanced the ambivalence of the position of *Periya Mēḷam* musicians, affecting their perceived relationship with Brahmans. In the third and last section, I examine the more recent performance contexts of *Periya Mēḷam* music which emerged during Rajarattinam Pillai's lifetime. They include those of concert hall recitals and radio programmes which provided the arenas for the innovations which Rajarattinam Pillai is believed to have brought to *Periya Mēḷam* music. A special emphasis is placed on the musical and social implications of these new contexts to *Periya Mēḷam* music.

Chapter 5 concerns the practitioners of *Periya Mēḷam* music who belong to several different *jātis* (caste groups), each with their distinct musical tradition and social position. I describe in the first section the *jāti* of *Isai Vēḷāḷars*, the presumed originators of *Periya Mēḷam* music, to which Rajarattinam Pillai belonged. I examine their ambivalent relationship with Brahman patrons and their unfavourable socio-economic conditions, both of which are important for the understanding of the prominence of Rajarattinam Pillai as a polysemic symbol. *Periya Mēḷam* musicians belonging to various barber *jātis* are described in the second section. I discuss the historical background for the conflict of interest between them and *Isai Vēḷāḷar* musicians, as well as Rajarattinam Pillai's connection to this conflict which is derived from his extended stay in Madras and manner of teaching. Finally, in the third section, I discuss the recent emergence of musicians belonging to *jātis* other than those described in the preceding two sections, and Rajarattinam Pillai's perceived role that contributed to their emergence. After describing each group of these musicians, I argue that the increasing prominence of these musicians has eroded the *Isai Vēḷāḷar's* previous hegemony of *Periya Mēḷam* music.

Chapter 6 advances the main argument of the present study. I first depict Rajarattinam Pillai's musical and personal attributes which contributed to the creation of charisma, as expressed by musicians and patrons, and then examine how different sets of Rajarattinam Pillai's attributes are arbitrarily chosen for manipulation by groups of musicians and patrons with varying social and musical backgrounds and motives. Based upon the previous discussion, I argue that Rajarattinam Pillai as a polysemic symbol embodies or summarizes the ambiguity and conflict in the relationship between two important musical traditions in South India.

TWO

The Life of T.N. Rajarattinam Pillai

THIS CHAPTER GIVES a brief account of the life of Rajarattinam Pillai. While the full implications of each event or attribute of his life cannot be delineated until we have the necessary contextual information that is given in succeeding chapters, a glimpse of Rajarattinam Pillai's life in the conception of musicians and patrons is a useful starting point. The description below is based upon N.R. Bhuvarahan's interview with Rajarattinam Pillai which appeared in 1942 in the Tamil weekly magazine, *Hanuman*[23] and biographical accounts by Sankaran (1961, 1981), Ellarvi (1967),[24] Nilam (1985), and Tumilan (1988)[25] as well as upon my own interviews with the practitioners and patrons of *Periya Mēḷam* music. Brief descriptions of his life and achievements by Malarvizhi (n.d.), Isaac (1964), Suttananda Baradiyar (1965), Natarajasundaram Pillai (1980), Pavadai (1980), and N. Rajagopalan (1990) are also incorporated into what follows, whenever appropriate. Although different sources agree with one another for the most part, some discrepancies do exist. These discrepancies are discussed in the main text when considered significant to the main thesis of the present study while others are indicated in the footnotes. I must emphasize that the description here is not given as empirical fact, but as the compendium of the available discourse on Rajarattinam Pillai's biographical events.

Tiruvavadudurai Natesan Rajarattinam Pillai was born in 1898 in Tiruvavadudurai, a small village in Tanjavur district (Mayiladuthurai taluk), to *Isai Vēḷāḷar* parents.[26] He was given the name Balasubramaniam. Available written accounts agree that his father, Tirumarugal Kuppusami Pillai, was a *nāgasvaram* musician of ordinary talent, who died only a few months after Rajarattinam Pillai was born, and that his mother was Govindammal (Ellarvi 1967: 97; Sankaran 1981: 290; Tumilan 1988: 12).[27] However, some *Periya Mēḷam* musicians suggest on

Figure 2-1: Tirumarugal Natesan
(Photo courtesy: B.M. Sundaram)

reflection that that Rajarattinam Pillai was born to a *dēvadāsi* (see Chapter 5) mother and her Brahman patron-husband. Although this belief may explain partly the strong patronage by some Brahman *rasikars* (connoisseurs) derived from kinship ties, it is not accepted among Brahman patrons today.

Rajarattinam Pillai was adopted when he was three by his childless maternal uncle, Tirumarugal Natesa Pillai (1874-1903), who was one of the best *nāgasvaram* players of his time (Sambamurthy 1985a: 93-5). It is said that Natesa Pillai gave his adopted son the new name of Rajarattinam. Natesa Pillai died soon afterwards, and Rajarattinam Pillai came under wings of his maternal grandfather, Tirumarugal Sivananam.[28] Rajarattinam Pillai eventually took Natesa Pillai's initial as part of his own name instead of that of his own father's, perhaps because of Natesa Pillai's fame as an extraordinary musician.[29]

Rajarattinam Pillai received much encouragement from the Tiruvavadudurai Madam (non-Brahman monastery) for learning music partly because Natesa Pillai was a musician attached to the Madam (*ādīṇa vittuvāṉ*).[30] Yet, it was another person, T.S. Ponnusami Pillai, who was responsible for Rajarattinam Pillai's musical training and specialization from the very beginning. Ponnusami Pillai was an administrator of the Madam and an enthusiastic and knowledgeable patron of classical music as was Srilasri Ambalavana Desikar (1888-1920), the head (*ādīnakarttar*) of the Tiruvavadudurai Madam, of whom he was a close associate (Tumilan 1988: 13). More importantly, Ponnusami Pillai was the patron-husband of Rajarattinam Pillai's elder sister (Dayalu), and took a special interest in Rajarattinam Pillai's development as a musician, perhaps because of this affinal relationship.[31] Dayalu was also a good singer, and Rajarattinam Pillai gave public concerts with her before switching to *nāgasvaram* (Sankaran 1981: 291; Tumilan 1988: 49). Dayalu's liaison with Ponnusami may also support the notion that she and Rajarattinam Pillai were born into a *dēvadāsi* lineage since it was rare for the daughter of a *Periya Mēlam* musician to become a *dēvadāsi*.

At five, Rajarattinam Pillai had rudimentary lessons in vocal music for about six months with a local *nāgasvaram* player (Tiruvavadudurai Markkandam Pillai) who was also attached to the Tiruvavadudurai Madam.[32] Then T.S. Ponnusami Pillai made an arrangement for Rajarattinam Pillai to study with Tirukkodikaval Krishna Iyer (1857-1913), a well-known Brahman violin player (Bhuvarahan 1987: 57).[33] Krishna Iyer was the chief *ādīna vittuvāṉ* at the Tiruvavadudurai Madam at that time, and accompanied musicians who were invited to perform there (Sambamurthy 1985a: 80-1). At nine, Rajarattinam Pillai was asked to sing for Ambalavana Desikar, who, impressed by his talent, ordered further training with Konerirajapuram Vaidyanatha Iyer (1878-1920), another Brahman musician (vocalist) of considerable repute (Visuvanadayyar 1980).[34] Shortly after studying under Vaidyanatha Iyer, Rajarattinam Pillai gave his first professional (paid) vocal concert at a wedding in Nannilam taluk.

Then, after studying *nāgasvaram* with Markkandam Pillai for about six months, Rajarattinam Pillai was sent in 1911 to Ammachattiram Kannusami Pillai (1876-1927),[35] who had been the regular *tavil* player for Tirumarugal Natesa Pillai, but who was also an excellent *nāgasvaram* player (B.M. Sundaram n.d.: 25, 1981; Tumilan 1988: 26-7).[36] While Tumilan states that Rajarattinam Pillai also studied *nāgasvaram* for one year with Kiranur Muttu Pillai, father of Kiranur Ramasami Pillai (1988: 29),[37] this part of apprenticeship is little known. The strict routine of early morning practice, for which Rajarattinam Pillai was famous, began at this early stage of training. Around 1910, Rajarattinam Pillai was appointed as a *nāgasvaram* musician (*ādīṉa vittuvāṉ*) at the Tiruvavadudurai Madam, and gave his first *nāgasvaram* performance outside of the Madam at the ten-day temple festival in Tirukkovilur for the remuneration of four hundred rupees (Bhuvarahan 1987: 59).[38]

When he was fourteen, shortly after his mother's death, Rajarattinam Pillai married his first wife Sarada, daughter of well-known merchant, Tanjai Saminada Pillai. Sarada's brother, Tanjai P.S. Venkatakrishna Pillai later became a famous Congress Party member.[39] Rajarattinam Pillai and Sarada's wedding was conducted on a grand scale in Tiruvavadudurai with financial assistance from the Madam itself. Mannargudi Chinna Pakkiri Pillai (1869-1915), one of the best *nāgasvaram* musicians of the time, performed for the ceremony. Rajarattinam Pillai, completely

Figure 2-2: Mannargudi Chinna Pakkiri as depicted in a painting in Konerirajapuram. Accompanying him on the *tavil* is Ammapet Pakkiri Pillai. (Photo courtesy: B.M. Sundaram)

absorbed in Chinna Pakkiri Pillai's performance on Saveri *rāgam*, is said to have forgotten to tie the *tāli* on Sarada, at the auspicious moment, to consecrate the marriage (Tumilan 1988: 6-9, 49). Rajarattinam Pillai himself recollects that Chinna Pakkiri Pillai asked him to play *nāgasvaram* and gave him a blessing on the second day of the wedding (Bhuvarahan 1987: 60).

The ten-day annual festival (Radasaptami Utsavam) at the Tiruvavadudurai Madam was one of the most prestigious performance contexts for *nāgasvaram* musicians. Each year most of the best players participated in this prestigious and competitive festival. Attached to the Madam, Rajarattinam Pillai was given frequent opportunities to come in contact with, and perform in competition with, the leading musicians of his time, such as Sembonnarkoyil Ramasami Pillai (1880-1923), Nagur Subbaiya Pillai, and Uraiyur Gopalasami Pillai (1876-1917) (Bhuvarahan 1987: 59). As Rangaramanuja Ayyangar recollects, Rajarattinam Pillai was already a rising star in *nāgasvaram* music in the late 1910s (1972: xi). Having performed on many prestigious occasions, his reputation was firmly established by 1930 (Tumilan 1988: 95).

After trying for several years, unsuccessfully, to have children with Sarada, Rajarattinam Pillai decided to take a second wife, Supputtayi, a girl from a well-established family of *nāgasvaram* musicians in Tirupparankunram.[40] The wedding was sumptuous with Madurai Ponnusami Pillai performing on the *nāgasvaram* for the occasion. The guests at the wedding asked Rajarattinam Pillai to play during the procession (Tumilan 1988: 78). When Supputtayi failed to

Figure 2-3: A rare photo with Pappammal, showing his jovial and burlesque side.
(Photo courtesy: Pappammal)

become pregnant, Rajarattinam Pillai married his third wife, Janakam, sister of a *nāgasvaram* musician, P.S. Sambandam Pillai. Eventually, he married his fourth wife, Pappammal, who was the sister of a *nāgasvaram* musician, Tiruvavadudurai Annamalai (Tumilan 1988: 138-40; B.M. Sundaram 1998: 20).

Unlike the case of his first four wives, Rajarattinam Pillai's encounter with his fifth and last wife was rather accidental. When he performed for a festival in Tiruchendur (Tirunelveli district), a young girl in the audience was listening to his music so intensely that he inquired about her after the performance. It is said that Rajarattinam Pillai proposed to her right then, married immediately, and they returned to Tiruvavadudurai together, much to the surprise of his other wives. She also became a disciple of Rajarattinam Pillai, and studied *nāgasvaram* (Sankaran 1981: 294; Tumilan 1988: 133).

Like many leading exponents of classical musicians who participated in films of the 1930s and 1940s, Rajarattinam Pillai acted and sang as a poet in the Tamil film, *Kāḷamēgam,* directed by Ellis R. Dungan in 1940 (Figure 2-4). The film, however, was a commercial failure, which ended Rajarattinam Pillai's career as a film star (Guy 1988/89: 71). Rajarattinam Pillai also appeared in a few films in scenes requiring a *nāgasvaram* musician, such as temple processions. One such film was *Kaviratna Kāḷidās* produced in 1936, and his name was mentioned prominently in the newspaper advertisement of the film, in fact, more prominently than those of the featured actors and actresses (Figure 2-5).[41]

Figure 2-4: A still image of the 1940 film *Kāḷamēgam* (Photo courtesy: Film News Anandan)

Figure 2-5: Newspaper Advertisement of a Film Announcing Rajarattinam Pillai's Participation (*The Hindu*, 18 September 1936)

As in the case of his own foster father, Rajarattinam Pillai had no children, although he had five wives.[42] He adopted a boy from outside of his own *jāti* of *Isai Vēḷāḷar*, and named him Sivaji. Despite Rajarattinam Pillai's attempt to teach him, Sivaji showed neither interest in nor aptitude for music. When Sivaji was eighteen, he married Hemamalini, sister of a well-known *Isai Vēḷāḷar* vocalist, Tiruvarur T.V. Namasivayam (1926-70). Sivaji's wedding was a lavish affair and conducted in the presence of many leading musicians (Tumilan 1988: 143-4) (Figure 2-6).

Rajarattinam Pillai received many titles and awards in recognition of his achievements. He especially liked the title, *Ahila Ulaha Nādasura Cakkaravartti* ('World Renowned Emperor

நிகழ்ச்சி நிரல்

30–11–54 முதல் **2–12–54** வரை இதில் கண்டுள்ள
வித்வான்களின் சங்கீதக்கச்சேரிகள் நடைபெறும்.

சங்கீத வித்வான்	அரியக்குடி	ஸ்ரீமான்	ராமாநுஜ அய்யங்கார்	அவர்கள்
,,	முசிரி	,,	சுப்பிரமணிய அய்யர்	,,
,,	மதுரை	,,	மணி அய்யர்	,,
,,		,,	G. N. பாலசுப்பிரமணிய அய்யர்	,,
,,		,,	M. M. தண்டபாணி தேசிகர்	,,
,,		,,	M. K. தியாகராஜ பாகவதர்	,,
,,		ஸ்ரீமதி	K. B. சுந்தராம்பாள் அம்மாள்	,,
பிடில் வித்வான்	கும்பகோணம்	ஸ்ரீமான்	ராஜமாணிக்கம் பிள்ளை	,,
,,	மைசூர்	,,	T. சௌடையா	,,
,,	திருவாலங்காடு	,,	N. சுந்தரேசய்யர்	,,
,,	சென்னை	,,	கோவிந்தசாமி நாயக்கர்	,,
,,	சென்னை	மாஸ்டர்	கிருஷ்ணன்	,,
,,	திருவள்ளூர்	ஸ்ரீமான்	சுப்பிரமணியம்	,,
,,	திருவிழிமிழலை	,,	சுப்பிரமணிய பிள்ளை	,,
மிருதங்க வித்வான்	பாலக்காடு	,,	மணி அய்யர்	,,
,,	பழனி	,,	சுப்பிரமணிய பிள்ளை	,,
,,	தஞ்சை	,,	ராமதாஸ் ராவ்	,,
,,	சென்னை	,,	S. V. S. நாராயணன்	,,
,,	தஞ்சை	மாஸ்டர்	T. K. மூர்த்தி	,,
கடம் வித்வான்	சென்னை	,,	வில்வாத்திரி அய்யர்	,,
,,	ஆலங்குடி	,,	ராமச்சந்திரன்	,,
கஞ்சிரா வித்வான்	மன்னார்குடி	,,	N. ஆறுமுகம் பிள்ளை	,,
முகர்சிங் வித்வான்	மன்னார்குடி	,,	நடேச பிள்ளை	,,
நாதஸ்வர வித்வான்	திருவெண்காடு	,,	T. P. சுப்பிரமணிய பிள்ளை	,,
,,	குளிக்கரை	,,	K. S. பிச்சப்பா பிள்ளை	,,
,,	காரக்குறிச்சி	,,	K. P. அருணாசலம் பிள்ளை	,,
,,	வல்லம்	,,	கிருஷ்ணன் பிள்ளை	,,
தவில் வித்வான்	திருமுக்கூடல் வாசல்	,,	முத்துகிருபிள்ளை	,,
,,	நாச்சியார்கோவில்	,,	N. P. ராகவம் பிள்ளை	,,
,,	வலங்கைமான்	,,	வெண்முககந்தரம் பிள்ளை	,,
,,	கோரநாடு	,,	கோவிந்தராஜ பிள்ளை	,,
,,	திருவெழுந்தூர்	,,	ராமதாஸ் பிள்ளை	,,

காவேரி கலர் பிரஸ், கும்பகோணம்.

Figure 2-6: The list of musicians who performed at Sivaji's three-day wedding (30 November-2 December 1954), which resembles the Who's Who in South Indian music at that time.

of *Nāgasvaram'*) given to him in the mid-1940s, on the suggestion of a Brahman connoisseur of music (Panchapakesa Iyer), after his performance at the annual festival at the Saṭṭayappar Temple in Nagapattinam. Thereafter, Rajarattinam Pillai started addressing himself with that title (or its shortened form, *Nādasura Cakkaravartti*) in his letterhead, as well as requesting others to do so (Tumilan 1988: 107-9).[43] In 1955, he became the first *nāgasvaram* musician to receive the Sangeet Natak Akademi Award (Malarvizhi n.d.: 58).

Rajarattinam Pillai was sent by the Tiruvavadudurai Madam as its delegate to the Independence Day Celebration in New Delhi in 1947 (Sankaran 1981: 297). He played *nāgasvaram* before personally handing a gift from the Madam to Jawaharlal Nehru, the first Prime Minister of India. Rajarattinam Pillai is believed to have been mistaken by Nehru for a state minister due to his dignified manner and appearance (B.M. Sundaram 1998: 8). Rajarattinam Pillai was also one of the first *nāgasvaram* musicians to perform abroad. After touring several times in Sri Lanka, he went to Malaysia in 1952 (Sankaran 1981: 296; Tumilan 1988: 147-8).[44]

After about 1950, he began to spend more time in Madras, and eventually moved there in 1954 following his differences with the Tiruvavadudurai Madam (Tumilan 1988: 153). At the very end of 1955, Rajarattinam Pillai had his first heart attack, and began to seek treatment periodically at a hospital in Madras. Many of Rajarattinam Pillai's friends donated money to help him with medical expenses.[45] Against the repeated warnings of his doctors and friends, however, Rajarattinam Pillai continued to perform actively. In between these performances, he suffered repeated heart attacks (Ellarvi 1967: 112; Sankaran 1981: 293, 297-8). His last public concert in Madras was held at the *Rasika Ranjani Sabha* in Mylapore on 1 December, followed by his last radio programme at the All India Radio Madras station the next day (Sankaran 1961: 53-4). On 12 December 1956, a day after his return from a performance (a wedding) in Alleppey (Kerala), he died of a massive heart attack at his rented house in Adayar (south Madras). His obituary was carried in all the major newspapers the following day.[46] His funeral procession in Madras was attended by a huge crowd, and his recorded music was played during the procession (Sankaran 1961: 47; Tumilan 1988: 155).[47] The first death anniversary ceremony of Rajarattinam Pillai was conducted by the South Indian Nadaswara Artists Association.

It is not difficult to gauge the popularity and importance of Rajarattinam Pillai as a symbol among musicians and patrons alike. In addition to their common perception that Rajarattinam Pillai was the best *nāgasvaram* musician of the twentieth century (or, often, of all time), his previous radio programmes continue to be re-broadcast, and his recordings continue to be released in commercial cassette tapes, more than thirty-five years after his death in 1956 (See Appendix 2). An annual function to commemorate his birth is performed by the Tamilnadu Eyal Isai Nataka Manram, a state agency of culture to protect and propagate the traditional arts of the state, and, in 1992, the DMK's cultural wing instituted an award to perpetuate the memory of Rajarattinam Pillai.

For *nāgasvaram* musicians, Rajarattinam Pillai was, and continues to be, an idol to admire and worship, and his name and image are continuously evoked in both public and private discourses. Not only did some of Rajarattinam Pillai's close associates idolize him, as his best-known disciple, Karukurichi Arunachalam, named his house as 'Rajarattina Vilasa' (Rajarattinam's Residence) (Tumilan 1988: 135) but even those who had little personal contact with Rajarattinam Pillai did

so, for example, by decorating their living room and family altar with his picture (Figure 2-7) or by naming their sons after him (Rajagopalan 1990: 225). One *nāgasvaram* musician decorated his house with pictures of three 'dignitaries' of India; Gandhi, Nehru, and Rajarattinam Pillai (Tumilan 1988: 71). After his death, Rajarattinam Pillai's portraits were commissioned in various places,

Figure 2-7: Rajarattinam Pillai's Picture Placed on a Family Altar (Nagapattinam, 1987)

வாணி விலாஸ சபா, கும்பகோணம்.

திருவுருவப்படத் திறப்பு விழா

—: அழைப்பிதழ் :—

அருகில 30—4—61 ஞாயிறன்று மாலை 4-மணிக்கு

முன்னாள் "நாதஸ்வர சக்ரவர்த்தி" திருவாவடுதுறை

திரு. T. N. இராஜரெத்தினம் பிள்ளை

அவர்களின் திருவுருவப்படத் திறப்பு விழா
நன்று நிகழப்பெறும்.

தாங்கள் வருகைதந்து சிறப்பிக்குமாறு கேட்டுக்கொள்ளப்படுகிறோம்.

Dr. T. S. சாஜன்,

கட்டணம்: ரூ. 2-00 1-50 0-50 0-25

Figure 2-8: Announcement for the Ceremony to Unviel Rajarattinam
Pillai's Portrait (Kumbakonam, 1961)

and the functions of their unveiling received much publicity (Figure 2-8). One of the very few books on music written by a *nāgasvaram* musician was dedicated to the memory of Rajarattinam Pillai, and a famous picture of Rajarattinam Pillai holding a *nāgasvaram* adorns the opening page of the book, although the author did not have a close relationship with him (Figure 2-9).

What was it that made the presence and image of Rajarattinam Pillai so popular and compelling to the musicians and patrons of his lifetime and to their contemporary counterparts alike? I will begin to explore this question in the next chapter by delineating the musical and social changes in *Periya Mēḷam* music for which he is credited.

Figure 2-9: A Well-known Portrait of Rajarattinam Pillai which Appeared in a Book on Music Theory by a *Nāgasvaram* Musician

THREE

Periya Mēḷam Music

THE FIRST HALF of the twentieth century, especially after the 1920s, witnessed the most dramatic changes in *Periya Mēḷam* music, and many important features of contemporary performance practice can be traced to these changes during this period. Not only did the period of Rajarattinam Pillai's performance career overlap that of greatest change in *Periya Mēḷam* music, he was often the focal point of them. Rajarattinam Pillai is believed to have been responsible, often single-handedly, for a number of changes, including the morphology of the instrument, the instrumentation of the *Periya Mēḷam* ensemble, and even the physical appearance of its practitioners. In this chapter, I will first describe the instruments and instrumentation of the contemporary *Periya Mēḷam* ensemble, and then discuss the changes which occurred both during and following Rajarattinam Pillai's lifetime and his perceived role in those changes.

I. INSTRUMENTS

Four different types of instruments are used in the *Periya Mēḷam* ensemble: 1) *nāgasvaram*, the double-reed aerophone that is the main instrument of the ensemble, 2) *tavil*, the double-headed drum which provides rhythmic accompaniment, 3) *tāḷam*, a pair of hand cymbals which delineates the rhythmic cycle, and 4) *srutipeṭṭi*, a bellows-pumped free-reed instrument which provides drone. A double-reed aerophone known as *ottu* was used in the past to provide the drone, but has been replaced by the *srutipeṭṭi*. This change is discussed in the next section.

1. *Nāgasvaram*

a. Construction

The *nāgasvaram* is a long double-reed aerophone with a conical bore. The body of the instrument is made of two separable parts: the main body (*uṟavu*), and the bell (*aṉaisu*). The body is made of hard wood, ideally of *āccāmaram* (a type of ebony: *diospyros ebenaster*), and has seven equidistant finger holes, while five additional holes are bored near the distal end of the pipe for tuning purposes, two on each side and one on top. The bell, often made of rosewood (*īṭṭimaram*) is attached to the distal end of the body around which a thin thread is wrapped to achieve the desired fit. The main body and the bell are further connected by a thick silk string (*kayaṟu*), which runs parallel to the body. One end of the *kayaṟu* is attached to the top end of the body which at one time was a separate piece of metal or wood, known as *mēlaṉaisu* (upper *aṉaisu*), and where several niches are carved around the pipe.

The *sīvāḷi* (reed piece) consists of a cane reed and fits over the copper staple (*keṇḍai* or *kaṇḍai*) on which it is permanently placed. Two thin rings made of coconut shell of slightly different size are placed on the staple. The diameters of these rings are made in such a way that they will rest on about one-third and two-thirds down from the top of the staple, which is a short pipe of two centimetres with its bottom slightly larger than its top part. These two rings are tied to the staple by very thin threads running around them, producing intricately patterned geometrical designs. The reed is then placed on the top ring, and

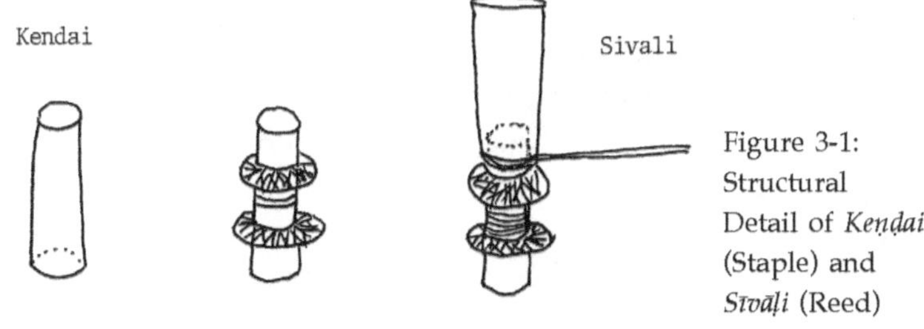

Figure 3-1: Structural Detail of *Keṇḍai* (Staple) and *Sīvāḷi* (Reed)

tied to the top part of the staple with a thicker thread (Figure 3-1). Although *sīvāḷi* means reed in the narrow sense, it also refers to the entire construction of the reed attached to the staple.

Many *sīvāḷis* are attached to the *nāgasvaram* by strings which hang down from where the *kayaṟu* is tied around the top part of the body.[48] A few ivory sticks (known as *kucci*), used for removing saliva from the reed and adjusting its interior shape, are also attached to these strings. Musicians insert a *sīvāḷi* into the top end of the body of the *nāgasvaram* each time the instrument is played, after checking the *sīvāḷi* by blowing into it. A very thin thread is wrapped around the portion of *keṇḍai* below the second ring so that the *sīvāḷi* is securely inserted into the top of the bore of the *uṟavu*. Golden coins given to *nāgasvaram* musicians as signs of appreciation by patrons are sometimes attached to the *kayaṟu* near the distal end of the instrument.

The instrument is carried in a cloth bag (*pai*) which is hung from a shoulder. In the past, only saffron-coloured bags without designs were used, but bags of a variety of colours, some with geometrical designs, are used today. When not used, the *nāgasvaram* is always hung on the wall rather than placed on the floor. This custom is said to comply with the respect due the instruments, and senior *Periya Mēḷam* musicians emphasize that the *nāgasvaram* and *tavil* were never kept or held below the level of one's navel. More practical reasons for this custom are to avoid damage from accidentally knocking down the instruments and to keep mice from gnawing at them. The measurements of the most frequently used type of *nāgasvaram* are given in Figure 3-2.

b. *Playing techniques*

A combination of fingering, tonguing and breathing techniques are utilized to play the *nāgasvaram*. Usually, three upper holes are manipulated by the three middle fingers of a player's left hand, whereas the remaining four holes by the last four fingers of the right hand. The basic fingerings of the *nāgasvaram* are shown in Figure 3-3. Although this basic fingering is identical

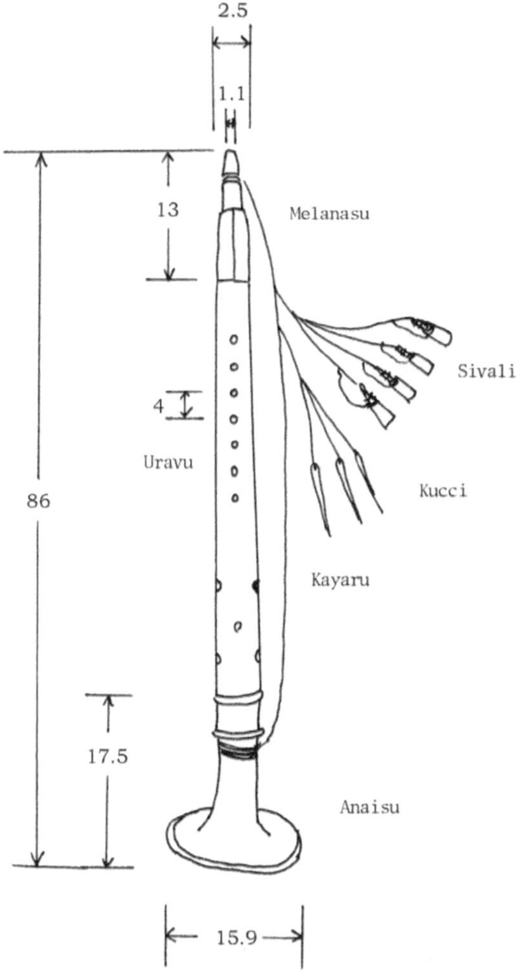

Figure 3-2: Measurements and Names of the Parts of Most Frequently
Used Type of *Nāgasvaram* (Pitch-2). Figures are in centimetres.

to that for the flute, intervals smaller than those obtained from
two adjacent finger holes are acquired differently in *nāgasvaram*.
While partial closing of the hole is used for this purpose in
flute playing, with *nāgasvaram*, small intervals are obtained by
a combination of several techniques which include changing
the shape of the oral cavity, the air pressure, and the depth of

Stayi (octave)		Mantara (low)	Matya (middle)	Tara (high)
Proximal End	Distal End			
● ● 0	0 0 0 0		*Sa*	*Sa*
● 0 0	0 0 0 0		*Ri*	*Ri*
0 0 0	0 0 0 0		*Ga*	*Ga*, *(Ma)*, *(Pa)*
● ● ●	● ● ● ●	*Ma*1 *(Ga)*	*Ma*1	
● ● ●	● ● ● 0	*Ma*2	*Ma*2	
● ● ●	● ● 0 0	*Pa*	*Pa*	
● ● ●	● 0 0 0	*Da*	*Da*	
● ● ●	0 0 0 0	*Ni*	*Ni*	

Key:
0		Finger hole (open)
●		Finger hole (close)

Sa	*Satjamam*	(c in the scale of c)
Ri	*Rishabam*	(d flat/d)
Ga	*Gandaram*	(e flat/e)
Ma1	*Sutta Mattiyamam*	(f)
Ma2	*Prati Mattiyamam*	(f sharp)
Pa	*Panjamam*	(g)
Da	*Daivadam*	(a flat/a)
Ni	*Nishadam*	(b flat/b)

Figure 3-3: Fingering Chart for *Nāgasvaram*

insertion of the reed into the mouth. Although partial closing of the hole is not used to obtain a certain sustained pitch, the technique of gradually opening and closing the hole is utilized to obtain the glide (*jāru*) from one pitch to the next in *nāgasvaram* playing. The technique of closing finger holes for a fraction of a second, known as *viraladi* (hitting with fingers), provides quick grace notes to the main pitch played.

Essentially, two blowing techniques are recognized in *nāgasvaram* playing. The technique known as *tuttukkāram* is similar to the single tonguing technique used in Western double-reed instruments. The player first touches his tongue to the reed, and then he quickly pulls it away as the air is pushed through the reed. *Ahāram* is a technique in which the tongue stays in the position detached from the reed. The movements involved in *tuttukkāram* and *ahāram* are similar to those employed in forming the syllables *tu* and *hu* respectively, and these syllables are used when the technique is explained or taught verbally. Both *tuttukkāram* and *ahāram* are played separately in scale exercise.[49] *Tuttukkāram* is always taught first, since it is easier to obtain the desired pitch than with *ahāram*.

Two distinct sound qualities can be obtained by rendering *tuttukkāram* and *ahāram*. In *tuttukkāram*, an attack [initial thrust] of sound can be obtained since the air is pushed through when the tongue comes away from the reed after a moment of non-movement of the air. As in the case of Western reed-instruments, the pitch is precisely delineated. In comparison, the passing of the air through the reed is more continuous in *ahāram*, and thus when two pitches are played consecutively, the dynamic and tonal change is more gradual than in *tuttukkāram*. The contrast of these two distinct sound qualities is utilized to delineate the text of the composition. The basic principle is that *tuttukkāram* is to be employed where syllables of the text fall, and *ahāram* otherwise. Faithful delineation of the text by means of blowing techniques is an important criterion for gauging a *nāgasvaram* player's musical knowledge and understanding, and therefore learning the text of compositions in vocal music is considered essential for *nāgasvaram* musicians. Criticism of a *nāgasvaram* musician often concerns the violation of this principle.

The playing of successive pitches in quick tempo utilizing mostly *ahāram* is called *briga*. The clear delineation of pitches in *briga* is extremely difficult, and greatly appreciated when it is executed well. The *briga* was one aspect of *nāgasvaram* playing in which Rajarattinam Pillai excelled, and musicians like to use metaphors such as 'lightning' to describe its speed.

c. *Nāgasvaram and Sīvāḷi makers*

Manufacture of the *nāgasvaram* and *sīvāḷi* involves a complicated set of procedures and requires a high degree of craftsmanship, with long years of training. They are made separately by professional craftsmen. While the *sīvāḷi* makers are *Isai Vēḷāḷars*, the most prominent group of *Periya Mēḷam* musicians (Chapter 5), the *nāgasvaram* makers belong to the separate artisan *jāti* of *Āccāri*.

Although a *nāgasvaram* can be purchased from music shops in urban centres, most musicians buy their instruments directly from the makers of their choice, and maintain a continuing relationship with them. Musicians are aware that their professions depend on the steady supply of well-crafted instruments and reeds. The *nāgasvaram* has a much shorter lifespan than the instruments of *Karnāṭak* music such as *vīṇa* and violin, which can be used for years, and sometimes even decades. Musicians agree that a *nāgasvaram* can maintain the preferred sound quality for one to two years. Many musicians express their appreciation by giving gifts or contributing to the important life-cycle rituals of the instrument and reed makers, such as their sixtieth birthday celebrations and the weddings of their children. Some *nāgasvaram* musicians send a gift of money during *Saraswati Puja*, as music disciples do to their *gurus* (teachers), and donate toward the makers' important social events. For a constant supply of high-quality *nāgasvaram* and *sīvāḷi* an amicable relationship with the maker is considered necessary.

The musician first orders the instrument by mail and the maker informs the musician when the instrument is ready to be picked up. Instruments are fragile and never sent by mail. When the musician comes to pick up his new *nāgasvaram*, he brings his own *sīvāḷi* to test the instrument. This way, if adjustments are required, they can be done prior to purchase.

One place known for producing high-quality *nāgasvarams* is Narasinganpettai, a small village near Kumbakonam (Tanjavur district), where there are three families, living adjacent, of *nāgasvaram* makers.[50] N.G.N. Renganada Accari, by far the most famous *nāgasvaram* maker for the last several decades, heads one of them. Many established *nāgasvaram* musicians buy instruments exclusively from him. Renganada Accari is proud of his association with many well-known *nāgasvaram* musicians, and their framed pictures fill the living room of his house. Because of Renganada Accari's reputation as the best *nāgasvaram* maker and the high price of his instruments, to play his *nāgasvaram* has become a status symbol among musicians. As later explained, his fame was created largely by his close association with Rajarattinam Pillai.

Figure 3-4: Renganatha Accari at work.
(Narasinganpettai, 1986)

With a few exceptions, *nāgasvaram* musicians buy *sīvāḷis* from professional *sīvāḷi* makers.[51] Unlike the *nāgasvaram*, *sīvāḷis* are usually both ordered and delivered by mail. Since *nāgasvaram* musicians consume many *sīvāḷis*, they order them by the dozens. Those with active performing careers will consume eight to ten dozen *sīvāḷis* per year. Many musicians agree that out of each dozen new *sīvāḷis* a few are not suitable for actual public performances. New *sīvāḷis* are hard, and unsuitable for performance, and musicians use them for practice for a few weeks before using them for performance. Repeated contact with saliva (*eccil*) provides the *sīvāḷi* with the desirable texture and elasticity. There are many more *sīvāḷi* makers than *nāgasvaram* makers and they are scattered all over South India. However, many established *nāgasvaram* musicians agree that the best *sīvāḷi* maker today is S. Natarajasundaram in Tiruvavadudurai, though they may not all buy his *sīvāḷis* which are considerably more expensive than others.[52]

2. *Tavil*

The *tavil* is a two-headed drum which provides complex rhythmic accompaniment to *nāgasvaram*. Its barrel-shaped body (*kaṭṭai*) is hollowed out of a solid block of hard wood such as jackwood. Female goat hide is stretched over hoops (*valai*) made of hemp or several bamboo sticks bundled together. These hoops are fastened to the body by interlaced leather thongs. The higher-pitched head (*valantalai*, 'right head') is played with one hand with *kūḍus* (thimbles made of a piece of cloth and rice paste) on four fingers,[53] whereas the lower-pitched head (*toppi*, 'hat'; or *iḍantalai*, 'left head') is played by the other hand with a light wooden stick (*kaḷi*).[54] The use of *kūḍu* for playing *tavil* began only in the 1930s,[55] and the *valantalai* is played with a bare hand even today when used for temple daily rituals. Louder and brighter sounds can be produced on the *tavil* when the player uses the *kūḍus* on his fingers rather than his bare hands. Since the relative volume of *nāgasvaram* and *tavil* musicians was, and is, a manifestation of their social hierarchy, the dissemination of the use of the *kūḍus* may be an indication of the increasing popularity and social prominence of *tavil* players in relation to *nāgasvaram* musicians.

The tuning of the *tavil* is a complex and strenuous process which involves pulling the interlaced thongs to achieve balanced tension of the drum heads. The instrument usually takes about one hour to tune. Unlike the *mridaṅgam*,[56] the *tavil* cannot be tuned during the performance, and the tuning prior to the performance has to be done with the greatest care, although the *tavil* is not tuned to any definite pitches.[57] In the 1990s, a new mechanism was invented to facilitate the tuning of the instrument. Instead of the interlacing leather thongs, thin strips of steel are individually attached to the large steel ring placed around the middle of the body of the *tavil*. One end of each *kambi* is attached to the hoop (*valai*), while the other end is connected to the steel ring with a nut and bolt. By tightening or loosening the nut, the head of the *tavil* can be easily tuned. Those who use this type of *tavil* cover the middle part of the instrument with a cloth or plastic, to hide the metal mechanism. The *kambi* are often wrapped with brightly-coloured plastic or vinyl covers which makes a sharp visual contrast to the traditional leather thongs. *Tavils* with this new tuning mechanism were used initially by younger players only, because older musicians preferred the instrument's traditional appearance, but it has completely overtaken the instruments with leather thongs now.

3. *Tāḷam*

The *tāḷam* is a pair of hand cymbals made of bronze, which is about 7.5 centimetres in diameter. The *tāḷam* used in *Periya Mēḷam* is bigger, heavier, and thus has a lower pitch and duller timbre, than the hand cymbals used for Bharata Natyam and *tēvāram* (Saivite devotional hymns) singing, also known as *tāḷam* (Higgins 1973: 30; Peterson 1989: 61).[58] Nachiyarkoyil, near Kumbakonam in Tanjavur district is known for high-quality *tāḷam* as well as other bronze wares. The *tāḷam* is played to mark the structure of rhythmic cycles, also known as *tāḷam*. In fact, the *tāḷam* is a term signifying a musical instrument and a musical function alike. Playing the *tāḷam* (as a cymbal) is conceptually identical to keeping the *tāḷam* (as a rhythmic cycle), in that an expression '*tāḷampoḍu*' (to place/put *tāḷam*) simultaneously refers to the act of hitting cymbals and providing a rhythmic reference by doing so.

The *tāḷam* is held horizontally with one of its cymbals resting on the player's palm against which the other is struck. Two different kinds of timbre are utilized to mark the section of a rhythmic cycle: open and closed. Open sound is obtained when the upper cymbal is left free immediately after cymbals are struck together, and closed sound when they stay in contact with each other, thereby preventing free vibration. Playing the *tāḷam* is the equivalent of hand and finger counts in *Karnāṭak* music.

Generally, the open sound of the *tāḷam* corresponds to a clap, and its closed sound to a wave of the hand. The *tāḷam* player also counts the individual beats of a larger section of a rhythmic cycle by the fingers of the hand holding the upper cymbal, much like finger counts in *Karnāṭak* music. However, playing the *tāḷam* in *Periya Mēḷam* music and hand counts in *Karnāṭak* music have an important functional difference. The former is an audible rhythmic reference provided as an accompaniment by a separate player for the *nāgasvaram* and *tavil* players, whereas the latter is essentially a device to maintain rhythmic accuracy on the part of the participant him/herself, whether as a performer or listener. The complex cross-rhythm which developed most extensively in *Periya Mēḷam* music may have contributed to the presence of an external rhythmic reference against which musicians could accurately try the most complex rhythmic patterns.

4. *Srutipeṭṭi*

The drone (*sruti*) which provides a melodic reference to soloists and accompanists alike is an essential component of Indian music.[59] At present, the instrument that provides the drone in the *Periya Mēḷam* ensemble is called the *srutipeṭṭi* (*sruti* box). *Srutipeṭṭi* consists of a rectangular wooden box in which free-reeds and bellow are attached. By pumping a bellow back and forth, a constant flow of air is provided into free reeds tuned to *Sa* (tonic), *Pa* (dominant), and *Sa* (an octave above the tonic).

Some *srutipeṭṭi* are tuned to only one tonic pitch; pitch-2, pitch-3 etc., while others have an adjustable switch that gives the option of playing to more than one tonic pitch. Although most *nāgasvaram* musicians play to one *sruti* they prefer, the *srutipeṭṭi* of the second type is handy for those who have to change *srutis*, depending upon the situation, such as in accompanying singers for cinemas.

II. CONTEMPORARY *PERIYA MĒḶAM* ENSEMBLE

The *Periya Mēḷam* ensemble that is preferred and considered complete by musicians and patrons today consist of six players including the main *nāgasvaram* player as its leader and soloist, and five accompanists consisting of the second *nāgasvaram*, two *tavil*, *tāḷam*, and *srutipeṭṭi* players. The ensemble is considered the main *nāgasvaram* player's group, and it is often referred to as his ensemble such as 'Rajarattinam Pillai and his party.'[60] The soloist generally has a regular set of accompanists, and the ensemble performs on a regular basis as a self-contained unit. The group-oriented *Periya Mēḷam* music presents a sharp contrast to *Karnāṭak* music performances in which the musicians are individually engaged and typically meet only at the performance.[61]

The main *nāgasvaram* player has the authority concerning all matters relating to his ensemble, musical or otherwise. He has the right to select his accompanists to form an ensemble (with an exception of the second *tavil* player who is selected by the main *tavil* player), to accept or deny engagements, to negotiate the performance fees for the ensemble, and to distribute remuneration among his accompanists in the prescribed rate they have agreed upon at the time of hiring. As the leader responsible for the musical output of his ensemble, he determines the selection of *rāgams* and compositions to be played, the length of performance, and the rhythmic framework (*tāḷam* and *eḍuppu*) for the *tavil* solo.[62]

The second *nāgasvaram* player is often a senior disciple of the main *nāgasvaram* musician. Being a second *nāgasvaram* player is often considered the last stage of musical training in which to learn the essence of the improvisational portion of music (*manōdharma saṅgīta*) by playing with and observing one's *guru* closely and intensively for an extended period of time. Many *nāgasvaram* musicians consider this final stage of discipleship indispensable to achieve high musicianship, and they often emphasize the importance of this final stage of training. The disciple may spend as long as fifteen years playing the second *nāgasvaram* before he forms his own group.

The main performance responsibility of a second *nāgasvaram* musician is to play the composed portions of music in unison with the main musician. When the soloist plays in upper register, he sometimes plays the same melody one octave lower. The soloist often elaborates on a *rāgam* before starting a composition,[63] and the second *nāgasvaram* player should know the general progression of the *rāgam* improvisation in terms of register and style so that the reed (*sīvāḷi*) is in playing condition and he can join in as soon as the soloist starts the composition. The second *nāgasvaram* player usually does not engage in *rāgam* elaboration prior to compositions. However, if he is considered capable by the main *nāgasvaram* player, he is often expected to play *svarakalpana* (improvisation within the framework of compositions), imitating the improvised phrases of the main player. When the soloist plays short improvisatory phrases after each section of a composition, the second player often provides a long sustained tonic pitch much like the *ottu* (drone pipe, explained later) player did in the past, though circular breathing is not utilized.

Two brothers may play *nāgasvaram*s together as a team.[64] Such ensembles are referred to as the '...Brothers (*Sahōdararhal*)' with the name of their ancestral home, such as the Tiruvizhimizhalai Brothers. If one of the brothers is known as a particularly good player, his name is sometimes added to the name of the ensemble, as seen in the case of the Sembonnarkoyil Govindasami Brothers. The second *nāgasvaram* player who is most often, though not without exception, a younger brother, is given more room to display his talent within this format than those who are disciples of the first *nāgasvaram* players, but the main *nāgasvaram* player still retains authority as the leader and soloist of the ensemble. As explained in the following section, this ensemble format of two brothers playing *nāgasvaram*s together was popularized by the immense success of the Tiruvizhimizhalai Brothers (Subramaniyam and Natarajasundaram), who, beginning in the late 1920s, specialized in the renderings of *kīrttanais*.[65]

The *tavil* players provide rhythmic accompaniment throughout the *nāgasvaram* performance. The main *tavil* player always initiates the *Periya Mēḷam* performance by playing the prescribed beginning pattern on the *toppi* and a short prelude. In sharp contrast to *Karnāṭak* music, the rhythmic accompaniment, though unobtrusive and in loosely regulated pulses, is provided on *tavil* throughout the *rāgam* elaboration. Between sections of *rāgam* elaboration, rhythmically dense interludes known as *uruṭṭuccol* are played by the *tavil* players. This unique performance practice probably developed out of the heavy emphasis on *rāgam* elaboration in *Periya Mēḷam* music and was originally meant to provide a break for *nāgasvaram* musicians with interludes by *tavil* players.

The second *tavil* player is often a senior disciple of the main *tavil* musician. Similar to the second *nāgasvaram* musician, performing with his *guru* is the final stage of discipleship before becoming the main player himself. The main *tavil* musician selects the second *tavil* player. While playing compositions, the two *tavil* players take turns accompanying the *nāgasvaram* players, roughly section by section of a composition. With the exceptions of some light compositions and the ending part of *taṇi arttaṇam* (or simply *taṇi*, solo by rhythmic accompanist), the two *tavils* are not played simultaneously. An example is the *kīrttaṇai*, the most commonly performed compositional form consisting of three sections (*pallavi, aṇupallavi, caraṇam*). If the first *tavil* player accompanies the *rāgam* elaboration through the end of the first section (*pallavi*) of a composition, then the second player accompanies the second section (*aṇupallavi*). The third section (*caraṇam*) is again accompanied by the first *tavil* player, and so on. In *svarakalpana*, the first *tavil* player teams up with the main *nāgasvaram* player, and the second *tavil* with the second *nāgasvaram*.

During the *taṇi*, the main *tavil* musician is given a chance to display his musical imagination and dexterity. He is free to play anything within the confines of the *tāḷam* and *eḍuppu* selected by the main *nāgasvaram* musician through his choice of the composition (*kīrttaṇai*) or the musical theme for *pallavi* preceding the *tani*. The second *tavil* player, on the other hand, is expected to alternate with the main player and reproduce what he plays. The ability of the second player is publicly tested in a competitive atmosphere. Since an exact reproduction is anticipated, minute mistakes or the inability to reproduce the pattern is apparent even to the uninitiated audience, and thus all the more embarrassing to the player who is unable to do it. Guest *tavil* players who came to be known as *sirappu tavil* or special *tavil* are occasionally hired for performances in addition to the regular *nāgasvaram* ensemble. These guest *tavil* players often become the centre of attraction, sitting at the front of the stage where the ensemble's regular *tavil* players would normally sit. The implications of the emergence of this new phenomenon will be discussed in the next section.

The *tāḷam* player is often a student of the *nāgasvaram* musician. Keeping rhythm with the *tāḷam* is much more difficult than it appears on stage, and it is considered an important learning experience for students. The *tāḷam* player is sometimes corrected by the other musicians when he is out of rhythm. Practically all *nāgasvaram* musicians begin their performing careers by accompanying their *gurus* on the *tāḷam*.[66]

The last instrument of the ensemble is the *srutipeṭṭi*. Since this instrument is simply played by pumping the bellows, it takes no skill and is often played by a young son or relative of the *nāgasvaram* musician.

The hierarchy among musicians is manifested in the spatial arrangement of the ensemble during performances. There are two basic positions *Periya Mēḷam* musicians take: standing and sitting positions. The act of standing indicates reverence, and the standing position of *Periya Mēḷam* music has a strong association with the ritual context in which musicians show reverence toward the deity. Conversely, the sitting position was initiated in secular performance contexts such as concert-hall recitals and domestic functions. In the standing position, the positions of the accompanists are determined in relation to the main *nāgasvaram* musician, who initiates moves according to ritual requirements. Musicians form a semi-circle facing the object of the performance (an image of the deity or the bridegroom). To whatever direction the main *nāgasvaram* musician may play, the second *nāgasvaram* player stands close to the main player and slightly behind him, if he is his student. The *tavil* musicians stand on both sides of the *nāgasvaram* musicians, usually slightly ahead of them. The main *tavil* player usually stands closer to the main *nāgasvaram* musician than the second *tavil* player. The *tāḷam* and *srutipeṭṭi* players can stand near the other musicians, as long as they are not blocking the direction of the performance.

The spatial arrangement in the sitting position is basically identical to that in the standing position, although it is more rigidly enforced since the direction of performance is fixed in this context. The main *nāgasvaram* player sits in the centre of the stage, whereas the second player usually locates himself to the soloist's left and slightly behind him. Two players of similar musical standing share the centre of the stage. The *tavil* players sit on both sides of the *nāgasvaram* musicians, slightly closer to the audience and facing each other. The main *tavil* player usually locates himself to their right and the second player to their left. When the main *tavil* player is left-handed, he sits to their left so that his quick hand movements on the *valantalai* are shown to the audience.[67] The *tāḷam* player usually sits behind the main *tavil* player, and the *srutipeṭṭi* player sits behind the *nāgasvaram* musicians.

III. CHANGES DURING RAJARATTINAM PILLAI'S LIFETIME (1898-1956)

Having surveyed the instruments and instrumentation of contemporary *Periya Mēḷam* music, I now turn to some of the major changes which occurred during the twentieth century. The periods prior to and following Rajarattinam Pillai's death in 1956 are distinct in terms of the nature of these changes, and will be discussed separately.

The first half of the twentieth century roughly coincides with the lifetime of Rajarattinam Pillai, whose charismatic ascent appears determined by the situation of the *Periya Mēḷam* tradition as perceived by his fellow musicians and patrons. This period may be described as having generated the greatest change in the recent history of *Periya Mēḷam* music as well as of *Karnāṭak* music. Beneath the many changes which occurred during this period were the encompassing socio-economic currents in South India, and these changes may be interpreted as the *Periya Mēḷam* musicians' adaptive strategies for survival. I have selected five interrelated areas of inquiry in which several of the most important changes are examined: 1) repertoire 2) lowering of the tonic pitch, 3) disappearance of the drone pipe, 4) the emergence of *siṟappu tavil*, and 5) physical appearance and paraphernalia of musicians. Although the implication of Rajarattinam Pillai's overall impact on these changes will be discussed in detail in Chapter 6, his relationship to each of the five areas above is touched upon in this section, wherever appropriate.

1. Repertoire

Extensive *rāgam* elaboration predominantly constituted the repertoire of *Periya Mēḷam* music up until the early decades of the twentieth century.[68] Experiences of listening to a *rāgam* elaborated during all-night temple processions are fondly discussed among musicians and patrons alike. The musical knowledge (*ñāṉam*) and imagination (*karpaṉai*) necessary to sustain this type of extensive elaboration is attributed to the tradition of *nāgasvaram* players, and many eminent vocalists of our time acknowledge its influence in their music and regard this as its major contribution to *Karnāṭak* music.[69] Such *rāgam* elaboration by Rajarattinam Pillai is a frequent topic of discussion. The vivid image of his all-night performances, at various temples with large crowds in attendance, is shared among those who witnessed them. A musician's skill is often described in terms of the duration of his performance, without exhausting new ideas. One story relates his playing of Todi *rāgam* for four consecutive nights, without repeating himself, during the annual temple festival in Kerala. Apart from the *rāgam* elaboration, some compositional forms which allow extensive improvisation, such as *pallavi* and *rakti mēḷam* (both explained in the next chapter), are also considered to have been an expertise of *nāgasvaram* musicians.

The high level of interest in *rāgam* elaboration among the general public in the first half of the twentieth century is often contrasted with some dismay to the public's increasing alienation from such elaboration and its predilection for film songs. Apart from the increased popularity of film songs, the commencement in the 1920s of various mass media such as disc recordings and radio programmes, both with their limited time for performance, contributed to the movement towards a composition-oriented repertoire.[70] In the 1940s, performances consisting primarily of extensive *rāgam* improvisation were already noticeably less frequent, and the time allocated to *rāgam* elaboration and other improvisational forms shorter.

The shift in the audiences' preference is reflected in the instrumentation of the *Periya Mēḷam* ensemble. Until the 1920s, the *Periya Mēḷam* ensemble included only one *nāgasvaram* and one *tavil*, as well as one *tāḷam* and one *ottu* (drone pipe). It was a suitable format in which a master *nāgasvaram* musician played extensive improvisation. The *nāgasvaram* musician played one *rāgam* for a long time with only short rhythmic interludes on *tavil* that enabled him to catch his breath. Extraordinary stamina was required for *nāgasvaram* musicians, since they had to play continuously in temple processions, which lasted for as long as ten hours.

The initial inclusion of a second *nāgasvaram* player on a regular basis is attributed to Tiruppamburam Natarajasundaram Pillai (1869-1938), who, inspired by the sound of four *nāgasvarams* played together at the annual festival in Tiruvarur,[71] began playing with his brother, Sivasubramania Pillai, in an ensemble. It was the Tiruvizhimizhalai Brothers, however, who popularized this format with their immense demand at marriage ceremonies.[72] Judging from recordings of *Periya Mēḷam* music of this period and pictures of ensembles, two *nāgasvarams* per ensemble became the preferred format, at least by the mid-1930s.[73] The main intent of this new format was to play compositions on two *nāgasvarams* in precise unison and therefore, as the new format became common, the improvisational portion of the performance gradually became less prominent.[74] Prior to the advent of this new format, the number of compositions played by *Periya Mēḷam* musicians was much less than in *Karnāṭak* music, since the repertoire of *Periya Mēḷam* music consisted largely of forms which allowed extensive improvisation. In order to expand their repertoire, the Tiruvizhimizhalai Brothers learned many compositions from Konerirajapuram Vaidyanatha Iyer, a renowned Brahman vocalist who also taught Rajarattinam Pillai.

2. Lowering to Tonic Pitch

The sizes of the *nāgasvaram* became larger in stages corresponding to the lowering of its pitch in the period between the 1920s and the 1950s. Since the 1950s, its size has remained constant. *Nāgasvarams* in pitch-5 (g above the middle c) were most commonly used until the 1920s.[75] The high pitch enabled the sound of the instrument to carry a great distance. The pitch was lowered gradually and by the mid-1940s, the majority of musicians were playing *nāgasvaram* in pitch 2, 2½ and 3 (d, d#, and e). Although the pitch-1 *nāgasvaram* has been tested by a few performers, most musicians play the pitch-2 *nāgasvaram*, with a fewer number performing in pitches 2½ and 3.[76]

The pitch-2 *nāgasvaram*, the most frequently used type today, is often called *bāri nāgasvaram* (or simply *bāri*), in opposition to *timiri nāgasvaram* (or *timiri*), which usually refers to all the higher-pitched types of *nāgasvaram*.[77] Although the *bāri nāgasvaram* is used today as a synonym to pitch-2 *nāgasvaram*, the *bāri* and *timiri* only point to relative pitch relation, and the actual pitches to which they refer depend upon the context. For example, the pitch-3 *nāgasvaram* is called *timiri* as opposed to pitch-2 *nāgasvaram* today, but it was referred to as *bāri* when it was compared to pitch-4 or pitch-5 *nāgasvaram*.[78] The only exception to this usage of *bāri* is the special type of *nāgasvaram* played exclusively for rituals at the Tyagaraja Swamy Temple in Tiruvarur. Although it is much shorter (approximately two feet) than pitch-2 *nāgasvaram*, it is known as *bāri nāgasvaram* or *Tiruvārūr bāri*.[79]

The pitch-2 *nāgasvaram*, or *bāri nāgasvaram*, believed to have been initiated by Rajarattinam Pillai, is conceptually linked with him and with his musical achievements, though he played instruments in all the other pitches at different stages of his life (Sankaran 1990b: 39).[80] For this reason, musicians who play the pitch-2 *nāgasvaram* generally attribute their selection of the instrument to the unmistakable sound quality Rajarattinam Pillai achieved on this instrument.[81]

A corresponding lowering of the tonic pitch is reported in *Karnāṭak* music during the same period (Higgins 1976; Rangaramanuja Ayyangar 1972: 320-1). The introduction of microphones on the concert stage enabling lower-pitched musicians audible in performance is considered chiefly responsible for the change (Venkataramaiyar 1971). In the case of *nāgasvaram*, however, this explanation is not completely convincing since the frequent use of microphones for *Periya Mēḷam* performances did not take place until much later. Nevertheless, the prestige associated with vocal music might have encouraged *nāgasvaram* musicians to emulate the change in vocal music. The dissemination of lower-pitched *nāgasvaram* among musicians may also be a result of the facility of these instruments which require less strenuous blowing.[82] Furthermore, *nāgasvaram* musicians' desire to be identified with Rajarattinam Pillai is likely to have contributed to the wide distribution of the pitch-2 *nāgasvaram*.

In contrast, some older patrons of *nāgasvaram* music still prefer the *timiri* type. For them, its piercing sound was the very manifestation of the deity's majesty, and they tend to regard the lowering of the pitch of the instrument detrimental to the overall musical and spiritual effect (Rangaramanuja Ayyangar 1977: 8). Because the finger holes of the pitch-2 *nāgasvaram* are far apart and more difficult to manipulate properly, it is argued that the quality of *nāgasvaram* music suffered. To these patrons of the older generation, Rajarattinam Pillai was a rare genius who conquered this disadvantage with his unusual technique and musicality (Mahadevan 1988: 34-5).

It is widely known among *nāgasvaram* musicians that the pitch-2 *nāgasvaram* was successfully manufactured by N.G.N. Renganada Accari in the early 1940s, in collaboration with Rajarattinam Pillai. The few others who attempted to make pitch-2 *nāgasvarams* had problems producing the correct pitch for *sutta matyamam* (*suddha madhyama*, perfect fourth above the tonic pitch). Renganada Accari's reputation as the best *nāgasvaram* maker can be traced to his long association with Rajarattinam Pillai, who, satisfied with the sound of the pitch-2 *nāgasvaram*, repeatedly praised Accari's skill publicly and gave him the title of Nadasvara Sirpi (Architect of *Nāgasvaram*). Rajarattinam Pillai has even been quoted to attribute his success to Renganada Accari's *nāgasvaram*. Renganada Accari's great skill, symbolized in his ability to manufacture the instrument with the right *sutta matyamam* pitch and his association with Rajarattinam Pillai, is proudly stated in his letterhead (Figure 3-4).

3. Drone Instrument

The instrument which provided the drone in the ensemble in the past was the *ottu*, a double-reed instrument that resembled the *nāgasvaram* in size, shape, and construction, but that had no finger-holes.[83] It was an indispensable part of the *Periya Mēḷam* ensemble until the 1940s. The substitution of the *srutipeṭṭi* for the *ottu* in the ensemble is widely believed to have been initiated by Rajarattinam Pillai. The dissemination of the new format with *srutipeṭṭi* is also attributed to Rajarattinam Pillai whose popularity compelled many musicians to imitate him. Its gradual takeover was completed in the late 1960s by which time very few *ottu* players were actively involved in performance.[84]

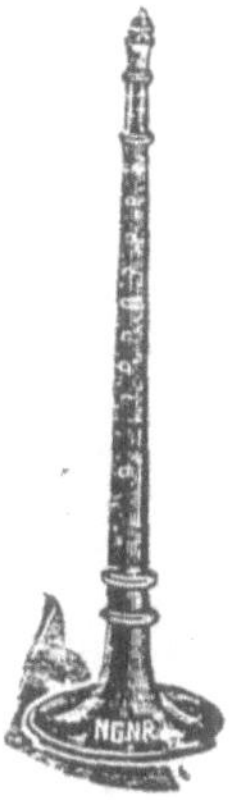

உ

மங்கள வாத்தியம் இசைக்கருவி சுத்த மத்திமம் பேசும் நாதஸ்வாம் செய்யும் மேதை நாதஸ்வரம் ஏற்பட்டதிலிருந்து யாரும் செய்யாததை சுத்த மத்திமம பேசும நாதஸ்வரத்தை புதுப்பித்து உலகம் முழுவதும் புகழும்படி செய்து, நாதஸ்வா எக சக்ராதிபதி T. N. R. அவர்களால் அகில இந்திய நாதஸ்வா சிற்பி என்ற பட்டமும், நற்சாட்சி பத்திரமும் பெற்று, சென்னையில் முதல் அமைச்சர் காமராஜ் அவர்களால் பரிசும் பெற்று, மதுரை நாதஸ்வா கோஷ்டியாரால் தங்க மெடலும் பெற்று, அனேக வித்வ சிரோன்மணிகளால் சன்மானங்களும் பெற்ற உலக புகழ் நாதஸ்வரம் செய்யும் கலைஞர்

என். ஜி. என். ரெங்கனுத ஆச்சாரி,
நாதஸ்வர சிற்பி,
நரசிங்கன்பேட்டை - 609 802.
(தஞ்சாவூர் ஜில்லா)

The artist who makes the *nādasvaram*, the auspicious musical instrument, with the right *suttamattimam*.

The artist who became world-famous, having made *nādasvaram* with the right *suttamattimam* pitch which nobody has ever done, who received the title of *Ahila Indiya Nadasvara Sirpi* (World-Famous *Nadasvaram* Artist) and a testifying certificate from T.N.R., the only authority of the instrument, who received a gift from the Chief Minister, Kamaraj in Madras, who received a gold medal from *nādasvaram* musicians in Madurai, who received awards from many distinguished musicians, who makes the world-famous *nādasvaram*

N.G.N. Renganada Accari, *Nadasvara Sirpi*,
Narasinganpettai-609 802 (Tanjavur District)

Figure 3-5: Letterhead of N.G.N. Renganada Accari
(English translation mine)

One distinguishing feature of this instrument is the use of circular breathing to provide an uninterrupted drone. This breathing technique has never been utilized to play the *nāgasvaram* within the living memory of contemporary *Periya Mēḷam* musicians,[85] although it is commonly found among many double-reed instrument performers in both West and Southeast Asia as well as rural traditions in South Asia (Flora 1986; Bryant 1990: 147-9).

Figure 3-6: An *ottu* player
(Kanchipuram, 1987)

In places where the musical traditions at temples are known to be systematized, such as Tiruvarur and Chidambaram, there were families whose traditional occupation was exclusively to play the *ottu* as part of *Periya Mēḷam* at the temple rituals and processions. Occasionally, less talented offspring in the family of *nāgasvaram* players were encouraged to learn the *ottu*. Mannargudi Chinna Pakkiri (1869-1915), considered one of the best *nāgasvaram* musicians of his time, in fact started his career as an *ottu* player (B.M. Sundaram 2001: 59). However, his case appears rather exceptional, and most of those who switched to the *nāgasvaram* achieved neither a high level of musicianship nor popularity.

Apart from Rajarattinam Pillai's popularity, the substitution of the *ottu* with the *srutipeṭṭi* is also attributed to the unfavourable economic condition of temple finances. On the one hand, the *ottu* player suffered from the relative decrease of the entire ensemble's salary much more because they received a considerably smaller portion of the remuneration than the *nāgasvaram* or *tavil* musicians to begin with, and they were forced to seek other means of livelihood, as the prospect for improvement gradually appeared remote. On the other hand, the *nāgasvaram* player was encouraged or more frequently compelled to switch over to the *srutipeṭṭi*, for economic reasons. Unlike the *ottu*, the *srutipeṭṭi* requires little performance skill and can be easily handled by the *nāgasvaram* player's own young son or a disciple living in the same household. Therefore, the inclusion of the *srutipeṭṭi* proved a way to increase the share of the *nāgasvaram* player and to cope with the decreasing net income.

The shift from the *ottu* to the *srutipeṭṭi* has induced a notable musical change. Because the reed used for the *nāgasvaram* and *ottu* absorb much moisture while being played, the pitch of the instrument will descend slightly. Since the pitch of the *ottu* will descend along with that of the *nāgasvaram*, and it is adjustable with the change in air pressure and the position of the lips in relation to the reed, the *nāgasvaram* player can perform for a much longer duration in tune with the drone without changing his reed (Sankaran 1990b: 39-40). With the stable drone provided by the *srutipeṭṭi*, on the other hand, reeds have to be replaced frequently. As many as fifty reeds are attached to the string (*kayaṟu*) which runs parallel to the body of the *nāgasvaram*, and *nāgasvaram* players often check the condition of the reed by blowing into it during the performance.

Despite the complete substitution of *ottu* with *srutipeṭṭi* in *Periya Mēḷam* ensemble, the drone pipe continues to be a part of various folk ensembles such as *naiyāṇḍi mēḷam*[86] and *urumi mēḷam*[87] in Tamil Nadu and *nagasvara vādana*[88] in Karnataka.

4. The Emergence of *Siṟappu Tavil*

The increasing popularity of the *tavil* in relation to that of the *nāgasvaram* is another gradual change which has occurred since approximately the turn of the century. The elevated status of *tavil* players resulting from their increasing popularity disturbed the previous hierarchical structure among *Periya Mēḷam* musicians, which was in turn manifested in some significant changes in musical content and performance practices. The most tangible manifestation of the growing prominence of *tavil* players is the emergence of the guest *tavil* players who came to be known as *siṟappu tavil* or special *tavil*. They are independent *tavil* musicians who do not belong to any specific ensembles, and who are instead hired as guest musicians in addition to and separately from the regular *Periya Mēḷam* ensemble.

Nidamangalam Minakshisundaram Pillai (1894-1949), one of the greatest and most popular *tavil* musicians of the twentieth century, is said to have been the first player to perform as a *sirappu tavil* (B.M. Sundaram n.d.: 27-8). According to one story, Minakshisundaram Pillai decided in the late 1930s to break away from the *Periya Mēlam* ensemble to which he had belonged due to ill-treatment by the *nāgasvaram* players over the use of a gift presumably given to the entire ensemble. Minakshisundaram Pillai then vowed never to be a regular member of an ensemble, disgusted by the inferior position of the *tavil* players which he interpreted to be the root cause of the humiliating incident.

The one *nāgasvaram*-one *tavil* ensemble format was the norm until the 1920s, as mentioned above, and the superior position of the *nāgasvaram* player in the hierarchy of *Periya Mēlam* ensemble was manifested in the distribution of income from temple service and outside performances, as well as the right to make decisions in musical matters. The *nāgasvaram* player received as much as 80 per cent of the entire remuneration, while the remainder was shared by the three other members of the ensemble with slightly more going to the *tavil* player than to the *tālam* and *ottu* players.[89] While the musical and religious importance of the *tavil* was well recognized even by the *nāgasvaram* players themselves, the dominance by *nāgasvaram* players in ensemble management was absolute.

By the time of Minakshisundaram Pillai's decision to become independent, the *tavil* must have acquired considerable popularity of its own among patrons. Hiring a *sirappu tavil* player required additional funds from the sponsor of the event, religious or social, and the prestige of hiring *sirappu tavil* players supported by a widening appreciation of their playing made this new phenomenon feasible. The increased popularity of the *tavil* was perhaps related to the shift of emphasis in repertoire from improvisation to composed music in *Periya Mēlam* music. Although, unlike in *Karnāṭak* music, rhythmic accompaniment is provided during *rāgam* elaboration in *Periya Mēlam*, it is generally more subdued and limited than the accompaniment during the composed music. This shift created more opportunities for *tavil* players to exhibit their dexterity.

With the relative decrease in the popularity of *nāgasvaram* in relation to *tavil*, the *siṟappu tavil* format has produced a handful of star players since around 1940. They have been in great demand for annual festivals at well-known temples, prestigious music festivals such as the one at the Music Academy in Madras, and highly-publicized weddings by wealthy families. Their names are recognized even among those with marginal interest in *Periya Mēḷam* music. Some players are known for demanding high performance fees, which sometimes equal or surpass that paid to the *Periya Mēḷam* ensemble. While some *nāgasvaram* musicians are wary of the popularity of *siṟappu tavil* musicians and the loss of customary respect to *nāgasvaram* musicians, others, especially younger upcoming players, express their appreciation for playing with such *tavil* players, fully aware that their association with famous *siṟappu tavil* players is beneficial to their own careers.

The growing social prominence of *tavil* players is discernible in musical interaction during performances. *Tavil* accompaniment during the *rāgam* elaboration was characterized by a subtle and subdued manner of performance, but showy interference has become more noticeable. Some *siṟappu tavil* players are demanding the right to make musical decisions which previously belonged to *nāgasvaram* musicians alone. For instance, when given a chance to play solo, the *tavil* player would conventionally perform in the rhythmic setting used in the composition the *nāgasvaram* had selected to play. Now some players play solo in the rhythmic setting of their own choice regardless of what precedes it, or even instruct the *nāgasvaram* player to select a composition with the rhythmic setting they prefer.

The increasing prominence of *tavil* players has an audible manifestation, in a change of the tone quality of their instruments. As mentioned earlier, the use of thimbles which began in the 1930s resulted in a louder and brighter sound on *tavil*, and, despite initial criticism from *nāgasvaram* musicians and patrons of *Periya Mēḷam* music, virtually all *tavil* players use the thimbles in performance excepting in daily temple rituals. This increased sonic prominence was pushed even further when some young *tavil* players experimented in the 1980s with thimbles made of plaster instead of rice powder and a piece of cloth (B.M. Sundaram 1986: 82).

The rising status of *tavil* musicians is also observable in their verbal interaction with *nāgasvaram* musicians. In the past, the accompanists, including the *tavil* players, always addressed the *nāgasvaram* musician with the honorific personal pronoun, *nīnga* (*nīngaḷ*), and its corresponding verbal endings whereas they were addressed with the less honorific '*nī*'. In contrast, *siṟappu tavil* musicians are generally addressed with *nīnga* by *nāgasvaram* musicians and patrons today, while the choice of different address terms in a given situation continues to be a focal point of disagreement among musicians.

The elevation of *tavil* players in relation to *nāgasvaram* musicians has a parallel in North Indian classical music. Neuman reports *tablā* players' increasing reluctance to take a subordinate role to the soloists.[90] He attributed this phenomenon to their newly-assumed prominence acquired on foreign tours where rhythmic accompanists are given equal attention by Western audiences, and the increasing tendency for rhythm-oriented performance which heightens the demands for good *tablā* players (1980: 141-2).[91] While the first factor mentioned by Neuman is not applicable to the case of *Periya Mēḷam*, since foreign tours were still rare, the increasing emphasis on the rhythmic aspect of performance has been observed in South Indian classical music in general.

5. Appearance of Musicians

The physical appearance of *Periya Mēḷam* musicians during performance changed drastically during Rajarattinam Pillai's lifetime, and he is credited unanimously for many changes. He was the first *nāgasvaram* player to adopt a Western hairstyle replacing the traditional *kuḍumi*,[92] and to wear a Western-style silk shirt during performances. The *kuḍumi* and bare upper torso, considered important ways of expressing one's devotion and obeisance to god, have a strong spiritual and ritual connotation, and were strictly observed by *Periya Mēḷam* musicians prior to Rajarattinam Pillai's alleged innovation. While Rajarattinam Pillai's decisions to abandon the traditional appearance was, at least in part, his way of challenging the discrimination against *Isai Vēḷāḷar* musicians by Brahmans by explicitly adopting their performance practice, he also paved the way for *Periya Mēḷam* music to break away from the original ritual context by discarding the physical appearance and customs associated with it.

IV. CHANGES AFTER RAJARATTINAM PILLAI'S DEATH (1956-PRESENT)

The period after Rajarattinam Pillai's death is best characterized by relative stability with few drastic innovations to the tradition compared to that during his lifetime. Performance practice and instrumentation remained virtually identical. However, it has also seen a gradual intensification of some of the tendencies initiated during Rajarattinam Pillai's lifetime. With the continuing deterioration of the temple tradition, which will be discussed in detail in the next chapter, the performance contexts for extended improvisation have become even more scarce. As remunerative support from temples has further worsened, sons from families of musicians find less incentive to succeed their hereditary profession and are opting for other possibilities.[93] Many senior *nāgasvaram* musicians predict the complete disappearance of the repertoire and performance practice peculiar to temple contexts in a few generations.

The two most significant changes in *Periya Mēḷam* music during this period may be the increasing prominence of non-*Isai Vēḷāḷar nāgasvaram* musicians and the emergence of institutionalized learning. Since the first change will be examined in detail in Chapter 5 (Section 3), it will suffice here to mention that it was Rajarattinam Pillai who triggered this phenomenon through his de facto endorsement of Karukurichi Arunachalam (1921-64), the very first non-*Isai Vēḷāḷar nāgasvaram* musician who achieved fame all over South India, as his musical heir.[94]

The institutional transmission of musical knowledge in *Periya Mēḷam* music began in 1957 with the establishment of the diploma course in *nāgasvaram* and *tavil* at the Tamil Nadu Government Music College (then known as Central College of Carnatic Music) in Madras. A well-known Brahman film director, K. Subramaniam, who was also an enthusiast of *Periya Mēḷam* music and an advocate of social reform, is believed to have lobbied extensively toward this end. By establishing a diploma course at the government school, Subramanian attempted to raise the social respectability of *Periya Mēḷam* music, as well as to erase the inferiority complex among its practitioners.[95]

Since then, at least five other public, and several privately owned institutions in which *Periya Mēḷam* music can be learned have opened. In addition to the one in Madras, the Tamil Nadu state government opened a second music school in Madurai in 1979. Diploma courses in *nāgasvaram* and *tavil* performance were established in the music department at a large university (the Annamalai University in Chidambaram, South Arcot in the 1970s)[96] as well as at a small college (*Arasar Kallūri* in Tiruvaiyaru, Tanjavur district, in 1966).[97] Two extremely wealthy temples have also opened music schools in which *Periya Mēḷam* music can be learned: the Daṇḍāyudapāṇi Temple in Palani (Madurai district) in 1958 and the Veṅkaṭēsvarā Temple in Tirumala (Chittoor district, Andhra Pradesh) in 1959 (Clothey 1983: 119).[98] In addition, a few small *nāgasvaram* schools are run by individual musicians.[99]

In comparison to the situation of *Periya Mēḷam*, music schools emerged much earlier in *Karnāṭak* music, at least by the late 1920s (T. Viswanathan 1966: 186).[100] L'Armand and L'Armand report that the number of music schools increased substantially in the 1920s and 1930s (1983: 432). The increase in the number of music schools corresponded to the emerging notion of music learning as a socially acceptable avocation, especially among women from Brahman and other high-ranking castes, and the parallel decrease of social stigma attached to public performances by women. At present, a majority of students in music schools are female. Although some go to music schools intending to become professional, many others learn music and dance as part of the general education, training highly valued when seeking a husband. In contrast, all *Periya Mēḷam* schools are vocational by nature, and the students are virtually all males, reflecting the male-oriented profession of *Periya Mēḷam* music. Excepting those who cannot attain the minimal skill required for performance, all the students intend to earn their livelihood based upon their training in these schools.

Before the emergence of institutional learning, musical knowledge in *Periya Mēḷam* was transmitted through a traditional method known as *gurukulavāsam*. In *gurukulavāsam*, an aspiring student typically lived in his *guru's* household, much as his adopted son. He was responsible for many daily chores including shopping, washing clothes, sweeping, and other miscellaneous errands. For this reason, a student was expected to practice early in the morning every day, typically before dawn, when no other obligations were assigned to him.[101] Many musicians continued to practice at early hours of the day after going through *gurukulavāsam*, as Rajarattinam Pillai is believed to have done.

The content and frequency of lessons depend totally upon the *guru's* schedule and mood. Some *gurus* did not teach at all in the sense of providing structured lessons. What was considered important was the constant exposure to the *guru's* music and a total immersion in the *guru's* life. A student was expected to acquire musical knowledge from repeated listening (*kēḷvi ñaṉam*). This expectation was also based upon the belief that the essence of *Periya Mēḷam* music (extensive *rāgam* elaboration) was unteachable, and that the *guru's* primary responsibility was to provide an environment in which the students could learn themselves through attentive listening. When a composition was taught, students were expected to first learn the composition vocally with its text, then figure out the *svaras* (pitches) of the melody themselves. This method ensured that students would memorize the text of a composition, the correct delineation of which was vital for *nāgasvaram* playing.

Nāgasvaram musicians considered it their duty to take a disciple and pass down the art to the next generation, and they seldom denied incoming disciples unless they showed no musical aptitude. Among the *Isai Vēḷāḷars,* tuition fees were neither required nor expected, and in some cases the *guru* even provided his poor students with clothes and a small allowance. If the family of the disciple was wealthy enough, money was presented occasionally as a gift to defray his living expenses.

Differences between the *gurukulavāsam* and institutional leaning are many and fundamental. First of all, the length and pace of training has been considerably altered. The institutions mentioned above all have either a three or four year diploma course, and the curriculum dictates the content and pace of instruction, sometimes regardless of the students' progress.[102] Many *Periya Mēḷam* musicians welcome the idea of government patronage of *Periya Mēḷam* music (Virusvami Pillai 1962: 17), but believe that institutional learning is useful only if after graduation a student seeks further training in a *gurukulavāsam,* in which the finer aspects of music can be learned.

What has promoted the recruitment of students is a monthly stipend that is provided to them at all the institutions mentioned above.[103] Although *Isai Vēḷāḷar* musicians usually support and welcome the idea of financial assistance by the government, they believe that the stipend attracts students from poor families of non-*Isai Vēḷāḷar jātis* who are less dedicated to, or worse, uninterested in, the tradition. These institutions screen applicants not only by testing their musical aptitude for learning *Periya Mēḷam* music, but by requiring the school education (eighth standard) for incoming students. Since *Isai Vēḷāḷar* musicians previously have given little importance to formal school education, many of their artistically qualified sons are not eligible for institutional learning of *Periya Mēḷam* music.

A related problem which many senior *Periya Mēḷam* musicians cite regarding institutional setting is a shift in the nature of the teacher-student relationship. The lack of respect among young students for the tradition of *Periya Mēḷam* music and its senior practitioners is often connected to this new setting of learning. In *gurukulavāsam*, the *guru* had an absolute command on all aspects of his students' life, and physical punishment was not uncommon if students could not meet the *guru's* code or expectation.[104] In the institutional setting, on the other hand, the teacher is only responsible for the content of lessons, and the strict behavioural code and fearful respect for the *guru* which for senior *Periya Mēḷam* musicians was essential for learning are largely absent.[105] This situation is seen as one factor which allows students to start giving public performances before they have gained a certain competence.

Yet, the introduction of institutional learning has not replaced the traditional *gurukulavāsam* altogether, since the number of students who can be admitted to these schools is small. For example, only twelve to twenty students are accepted to each government school every three years, and the efficiency of the system is often criticized by *Periya Mēḷam* musicians themselves. Nevertheless, it has created opportunities for non-*Isai Vēḷāḷar* students to study with accomplished *Isai Vēḷāḷar* musicians who have largely monopolized the institutional positions. This situation is especially evident in the schools in Madras and Tirupati where a majority of students belong to barber *jātis*. For example, at the Government College in Madras where a majority of students belong to the Tamil-speaking barber *jāti* known as *Maruttuvar*, all five teachers who have taught since its inception in 1957 are *Isai Vēḷāḷars* from the Tanjavur area. Although almost all students are from families of *Periya Mēḷam* musicians, and they would likely become professionals regardless of them attending these schools, many *Isai Vēḷāḷar* musicians believe that people from other *jātis* entered the profession of *Periya Mēḷam* music through these colleges.

The period between 1920 and 1950, which roughly

corresponds to Rajarattinam Pillai's active performing career, may be termed the period of greatest change in *Periya Mēḷam* music. The changes which occurred during this period were drastic and pervasive, and were found in many aspects of the *Periya Mēḷam* tradition including the size and sound of the instrument, the instrumentation of the ensemble, styles and techniques of playing, repertoire, hierarchy among musicians, and their physical appearance.

Rajarattinam Pillai is perceived to have played the decisive role not only in initiating most of the important changes during this period, but also in stabilizing or perpetuating them by his charisma which commanded imitation among his followers.

FOUR

Performance Contexts of *Periya Mēḷam*

INTERCONNECTED TO THE changes in instrument and instrumentation discussed in the previous chapter, the performance contexts of *Periya Mēḷam* music underwent a considerable change during the period of Rajarattinam Pillai's active performing career. This chapter describes the different performance contexts in which Rajarattinam Pillai operated and gained recognition, then places his perceived role in the changes during his lifetime. The chapter is divided into three sections, which deal respectively with three categories of performance contexts for *Periya Mēḷam* music: 1) the temple rituals and festivals, 2) domestic life-cycle functions, and 3) new contexts. The nature of the importance of each performance context to the tradition of *Periya Mēḷam* music is distinct, and has changed during the period in question.

I. TEMPLE TRADITION (*KŌYIL SAMPRADĀYAM*)

The unfamiliar music flowing inside and around the temples has aroused the curiosity of many travellers to South India for centuries. Their reactions to these strange sounds were mixed with bewilderment and uneasiness at best, and usually characterized by impulsive but relatively mild criticism and naive ethnocentrism.

Mrs Murray Mitchell, the wife of an English missionary, provides a typical example of the European reaction to this music when she describes the music she heard in 1882 at the famous Meenakshi Sundareswarar Temple in Madurai as follows.

> The whole place, too, was filled with the horrid din of tom-
> toms, and the shrill noise of pipes, reverberating through the
> weird gloom of the passages, and giving one quite an uncanny
> feeling. (M. Mitchell 1885: 140-1)[106]

The music which Mitchell heard was in all probability that of
the *Periya Mēḷam* ensemble, featuring the *nāgasvaram* and *tavil*.

In sharp contrast to the European travellers' typical
characterization of the music as weird and dreadful, the sound
of the *Periya Mēḷam* is considered to possess auspiciousness
(*maṅgalam*) and majesty (*gambīram*) for South Indian Hindus.
Periya Mēḷam music is believed to be the sonic manifestation
of the deity, and it makes the deity's presence immediate
and audible to worshippers. For this reason, *Periya Mēḷam* is
considered an essential element of temple rituals and festivals,
as indicated in a common saying, 'There is no village without a
temple, and there is no temple without the *nāgasvaram*.' (Krishna
Iyer 1933: 71).

The religious and social importance of this music in the past
can also be detected from the references to such ensembles in
numerous accounts left by Europeans, as well as from the stone
inscriptions found widely in South India. Although the musical
content and performance practice might well have significantly
changed over time, the degree to which a musical ensemble
featuring reed aerophones and drums is given importance in
the religious and social life of South Indian people has not
qualitatively changed.

1. Historical Evidence

The origin and development of *Periya Mēḷam* music is traced
by musicians and patrons alike to temple rituals and festivals.
However, it is difficult either to support this theory with
concrete evidence, or to determine the historical depth of this
tradition, if, in fact, that was the case, due to the paucity of the
historical evidence pointing to the existence of *nāgasvaram*. Given
the current knowledge of this issue, it is important to survey

presently available evidence, and to suggest the orientation of future research in this regard.

A group of scholars maintain that it was during the time of the Vijayanagara Empire (14th to 17th centuries) when the tradition of *Periya Mēḷam* began, on the ground that available historical evidence is dated only after the time of Vijayanagara (Raghavan 1949, 1955; Isaac 1964; Sambamurthy 1983). The term *nāgasvaram* in the form of its cognates (*nāgasara/nāgasura*) began to appear in literary works from the early fifteenth century. *Nāgasura* or *nāgasara* is the far more common term applied to the instrument than *nāgasvaram* in the evidence from this period, while the accompanying drum is referred to as *dolu, dola* or *dol,* instead of *tavil,* indicating the connection to North Indian drums with similar names.[107] A Telugu work, Kridabhirama (c. 1400), is probably the first historical evidence which includes a reference to the instrument, and it is stated under the term *nāgasara* (Raghavan 1949: 156).

Several inscriptions speak of gifts of land or of a village made to the temple to appoint or support *nāgasvaram* and *tavil* musicians. Although Raghavan states that *nāgasvaram* was well-known in the fifteenth century (1949: 159), the earliest inscription which refers to these instruments is dated 1496 and is found in Tirumala (Chittoor district, Andhra Pradesh; see Map 1). This inscription in Tamil records that an equal amount of money (2 *paṉam*) was to be paid to the *naṭṭuvaṉār* (dance-master) and *muttukkārar* (time-keeper), *emperumāṉaḍiyār* (temple dancers), and the players of *dola* and *nāgasara*.[108] Another Tamil inscription found inside the Govindarajaswami Temple in Tirupati records the employment of two *nāgasvaram* (*nāgasuram*) musicians with the contractual terms of remuneration (36 *rekhai-pon* per year).[109] An inscription (dated AD 1549) found at the Nilakantha Temple in the village of Nitturu (Anantapur district, Andhra Pradesh), reports a gift of lands donated to the temple for the maintenance of service by six dancing girls, Bhavagata chanters and *nāgasara* musicians (Mackenzie in Raghavan 1949: 157). A Kannada inscription (dated AD 1552) found at the ruined

Vasanta-Mallikaijuna Temple in Devalapura (Bellary district, Karnataka) records the appointment of a *nāgasvaram* musician (*nāgasvaravanu*), Musiya-Ravuta, at the temple.[110]

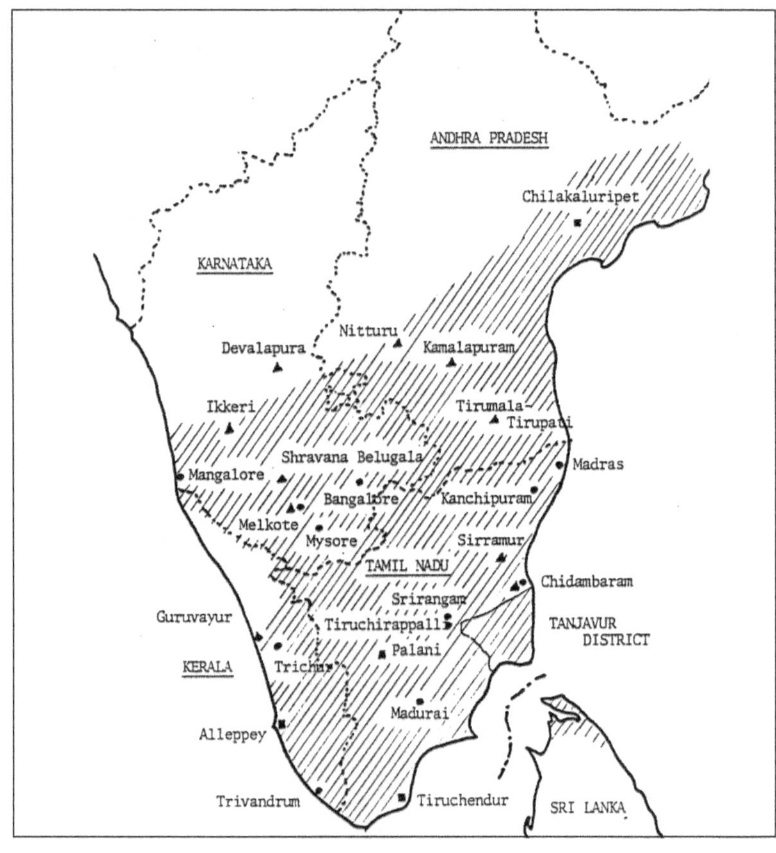

Key:

....	State division
TAMIL NADU	State name
Madras	City/town name
	Locations for historical evidence
	Locations of ethnographic interviews
	Other locations referred to in the text
shaded areas	Distribution of *Periya Melam* music
	(see Map 3 for the details of Tanjavur district)

Map 1: South India (Locations of Historical Evidence and Distribution of *Periya Mēḷam* Music)

The *nāgasvaram* music was probably played widely across the realm of Vijayanagara, considering the scattered locations where these inscriptions are found. Moreover, it was played not only at Hindu temples, but also at Jain temples, as indicated by an example of inscriptional evidence dated AD 1582 from Sirramur (South Arcot district),[111] and by miniature paintings at the Jain monastery in Shravana Belugala (Hassan district, Karnataka) which portray '*nagasvaram* musicians in procession' (Kuppuswamy and Hariharan 1985: 50).

Since inscriptions were incised mainly to keep official records of grants and donations, the information gleaned from them is often confined to the names of instruments current at the time and the general nature of their performing context. Foreign visitors to India often had access to ruling kings and their courts, and left us valuable data concerning their socio-cultural life including accounts on music and dance. Although often tainted by ethnocentrism, the accounts by foreign visitors provide vivid observations of performance practice, based on their own first-hand participation in the events, which complements the information from inscriptions.

Two Portuguese traders, Domingo Paes and Femao Nuniz, visited Vijayanagara during the reign of Krishnadeva Raya (1509-30), shortly before the above Sirramur inscriptions were cut. While both travelers make a number of references to music and dance, Paes especially provides us with vivid observations of the Vijayanagara court where music and dance played important roles.[112] Apart from these accounts on court life, Paes also mentioned that the 'dancing-girls and other women with music' accompanied the 'triumphal cars which run on wheels' when it was taken out for procession (Sewell 1980: 262), and that during the annual nine-day festival, women performed on 'trumpets, drums, viols, and pipes' (Ibid: 273).

Although Paes provided no further description of the pipes except to say that they were 'not like ours' (Ibid: 273), he distinguished them from trumpets, and they may well have been some type of reed aerophones, especially when considering their use for *tēr* processions,[113] an important performing context for the contemporary *Periya Mēḷam* ensemble. Unfortunately, Paes did not further describe the music played inside the temple, in the manner of the detailed observations he made on other subjects.

About a century later, a noble Italian traveller, Sig Pietro della Valle (1586-1652) who visited the realm of Vijayanagara between 1623 and 1625, left an invaluable description of the music in temples. When he visited a temple in Ikkeri (Shimoga district, Karnataka) in 1623, he wrote,

> At day-break the Ministers of the Temple where we lodged, Sounded [sic] Pipes and Drums for a good while in the Temple, without other Ceremony. The like they did again about Noon, and at Evening. (della Valle 1665: 119)

At another temple in Ikkeri, della Valle described what he saw as,

> The same Evening Lights being set up in all the Temples, and usual Musick of Drums and Pipes sounding, I saw in one Temple, which was none of the greatest, a Minister or Priest dance before the idol all naked, saving that he had a small piece of Linnen over his Privities, as many of them continually go. (della Valle 1665: 137)

From these, we learn that the use of an instrumental ensemble featuring wind instruments and drums to provide music in the temples was common, even at smaller temples. He described elsewhere the temple instrumental ensemble as producing 'a great noise' (138), and the pipes in his description may well be a type of double-reed instrument akin to the *nāgasvaram*. Furthermore, the music was probably played periodically at the prescribed times of the day, reminiscent of the music played by the *Periya Mēḷam* ensemble as part of the daily temple ritual discussed below. The dance before the deity to the musical accompaniment described above also reminds one of the practice of temple dancers (*dēvadāsis*), though of a different sex, before the abolition of temple dancing.[114]

The sculptures and paintings offer important visual information on the morphology of musical instruments as well as on the performance practice and context. The South Indian temples prove to be an indispensable repository of the iconographic representations of music culture, with literally thousands of specimens exhibiting important visual information (Sambamurthy 1982b: 220-3; Tarlekar and Tarlekar 1972; Kuppuswamy and Hariharan 1985).

As in the case of inscriptions, however, the visual representations of *Periya Mēḷam* music are few in number. The dearth of such evidence presents a stark contrast to the abundance of inscriptions of other aerophones such as flutes and trumpets (Isaac 1964). It also appears to conflict with the commonly held belief among musicians and the general public that *Periya Mēḷam* music has been an indispensable part of temple rituals since the inception of temples.

One difficulty in using iconographical representations for historical evidence centers around the determination of the date of a specimen. Unlike the inscriptions which often give the precise date of the document, iconographic representations are rarely dated, and most temples experienced a series of renovations at different points of history. Although the general stylistic features peculiar to each period can be useful, to determine when each specimen was created remains difficult.

Iconographic examples depicting *nāgasvaram*-type instruments from the Vijayanagara territory are found at the Cheluva Narayana Swamy Temple in Melkote (Mandya district, Karnataka) (Figure 4-1: a). At the bottom foundation of a hall facing the temple tank, there are five panels of sculptural representations, each portraying the figure of a dwarf playing an aerophone. Two of them are seen playing instruments resembling *nāgasvaram* with clearly conical bodies, whereas the other two are playing snake charmers (single-reed aerophone) known today as *mahuḍi* or *puṅgi* with the last remaining musician blowing into a bent horn (Figure 4-1: b, c).

a.

b.

c.

Figure 4-1: Sculpted Panels of the Instruments Resembling *Nāgasvaram* (Melkote, Mandya district, Karnataka) a: Overview

Probably the best sculptural examples of a *nāgasvaram*-type instrument are the three panels found at the bottom of the inside wall surrounding the Kanakasabha at the Nataraja Temple in Chidambaram (Figure 4-2: a). The first panel (Figure 4-2: b) shows two male musicians playing what appear to be a *nāgasvaram* and an *ottu*. One instrument is held downward parallel to the player's body, while the other is held at an angle away from the player. In the first one, the fingers of the player placed on his instrument look as if they were opening and closing finger holes, whereas in the second the position of hands and fingers suggests that the player is merely holding his instrument much like an *ottu* player does. The second panel (Figure 4-2: c) shows two more male figures, both standing straight and facing forward. The figure on the left appears to be blowing into a conical pipe much like *nāgasvaram*, although the distal end (bell) of the instrument is broken off. In this sample, the reed and staple can be clearly seen. The figure on the right is about to hit his hand cymbals, which resemble the present-day *tāḷam*. The third panel (Figure 4-2: d) shows yet another set of two male musicians. The player on the left plays a barrel-shaped drum which is hung from his left shoulder, much as the present-day *tavil*. He plays the two heads of the drum with his hands. Facing the drummer, the musician on the right plays a clearly conical pipe. He holds the instrument away from his body as if he was projecting the sound toward the drummer. Compared to the first two panels, the musicians on the third exhibit much more movement. The drummer appears to be concentrating in his performance with his legs slightly apart and bent, and the reed-pipe player's positioning of his instrument may be a freeze of the swinging of the instrument commonly seen among contemporary *nāgasvaram* players. All the six figures in these panels wear a loose lower-body garment resembling the present-day *vēṭṭi*, with their upper torso bare. They all decorate themselves with necklaces, armbands, and bracelets.

The innermost wall where these sculptured panels are found is known as Kulottunga Cholan Tirumaligai, after the Cholan

a.

b.   c.

Figure 4-2: Sculpted Panels of the Instruments Resembling Those Used in *Periya Mēḷam* Ensemble (Chidambaram, South Arcot district, Tamil Nadu)
a: Overview

king, Kulottunga I (1070-1120), who initiated the construction of the structure. The wall is believed to have been completed during the reign of his son and successor, Vikrama (1118-35) (Swamy 1979: 57). If this theory is to be accepted, the earliest possible date for the panels and the instruments depicted on them would be the beginning of the twelfth century. S.R. Balasubramanyam, a noted art historian, ascribes the present structure of the Nataraja Temple to the Later Chola period (1070-1270), perhaps suggesting that no renovations were made since the construction by Vikrama (1966: 65). However, these sculptural panels appear to be too little damaged to have been made in the twelfth century. Seeming to agree with my observation, Isaac concludes that *nāgasvaram* and *ottu* came into being by the fourteenth century, although she cites this iconographic evidence from Nataraja Temple (1964: 325).

In contrast to those who believe in the Vijayanagara origin of *Periya Mēḷam* music, a few other scholars accord its beginning to much earlier periods. Malarvizhi emphasizes the ancient origin of *nāgasvaram* on the ground that the *uttalavenu* mentioned in the Rig Veda, the *vaṅgiyam* in Adiyaruku Nallar's commentary to *Silappadikāram* (second century AD), and the *peruvaṅgiyam* in the Sangam literature are direct predecessors of the present-day *nāgasvaram* (n.d.: 7-11).[115] Citing the sculptural evidence at the Nataraja Temple mentioned above, Malarvizhi also argues that the structure where the sculptures are found was built in the sixth century AD by Simhavarman, and that *nāgasvaram* existed then (n.d.: 11-3), discounting the possibility of the changes due to renovations. Kuppuswamy and Hariharan (1985), on the other hand, believe that the frescoes of the Ajanta caves are the first representations of the *nāgasvaram*, presumably suggesting its North Indian origin. However, their findings must be placed in the context of the history of reed instruments in general in South Asia, and the use of the term *nāgasvaram* to refer to prototypic aerophones is confusing.[116]

It is evident from the names of instruments mentioned in the ritual manuals and the abundance of their iconographical representations in the temple that a wide variety of instruments were once used as part of temple rituals (Isaac 1964; Sambamurthy 1976).[117] A number of musical instruments are also mentioned in conjunction with temple ritual in inscriptions since the Chola period.[118] *Periya Mēlam* music can be seen as the sole intact survivor among the many traditions of instrumental music which flourished at various periods in history, since all the other traditions of the immediate past have been recently discontinued or are on the verge of extinction. For an example of the latter case, only one competent player of the *pañjamuhavāttiyam* ('five-faced instrument') is known to be available at present, although presumably it was at one time an important instrument for many Siva temples in the Tanjavur area.[119] While insufficient salaries for temple musicians have caused the discontinuation of these traditions, the survival of *Periya Mēlam* music is indebted to the suitability of the instruments for playing *Karnāṭak* music and the acquisition of the status as the indispensable element at domestic functions.

2. The *Nāgasvaram* Tradition in Tiruvarur

Periya Mēlam musicians, especially those of the older generation, assert that *nāgasvaram* and *tavil* came into existence simultaneously when the very first temple was established in South India (Sankaran 1976: 17; B.M. Sundaram 1986: 76). Although the historical depth of the *Periya Mēlam's* association with the temple rituals cannot be determined from this belief, it clearly reflects the widely held notion of the *Periya Mēlam's* initial connection with temple rituals and festivals.

A more specific story is handed down by musicians from Tiruvarur and many others from the Tanjavur area. They claim that the temple *Periya Mēlam* tradition developed in Tiruvarur, more precisely at the temple built for the deity Tyagaraja,[120] where hereditary musicians have, as they believe, served the temple since the Chola period (850-1278). Presumed descendants of such a family, who still play the *nāgasvaram* for the temple, possess palm-leaf manuscripts which give their genealogy for the last twenty generations.[121]

According to the same manuscript, the *nāgasvaram* was bestowed by Siva from Kailash at the request of a mythical Chola emperor, Musukunda, when Siva visited Tiruvarur manifesting himself as Tyagaraja. This mono-genetic origin myth of *nāgasvaram* is followed by a story which explains the dissemination of *nāgasvaram* music to other temples in the Chola kingdom. The musicians in Tiruvarur maintain that when rain was successfully induced by the performance of *nāgasvaram* musicians from Tiruvarur during a severe drought, Rajendra Chola I (1012-44), the ruler of the Cholas, recognized the power (*sakti*) inherent in the instrument and ordered the other temples in his territory to establish similar traditions.[122] As a sign of his appreciation of this miraculous performance, Rajendra Chola presented the musicians with two ivory *nāgasvarams*, which have survived until today.[123]

Although no historical evidence has so far been found to support the incident surrounding Rajendra Chola I's gift, this origin myth constitutes a part of the strong conceptual association of *nāgasvaram* music with the deity Siva. Although the *nāgasvaram* is played both at Saiva and Vaishnava temples today, its primary connection with Siva is emphasized by musicians in their explanations concerning the construction of the instrument and the sound organization of its music. The term *sīvāḷi*, the reed of the *nāgasvaram*, is said to derive either from Siva *liṅgam*, the phallic symbol of Siva which the shape of the staple of the reed (*keṇḍai*) resembles, or from *sivaoli*, the sounds of Siva. Another symbolic association of *nāgasvaram* music with Siva is manifested in the importance of the number five which represents the five aspects of Siva. The *sīvāḷi* is explained to be composed of five parts, each representing *namasivāyā* ('obeisance to Siva'), the five sacred syllables (*pañjaksara*) of Siva. The *tavil* also has its own story which connects the instrument to the Hindu pantheon. The Abhinava Bharata Sara Sangraham by Mummadi Chikka Bhupala (c.AD 1670) explains that the *dolu* was created by the ten-faced demon, Ravana or Ravanesvara, to awake his brother, Kumbhakama, from his deep slumber (B.M. Sundaram 1986: 78). As Ravana is usually depicted as a devotee of Siva, the association of *nāgasvaram* music with Siva is once again emphasized.

Regardless of the legitimacy of a claim that Tiruvarur has been the centre of *Periya Mēlam* music since the Chola period, *Periya Mēlam* musicians and patrons all believe that the Tyagaraja Swamy Temple in Tiruvarur has been practicing the most elaborate and systematized temple tradition for the last two centuries, and that the tradition of many other temples is based upon the practice in Tiruvarur (Sankaran 1990b: 34). For most patrons of *Karnāṭak* music, Tiruvarur is well known as the birth place of the three most influential saint-composers of the early nineteenth century (Tyagaraja, Muttusvami Diksitar, and Syama Sastri), collectively known as the *mummūrttihal* or in English, 'The Musical Trinity' or simply 'The Trinity'. The time of these three composers is widely considered the highest point in the history of South Indian music (Rangaramanuja Ayyangar 1972; Sambamurthy 1985b: 66-8), and their compositions still constitute the most important repertoire in *Karnāṭak* music today.

Much less known is the father of one of the Trinity (Muttusvami Diksitar 1775-1835), Ramasami Diksitar (1735-1817) who is credited for the systematization and codification of the most immediate *Periya Mēlam* tradition at the Tyagaraja Swamy Temple (Sankaran 1976; Sambamurthy 1985b: 125). Ramasami Diksitar, was an orthodox Smarta Brahman from Virinchipuram (North Arcot district), besides a musician and Sanskrit scholar conversant in the religious scripture known as *āhamam* (*āgama*) (Venkatarama Aiyar 1968: 3). He moved to Tiruvarur mainly due to the unstable political situation caused by the Anglo-French conflict in northern Tamil Nadu in the late eighteenth century. This conflict resulted in the migration of many scholars and musicians to other areas, especially to the Tanjavur area, where they were generously patronized by Maratha rulers. Ramasami is also said to have studied music theory with Venkatavaidyanatha

Diksitar, a descendent of the famous seventeenth century scholar of music, Venkatamakhi (Raghavan 1975a: 1).

Ramasami Diksitar is believed to have codified the system of playing *rāgams* according to the time of the day, and set the special compositions to be played at particular stages of daily rituals and processions (Raghavan 1975a: 2; Sankaran 1976: 16).[124] Although no written records of the content of his codification are available, the present performance practice of the *Periya Mēḷam* at the Tyagaraja Swamy Temple is believed to have been firmly established at that time.

Like his father Ramasami, Muttusvami Diksitar also composed a number of songs which were to be performed for different deities enshrined in the temple. He also contributed to the perpetuation of the musical tradition at the Tyagaraja Swamy Temple by training *Periya Mēḷam* musicians and *dēvadāsis* (Raghavan 1975a: 7).[125] The *Periya Mēḷam* musicians and *dēvadāsis*, in turn, have been important carriers of the Diksitars' repertoire to the present generation (Raghavan 1975a: 35-7; Sankaran 1976).[126] While Muttusvami Diksitar is usually described in literature as a teacher who trained them, many *Periya Mēḷam* musicians emphasize that his music was influenced heavily by their tradition. Some even claim that in many compositions Diksitar provided only the text which his *nāgasvaram* or *dēvadāsi* associates set to music (cf. Kersenboom-Story 1987: 42-3).

3. Daily Rituals

When the temple tradition (*kōyil sampradāyam*) of *Periya Mēḷam* music is spoken of by its practitioners, it is divided into the following two categories: the daily rituals (*pujas*) performed inside the temple, and the annual festivals featuring processions (*ūrvalams*) around the temple. In both categories, the centre of attention to whom worship is directed is the deity of the respective temple. The temples generally have a set of two images for each deity. A stone image (*mūlamūrtti*) permanently placed in the sanctum sanctorum (*mūlāstāṇam*) receives the main daily rituals, whereas a metal image (*uṟsavamūrtti*) which is also offered daily worship is meant primarily to be taken out for the procession. During each of the six daily rituals performed at prescribed times, the deity is treated as a royal personage with sixteen rites of adoration, including *vāttiyam* (instrumental music).[127] *Periya Mēḷam* is the instrumental music common to all the temples, although other instruments are often used in conjunction with the *Periya Mēḷam* ensemble at certain rituals according to the performance customs of individual temples.

Figure 4-3: Daily ritual at a temple (Kumbakonam, 1986/87)

The most pervasive feature of playing the *nāgasvaram* in temples is a system of playing *rāgams* appropriate to the time or time period of the day, which in all probability developed out of the system of six daily rituals (*shatkālapūja*). At each *pūja*, a *nāgasvaram* player elaborates on a *rāgam* he has chosen from those considered suitable for the time. The performance for each daily *pūja* typically consisted of the elaboration of a *rāgam* until approximately the 1920s. Since then, a composition on the same *rāgam* has also been played after the elaboration of a *rāgam*, influenced by the general trend toward composition-oriented repertoire.

The names of the six daily rituals, the approximate time when each ritual takes place, and the list of *rāgams* appropriate to each of six daily rituals is provided in Table 1. The data given in this table is based on the information I gathered from ten senior *nāgasvaram* musicians. Some discrepancies can be observed among musicians and scholars as to the allocation of *rāgams* to ritual time. The *rāgams* used in the temple can be classified into three categories according to the degree of their specificity to ritual or the time of the day. At one end of the spectrum, there are a few *rāgams* which have particularly strong associations with, and are thus played only for, specific rituals. For example, Bupalam *rāgam* is played only at the ritual called *tiruppaḷḷiyaraiyeḷucci* in which the deity is woken up early in the morning, whereas Nilambari is rendered when He is lulled to sleep at night (*paḷḷiyaraisēvai*). The performance of Bupalam and Nilambari *rāgams* derived from the previous practice of *dēvadāsis*

Table 1: Six Daily Rituals and *Rāgams*

Ritual	Time	*Rāgams*
1. *Tiruvaṉantāl* (*Veshakkalam*)	5-6 a.m.	Bupalam (*tirupaḷḷiyaraiyeḷucci*) Bauli, Mayamalavagaula Nadanamakriya, Valaji Malayamarutam, Revagutti
2. *Kālasanti*	730-8/9 a.m.	Kedaram, Saveri Sudda Saveri, Danyasi Sudda Danyasi, Surati Abogi, Sudda Bangalaa Arabi, Bilahari Asaveri, Devagandari
3. *Uccikālam*	12-1 p.m.	Sri Rāgam, Manirangu Bangala, Madyamavati
4. *Sāyaraccai*	5-7 p.m.	Purvikalyani, Kalyani Shanmukapriya, Todi Panduvarali, Kamas Natakurinji Harikamboji, Kamboji Ramapriya, Bhairavi Sankarabaranam Karaharapriya
5. *Iraṇḍāṅkālam*	9-10 p.m.	Aberi, Ananda Bhairavi Mohanam, Kedaragaula Atana, Begada Kanada, Simendramadyamam

Ritual	Time	*Rāgams*
6. *Arttajāmam*	11-12 p.m.	Nilambari (*paḷḷiyaraisēvai*) Lalita, Navaroj. Some musicians consider *Sudda Bangala rāgam* most suitable for the *Uccikkalam* ritual.

singing songs composed in these *rāgams* at various rituals.[128] Since the abolition of the institution of *dēvadāsis*, *nāgasvaram* musicians have absorbed that function. The *tavil* and *tāḷam* are not played at these rituals, and the *nāgasvaram* player usually improvises freely on these *rāgams* rather than playing the songs previously sung by *dēvadāsis*. Another example of the first category is Gambira Nattai, played only at the commencement of the procession, which will be discussed in the next section.

In the second group, which includes most *rāgams*, a *rāgam* is associated with one of the six daily rituals, and is not played at any other time of the day. However, it is the *nāgasvaram* musician's decision whether that *rāgam* is to be actually played, since there are at least several other *rāgams* considered appropriate to same ritual time period.

The third type consists of a few *rāgams* considered suitable for any ritual time of the day, although they are performed more frequently at a certain ritual time. For example, Natakurinji *rāgam* can be played at any time of the day, although it still assumes some association with the *Sāyaraccai* ritual and is played more frequently during that ritual. Hamsadvani *rāgam*, in contrast, has no particular association with any ritual time, although musicians agree that it sounds best in the evening. Since Hamsadvani is a relatively new *rāgam*, and in fact is believed to have been created by Ramasami Diksitar himself, it might not have been codified into the system.

According to *nāgasvaram* musicians, this system of playing *rāgams* appropriate to the times of the day was observed in most temples in the Tanjavur area until around the time of Rajarattinam Pillai's death, and it is still maintained in some temples where older orthodox *nāgasvaram* musicians provide music.[129] The practice of offering a *puja* with *Periya Mēḷam* music six times a day is now maintained only at a handful of temples,[130] and less important daily rituals have been either discontinued altogether or exercised in a simplified manner without *Periya Mēḷam* accompaniment. Among the daily rituals, *Sāyaraccai* is the longest, the most elaborate, and the most important both for worshippers and *Periya Mēḷam* musicians. Should the accompaniment of *Periya Mēḷam* music be omitted for any of the daily rituals at a given temple, the *Sāyaraccai puja* would be the last one to be eliminated.[131] It is an evening *puja* which starts around 5 p.m., and lasts about one and half to two hours. More worshippers visit the temple during the *Sāyaraccai* than at any other of the daily rituals (Kersenboom-Story 1987: 112-3).

4. Calendrical Festivals

Another important performing context for *Periya Mēḷam* music in temples is the periodical festivals. Although each temple has a set of festivals peculiar to it, the annually performed *tiruviḻā* (Skt. *Bramotsva*) is the most important festival not only for each temple but also for *Periya Mēḷam* musicians. The *tiruviḻā* usually lasts for ten days, and ends on the Panguni Uttiram (the full moon day in the month of Panguni: March/April). A different *Periya Mēḷam* ensemble is engaged for each day of the festival. Regardless of the fame and ability of the *dēvastāṉa vittuvāṉ* at the temple, he and his group are assigned for the performance for at least one day during the festival.

This custom is usually explained as giving due respect to the *dēvastāṉa vittuvāṉ*. The performance responsibility of a visiting ensemble is confined to the music for the procession, and sometimes a musical concert (*kaccēri*) on the platform within the temple compound at night.[132] The daily *puja* is performed as usual to the accompaniment of the *dēvastāṉa vittuvāṉ* of the temple during the festival.

The selection of the visiting *Periya Mēḷam* ensemble is made by the trustees of the temple on the basis of the musicians' reputation. In some cases, the *dēvastāṉa vittuvāṉ* of the temple and *rasikars* of *Periya Mēḷam* music make suggestions concerning potential candidates to the less musically-inclined trustees, who are ignorant of or indifferent to the relative competence of different musicians.[133] *Periya Mēḷam* musicians contrast the temple trustees in the past who kept the quality of music high with their knowledge and interest, to those today who show no interest in music at all. Apart from a handful of well-established musicians with state-wide popularity, many musicians seek performance opportunities by writing to temple trustees. Since the annual festival, especially at a well-known temple, is an extremely public event, drawing thousands of worshippers from wide areas, participation in such festival is highly prestigious and provides the musicians with effective publicity. A list of participating ensembles is displayed within the temple compound (Figure 4-5) or included in the written announcements circulated before the festival (Figure 4-6).

The highlight of the annual festivals is the daily procession (*ūrvalam*) of the deity on a palanquin or on a variety of vehicles (*vāhaṉam*), depicting aspects of the deity's qualities and deeds. For worshippers, seeing the deity during the procession is extremely auspicious. The temple compound is considered the deity's territory, and people

Figure 4-4: A temple procession led by a *nāgasvaram* musician (Madurai, 1989)

go there to see the deity in ordinary circumstances, whereas, during the procession, the deity bestows a special favour by visiting the sphere of the humans.

Figure 4-5: Display of the List of Invited *Nāgasvaram*
Musicians for the Annual Festival at the Kapaleeshwarar
Temple in Mylapore, Madras (1987)

As mentioned earlier, temples have a set of two images for the deity: the metal image of the deity taken out for the procession (*uṛsavamūrtti*) and the stone image of the same deity permanently placed in the sanctum sanctorum. The *uṛsavamūrtti* is placed on the palanquin or a vehicle prescribed for the day, and decorated elaborately with flower garlands before the procession.[134] The procession goes along on the four streets surrounding the temple compound, always in the direction of circumambulation, keeping its right side toward the temple, and is accompanied by royal umbrellas, fans, and *Periya Mēḷam* music.

In describing the *Periya Mēḷam* music during the procession, I will first discuss the practices prevalent until around the 1930s, when Rajarattinam Pillai and other musicians of his generation performed, and then some of the important changes which have occurred in recent years. While changes in the performance

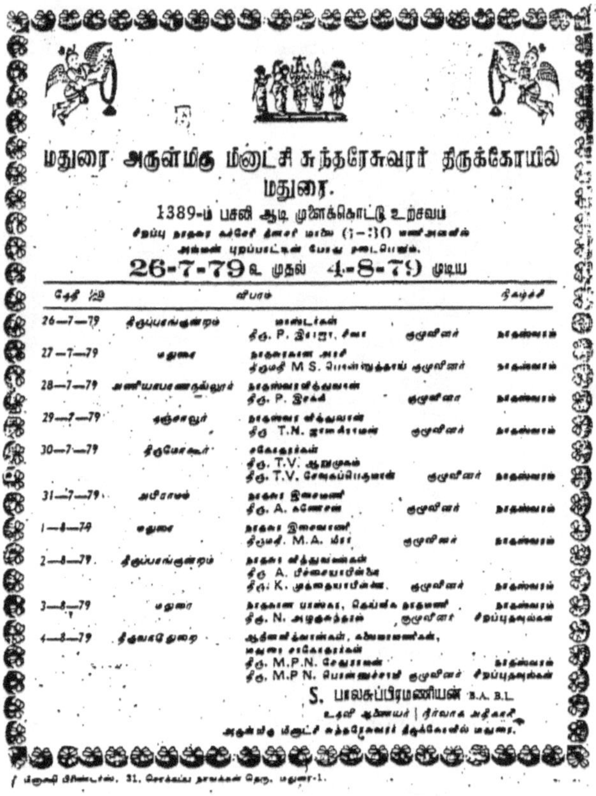
மதுரை அருள்மிகு மீனாட்சி சுந்தரேசுவரர் திருக்கோயில்
மதுரை.
1389-ம் பசலி ஆடி முளைக்கொட்டு உற்சவம்
26-7-79 உ முதல் 4-8-79 முடிய
S. பாலசுப்பிரமணியன் B.A. B.L.

Figure 4-6: Printed Announcement of *Periya Mēḷam* Performances for the Annual Festival at the Meenakshi Sundareswarar Temple in Madurai (1979)

practice of the procession and the accompanying *nāgasvaram* have been gradual, the description of the past practice given below is a prototypical one which musicians and lay worshippers tend to provide. Since the temple procession is the performance context in which musicians and patrons have provided discourses on Rajarattinam Pillai's musical ability with the most frequency and detail, the following description is meant to give a sense of what it might have been like to witness him in performance.

The procession in the past started around 9 p.m., moved in a leisurely pace, making several stops along the route and ended at dawn.[135] From the point of view of musicians and *rasikars*, the temple procession is the most suitable performance context for *Periya Mēḷam* music because of the sheer length of time available for performance and the absence of distraction. In this context, musicians could display their talents and compete with each other, and the method of playing extensive *rāgam* elaborations and other highly improvisational forms developed. Although back-to-back performances involving more than one ensemble in a given procession was not the norm, the presence of rival musicians created a fiercely competitive atmosphere among musicians, particularly between hosting *dēvastāṉa vittuvāṉs* and visiting musicians.

The performance rules maintained at certain temples also accelerated the competitive atmosphere of performances during the procession. For example, at the famous temple of Nataraja in Chidambaram, it is still customary that at the beginning of the procession the *dēvastāṉa vittuvāṉ* plays a *rāgam* of his choice for a short while, which has to be played by the visiting *nāgasvaram* musician extensively, no matter how little scope the *rāgam* may have for extensive elaboration.

When taken out through the east gate tower (*gōpuram*) of the temple for the procession, the deity stopped just outside the entrance. This moment marks the beginning of the procession of the deity (*sāmipuṟappāḍu* or *puṟappāḍu*). The *tavil* player rendered the short rhythmic prelude known as *alārippu* in *kaṇḍa naḍai* (the sub-division of a beat into five segments), which was believed to correspond to the five faces of Siva.[136] Immediately following this, the instrumental composition known as *mallāri* was played by the entire ensemble, consisting of a *nāgasvaram*, a *tavil*, an *ottu*, and a *tāḷam*.[137] While a *mallāri* was set in different *tāḷams*, the *rāgam* in which it was played was always Gambira Nattai.[138] The *mallāri* had a relatively simple and short melodic line, which was to be played in three different speeds (*kālams*) and in different sub-divisions of beats (*naḍais*).[139] With the exception of the performance in the slowest speed, the *gamakams* (melodic embellishments) were kept to a minimum, and precision in executing complex cross-rhythms in relation to the chosen *tāḷam* (rhythmic cycle) was the most important criterion of the successful rendition. The *mallāri* was to be played exclusively at the beginning of the procession on *nāgasvaram*, and never at any other stages of the procession nor in other contexts in which *nāgasvaram* might be heard.[140] Often a short exposition in the same *rāgam* proceeded the rendition of the *mallāri*.[141]

After the *mallāri*, the *nāgasvaram* musicians turned around and led the procession out to the street, as the *nāgasvaram* player started playing the main *rāgam* of his choice for the day. A *rāgam* suitable for extensive improvisation was usually chosen, for he would elaborate on the *rāgam* for one to two hours or even longer, depending upon his ability.[142] Unlike in *Karnāṭak* music, the *tavil* player provides rhythmic accompaniment, albeit sporadic and unobtrusive, during the *rāgam* elaboration by the *nāgasvaram* player. Between sections of the *nāgasvaram* playing, short but rhythmically dense interludes (*uruṭṭuccol*) are occasionally played.

The ensemble then typically played a *pallavi* in the same *rāgam*, which would last for another two hours or so. The *pallavi* employs a single line of text, often set in an unusual and difficult *tāḷam, naḍai,* and *eḍuppu,*[143] as the basis of extensive improvisation. The *pallavi* is a form in which a musician's technical skills and knowledge for improvisation are rigorously tested. Along with *rāgam* elaboration, the *pallavi* is considered the specialty of *Periya Mēḷam* musicians, and some believe the performance practice of this form itself was developed by them.[144] A long extended *pallavi* was usually followed by a *tavil* solo, which was customarily set in the *tāḷam* of the *pallavi* just completed. This was the only time for the *tavil* player to show his skill extensively since he was an accompanist in the embryonic sense of the word and no flashy interruption in any other parts of the procession was tolerated by the *nāgasvaram* musician. Perhaps the insertion of a *tavil* solo itself was originally meant to give some rest to the *nāgasvaram* player around the mid-point of the procession, by which time he had continuously played for three to four hours. The *tavil* solo typically lasted about one hour. Only after this were a few *kīrttaṉais* played with shorter *rāgam* elaborations preceding them. At this point, a form known as *rakti mēḷam* (or simply *rakti*, 'charm'),[145] which allowed an extensive improvisation, might also be played. As in the case of the *mallāri*, the *rakti mēḷam* was a repertoire exclusive to *Periya Mēḷam* musicians. In this form, the set rhythmic formula (*tin taka ta dit tai*) and the infinite number of its variations are played exclusively in *Misra Chapu tāḷam*. While any *rāgam* may be selected, *rāgams* such as *Natakurinji, Kiravani, Kamboji*, and Todi are considered suitable for the *rakti mēḷam* (Sankaran 1986a: 68).[146] The *rakti mēḷam* was regarded as the most technically demanding form in *Periya Mēḷam* music, and some believe it to be the predecessor of the *pallavi* (B.M. Sundaram 1977). The performance of the *rakti mēḷam* was confined to the Tanjavur area, and one family of *nāgasvaram* musicians associated with Sembonnarkoyil, a small village in Tanjavur district, was particularly known for their expertise in this repertoire.[147] Although the performance of the *rakti mēḷam* was optional at a given procession, a few temples had a unwritten performance code which required the inclusion of the *rakti mēḷam* for participating musicians.[148] Toward the end of the procession, a few light compositions such as *padam*,[149] *jāvaḷi*,[150] and *tiruppugaḷ*[151] were played. Just as the beginning of the procession was marked by the *mallāri*, its end was also highlighted by a special composition as the deity went back into the temple. In many Sivaite temples, a *kīrttaṉai* by Tyagaraja in Yadukulakamboji *rāgam*, Heccarika,[152] was played whereas an instrumental composition called *paḍi* in Saveri *rāgam* was performed in some Vaishnavite temples.[153]

If we are to accept the concept of *nādam* (sound) as the manifestation of the deity, the performance of the *Periya Mēḷam* during the procession of the deity may be its prime example. Many of those who witnessed the all-night processions with *nāgasvaram* music confess to have felt the very presence of the deity in the music itself. For this reason, some even claim that the *nāgasvaram* is the most important element of the festival, in fact, more important than the image of the deity (*uṛsavamūrtti*) since the sound of the *Periya Mēḷam* is regarded as the very manifestation of god's presence.[154]

A number of differences can be pointed out between the temple procession up until about the 1930s as described above and the present practice. In fact, in no other context are the changes which have occurred in *Periya Mēḷam* music more marked in magnitude and symptomatic of the general trend than in temple procession. First of all, the duration of the procession as a whole has become considerably shorter. The all-night procession in the past has been shortened to the one which ends around 1 or 2 a.m., giving musicians only about half as much of time as before for their performance. The poor attendance after midnight and the changing taste of the patrons are said to be the main reason for finishing up the procession earlier. However, the change which has had the most effect is the shift of emphasis in repertoire from extended improvisation to compositions. The *rāgam* elaboration and other improvisational forms are no longer main items of performance. The *rāgam* elaboration has become more of a prelude to the composition which follows. The frequency of rendering a *pallavi* which was the essential item during the procession before has notably decreased, whereas the *rakti mēḷam* is rarely performed at present. Even when *kīrttaṉais* were played, they were essentially the vehicle for improvisation, whereas today many compositions are played in succession without extensive improvisation, and some musicians even play popular film songs.

5. Temple Musicians (*Dēvastāṉa Vittuvāṉ*)

The *Periya Mēḷam* musicians attached to the temple and responsible for providing music for the ritual occasions requiring it are known as *dēvastāṉa vittuvāṉs*. As the leader of the ensemble, the *nāgasvaram* musician receives from the temple management the monthly monetary remuneration (*sambaḷam*) for the entire ensemble, which he then distributes to his accompanists at the mutually agreed rate (*paṅgu*). The *nāgasvaram* musician also has the right to select his accompanists, although he usually plays with a *tavil* musician from the family with which his family has been associated. In other words, when a *nāgasvaram* musician leaves his position of *dēvastāṉa vittuvāṉ*, his son or other successor will play with the *tavil* musician who has played with the retiring player.

For practical reasons, the *dēvastāṉa vittuvāṉs* live within walking distance of the temple they serve on the daily basis. When the house is given by the temple, it is often located on one of the four streets surrounding the temple compound. Although many temples customarily provided *dēvastāṉa vittuvāṉs* with land, a house, provisions and a share of *prasādam* (food offering to the deity), only a handful of wealthy temples provide these privileges to musicians today.[155]

The *nāgasvaram* musician, especially if he is well-known, usually does not play for daily rituals himself, but instead sends one of his disciples. It is true that some senior *nāgasvaram* musicians emphasize the importance of their daily service at the temple as a sacred duty, and that they do not fail to play for daily rituals themselves. However, the presence of the *dēvastāṉa vittuvāṉ* is mandatory only at the calendrical festivals and other important occasions. By sending his disciple to fulfill his daily performance responsibility, he also makes himself available for domestic functions.[156]

Although the majority of temples today employ only one set of *Periya Mēḷam* musicians, some wealthy temples, such as the Meenakshi Sundareswarar Temple in Madurai have two sets. In this case, each set has a responsibility to provide music every half month, and both ensembles are expected to participate in annual festivals and other special occasions.[157] In the Tyagaraja Swamy Temple in Tiruvarur, four families of *nāgasvaram* musicians were responsible for temple service for seven to eight days a month until the early decades of the twentieth century. Two families became defunct since then with no successors, and the remaining two families have absorbed their duties.

The position of the *dēvastāṉa vittuvāṉ* is ambivalent in several important ways. On the one hand, service at temples is regarded as a sacred privilege and responsibility given to the *Periya Mēḷam* musicians by the deity, and much pride in their association with their temples and their continuous contribution through a number of generations is discernible especially among senior musicians. On the other hand, negative connotations have been attached to the *dēvastāṉa vittuvāṉs* who perform only at the temple, as compared to those who play for various other contexts and non-*dēvastāṉa vittuvāṉs* who can afford not to be attached to the temples. The usage of the term *dēvastāṉa vittuvāṉ* assumes a slight air of ostentation for those musicians without sufficient recognition, and only accomplished musicians are addressed or address themselves as such without drawing a comment or gesture of disapproval.

The appointment of the *dēvastāṉa vittuvāṉ* was mostly hereditary until about fifty years ago when a son of a *nāgasvaram* musician had few occupational options or desires other than to succeed his father. Many families have had the hereditary positions at the temple at least for several generations in direct patrilineal transmission, even if only the traceable predecessors are counted. Many widely-recognized families of *nāgasvaram* musicians trace their traditions for four to five generations. Although an exceptional case, a family of musicians attached to the Tyagaraja Swamy Temple in Tiruvarur possess, as mentioned earlier, a manuscript containing the names of musicians of the last twenty generations.

However, while the eldest son's right to succeed his father's position was observed in principle, the difficulty of and the varying aptitude toward the instrument prevented the automatic transmission of the temple position to him in practice. When the eldest son did not achieve enough proficiency, one of the other able younger sons or a close relative succeeded to the position.

The present generation, however, is witnessing the finale of such hereditary transmission of the temple position. Monthly remuneration from the temples where musicians serve has become increasingly insufficient, and this economic depression has forced many hereditary musicians out of their profession. *Periya Mēḷam* musicians claim that this explains the discontinuation of the profession in many of their lineages, including, as its extreme case, the virtual extinction of *ottu* players, who obtained a much smaller share of remuneration. Poor living conditions resulting from the insufficient remuneration have fueled the decreasing respect towards *Periya Mēḷam* musicians.

The monthly salary to the *Periya Mēḷam* musicians is meagre, except at a handful of wealthy temples. At the time of research (1986-9), the monthly remuneration from most temples ranged between Rs. 150 and Rs. 500, which was usually less than a musician would receive from one engagement at domestic functions. The amount of remuneration has often remained the same for as long as twenty years. The actual decrease of income from temples has affected the entire community of *Periya Mēḷam* musicians, but especially threatened the life of the less talented musicians who are not employed for lucrative performances outside the temple. *Periya Mēḷam* musicians believe that this is the main cause for the tendency among the younger generation to abandon their hereditary profession. Although public pleas have been made by influential *nāgasvaram* musicians, caste organizations, and *rasikars* of *Periya Mēḷam* music for governmental support to remedy the insufficient salary from temples, the situation has not yet noticeably improved.[158]

The present dire economic conditions of temple staff, including *Periya Mēḷam* musicians, can be regarded as an epiphenomenon of the continuous attempts by the non- Brahman political organizations to transfer the authority to control temple administration from Brahmans to the state (Rajagopal 1985: 66-82). One of the major targets of this religious reform movement was the hereditary trustees, many of whom were Brahmans and/or enthusiastic patrons of music (Raghavan 1958). The *Madras Religious Endowments Act of 1927*, though weak in its actual impact, marked the beginning of government control over powerful independent temples, and was extended by each revision and amendment. After 1970, the trusteeship became a position appointed by the state government (Kennedy 1974: 286).

Periya Mēḷam musicians claim that the inadequate salary from the temples is connected to the indifference of contemporary trustees who have the authority to fix salaries for *Periya Mēḷam* musicians as well as to hire or dismiss them (Shankari 1984: 173). Although the primary reason for government takeovers was to curtail allegedly widespread corruption and mismanagement of temple funds, the appointment of trustees became contingent mostly on party politics and often a form of rewarding faithful party members (Malhotra 1972: 11; Venkatramani 1984). Thus, the new trustees often exhibited little understanding of the significance of rituals and the music associated with them.

With the increasing options for other occupations and the insufficient remuneration from temples, little economic incentive exists for sons of *nāgasvaram* musicians to continue the family tradition, often leaving the hereditary temple position open. This has created an opportunity to become a *dēvastāṉa vittuvāṉ* for those who would previously have had less access to the position. When the position becomes vacant, the retiring *dēvastāṉa vittuvāṉ* attempts to recommend one of his competent relatives, often his son-in-law, to the temple trustee.[159]

Despite the meagre compensation from the temple they serve, however, the position of *dēvastāṉa vittuvāṉ* is important for musicians for a different reason. Apart from many older musicians' belief in playing music for the deity as a sacred privilege, the temple also serves as a venue for publicity for the musician. Musicians are aware that impressive performances at temple rituals and festivals, or even their mere presence there, are noticed by potential sponsors and bring opportunities for more lucrative engagements for marriage ceremonies.

As in the case of temples, many monasteries known as Madams have *Periya Mēḷam* musicians who play for the daily *puja*. In addition, three non-Brahman *ādīnams* (monastic centers) in Tanjavur district, which are important parental Madams exercising control over subordinate Madams also appoint *Periya*

Mēḷam musicians as *ādīna vittuvāṉs* in addition to those who play for the daily service.[160] The performance responsibility of *ādīna vittuvāṉs* is confined to the annual festivals and other special occasions. For example, in the *ādīnam* in Tiruvavadudurai (Mayiladuthurai taluk) to which Rajarattinam Pillai was attached for many years,[161] the *ādīna vittuvāṉs* are expected to play only at two types of special occasions: the ten-day annual festival known as *Radasaptami Utsavam* in the month of *Tai* (January/February), and at the bi-monthly *Nataraja Abisekam* which lasts only for one day. The *ādīna vittuvāṉs* are given *gaurava sambaḷam* (honorary salary in cash) each month as a tangible token or acknowledgement of their association with the *ādīnam*. They are paid throughout the year, including the months when they have no performance obligations. A considerable amount of unhusked rice (net) is also given to them once a year after the harvest season.[162] During the annual festivals, other *Periya Mēḷam* ensembles (*siṟappu mēḷam*) are invited, usually one per day, and the *ādīna vittuvāṉs* (*ādīna mēḷam* or *maḍattu mēḷam*) serve as the host to the other visiting musicians during performances.

The position of *ādīna vittuvāṉ* brings much higher prestige to *nāgasvaram* musicians than that of *dēvastāṉa vittuvāṉ*. In turn, the *ādīna vittuvāṉs* are the pride of their *ādīnams*, as is clearly seen in the case of Rajarattinam Pillai. Only some of the best musicians in the past were appointed to these positions, and that was perhaps instigated by the rivalry among three *ādīnams* or between these three non-Brahman *ādīnams* and the Brahman-oriented Sankaracharya *ādīnams*, such as the ones in Kanchipuram and Kumbakonam. The positions of *ādīna vittuvāṉ* were not generally hereditary and were filled according to musicians' ability and fame, although the close association, either by blood or through discipleship, with the previous *ādīna vittuvāṉ* may have well influenced the decision.

Rajarattinam Pillai's association with the Tiruvavadudurai Adīnam which lasted for more than thirty years was initiated by his own relatives. First, Tirumarugal Natesa Pillai, who adopted

Rajarattinam Pillai, was a famous *nāgasvaram* musician attached to the *ādīnam*. Although Natesa Pillai died when Rajarattinam Pillai was still a small child, he had an advantage of being an adopted son of the previous *ādīna vittuvāṉ*. Second, the patron-husband of Rajarattinam Pillai's sister, who was a trustee at the *ādīnam*, not only gave encouragement to Rajarattinam Pillai but arranged well-known musicians to teach him. In this environment, Rajarattinam Pillai had a chance at a very early age to perform for the head of the *ādīnam*, who encouraged him in his studies. After Rajarattinam Pillai's talent was detected, his musical training and development was carefully monitored by the *ādīnam* itself through these two enthusiastic and influential supporters.

The generous gifts, such as a gold coin and the *nāgasvaram* covered with gold or silver foil, have been bestowed by the *ādīnams* both to the *ādīna vittuvāṉs* and visiting musicians, either as an appreciation of a particularly fine performance or more commonly as the recognition of a musician's accumulated achievements. Rajarattinam Pillai was the only musician who was presented with a gold-covered *nāgasvaram* by the Tiruvavadudurai Adinam, whereas three other eminent *nāgasvaram* musicians have been given silver covered *nāgasvarams* by them (Malarvizhi n.d.: 28-9).

Princely courts had a number of musicians on their payroll, including those who played *nāgasvaram*. As in the case of *ādīna vittuvāṉs*, the responsibility of court *nāgasvaram* musicians (*āstāṉa vittuvāṉ*) was confined to a few special occasions, while a monthly salary was paid to them throughout the year. Madurai Ponnusami Pillai (1879-1930), who was attached to the Mysore court during the reign of Krishnaraja Wodeyar IV (1897-1940), travelled to Mysore only twice a year on the Maharaja's birthday and Dasara festival from Madurai, where he lived all his life. Ponnusami Pillai was a pride of the Mysore court, and he was given a number of monetary awards and expensive gifts from the Maharaja (Anon. 1980).[163]

6. Individual Traditions

Apart from the performance practice that they share, many individual temples have distinct features which relate to the compositions, *rāgams*, and instruments to be played as part of their daily rituals and calendrical festivals. The Hindu saints have, for centuries, made pilgrimages to a number of temples where, inspired by the divine presence, they wrote songs praising the presiding deities. The tradition of praising the deity in song form dates back at least to the period of the early *Bhakti* movement in South India (sixth to ninth centuries AD) when a number of poet-saints composed hymns with fervid devotion (*bhakti*) at the various sacred sites they visited (Nilakanta Sastri 1963: 35-48). Today, these hymns are sung by a group of temple servants known as *ōduvārs* and *araiyars* attached to the Siva and Vishnu temples respectively.[164] Many compositions by the *mummūrttihal*, which constitute the major portion of the repertoire of present-day *Karnāṭak* music, are believed to have been composed in this manner either at the temples themselves or at the places where the temples are located (Sambamurthy 1970, 1985b).

Playing the compositions in praise of the deity appears appropriate not only because the deity in question is the object and *raison d'être* of these compositions, but also because the composer's devotion and spiritual relationship with the deity can be transcended through time and re-experienced through its performance. Some of these compositions have achieved sanctity in themselves and have become associated with part of the status of the deity's personal property, not to be utilized for any other purposes. The performance of these compositions is restricted only for the deity in question. For example, when Muttusvami Diksitar visited the Akshayalinga Swamy Temple in Kilvelur (Tiruvarur taluk), he composed a *kīrttaṉai* in Sankarabharanam *rāgam* (*Akshayalingavibho*) praising its presiding deity.[165] While this composition is played daily in the temple by *Periya Mēḷam* musicians, the performance of this composition for domestic functions is consciously avoided in Kilvelur and the surrounding area.[166]

Another example is found at the Padmanabhaswamy Temple in Trivandrum (Kerala) where nothing but Swati Tirunal's compositions on his *iṣṭa deivam* (guardian deity), Padmanabhaswamy, may be played on *nāgasvaram*, except for the textually neutral *rāgam* elaboration and purely instrumental compositions such as *mallāri*. The Padmanabhaswamy Temple is one of the few temples which still retain the highly systematized *nāgasvaram* tradition in practice. Musicians play only a *rāgam* or a *rāgam* and the *kīrttaṇai* in the same *rāgam* prescribed for each of four daily rituals. For example, there is a list of four *kīrttaṇais* (in Mayamalavagaula, Bilahari, Nadanamakriya, and Mohanam *rāgams*) prescribed for the first ritual of the day around 4.30 a.m., of which one *kīrttaṇai* is selected by the *nāgasvaram* musician depending on his mood. The *rāgam* of the chosen *kīrttaṇai* is played for ten to fifteen minutes first. In contrast, at the second *puja* of the day around 10.30 a.m., one of the five *rāgams* (Danyasi, Saveri, Sri, Simendramadyamam, and Madyamavati) is played for about thirty minutes, and no compositions are played then.[167] The *nāgasvarams* played in this temple are higher in pitch (5½ *kaṭṭai* or G# as tonic pitch) and shorter (about two feet long) than the kinds most commonly used today. When not in use, they are always kept in a room inside the temple, and taking them out of the temple compound is strictly prohibited.[168]

Certain *rāgams* may be considered appropriate for a deity on the basis of the compatibility between the *rasa* which a *rāgam* evokes and the disposition of a deity. Mohanam *rāgam* is played only for the deity Aghoramurthy at the Swetharanyeswarar Temple in Tiruvengadu (Sirkazhi taluk, Tanjavur district) (Narayanaswamy 1982; Sambamurthy 1982b: 230), and playing of this *rāgam*, either its improvisational elaboration or compositions outside of the temple contexts is forbidden in Tiruvengadu. In this case, the *vīra rasa* with which Mohanam *rāgam* has a strong association, is believed to be suited to the deity's disposition.[169]

Special types of instruments may be employed according to the tradition of individual temples. The Kumbeswarar Temple in Kumbakonam (Tanjavur district) was known for its regular performance on a *nāgasvaram* made of soap stone until the death of its last player Kunjidapadam Pillai in the early 1980s.[170]

Some temples have a tradition of playing the *muhavīṇai,* a small double-reed instrument with a limited range (one and half octave), as part of the temple ritual with the *tavil* accompaniment. The *muhavīṇai* is used as part of the ensemble accompanying the *terukkūttu* dance drama, and was once used to accompany temple dance until it was replaced by flute and clarinet.[171] Presumably, the use of the *muhavīṇai* was prevalent until the early decades of the twentieth century, but only a handful of temples use this instrument today. One such example is the Vaidhyanatha Swamy Temple in Vaidesvarankoyil (Tanjavur district) where the *muhavīṇai* is played once a day by a *nāgasvaram* musician attached to the temple. The Sankaracharya Adinam in Kanchipuram also had an *ādīna vittuvāṉ* who played the *muhavīṇai* until around 1980.[172]

In some Saiva temples, different types of drums are used either augmenting the *Periya Mēḷam* ensemble or replacing the *tavil*. In the area around Tiruvarur, a pair of kettledrums known as *koḍukoṭṭi* or *kiḍikeṭṭi* is sometimes used as a rhythmic accompaniment instrument replacing the *tavil*. It is played with a pair of two bamboo sticks with their playing ends shaped like a loop. The *koḍukoṭṭi* is already mentioned in *tēvāram* hymns (6th to 9th centuries) and *Silappadikāram* as a type of drum, though no morphological

Figure 4-7: *Koḍukoṭṭi* (Tiruvarur)

description is given (Dorai Rangaswamy 1958: 394-6). The name of the instrument may well derive from a Siva's dance with the same name (Pillay 1969: 462, 492; Peterson 1989: 99). The *koḍukoṭṭi* is still used at the Tyagaraja Swamy Temple in

Tiruvarur during the procession of the deity on temple car (*tērursavam*) (Balasubramaniyan 1988: 265). Additionally, a pair of kettledrums known as *sammela* which resembles the *koḍukoṭṭi* is used in several temples in the Dakshin Kanara district of Karnataka state.

In some temples, the *Periya Mēḷam* ensemble employs an additional drum which marks the different divisions of the *tāḷam* rhythmic cycle, either augmenting or replacing the *tāḷam* (hand cymbals). At the Ekambaranathar Temple in Kanchipuram (Chingleput district), a barrel-shaped drum called *ōḍal* is used in place of the *tāḷam*, whereas at the Krishna Temple in Guruvayur (Trichur district, Kerala), a kettledrum called *iruduri* is added to the ensemble during the daily *puja* to augment the rhythmic pattern played on the *tāḷam*.

II. DOMESTIC FUNCTIONS AND MARRIAGE CEREMONY

During the months considered appropriate for conducting marriage ceremonies, any locality in Tamil Nadu is filled with the music of *Periya Mēḷam* ensemble. Its sound will be heard flowing from the inside of a marriage hall early in the morning, or an ensemble may be observed at night leading the procession of a bridegroom or bride decorated with bright-coloured garlands. People are dressed up in expensive silk garments, and the atmosphere is exuberant and jovial. Going through a densely-populated area such as Mylapore in Madras, one might encounter such an event at almost every block.

Apart from the performance at temples, the domestic rituals which mark the transitions of one's life collectively provide the economically most important performance contexts for *Periya Mēḷam* musicians. As the salaries from temples they serve become increasingly inadequate, the remuneration from playing for these domestic functions has served as a major source of their income.

Despite this increasing economic dependence on domestic functions, however, it is the status of *Periya Mēḷam* musicians as god's servants at temples which provides them with the ultimate legitimacy for being invited at such occasions. The mere presence of *Periya Mēḷam* musicians is considered to emanate auspiciousness which they acquire through constant contact with the deity in temple services.[173]

The more specific reason for the inclusion of *Periya Mēḷam* on such occasions is the auspiciousness (*mangalam*) with which its sound is strongly associated.[174] The sound of the *Periya Mēḷam* functions at two different levels, promotive and preventive, for a successful completion of the ceremony. The ceremony which marks the transition from one stage of life to the next is ritually dangerous as a whole due to its unstableness (Gennep 1960; Douglas 1966), and it is considered important to fill the ritual space with the auspiciousness emanating from the sound of the *Periya Mēḷam*. The selection of *rāgams* and compositions taken to be auspicious for the occasion are also made for this reason. Therefore, the sounds and presence of *Periya Mēḷam* ensemble provides and intensifies the auspiciousness at the entire ceremony with its innate propitious quality. On the other hand, the crucial moments during the ceremony which symbolize the transition between stages are particularly susceptible to undesirable forces, which can be prevented by the use of *Periya Mēḷam* music. Such forces can take damaging effect only when undesirable sensory phenomena are perceived. In the aural sensorial domain, the misfortune is believed to manifest to those who hear the inauspicious sounds such as coughing and sneezing (Padfield 1975: 106; Diehl 1956: 97, 189; Allison 1980: 371). The *Periya Mēḷam* is believed to prevent the various sounds culturally defined as undesirable from being heard by overpowering them with extremely loud music during those crucial moments, thus circumventing the consequent misfortunes. In addition, P.V. Jagadisa Ayyar mentions that *Periya Mēḷam* music scares undesirable invisible beings away both from the marriage dais and the premises (1925: 63).

Up to a few generations ago, more importance was given to the execution of the domestic rituals as prescribed by the tradition, and *Periya Mēḷam* ensembles were hired as an indispensable part of all the major functions. Table 2 shows the names and occasions of the major rituals among Tamil Brahmans which traditionally called for the inclusion of *Periya Mēlam* music.[175]

Even among Brahmans, who generally give much more importance to the rigid execution of domestic rituals, there has been a tendency to simplify ritual procedures or abolish certain

---

Table 2: Brahman Life-Cycle Rituals

A. Pre-natal Rituals (only for mothers-to-be)

| 1) *valaikkāppu* | Fifth month pregnancy ritual[a] |
| 2) *sīmandam* | Hair-parting ritual[b] |

B. Childhood Rituals

| 3) *aptapūrtti* | First birthday of a child[c] |

C. Educational Rituals (only for boys)

| 4) *atcarāppiyāsam* | Initial learning[d] |
| 5) *upanayanam* | Initiation ritual[e] |

D. Marriage-Related Rituals

6) *niccayattāmbūlam*	Betrothal ritual
7) *māppillai alaippu*	Invitation of bridegroom[f]
8) *muhūrttam*	Consecration of marriage
9) *grhapravesa*	Initial entry into the bridegroom's house

a   The *valaikkāppu* ('bangle protection') is a ritual in which many bangles are placed on the wrists of the pregnant woman (Reynolds 1980: 48). Pandian states that this ritual is done usually in the seventh month of pregnancy (1987: 126).

b   The *sīmandam* is a ritual performed usually on the seventh month of pregnancy to pray for the birth of a male child.

c   The child's ears are pierced during this ritual. For this reason, it is also known as *kādukkuttudal* ('piercing of ears'). This ritual is sometimes performed entirely at the temple compound. a It was originally performed when the boy was taught the Veda for the first time. It is performed today when he first goes to school.

e   The *upanayaṇam* is the ceremony in which a twice-born boy is initiated into Gayatri mantra, and the sacred thread is invested on him.

f   This term is used by *Periya Mēḷam* musicians. Brahmans generally prefer to use the term *jāṇavāsam* for the same ritual. Among some non-Brahman *jātis*, the bride is taken for a procession rather than the bridegroom, and the ritual is called *peṇ aḻaippu* (invitation of a girl/bride).

---

important domestic rituals altogether, as already observed by Singer (1972). This tendency is particularly noticeable in the big urban centers like Madras where Western values and lifestyles are adopted to a greater extent. For example, the marriage ceremony (7, 8) which lasted four to five days until around 1930 is now usually compressed into one or one and half days.[176]

The inclusion of the *Periya Mēḷam* ensemble in some rituals and its exclusion in others illustrates the hierarchical importance among these domestic rituals. While the *Periya Mēḷam* ensemble is rarely seen today at *vaḷaikkāppu, sīmandam, aṭcarāppiyāsam,* or *grhapravesa,* it is still considered essential at the more important ceremonies such as *upanayaṇam* and the other marriage-related ceremonies (*māppillai aḻaippu* and *muhūrttam*). The *aptapūrtti* and *niccayattāmbūlam* come in between these two categories. They are often celebrated with *Periya Mēḷam* ensemble, but its exclusion does not usually bring explicit social disgrace or disappointment among the participants.

1. Marriage-Related Ceremony

Marriage is the most important stage of one's life for Hindus, and the ceremony which marks the beginning of this stage is given the greatest importance, with the possible exception of the *upanayaṇam* (initiation ritual) in the case of male Brahmans. As is well documented, Hindu marriage is considered an act of duty and a matter of moral and religious obligation (Pandey 1969; Chatteijee 1978: 26; Devadoss 1979: 85). It is eloquently expressed and defined in the various rituals which constitute the marriage ceremony.

The ceremony which accompanies and marks this important transition in one's life is conducted on a grand scale, and *Periya Mēlam* and its music are regarded as an indispensable element of this ritual (Padfield 1975: 118). While still heard on a variety of auspicious occasions, the association of the sound of *Periya Mēlam* in general and *nāgasvaram* in particular with marriage has in fact become so well-established that it is effectively employed to symbolize marriage in literature, films, and advertisements.[177]

Despite this strong association today, to determine when the use of *Periya Mēlam* music in the marriage ceremony started is difficult. Abbe Dubois, a well-known French missionary who stayed in India between 1792 and 1823, speaks of the ubiquitous use of instrumental ensembles without mentioning names of instruments (1986: 587). Louis Marie Mousset (1808-88) mentions the prevalent use of *nāgasvaram* for weddings in her Tamil-French dictionary published in 1895 (Mousset and Deouius 1981: 203). F.R. Hemingway reports that *Periya Mēlam* is always present at weddings (1906: 78-82).

Among many ceremonies related to marriage, the most important are *niccayattāmbūlam* (betrothal ceremony) and the core marriage ceremony consisting of *māppillai alaippu* and *muhūrttam*. Both are still accompanied today by the music provided by *Periya Mēlam* ensemble. The *muhūrttam*, in particular, involves a number of rituals to be accompanied by *Periya Mēlam* music prescribed specifically for the occasion.

The description of the marriage ceremony among Tamil Brahmans and the performance practice of *Periya Mēlam* music as executed at present is provided here, to illustrate the knowledge, musical or otherwise, necessary for active musicianship in this performing context. The reason for choosing the Brahman marriage ceremony for description over that of other groups is multifold. The Brahman ceremony is probably the most elaborate and complex of all in general, and in a number of ways it serves as a model for the corresponding rituals among other groups. It also requires a special musical repertoire for *Periya Mēlam* musicians which is not included in non-Brahman ceremonies.

a.

b.

c.

Figure 4-8:
a. Advertisement for the
Wedding Facility at a Western-style
Hotel (*Aside,* 1988)
b. Advertisement for Wedding
Saris (*The Hindu,* 1991)
c. Announcement of the Drama
Production with a Theme on Marriage
(*Kalki,* 15 April 1990)

Most importantly, however, the Brahmans have been as a group the most appreciative and supportive patrons of *Periya Mēlam* music as well as of *Karnāṭak* music in general. The importance given to the *Periya Mēlam* in their marriage ceremonies is generally much greater than among non-Brahmans. A brief discussion on the general differences between Brahman and non-Brahman marriage ceremonies follows the description of the former.

Upon finalizing all the necessary arrangements, the wedding invitation which mentions the time and place of the function is printed out and either mailed or personally delivered in advance to the guests.[178] Although in the past, it was customarily included in the invitation, today the name of the *nagasvaram* player is mentioned only when he is considered prestigious (Figure 4-9: a,b).

a. Māppiḷḷai aḻaippu

The *māppiḷḷai aḻaippu* ('invitation of the bridegroom') is the ritual in which the bridegroom is taken in procession to the marriage hall where the ceremony is to take place. This ritual is always held in the evening before the *muhūrttam* day when the core marriage-related rituals are performed. The time and date of the ritual is usually not announced in the invitation. The attendance at this ritual is considerably smaller than that of the *muhūrttam*, since only relatives and close friends participate in it. For about one hour before the *māppiḷḷai aḻaippu* begins, the *Periya Mēlam* ensemble plays at the hall, while guests arrive for the occasion. No *rāgams* or compositions are specified except that the time theory described in the previous section is generally maintained. Usually several *kīrttaṉais* are played with relatively short *rāgam* elaborations preceding some of them. When the time to start the ritual comes, everyone, including the musicians, walks to the nearby temple where the bridegroom receives blessings from the deity while musicians play several more short compositions. The musicians lead the bridegroom around the inner enclosure (*prakāram*) with music. The bridegroom is given

Figure 4-9: a. Wedding Announcement in Tamil (1989) (The *nāgasvaram* player's name is mentioned in the second line from the bottom) b. Wedding Announcement (Back Page when Folded) in Tamil with a Drawing of *Periya Mēḷam* Musicians and the Names of Participating Musicians (1987)

Figure 4-10: Tanjavur Godandapani and his ensemble during the *Mappiḷḷai aḻaippu* (Chennai, 1989)

new clothes by the bride's family, often a western suit today, which he wears on the procession.[179]

The return procession to the hall then begins. A sports car, usually bright red in colour and decorated with flowers, is rented for the bridegroom.[180] Just as in a temple procession for the deity, several torch-carriers are hired, and the procession stops at several places on the way. The *Periya Mēḷam* musicians provide music continuously while leading the procession. They occasionally turn around to face the bridegroom when the car stops and play for sometime in that position until it starts moving again.[181] Upon returning to the hall, musicians sit where they were playing before the ritual and play for some time while the guests greet and chat with each other and gradually move into the dining hall for dinner. The musicians tend to play a number of short and light classical compositions like *tiruppugaḻ, jāvaḷi,* and 'English Note'.[182] When a majority of guests finish their dinner, the *Periya Mēḷam* musicians have their turn.

b. *Muhūrttam*

The *muhūrttam*, deriving from Sanskrit *mukurta*, refers in its narrowest sense to a division of time, which corresponds to one and half hours. It also means the auspicious time astrologically appropriate for doing something significant (Madan 1987: 51), such as the consecration of marriage, and by extension to the ceremony performed during that time and to the day when the ceremony is celebrated.[183] It usually takes place in the morning for the duration of seventy-five to ninety minutes. The exact time and duration of each *muhūrttam* depends upon the calculations based upon the astrological signs of the couple. In order to illustrate the role of *Periya Mēḷam* ensemble at this ceremony, the description of a typical Brahman *muhūrttam* as observed in Tamil Nadu in 1986-7 is provided here.[184] Comparison with past practices is provided wherever relevant.

The marriage ceremony used to take place at the house of the bride's family, who was responsible for its entire expense. While most marriage ceremonies of Brahmans and high-ranking non-Brahmans are presently held at rented halls built specifically for the purpose known as *kalyāna maṇḍapam* ('marriage hall'), the bride's family is still responsible for the arrangements and expenses necessary for the ceremony including the engagement of the *Periya Mēḷam* ensemble.[185]

The marriage ceremony consists of a series of rituals taking place one after the other. The rituals which require the *Periya Mēḷam* accompaniment include those preceding the *muhūrttam* per se (*kāsiyāttirai, mālaimaṟṟal, ūñjal*), and the entire *muhūrttam* ceremony. The *kāsiyāttirai* (*kāsi*, Banaras; *yāttirai*, pilgrimage) is a ritual in which a mock pilgrimage to Banaras is performed by the bridegroom (Sasivalli 1985: 200-1). In villages where many ceremonies still take place at the house of the bride's family, the bridegroom would dress as a pilgrim and walk to the boundary of his village as if he was going to Banaras to become a *sanniyāsi* (*sanyasi*, ascetic). He would be accompanied by his parents, friends, and relatives, and the procession would be preceded by a *Periya Mēḷam* ensemble. When he crossed the village boundary, the father of the bride would meet him and ask him to return to marry his daughter (Dubois 1986: 221-2). Accepting the request, the bridegroom would return to the bride's house for the marriage ceremony.

While the above description still holds true in villages, the ritual is much more simplified in urban areas where the majority of marriage ceremonies take place at wedding halls.[186] The *Periya Mēḷam* ensemble leads the bridegroom from his dressing room in the marriage hall to just outside its entrance, where he is greeted by the bride's father and heads back inside the hall. The entire ritual is completed within fifteen to twenty minutes. It is customary among many *nāgasvaram* players to improvise on Asaveri *rāgam* as they lead the procession to the outside of the hall, and to play a Tyagaraja *kīrttaṇai* of the same *rāgam*, Raramayintidaga, on the way back inside the hall.[187] The choice of Asaveri *rāgam* roughly follows the time theory of *rāgams* discussed in the previous section as part of temple *nāgasvaram* tradition. Asaveri is to be played in the late morning between 9 a.m. and noon (Sambamurthy 1952: 30) whereas most *muhūrttams* take place in the early morning.[188] The unbearable longing of the ideal bride to join her husband-to-be is superimposed onto Tyagaraja's plea in the composition to the deity Raghuvira to join him in his house, while the identification of the wife as a devotee to her husband is also effectively expressed.[189]

When the bridegroom returns to the hall from the *kāsiyāttirai*, the bride is brought out to stand face to face with him.[190] The *Periya Mēḷam* ensemble stops playing even though they have not finished Raramayintidaga, and stands aside to give more room for people to surround the couple, who then put garlands (*mālai*) on each other three times (*mālaimaṟṟal*).[191] *Nāgasvaram* musicians play a song known as *mālai maṟṟalpāṭṭu* (*pāṭṭu*, 'song') with no rhythmic accompaniment during the exchanges of garlands. The rendition of *mālai maṟṟal* songs is often omitted today, and musicians stand around and wait till the next ritual begins in such a case.

The couple then sits on the swing which is usually set close to the entrance of the marriage hall for the *ūñjal* ('swing') ritual.[192] Five married women, including the mothers of the bride and bridegroom, one by one face the couple and give a blessing by applying milk to the couple's feet, offering fruit to the couple, waving a tray of coloured rice balls (*paccaippiḍi*), and throwing a few of them into the air in the four cardinal directions to protect the couple from evil eyes while other women sing a variety of marriage songs such as *lāli* (lullaby) and *ūñjarpāṭṭu* ('swing song' or simply *ūñjal*) (Ramanathan 1984: 6).[193] Both *ūñjal* and *lāli* are song types,[194] and several songs for each type, set in a variety of *rāgams* and *tāḷams,* are frequently sung at the *ūñjal* ritual.[195] Immediately following the women's singing, the same songs are played on *nagasvaroms* in an unhurried tempo often without *tavil* or *tāḷam* accompaniment.[196]

The bride and bridegroom return to their respective dressing rooms, while guests sit on the chairs facing the marriage dais (*maṇamēḍai*) and wait for the *muhūrttam* to commence. Meanwhile, the *Periya Mēḷam* musicians sit at the designated place, either on an elevated stage specifically reserved for musicians or in one corner of the floor from where the ritual on the dais is easily observed. Now the marriage ceremony proper begins. When the marriage ceremony is ready to start, the officiating priest (*purōhidar*) signals the musicians to start playing. The bride and bridegroom return to the hall with *Periya Mēḷam* music played in the background and sit side by side on the dais.

Throughout the marriage ceremony, musicians play a series of compositions of their choice with a relatively short *rāgam* preceding some. While no specific compositions or *rāgams* are prescribed for the occasion until the very end of the ceremony, lighter compositions in *rāgams* with appropriate *rasas* are frequently selected for the occasion.[197] One exception occurs during the *tālikaṭṭudal,* which will be discussed later. Kalyani and Ananda Bhairavi are popular *rāgams* at weddings for their strong association with auspiciousness.[198] For the opposite reason, some *rāgams* like Muhari,[199] Ahiri,[200] Saveri, and Revati[201] are consciously avoided because their *rasas* are believed to be inappropriate to the auspicious occasion.[202]

A type of musical fanfare known as *geṭṭimēḷam* is played by the *Periya Mēḷam* ensemble to mark some important moments during the *muhūrttam.* Just as the reason for inviting a *Periya Mēḷam* ensemble to domestic functions in general, the main purpose of playing the *geṭṭimēḷam* is to protect these particularly vulnerable moments during the ceremony from inauspicious sound such as that of sneezing or coughing which might otherwise be heard.[203] In the *geṭṭimēḷam, nāgasvaram* musicians play high-pitched tremolo mainly on tonic (*Sa*) and dominant (*Pa*) pitches,[204] mixed with some *brigas* (fast passages) and *tavil* players play rapid alternations of selected strokes (Berberich 1974: 129), both in a rather loud (*geṭṭi*) and frenzied manner. Musicians start playing the *geṭṭimēlam* as soon as they notice the cue from the priest or those who surround the couple and watch the ceremony closely, no matter what they may be playing at that moment.[205] The *geṭṭimēlam* usually last only for a half to one minute, and when the particular moment in the ritual calling for it is over, musicians resume what was previously being played.

An important aspect to be observed here is that the *geṭṭimēlam* is a noise in the sense that it is not a structured sound, based on the system of *rāgam* and *tālam* which defines South Indian classical music. The use of noise to fill in the break in the cosmological sequence, or in the life-cycle transition from one stage to the next is widely exercised (Needham 1967; Levi-Strauss 1969).[206] In this light, it is probable that *geṭṭimēlam* was the original function of the *Periya Mēlam* ensemble to which music was later added, or that *geṭṭimēlam* was originally played by another ensemble specifically for that purpose but the *Periya Mēlam* ensemble later absorbed that function.

Two important rituals during the *muhūrttam* which require the *geṭṭimēlam* are *kūrai aṇidal* ('presenting marriage *sari*') and *tālikaṭṭudal* ('tying of marriage necklace'). The *kūrai aṇidal* is the ritual in which the bridegroom gives the marriage *sari* made of costly silk (*kūraipoḍavai*) to the bride. Upon receiving the *sari*, the bride goes back to her dressing room to change into the *sari* just presented, then returns to the dais for the *tālikaṭṭudal* ritual. The *kūraipoḍavai* is considered, along with the *tāli* described next, the symbol of their marital bond with *sakti* invested in it.[207] After the *muhūrttam*, it is to be kept in her possession throughout the rest of her life, and to be worn at important ritual occasions.[208]

The tying of the marriage necklace (*tāli*) is the final and most important act of consecrating the marriage, forming the climax of the marriage ceremony.[209] After putting on the *kūraipoḍavai*, the bride returns to the dais and sits on her father's lap. The bridegroom and one of his sisters tie the *tāli* around her neck,[210] and all the guests at the ceremony bless them by throwing rice, which has been distributed on a tray by the priest shortly prior to the ritual.[211] At the moment that the bridegroom starts tying the *tāli*, the musicians begin playing the *geṭṭimēḷam* which lasts about one minute or longer until the ritual is over. It is generally agreed that Natakurinji *rāgam* should be heard at the time of *tālikaṭṭudal* before the *geṭṭimēḷam* is played.[212] Musicians usually start playing Natakurinji *rāgam* sometime before the *tālikaṭṭudal* to make sure that this *rāgam* will be heard going into the ritual. The extensive elaboration and *pallavi* in Natakurinji *rāgam* was a common item to be heard during the *muhūrttam* in the past, and even the *rakti mēḷam* was occasionally played on the request of the host. These forms involving extensive improvisation have been replaced by shorter *rāgam* and *kīrttanais*.

The *tālikaṭṭudal* marks the end of the *muhūrttam*, immediately after which a composition type known as *ānandam* ('bliss') is played with great pomp. The successful completion of the event, which has required much preparation, care and coordination, often at this point brings smiles of accomplishment and relief on the faces of the newlyweds and their parents. The exhilarated guests approach the dais and individually congratulate the couple. The *ānandam* played by the *Periya Mēḷam* fills the entire marriage hall with a vibrant sense of exuberance. The *ānandam* composition most frequently performed today is the one in Kapi *rāgam*, which is also considered an auspicious *rāgam*.[213] After the *ānandam*, the musicians either play several short compositions or play the *maṅgalam* and a short exposition of Madyamavati *rāgam* to end the performance.[214] After the musicians finish playing, recorded music is played.

When the marriage ceremony lasted for four to five days, a ritual known as *nalaṅgu* ('anointing') was performed in the evenings. It was a ritual in which the couple sat on the floor and smeared the paste made with saffron, turmeric and oil onto each other's legs, while women surrounding them sang *nalaṅgu* songs (Jagadisa Ayyar 1925: 60-1). The *nalaṅgu* is now performed in the afternoon of the *muhūrttam* day since, as discussed in the following section, the reception usually takes place that same evening. Most women no longer know these songs, and usually *nāgasvaram* musicians play them without rhythmic accompaniment.

c. *Reception* (Varavērpu)

In addition to the marriage-related rituals, the hosts give a reception (*varavērpu*) frequently with a music recital on the evening of the *muhūrttam*.[215] It is the time for guests to enjoy the music while they congratulate and freely chat with the newly-wedded couple who position themselves at the designated area in the hall. The musical party may be the same *Periya Mēḷam* ensemble which played for the *muhūrttam*, another *Periya Mēḷam* ensemble who is better known than the first, or more frequently a *Karnāṭak* music ensemble featuring either a vocalist or an instrumental soloist. More than one group may occasionally be invited by those hosts who are enthusiastic *rasikars* of classical music and are wealthy enough to do so.

The wedding reception is a custom recently initiated by Brahmans, presumably after a Western model, and the English term 'reception' has passed into South Indian languages. Although Srinivas emphasizes the increased secularization of traditional culture as the chief reason for the great popularity of the reception (1971: 126), it should not be forgotten that the reception was also a kind of adaptive strategy for Brahmans to cope with their new economic role while maintaining traditional ritual purity. Many Brahmans had business relationships with the British as *dubāsh* ('two languages' in Sanskrit, translators), and also with wealthy non-Brahmans. The social necessity to invite guests from among wider caste, religious and national identities who might be ritually polluting was met by separating the ceremony into two segments, ritual and secular. Yet, it soon became fashionable even among those with no ritual necessity for the separation, since it proved to be a perfect context to display the status and influence of the two families involved.

The professional standing of the musicians thus is important for the host, as part of their power display, and the remuneration for well-known musicians can be quite high (Srinivas 1971: 126). The extraordinary sums of remuneration which Rajarattinam Pillai demanded and received at highly publicized weddings hosted by dignitaries of South India are still topics of discussion among performers and patrons of *Periya Mēḷam* music. Tumilan reports, for example, that Rajarattinam Pillai received a total of Rs. 10,000 (the agreed remuneration of Rs. 7,000 plus additional Rs. 3,000 as a token of appreciation) in the 1950s when he played for the wedding of the daughter of S.S. Vasan, a celebrated film director and founder of the Tamil weekly *Ananda Vikadan* (1988: 131-2). Ten thousand rupees was an enormous sum of money, considering that the average monthly income for the family of a middle-class government employee in the city of Madras was a mere Rs. 163.9 in the mid-1940s.[216] Rajarattinam Pillai's participation at highly publicized marriage ceremonies by political figures, business tycoons, and cultural dignitaries made him even more popular among those who aspire to move upwards socially. Rajarattinam Pillai was so popular, it is often said, that some families decided the date of the marriage ceremony only after securing his consent to perform.

For the same reason, a Bharata Natyam dance recital, which occurs much less frequently, is greatly valued due to its elaborateness and implied expense. Dancing by *dēvadāsis* was an important and popular part of the marriage ceremony of wealthy families in the past (Arudra 1986/87: 32), until the public dancing by the *dēvadāsis* became increasing stigmatized in the early decades of the twentieth century.[217] When a *Periya Mēḷam* ensemble plays for a reception, more emphasis is placed upon the improvisational portion of music (*manōdharma sangīta*) than compositions. Musicians have an opportunity to display their skills to a more attentive audience without the interruptions caused by ritual requirements, as in the case of the *muhūrttam.*

2. Arrangement and Remuneration

The responsibility to arrange the marriage ceremony and cover its entire expenses rests on the bride's family, and that includes the engagement of the *Periya Mēḷam* ensemble for the occasion. While some families have a specific *nāgasvaram* player and his ensemble whom they hire for all their domestic rituals requiring *Periya Mēḷam*, others make inquiries into potential players whenever necessary. With the decreasing number of domestic rituals requiring *Periya Mēḷam* and more frequent relocations of patrons in recent years, an ensemble is sought as the occasion arises. Many *kalyāṇa maṇḍapams*, and more recently Western-style hotels, arrange or recommend a *nāgasvaram* player as part of their service to assist their customers, and the business cards of *nāgasvaram* musicians may be seen at the office of the marriage halls.

Upon finalizing the date of the ceremony, the bride's parents send for the *nāgasvaram* player to inform him of their interest in hiring his ensemble for the occasion.[218] The musician visits the bride's family to discuss the scheduled date, the details of performance requirement, and the remuneration for the performance. When the musician lives far away, the initial contact may be made through the mail. If the arrangement is finalized, advance money (*muṉpaṇam*) is usually paid to the *nāgasvaram* player either at their first meeting or when the formal invitation is hand-delivered to the musician. Although not fixed in any formal way, the amount of the advance ranges anywhere from 10 to 20 percent of the entire remuneration. The rest is paid in cash as soon as the ceremony is over. As in the case of the monthly salary from the temple, the remuneration is given to the leader of the ensemble, who distributes the money to its members at the rate prescribed to the group.

Engaging a *Periya Mēḷam* ensemble has to be done well in advance, like the other arrangements to be made for the ceremony such as renting a marriage hall (*kalyāṇa maṇḍapam*), hiring an officiating priest (*purōhidar*), and engaging the kitchen crew. Hindu astrology prohibits the performance of marriage ceremonies at inauspicious times of the year or month, and this enhances the congestion of ceremonies during the limited auspicious times.[219] This also creates an uneven work load and income for the musicians throughout the year. During the months most suited for marriage, established musicians tend to get more performance offers than they can accept, while the same musicians may sometimes find it hard to make ends meet during the slack months.[220]

Some musicians have a fixed rate for the performance, while others accept an offer within a certain range, depending upon the economic standing of and their relationship with the sponsor as well as the location of the performance.[221] A few top *nāgasvaram* musicians in the past, such as Mannargudi Chinna Pakkiri, are said to have requested a certain percentage of the entire budget allocated for the ceremony.[222] The notion of monetary remuneration is problematic for classical musicians. On one hand, the idea of selling music like a commodity is regarded as anti-thetical to the Hindu ideal of saintly musicians, and is thus not appreciated, at least publicly. Musicians, therefore, often hesitate to take the initiative in discussing performance fees. On the other hand, the monetary remuneration is intricately woven into the artistic hierarchy among musicians. The logic goes that the more one gets, the better one is and vice versa. I have heard that in a few instances a musician may adamantly request even one more rupee given to him/her to maintain superiority over others.[223]

The on-going rate for a musician is relatively easy to find out even when he is not your regular musician because he is usually sought through one's relatives and friends. Therefore, the engaging party has a good estimate of what is expected by the time of their first meeting with the musician. The negotiation may take the form of the hosts suggesting the amount, which the *nāgasvaram* musician gratefully accepts. This format of negotiation reduces the embarrassment the musician may have in displaying his interest in monetary matters, thus deviating from the ideal type of the saintly musician. The dilemma of being caught between the need to manifest, or more importantly to project the image of, this ideal type and making a living in a capitalistic modern world is more immediate to *Periya Mēḷam* musicians who continue to hold the ritually sanctified status as god's servants at temples.

The *nāgasvaram* player can also accommodate a low payment engagement by changing the size of his ensemble, while maintaining his own expected fee. The second *tavil* player and the second *nāgasvaram* player are sometimes omitted for this purpose. Musicians who perform under these circumstances are not held in a high esteem due to the implied low payment which signifies a low standard of musicianship.

The remuneration is expected to be considerably higher for the engagement involving long-distance travel. The musicians in the Tanjavur area travel great distances during the marriage ceremony season. The invitation is often made to Tanjavur musicians by those who have migrated from Tanjavur to their respective areas. Brahmans and high-caste non-Brahmans who have settled in Madras and other urban centers in northern Tamil Nadu tend to have reservations about hiring barber *Periya Mēḷam* musicians for their social functions, since in the Tanjavur area barber (*Pariyāri*) musicians play only for the lifetime rituals of low-caste non-Brahmans. They often invite *Isai Vēḷāḷar* musicians from their own ancestral village or town, if the budget permits. Some Tanjavur *nāgasvaram* players have a contact person as a kind of performance agent in Madras to facilitate engagements. Several *nāgasvaram* and *tavil* musicians have moved from the Tanjavur area to Madras,[224] and they are sought afterby the immigrants from the same area for the identical reason.

When they travel to other areas, musicians stay either at a relative's house or in a room at the marriage hall where they are scheduled to perform. In some unusual cases, luxury hotel rooms are offered for visiting musicians. Even in such cases, musicians tend to decline the offer as a courtesy to their host, insisting on staying at the marriage hall. Travel expenses are included in the remuneration, and musicians usually travel in the most economic way.

In addition to the agreed remuneration, *Periya Mēḷam* musicians are customarily given a *vēṭṭi* (lower garment) together with the final payment by the bride's family. If the performance was much appreciated by the host, some extra money, an expensive shawl with gold embroidery (*poṉṉāḍai* or *sādarā*), or even a gold coin (*dalla* or *padakkam*) may be presented to the *nāgasvaram* musician as a token of their appreciation. These items are treasured by the musician, who wears the shawl at important festival engagements and attaches the gold coin to his *nāgasvaram*. Expensive garments and the number and size of gold coins attached to the instrument are two of the eloquent visual representations of a *nāgasvaram* musician's status among his peers.[225] The occasion and hosts associated with these gifts (*aṉbaḷippu*) are remembered fondly for the rest of his life. The bridegroom's family occasionally gives money as a gift to the musicians separately from that presented by the bride's family, but the amount tends to be within a certain range so as not to overpower and thus embarrass the bride's family.

As mentioned earlier, the remuneration from marriage ceremonies constitutes the largest portion of most *Periya Mēḷam* musicians' income. In fact, playing for these functions can be extremely lucrative for established *Periya Mēḷam* musicians. Jagadisa Ayyar, for example, reports with astonishment that as much as Rs. 300 was paid for one day's engagement (1925: 41). This was probably an extraordinary figure, given Rangaramanuja Ayyangar's statement that no musicians, including those of *Karnāṭak* music, received more than Rs. 200 until 1926 (1977: 22). At the time of my research (1986-7), the remuneration of the top-ranking *nāgasvaram* musicians and their ensembles for an engagement for the marriage ceremony was around Rs. 3,000, which roughly corresponded to a month's salary of a medium-level white collar worker or a college professor. The majority of *Periya Mēḷam* musicians received Rs. 500 to Rs. 2,000 per ensemble for an engagement.

'My, you've got a lot of medals hung on your *nāgasvaram*!
Who gave (them to you) and when?'
'I wanted (them) so much. I attached your coin necklace.'

Figure 4-11: Caricature of *Nāgasvaram* Musician
(*Kalki*, January 26, 1969 Issue)

3. Recent Trends

While the inclusion of a *Periya Mēḷam* ensemble at the marriage
ceremony is still considered an absolute necessity because of its
religious and social significance, the degree of its involvement
has declined in recent years. When the marriage ceremony
lasted for four to five days, wealthy patrons hired a different
Periya Mēḷam ensemble for each day of the ceremony, creating
more performing opportunities for musicians.[226] Although
normally no two groups played side by side on the same day,

the presence of accomplished musicians in the audience created a competitive atmosphere, which often triggered an exciting performance. Even when many well-known musicians were hired for a marriage ceremony, a local player was customarily engaged at least for one day, whatever his playing skill might be. This practice of giving due respect to a local player (*uḷḷūr vittuvāṉ*) was faithfully followed in the engagement of *Periya Mēḷam* ensembles for annual temple festivals as well.

In contrast, today only one *Periya Mēḷam* ensemble for the ceremony is likely to be found, with a second group possibly hired for the reception. The reception roughly corresponds in function to the last three or four days of the past marriage ceremony, when a variety of entertainments were provided for the guests. There is a growing tendency to play commercially available cassette tapes of *Periya Mēḷam* music during the reception, instead of hiring an ensemble for performance. Tapes which are meant to be played during the *muhūrttam*, containing the compositions played at various stages of the ceremony (elaboration of Asaveri *rāgam, ūñjal, lāli,* a composition in Natakurinji *rāgam, geṭṭimēḷam, āṉandam* etc.) have also been released.[227] While the vast majority of marriage ceremonies continue to employ *Periya Mēḷam* ensembles at least for the *muhūrttam* at present, the emergence of such recordings may anticipate its gradual disappearance in the future. Additionally, cassette tapes of *Periya Mēḷam* music has already replaced a live ensemble at many of the less important life-cycle rituals mentioned earlier.

4. Non-Brahman Marriage Ceremony

While the marriage ceremony differs in details from one non-Brahman *jāti* to the next, its basic format, including the constituent rituals and their sequence, remains largely the same. For this reason, non-Brahman marriage ceremonies will be discussed as a unit, distinguished from their Brahman counterpart. The most important structural difference between these two in relation to the *Periya Mēḷam* music is the absence of the *ūñjal* ritual at the non-Brahman ceremonies. The tradition of singing marriage songs is confined to older Brahman women at present, and it may be replaced by the rendition on *nāgasvaram* or may be totally forgotten in the next generation.[228]

The dichotomy of the ceremony into Brahman and non-Brahman reflects the different musical predilection of both groups, as seen by the *Periya Mēḷam* musicians themselves. The Brahmans' preference toward *Karnāṭak* music is contrasted to the immense popularity of film songs among non-Brahmans. The level of appreciation among non-Brahmans for *Karnāṭak* music is generally much lower and film songs are preferred during the marriage ceremony, with the exception of a small number of enthusiastic *rasikars*. The film songs which are popular at the time of ceremony may be requested by the hosts and guests. Some popular film songs may be set in the *rāgams* previously considered inappropriate for auspicious occasions, and *Periya Mēḷam* musicians deplore the current popularity of film songs, which they consider the evil source of the decline of classical music among the general public.[229]

In addition to requesting a *Periya Mēḷam* group to play film songs, instrumental ensembles specializing in such songs are often engaged by wealthy non-Brahmans at their ceremonies. There are two types: a light music group and 'Band' (or 'Band Set', *bāṇḍuvāttiyam*). The former group, often engaged during the reception, has instrumentation typical of film music including several electric instruments, a trap set, *tablā* and South Indian flute. It features at least two singers, one male and one female, and sometimes even a dancer. Hiring a light music group is expensive, and popular only among wealthy non-Brahman *jātis*, especially *Chettiars*.

A Western-style 'Band' may be hired along with a *Periya Mēḷam* ensemble on the *muhūrttam* day.[230] They usually play film songs and popular light classical compositions before the ceremony begins to welcome arriving guests. A *Periya Mēḷam* ensemble and a 'Band' are sometimes heard playing their own musics simultaneously, sounding as if they are trying to outdo each other. The bright-coloured Western-style uniforms of the 'Band' members also create a sharp visual contrast to the traditional attire of the *Periya Mēḷam* musicians in white *vēṭṭi* and white or light yellow shirts. Although *nāgasvaram* musicians themselves have veered away from traditional attire by starting to wear Western-style shirts since this innovation by Rajarattinam Pillai (see Chapter 3), their shirts tend to remain white or light-coloured.

Neither a film music group nor a 'Band' are to be seen at Brahman *muhūrttams* at present. In fact, many Brahmans express their disgust for the increased use of these ensembles. Yet, a 'Band' is sometimes hired for the *māppiḷḷai aḻaippu* at the Brahman marriage ceremony. This may be a precursor of further changes. A 'Band' is also a common feature at Muslim and Christian marriage ceremonies, for which the *Periya Mēḷam* ensemble is not commonly engaged.[231]

III. NEWLY-EMERGED CONTEXTS

In addition to the two major traditional performing contexts discussed in the previous two sections, several new contexts have emerged in the twentieth century. These include concert hall recitals, radio programmes, cinemas, conventions, public ceremonial functions, and commercial recordings. Although the performances at such contexts are restricted to a relatively small number of privileged musicians and take place much less frequently, they are important in three respects. First, these new performance contexts have absorbed certain functions of the two traditional contexts discussed in the previous chapters. Second, they have become the primary criteria according to which the artistic ability of musicians is expressed and evaluated. Third, they serve as the arenas in which novel performance practices are introduced into *Periya Mēḷam* music in general. Some of the innovations made in these new performance contexts have been gradually adopted in the traditional contexts. Although

Rajarattinam Pillai figured prominently in the two traditional contexts, it was in these newly-emerged contexts that he is believed to have brought about many innovations, which have remained essentially unchanged till today.

1. Concert-Hall Recitals

The concert-hall recital sponsored by voluntary associations of music lovers has been the most prestigious, though not the most numerous, performance context for *Karnāṭak* music since the early decades of the twentieth century (L'Armand and L'Armand 1983: 421-2). These associations, known as *sangitasabha* or simply *sabha,* filled the void created by the cessation of princely patronage (Higgins 1976: 22). Though much later than in *Karnāṭak* music, *Periya Mēḷam* music also began to be played in this setting from the 1930s.

The *kaccēri* is a generic term for a musical performance. The term *kaccēri* is believed to have derived from the Urdu *kachahri* whose etymological meaning is an office for any public transaction, but which also refers to a meeting and assembly for leisure in general (*Tamil Lexicon* 1982: 632). It is reported that the term *kaccēri* was used to refer to musical recitals as early as 1858 (G.R. 1986: 27).[232] The Tamil term *viṇihai* was used in Tamil newspapers and magazines to refer to musical recitals in the early decades of the twentieth century, but it has fallen into disuse since.[233]

In *Karnāṭak* music, the concert-hall recital sponsored by *sabhās* (*sabhā kaccēri*) is distinguished from two other major performance contexts, *kalyāṇa kaccēri* and *kōyil kaccēri*. *Kalyāṇa kaccēri* ('wedding recital'), performed at the reception during the marriage ceremony discussed in the previous section, is a significant source of income for many *Karnāṭak* musicians. *Kōyil kaccēri* ('temple recital'), by contrast, is essentially an offering of music to the deity without monetary remuneration. The term *kaccēri* has a strong association with the setting and performance practice of *Karnāṭak* music, and it is not generally used by *Periya*

Mēḷam musicians, except as in *sabhā kaccēri* in which *Periya Mēḷam* is performed in the setting associated with *Karnāṭak* music.

Periya Mēḷam music was first played in the concert hall at least by the 1930s.[234] Rajarattinam Pillai is widely believed to have initiated and established the *Periya Mēḷam* performance in this context, although the exact year of his first *sabhā kaccēri* performance can not be ascertained (Parthasarathy 1981; M. Srinivasan 1991: 44). Full-fledged *Periya Mēḷam* recitals in concert halls were sponsored, though never as frequently as *Karnāṭak* music, by *sabhās* in the 1940s and 1950s.

One important feature associated with this new context was the introduction of microphones to *Periya Mēḷam* music. This new practice is believed to have been started by Rajarattinam Pillai, who insisted on using them, just like in any other *Karnāṭak* music recital. Although continually criticized and resisted in *Karnāṭak* music itself, the use of microphones was equated to the prestige of *Karnāṭak* music, once it became the norm. Rajarattinam Pillai once requested that two microphones be set for his instrument, when he found out the previous performer (vocalist) used two microphones during the specially arranged performances for the Russian delegation in the late 1940s. *Periya Mēḷam* music, originally meant for outdoor performances, is extremely loud, and many patrons still consider any amplification acoustically unnecessary at best and accelerating the vulgarization of the art in the face of modern technology.

The other change which Rajarattinam Pillai is believed to have initiated in this context concerns the appearance of *nāgasvaram* musicians during performances. As explained in the previous chapter, the traditional appearance of *nāgasvaram* musicians featuring *kuḍumi* and bare upper torso was changed with the adoption of Western hair style and shirt. In the early years of the twentieth century, *Karnāṭak* musicians had a similar ritually sanctioned appearance, but they abandoned it earlier to adopt modern hairstyle and attire. The changes in *Periya Mēḷam* musicians' appearance were made initially in the modern context of concert hall recitals, but they gradually spread to other traditional contexts as well, albeit with persistent complaints from those with orthodox values.

Both the use of microphones and the modern attire were the direct imitation of the practice in *Karnāṭak* music. As many *Periya Mēḷam* musicians believe, Rajarattinam Pillai interpreted the difference in performance practice as part of an imposed restriction placed by Brahmans, and he challenged the inequality based on caste difference by emulating *Karnāṭak* musicians. For many Brahman patrons, Rajarattinam Pillai's initiative in these changes was childish and vulgar. Childish because the microphones were absolutely unnecessary, and vulgar on the ground that Rajarattinam Pillai stripped the *Periya Mēḷam* musicians of the privilege of their status as god's servants by discarding traditional attire.

Regardless of Rajarattinam Pillai's initial intention, just as the introduction of microphones induced a 'crooning' style of singing in *Karnāṭak* music (Higgins 1976: 24), a soft style of playing has developed for *nāgasvaram* as well, and some, such as B. Ramadasappa of Bangalore, have even come to specialize in it. Today, one rarely finds concert hall recitals of *Periya Mēḷam* music without microphones set up for both *nāgasvaram* and *tavil* players. It is probable that the lowering of the tonic pitch of *nāgasvaram* and the resultant lessening of carrying power has aided the dissemination of microphones. In addition to their use at concert-hall recitals, microphones are also employed during temple festivals and marriage ceremonies, although amplification through loud-speakers in these settings is meant to announce the event to the people outside the compound. It can be interpreted, conversely, that the presence of microphones encouraged the lowering of the tonic pitch.

In contrast to the prominence of *sabhā kaccēris* by Rajarattinam Pillai and his contemporaries from the 1930s through the 1950s, the *sabhā kaccēris* of *Periya Mēḷam* music today are largely reconciled to a ceremonial role. The *Periya Mēḷam* ensemble is engaged mainly to kick off the music festivals with its presumed auspiciousness, and plays on its first day, typically immediately prior to or following the opening ceremony, rather than as part of regular programmes.

The *sabha* officials who organize concerts tend to explain the current scarcity of *Periya Mēḷam* recitals for several reasons. Many claim that *Periya Mēḷam* music is meant for outdoor performances and that its loud sound is unsuitable to performance inside the concert halls, regardless of the use of microphones. This claim is often discredited by *Periya Mēḷam* musicians and *rasikars* who are quick to point out the loudness of current *Karnāṭak* music concerts through amplification. Nevertheless, many, including ardent patrons of *Periya Mēḷam* music, believe that the music sounds best when it is heard at some distance, and one often finds more of the audience at the back of the hall, away from the stage in *Periya Mēḷam* recitals.

Another reason given by *sabha* officials is the absence of the performers today of the calibre similar to that of Rajarattinam Pillai and other master musicians during their active performing careers. The notion of the general decline in the artistic standard of *Periya Mēḷam* music appears firmly established among most patrons of classical music. Some organizers claim that they would be quite willing to sponsor more *Periya Mēḷam* recitals if such musicians were available. For *Periya Mēḷam* musicians, this reasoning is only an excuse not to give them a chance to prove their ability, because most *sabhās* encourage young performers of *Karnāṭak* music by sponsoring concerts and competitions for them while similar events for upcoming *Periya Mēḷam* musicians are virtually non-existent.

Finally, the current lack of interest in *Periya Mēḷam* music among concert goers is claimed to be a major reason for the *sabhās'* reluctance to sponsor more recitals. A *sabha* is dependent for its existence upon the annual membership fees and the donations from supporting organizations, whose preference inevitably reflects the selection of the genre and musicians. It is often mentioned that many *sabhās* are forced to include dramas and comedy shows in their programmes, even if the officials themselves are devoted exclusively to classical music

(Subrahmanya Aiyar 1966: 145), and that finding a rationale for sponsoring *Periya Mēlam* recitals for which attendance is invariably low is all the more difficult.

The lack of interest in sponsoring *Periya Mēlam* music on the part of *sabha* officials is often interpreted by its practitioners as a manifestation of the categorical neglect of the genre.[235] It is sometimes spoken of as an example of the discrimination by Brahmans, who constitute the majority of concert organizers and patrons in general, against *Periya Mēlam* musicians, who are virtually all non-Brahmans.

In contrast to Brahman controlled musical *sabhās*, several governmental or other non-Brahman oriented organizations have been sponsoring *Periya Mēlam* recitals, although these organizations themselves are considered somewhat outside of the mainstream of music culture in Madras. The most influential organization is the Tamil Isai Sangam, which was established in 1943 as an institutional base for what came to be known as *Tamil Isai Iyakkam* (Tamil Music Movement, see Chapter 6). Tamil Isai Sangam not only holds several full-fledged *Periya Mēlam* recitals during its annual music festival in December, but also attempts to encourage upcoming *nāgasvaram* players by sponsoring an annual competition. Another non-Brahman-oriented organization, Muttamir Peravai, is the cultural wing of the Dravida Munnerra Kazhagam (DMK), one of the two major political parties in Tamil Nadu, and it has been sponsoring *Periya Mēlam* concerts since the 1960s. M. Karunanidhi (1924-2018), who was the leader of the DMK since 1969, and five-time Chief Minister of Tamil Nadu, between 1969 and 2011, is the son of a *nāgasvaram* player from near Tiruvarur (Tanjavur district) and belongs to the *Isai Vēḷāḷar jāti*.[236] *Isai Vēḷāḷar Periya Mēlam* musicians believe that Karunanidhi is personally responsible for the advent of Muttamir Peravai. Muttamir Peravai recently instituted the 'Rajarattinam Award,' an award given annually to distinguished *nāgasvaram* musicians 'to perpetuate the memory' of Rajarattinam Pillai. Presiding over the function, Karunanidhi himself presented the first 'Rajarattinam Award' to the Madurai

Brothers (Sethuraman and Ponnusami).[237] In addition, a state agency called Tamil Nadu Eyal Isai Nataka Manram has attempted to bring more public recognition to *Periya Mēḷam* musicians by arranging concerts through pre-existing *sabhās*, by conferring a musical title (*Kalaimāmaṇi*) to selected musicians since 1955,[238] and by sponsoring the annual function which commemorates Rajarattinam Pillai's birthday.

2. Radio Programmes

The close relationship between radio programmes and classical music was established in earnest in 1938 when All India Radio (AIR) opened its Madras station, the first in South India, although the history of radio programmes in this region goes back to 1924 when the Madras Radio Club began broadcasting with limited facility and air time. Two and half hours of music and talk were broadcast every evening between 1924 and 1927. The Madras Corporation resumed the service in 1930 until it was taken over by AIR in 1938 (Baruah 1983: 1).[239] The Tiruchirappalli station which opened in 1939, only a year after the Madras station, is to this day the closest to the Tanjavur district and the most important for *Isai Vēḷāḷar Periya Mēḷam* musicians in the area.[240] Many of Rajarattinam Pillai's performances were broadcast from this station.[241]

The AIR is probably the largest single patron of classical music today. More than three thousand South Indian classical musicians were on the AIR payroll for their performances on its radio programmes in 1982 (Baruah 1983: 55). Although the official number of *Periya Mēḷam* musicians in this figure is not available, I estimate it at around five hundred, based upon information from musicians and officers at several AIR stations.

Two types of musicians perform for AIR programmes: staff artists and casual artists. Staff artists are salaried musicians, who spend a specified number of hours at the station, performing on the AIR programmes as well as doing some administrative duties.[242] Casual artists come to the station only when they perform for the programme, and they get paid for the performance each time it takes place. In *Karnāṭak* music, the majority of staff artists are instrumentalists whose responsibility is to provide accompaniment for the soloists, who are mostly casual artists. In contrast, virtually all the *Periya Mēḷam* musicians who perform for AIR programmes are casual artists, since the *Periya Mēḷam* ensemble is a self-contained unit of musicians and performs as a group on a regular basis.[243] Neither *nāgasvaram* nor *tavil* musicians play with *Karnāṭak* musicians except for special experimental programmes. The *nāgasvaram* musician is usually expected to bring his own ensemble for the performance.[244]

In order to perform for AIR programmes, musicians first have to be graded into four categories (B, B-High, A, and A-Top in ascending order) according to their skill. The lower three grades are determined by auditions, whereas the highest grade (A-Top) is honorary and is given to eminent musicians after a recommendation from the selection committee at the AIR's headquarters in Delhi (Baruah 1983: 56-9). Though an essential part of the life of South Indian classical musicians today, the AIR's grading system through auditions was not instituted in the early 1950s without objection. Some old masters questioned the validity of auditions in which their musical merits were to be judged by people they considered musically inferior, and refused to take an audition. For example, M. Kodandaram, a prominent *nāgasvaram* musician in Bangalore, recalls the boycott of AIR auditions by his *guru*, R. Mamundiya Pillai and his brother R. Subramania Pillai of Mayiladuthurai (Tanjavur district), both well-known *nāgasvaram* musicians. Sankaran (1988) also reports that eighteen musicians including Ariyakkudi Ramanuja Iyengar (1890-1967), one of the top vocalists of his time, refused to perform for the radio programmes when the audition system was instituted. Similar resistance from the *Hindustani* musicians is also documented (Luthra 1986: 308).

The Local Audition Committee (LAC) of each station, a panel of six to seven experts, is authorized to give the lowest grade (B) based on the audition result, whereas, in the case of the two higher grades (B-high and A), the decision is made by the Music Audition Board (MAB) in New Delhi with the Director General of AIR as its chairperson. Many members of MAB are respected musicologists and musicians with the highest grade (A-Top), and the audition tape of a candidate is sent for their appraisal (Baruah 1983: 56-7).[245] Although the identity of the candidate is kept secret by the AIR, the stylistic preference of the MAB members sometimes influences the results.[246] Musicians with B and B-high grades can perform only at the station where they are auditioned, whereas musicians with higher grades are entitled to perform at any other stations if so they desire.

The engagement of a *nāgasvaram* musician and his ensemble begins with a written notice from the station of the time and conditions of his next proposed programme. This is done about three weeks before the programmes, most of which are broadcasted live. A list of compositions, about three times as many as he can perform for the time allotted for his programme, is requested by the station. After consulting the list submitted by the musician, the station selects compositions from the list to avoid redundancy in a day's programme and informs the musician of its choices, at least several days before the engagement.[247] No further communication is made until the day of the performance, when musicians are expected to appear about one hour prior to their programme, with the letter previously sent by the station as his identification. The performance fees as well as the duration and time slot of performance are determined by the grades of musicians. The fee scales according to musicians' grades for classical musicians, as effective September 1985 are shown in Table 3.

Unlike *Karnāṭak* soloists to whom accompaniment is provided by the staff artists of the station or by guest artists separately engaged, the *nāgasvaram* player is usually asked to bring his own accompanists. The fees are paid according to the size and instrumentation of the ensemble specified by the station. For instance, a *nāgasvaram* musician in Madras with the B-high grade was asked to bring three accompanists (one *tavil*, one *tāḷam*, and one *srutipeṭṭi*) for a radio performance in early 1989, for which he received Rs. 460. This amount consisted of his own share (Rs. 250) as a leader of the ensemble, and that for his three accompanists (Rs. 70 x 3 = Rs. 210). As is always done, the payment was made in cheque immediately after the performance to *nāgasvaram* player, who later distributed it to his accompanists in cash.

Table 3: Pay-Scale for AIR Performance

Grade	*Leader*	*Member*
A-top	750	100
A	350-500	80
B-high	200-275	70
B	100-160	60

The AIR has an unwritten policy that a musician cannot perform for its programmes more than four times a year, presumably as part of their democratic policy to give performance opportunities to as many deserving musicians as it can. Due to this restriction, the net remuneration from radio performances of any given musician constitutes a relatively small portion of his annual income. Yet, radio programmes are extremely important to musicians because of the benefits created by the far-reaching publicity. High grades and well-received performances can legitimize musicians' demands for higher remuneration for other engagements.

Although the AIR does not reveal the audition results, finding out a musician's grade is not difficult, because the time slot and the duration of programmes are systematically determined by the grade. The grades given to the musicians based upon the audition at the AIR have become an important criteria for judging their musical calibre and fame. Musicians utilize, whenever possible, their grades to enhance their musical standing among their rivals.

AIR is often considered the origin of a new performance format for *Periya Mēḷam* music. Rajarattinam Pillai is widely, albeit not unanimously, believed to have been the first *nāgasvaram* player to perform to the accompaniment of violin, *mridaṅgam*, and *tamburā*, the standard format in *Karnāṭak* music.[248] Since the *tamburā* is the preferred drone instrument for *Karnāṭak* music, this accompaniment format is known as *tamburā sruti*, even when the *srutipeṭṭi* substitutes for the *tamburā*, as it often does today. It is usually believed that Rajarattinam Pillai originated the idea of playing *nāgasvaram* to the *tamburā sruti* himself and that he gave such a performance for AIR for the first time, but some opine that AIR officers at the Tiruchirappalli station advanced the idea to Rajarattinam Pillai, who agreed to this suggestion. However, whether or not Rajarattinam Pillai came up with the idea of playing the *nāgasvaram* with the *tamburā sruti*, there is evidence that he planned a concert-hall recital with the *tamburā sruti* in Madras at least on one occasion in 1937 prior to the beginning of AIR in South India.[249] Furthermore, it has been recorded that a *nāgasvaram* musician named Mannargudi Manickam Pillai played twice for Madras Corporation Radio programmes with *tamburā sruti* in 1935.[250] While either evidence refutes the popular belief concerning the origin of *tamburā sruti* performance on AIR stations, it is likely that most musicians in Tanjavur came to know about the new performance format through AIR programmes. Rajarattinam Pillai also performed as a vocalist on radio programmes, either as a soloist or in duet with another vocalist, such as Tiruppamburam Swaminatha Pillai (1900-61), a reputed *Isai Vēḷāḷar* flute player, who was also known for his ability in vocal music, much like Rajarattinam Pillai.

3. Film

The Indian film industry is well-known as being one of the most prolific. It ranks second, globally, with an annual production of about seven hundred feature films (Manuel 1988: 173). Yet, the significance of films in India lies in the extent of their impact on its socio-cultural life.

Since the *Periya Mēḷam* is an essential element both of temple and domestic rituals, which are themselves prominent themes in South Indian culture, the scenes requiring the *Periya Mēḷam* music are many. Many films in South Indian languages have at least one wedding scene with *Periya Mēḷam* music, and a number of *Periya Mēḷam* musicians have provided music for film productions. In these films, the *Periya Mēḷam* music is played either as part of the scenes involving its traditional contexts of marriage ceremonies or temple rituals, or as an accompanying instrument for vocal numbers. In the former, musicians are either totally absent on the screen, or appear in a very short sequence much as a paraphernalia of the setting. When used as an accompanying instrument, the pitch of the instrument has to be identical to that of the singer, and this necessitates that *nāgasvaram* musicians play in different tonic pitches (*sruti*) as the occasions arise. Since instrumental parts are added each time in separate sessions in recording studios, *nāgasvaram* players often do not meet other musicians.

Music and dance have always been essential elements of the majority of South Indian films, but it was particularly prominent in the period between the advent of the talkie in 1931 and around 1945. A Tamil film made during this period contained as many as thirty songs, and one film even contained sixty-five songs (Guy 1985: 465). Many well-known *Karnāṭak* musicians were lured into cinema, not only because the technological limitations forced actors and actresses to sing on the set themselves (L'Armand and L'Armand 1978: 132), but also to elevate the medium of cinema, then considered vulgar and sinful, to a socially respectable form of entertainment. G.N. Balasubramaniam, a handsome and promising Brahman singer, with a college degree, was probably a perfect candidate to play the latter role. He sang and acted in many films (Baskaran 1976: 19-20; Guy 1988/89: 67). That film songs in the early years were much more akin to classical music in musical form and literary content explains the ease with which *Karnāṭak* vocalists entered into film. Rajarattinam Pillai acted, sang, and played *nāgasvaram* as a poet in the film called *Kalameham* in 1940, and remains till today the only *nāgasvaram* musician who appeared as a main figure in a film. Nevertheless, the film was a commercial flop, which ended Rajarattinam Pillai's career as a film star (Guy 1988/89: 107).

Apart from these films, at least two films have been produced based upon the story of a *nāgasvaram* musician. In *Koñjum Salaṅgai,* produced in 1962, the story revolves around a love triangle between a young *nāgasvaram* musician, a poor but talented singer, and a dancer. The *nāgasvaram* music was provided by a well-known player, Karukurichi Arunachalam (1921-64), when he was at the height of his popularity. Although Arunachalam's *nāgasvaram* music for this film was viewed favourably by patrons of classical music, the film itself was a commercial failure, despite the high expectations before its release (Guy 1990: 42-3).

The best-known film which either has *nāgasvaram* music in it or is about a *nāgasvaram* musician is without doubt *Tillānā Mōhaṉāmbāḷ.* It is a film based on the popular serial novel which

Figure 4-12: A still from the 1968 film *Tillāṉā Mōhaṉāmbāḷ*
(Photo courtesy: Film News Anandan)

appeared in the Tamil weekly *Ananda Vikatan,* and became a smash hit when it was released in 1968. The continuing popularity of this film may be detected from the repeated re-runs on TV and the recent release of a commercial video version. The success of this film is partly due to the all-star casting, especially the two immensely popular stars for its main roles: Sivaji Ganesan, one of the two most popular and influential actors in Tamil cinema between the 1950s and 1970s (Guy 1985: 471), as a talented and handsome *nāgasvaram* musician (Sanmukasundaram) from Sikkal (Tanjavur district), and Padmini, a heart-throb of South India, as a young *dēvadāsi* (Mohanam) from Tiruvarur who refused to take any patron-husbands because of her love for him.

Both Sivaji Ganesan and T.S. Balaiah, who acted as the main *tavil* player, have been praised for their faithful imitation of musicians' movements and gestures in performance.[251] Like *Koñjum Salaṅgai,* the story revolves around the relationship between a *nāgasvaram* player and a dancer, but the depiction of the customs and habits among the *Periya Mēḷam* musicians in Tanjavur district are judged by musicians themselves and patrons from the same area to be detailed and well researched. The *Periya Mēḷam* music was played by the Madurai Brothers (Sethuraman and Ponnusami) who were already the established musicians in Madurai, but the immense success of this film drastically accelerated their popularity all over South India. The choice of the Madurai Brothers is somewhat ironic because the main characters of the story are supposed to be from Tanjavur district, and the style of musicians from Madurai is considered by Tanjavur musicians quite distinct from their own.

Some believe that the character of the *nāgasvaram* musician in *Tillānā Mōhanāmbāḷ* was modelled after Rajarattinam Pillai, although it is a considerably more idealized and romanticized version than what he is generally known for. This belief derives from the fact that the hero *nāgasvaram* player of the film is sometimes referred to as *Nāgasvara Cakkaravartti,* the well-known title with which Rajarattinam Pillai was known and addressed.

It is notable that this film's immense popularity hinges, not exclusively but substantially, on its evocation of the pathos of the bygone era (Guy 1991). The success of the film and the choice of characters for the protagonists of the story are not coincidences. *Periya Mēḷam* musicians and *dēvadāsis* are integral parts of the landscape of a bygone period which continues to evoke nostalgia among Tamils.

4. Disc Recordings

The history of music recording in India began in 1902 when Fred Gaisberg recorded several hundred titles in Calcutta for the Gramophone Company of India, which had been established the year before (Perkins, Kelly, and Nard 1976: 72). The Company had some titles in South Indian languages from its early years (Granow 1981: 257). Although the exact year of the first recording of South Indian classical music is unknown, many 78 rpm disc recordings of *Karnāṭak* and *Periya Mēḷam* music were available by the early 1920s. Two *nāgasvaram* musicians, who were among the very first to be recorded extensively, were Madurai Ponnusami Pillai (1879-1930) and Sembonnarkoyil Ramasami Pillai (1880-1923).[252] They each made at least fifteen disc recordings for the HMV (His Master's Voice) label.

Rajarattinam Pillai was probably the most frequently recorded *nāgasvaram* musician on 78 rpm discs. I have identified twenty-nine disc recordings of his music, which are listed along with more recently released cassette recordings in Appendix 2. Rajarattinam Pillai's very first recording was a elaboration of Todi *rāgam*, the *rāgam* for which he was best-known, and it was released in 1934 on the Odeon label. During Rajarattinam Pillai's lifetime, owning a phonograph or radio was a luxury which only a small number of wealthy patrons could afford, but the influence of his recordings has transcended time. They have acquired many ardent listeners among young musicians today, who never had a chance to listen to his music in person. For many younger *nāgasvaram* musicians, these recordings, along with the rebroadcasts of Rajarattinam Pillai's previous AIR programmes, continue to be a source of inspiration and validate the high opinion of Rajarattinam Pillai held by older musicians.

Cassette tapes became a powerful medium of music transaction when the mass production of cheap cassettes began in the late 1970s and the reduction of import tariffs were reduced in the early 1980s (Manuel 1988: 190). The impact of cassette tapes is most prominent in film music and other forms of popular music, but classical music is no exception. A few most popular *nāgasvaram* musicians today, like their *Karnāṭak* music counterparts, are producing cassette tapes at a rate never seen before. Yet, while these few musicians acquire more popularity with this new medium, the easy access to these cassette tapes has also prompted the replacement of a live *Periya Mēḷam* ensemble with cassette tapes at the domestic functions, depriving jobs from many musicians.

The temple rituals and festivals are considered the original context and *raison d'être* of *Periya Mēḷam* music. Daily rituals in the temple maintained a specific sense of *rāgam*-time correspondence among the worshippers, whereas the improvisational aspect of music was pursued to the maximum during the procession, as Rajarattinam Pillai was believed to have done. Although Rajarattinam Pillai was never attached to temples, the discourse on his musical excellence centers around the specific *rāgam* elaboration or *pallavi* during a temple procession. In contrast to the glory attached to the temple performances in the past, the insufficient remuneration has threatened the foundation of the community of hereditary *Periya Mēḷam* musicians.

The auspicious quality of the *Periya Mēḷam* ensemble is the reason which explains its inclusion in various domestic occasions. Although the degree to which the *Periya Mēḷam* ensemble is utilized at the domestic functions has decreased in recent years, its presence at selected important ceremonies is still considered indispensable. Unlike the other ceremonies, the performance at *muhūrttam* includes a special repertoire exclusive to the ritual, and its knowledge is essential for active musicianship. While the *muhūrttam* ritual may not provide the most satisfying atmosphere to musicians themselves because of the inattentiveness of the audience, little opportunity for extensive improvisation, and interruptions due to necessary coordination with ritual sequences, it provides the major source of income with which they cannot dispense to sustain their profession. Rajarattinam Pillai became the most prestigious *nāgasvaram* musician to hire for marriage ceremonies, with an extraordinary remuneration.

The performance contexts which emerged in the twentieth century have not only diversified *Periya Mēḷam* musicians' activities, but also provided them with different media for self-promotion. The participation and ranking in these contexts became a decisive criterion for musicians' musical ability and popularity, which then determine the remuneration rate from the traditional contexts, especially that of marriage ceremonies. The new performance contexts also served as a medium through which a number of important innovations were introduced and spread to other contexts of the *Periya Mēḷam* music. Many changes are thought to have been initiated by Rajarattinam Pillai with his keen sense of the unequal treatment of *Periya Mēḷam* musicians, who were all non-Brahmans, by the heavily Brahman-dominated *Karnāṭak* musicians and patrons.

FIVE

Practitioners of *Periya Mēḷam*

HAVING DESCRIBED THE performance practice (Chapter 3) and the contexts of *Periya Mēḷam* music (Chapter 4), I now turn to a discussion of different *jātis* (caste groups) whose members are performers of *Periya Mēḷam* music. The multiple interpretations of Rajarattinam Pillai as a symbol and the peculiarities of the *Isai Vēḷāḷar jāti* to which he belonged are dialectically connected. If we exclude *Karnāṭak* music and its practitioners/patrons from discussion for the time being, the peculiarities concerning the *Isai Vēḷāḷar jāti* can be observed in two related dimensions: the intra-*jāti* social organization and concomitant structural tension within the *Isai Vēḷāḷar jāti*, and the nature of the inter-*jāti* relationship between the *Isai Vēḷāḷars* and others associated with *Periya Mēḷam* music. Both of these dimensions precondition the parameters of the interpretations of Rajarattinam Pillai by different groups of musicians and patrons, while the peculiarities are most clearly manifest in the interpretations themselves.

Although *Periya Mēḷam* music has been played by musicians belonging to several *jātis*, I will focus upon the two most prominent *jātis* in Tamil Nadu: *Isai Vēḷāḷar* and *Maruttuvar*. The *Isai Vēḷāḷars* are prominent in central Tamil Nadu, particularly in Tanjavur district, whereas, *Maruttuvars*, although found all over the state, are especially prominent in the northern districts of Tamil Nadu including Madras. These two groups are discussed in the two succeeding sections, while the last section deals with other smaller groups of practitioners of *Periya Mēḷam* music.

I. *ISAI VĒḶĀḶAR* MUSICIANS IN TANJAVUR

1. Tanjavur

Isai Vēḷāḷars are the musicians most closely identified with *Periya Mēḷam* among the many different caste groups associated with it. They are the ritual music specialists prominent in central districts of Tamil Nadu, and particularly concentrated in Tanjavur district. Much of this district lies in the fertile deltaic area of the Kaveri river and its many branches. Its rich agriculture not only provided the ideal seat for one of the great kingdoms of ancient and medieval South India, but also is the primary reason for the district's continuing economic significance. Given its economic prosperity, Tanjavur has also been a centre of Brahmanical culture (Gough 1955). The heavy concentration of temples provided the religious *raison d'être* as well as patronage to the high level of cultural activity.[253]

Just as Tanjavur is considered the cradle of contemporary *Karnāṭak* music, it is also regarded as the artistic centre of *Periya Mēḷam* music in the past. The belief that *Periya Mēḷam* music originated in the Tanjavur area is unanimous among musicians and patrons of classical music, regardless of their natal associations (Cf. Shelvankar 1937: 162). In fact, this notion is so strong that some scholars misleadingly call the *Periya Mēḷam* ensemble the 'Tanjore Band' (Isaac 1964: 381; Sambamurthy 1976: 16).[254]

Among the three distinct *jāti* groups which can be identified in this area as associated with *Periya Mēḷam* are the *Isai Vēḷāḷar, Maruttuvar (Pariyāri),* and *Nāidu*—the first will be discussed in this section, and the last two as part of the following section. *Isai Vēḷāḷars* perform for rituals and festivals at Brahmanical temples and for the domestic rituals of Brahmans and high-ranking non-Brahmans. The reputation of Tanjavur as the centre of *Periya Mēḷam* music among musicians and patrons of classical music derives almost exclusively from the contribution of this group. Both *Maruttuvar (Pariyāri)* and *Nāidu* have a primary occupational association with barbering, and some members of these two groups are found attached to non-Brahmanical temples and perform for domestic rituals among low-ranking non-Brahmans.

The alleged importance of the Tanjavur area as a cultural centre in Tamil Nadu, and often of all South India by extension, is linked with the unanimously accepted notion that Tanjavur was the political and economic centre during the period of the Chola kingdom (9th to 11th centuries) and the domination by Nayak and Maratha kings (16th to 19th centuries) (Nilakanta Sastri 1966; Subrahmanian 1984). A great deal of contemporary art forms, whether in performing arts (music, dance, drama) or visual arts (painting, sculpture, architecture), it is generally believed, developed under the strong patronage of succeeding rulers during these two different historical periods.

In the field of music, more specifically, the Tanjavur area is often considered the 'brightest spot' or 'cradle' of South Indian music (Appaji Rao 1937: 164; Seetha 1981; Sambamurthy 1982d: 134), on the ground that much of present-day performance practice and repertoire developed in this area. While iconographical and epigraphical evidence from the Chola period can be amply identified indicating the high degree of musical attainment and activity and the existence of royal patrons, the degree of its continuity into the present-day tradition remains uncertain. The genesis of contemporary *Karnāṭak* music is generally traced to the period of the Vijayanagara empire (14th to 17th centuries), to which the cultural as well as political centre of South India shifted after the decline of the Chola dynasty. Purandaradasa (1484-1564), a prolific Brahman saint-composer, who was patronized by Vijayanagara rulers, is said to have contributed to the systematization of graded rudimentary exercises (*saraḷi varisai, jaṇṭa varisai, alaṅkāram,* and *gītam*) used in both *Karnāṭak* music and *Periya Mēḷam* music today. The use of Mayamalavagaula *rāgam* for beginning students when they practice these exercises at the initial stage of learning is also attributed to Purandaradasa (Sitaramiah 1971: 123-4; Sambamurthy 1985b: 33-4).[255]

It is, however, during the domination by Nayak and

Maratha kings in the Tanjavur area (16th to 19th centuries) that the foundation of the present-day *Karnāṭak* music is believed to have been firmly established. The succeeding rulers during this period were not only ardent patrons of music, but also musicians, composers, and music scholars themselves (Seetha 1981; Kuppuswamy and Hariharan 1984). Many musicians were attached to their courts, performing regularly and teaching interested members of the royal family. More importantly, this period produced the three saint-composers, known today as *mummūrttihal* or the Musical Trinity, whose compositions still constitute the major portion of the repertoire in classical music today.

The claim that the foundation of *Karnāṭak* music developed in the Tanjavur area is often utilized, quite naturally, by those associated with Tanjavur, as a means of legitimizing their artistic superiority over other regional styles and their practitioners. This what may be termed as 'Tanjavur-centricism' is a major source of discontent on the part of musicians and patrons not associated with Tanjavur.

It is important that the notion of Tanjavur as the main artistic centre of *Periya Mēḷam* music is based largely on the region's prestige as the most important centre in *Karnāṭak* music. In the eyes of most Brahman patrons, the *Periya Mēḷam* tradition in the Tanjavur area was an integral part of the idealized past in South Indian classical music from the time of the Musical Trinity to the early decades of the twentieth century. The merit of *Periya Mēḷam* music is, for them, inseparable from the achievements of *Karnāṭak* music in this area.

The musical style of performance developed in this area is known as Tanjavur *bāṇi* ('style'), which is based on the primacy of vocal music and the extensive use of difficult ornamentations (*gamakams*). Since the *nāgasvaram* is often considered the most effective instrument to reproduce the styles of ornamentations developed in vocal music, the prestige of the Tanjavur *bāṇi* in *Karnāṭak* music is easily transferable to *Periya Mēḷam* music.[256]

Interestingly, however, the degree to which the authenticity of music content is accorded to Tanjavur is even larger in *Periya Mēlam* music than in *Karnāṭak* music. In contrast to the existence of strong regional styles, such as Mysore or Travancore, other than that of Tanjavur in *Karnāṭak* music, Tanjavur was the sole uncontested centre of *Periya Mēlam* music in the past. It is true that the hegemony of Tanjavur *Periya Mēlam* tradition has been recently challenged by the influx of accomplished players from other areas, who may insist on a rather uniform performance standard all over Tamil Nadu today. Yet, the role which the Tanjavur area played in the past is almost never questioned.

The importance of Tanjavur both for *Karnāṭak* music and *Periya Mēlam* music derives from the cultural and demographic characteristics peculiar to this region. The Tanjavur area has been a centre of Brahmanical culture with the highest concentration of Brahmans as well as Brahmanical temples in Tamil Nadu (Beteille 1969: 168). According to the 1871 Census, Brahmans comprise 6.4 percent of the population in Tanjavur district while they constitute only 3.5 per cent in the Madras Presidency. The contrast is even sharper if the figure for Tanjavur district is compared to those of its neighbouring districts such as South Arcot (1.8 percent) and Tiruchirappalli (2.6 percent).[257] Yet, it was not simply their larger representation in the population, but the Brahmans' economic prosperity which made them prominent in Tanjavur. They were often wealthy *mirāsudārs* (joint landholders), politically dominant over other castes (Rao 1989: 31). The Brahmans' gradual loss of dominance at the village level in Tanjavur and the increasing migration to urban centres, including those outside the district, have had grave consequences on the patronage of *Periya Mēlam* music in the district (Bouton 1985: 89).

The prominence of Brahmans and Brahmanical culture explains the heavy concentration of the *Isai Vēḷāḷars* in Tanjavur district, although *Isai Vēḷāḷars* are found in other districts of Tamil Nadu. In the 1971 estimation, half of the entire *Isai Vēḷāḷar* population (150,000) lived in Tanjavur district.[258] *Isai Vēḷāḷars* are also found in the areas surrounding the Tanjavur district, in central and southern parts of Tamil Nadu, particularly Tiruchirappalli and Madurai districts. A small number of *Isai Vēḷāḷars* are also found in the Chingleput, Coimbatore, Pudukkottai, Ramanathapuram, South Arcot, and Tirunelveli districts (see Map 2).

Key:
————	State division
············	District division
TAMIL NADU	State name
TANJAVUR	District (*mavattam*) name
Madras	City/town name

Map 2: Tamil Nadu State (District Locations)
[Administrative Divisions Based on 1981 Census of India]

Although Tanjavur district has been so far discussed as a unit, the areas comprising its hinterland are by no means homogeneous. The importance of Brahman patronage to *Periya Mēḷam* music may in one way be measured by the pattern of distribution of Brahmans and *Isai Vēḷāḷars* within the district as well. The Brahmans were concentrated in northern and eastern parts of the district (Beteille 1974: 150). The northern section of the district, especially found many wealthy Brahman landowners (Bouton 1985: 122).[259] While a statistical breakdown of the *Isai Vēḷāḷar* population within the district is not available, well-known *Isai Vēḷāḷar Periya Mēḷam* musicians have hailed almost invariably from these areas. In this study, the northern and eastern parts of Tanjavur district, where Brahmanical culture was prominent, is referred to as the Tanjavur area.

2. *Isai Vēḷāḷars*

The term *Isai Vēḷāḷar* to refer to a *jāti* of *Periya Mēḷam* musicians in Tanjavur and its surrounding districts is of recent origin. According to Srinivasan, this term was officially adopted by the caste association (Isai Vellala Sangam) in Kumbakonam in 1948 to replace its previous designation, *Mēḷakkārar* (1985: 1876).[260] The new name came to be accepted for the purpose of government classifications at least by 1950, as it appeared in the list of Backward Classes in Madras Education Rules (Saraswathi 1974: 216-7).[261]

It is difficult to determine, however, whether the term was used previous to its official adoption, or how quickly it was accepted by the society. Eugene Irschick discounts the usage of this term prior to the twentieth century, without providing a specific time of its beginning (1986: 215). Two scholars who conducted anthropological research in northern Tanjavur district, Kathleen Gough (1955, 1981; fieldwork in 1951-3), and Andre Beteille (1965a; fieldwork in 1961-2) both use the term *Mēḷakkār* or *Mēḷakkāran* to the exclusion of the *Isai Vēḷāḷar*, although Beteille mentions that the *Mēḷakkārans* claimed the status of *Vēḷāḷars* (1965: 89). Louis Dumont who did field research in 1948-50, though not in Tanjavur district but mostly in Madurai district, also used only the term *Mēḷakkārar* (1986). The exclusive use of the term *Mēḷakkārar* by these authors may indicate the low prevalence of the term *Isai Vēḷāḷar* in common parlance at the time of their research. While the new term, *Isai Vēḷāḷar*, appears widely accepted as a *jāti* name in public accounts today, its previous name, *Mēḷakkārar*, is still often used by patrons as a descriptive occupational term to refer to *Periya Mēḷam* musicians.[262] The 1970 state governmental commission which surveyed the condition of disadvantaged *jātis* used both *Isai Vēḷāḷar* and *Mēḷakkārar*.[263]

Adopting a new *jāti* name to avoid the negative connotation or stigma attached to its previous term, and thus to seek upward social mobility, is a common phenomenon all over India (Bhat 1984: 197). It will suffice to give only two examples here. The members of a *Nāḍār jāti*, prominent in Ramanathapuram and Tirunelveli districts of Tamil Nadu, disassociated themselves from the derogatory term *Shanan*, synonymous to their ritually polluting occupation of toddy-tapping. Their effort was made successful largely through organized attempts by their caste association to obtain official recognition of the word *Nāḍār* ('Lord of the Land'), the designation of their preference (Hardgrave 1969). Similarly, with a concerted effort by their caste association, the *Waddars* in Karnataka state were allowed by the government in 1946 to change their name to *Bhovi*, a more respectable term, which appears in the pan-Indian epic, *Mahabharata* (Bhat 1984: 177-8).

In the case of *Isai Vēḷāḷars*, the designatory change may be attributed to their need to differentiate themselves from barber musicians, who, as discussed in detail in the next section, are the chief practitioners of *Periya Mēḷam* music in vast areas of Tamil Nadu, and monopolize the profession in its northern districts including Madras. The need for differentiation is closely related to the use of the term *mēḷam*. Since the *Mēḷakkārar* simply means a musician ('the one who plays *mēḷam*'), *Periya Mēḷam* musicians belonging to barber *jātis* were referred to as such in recent years.[264] As the association between the designation

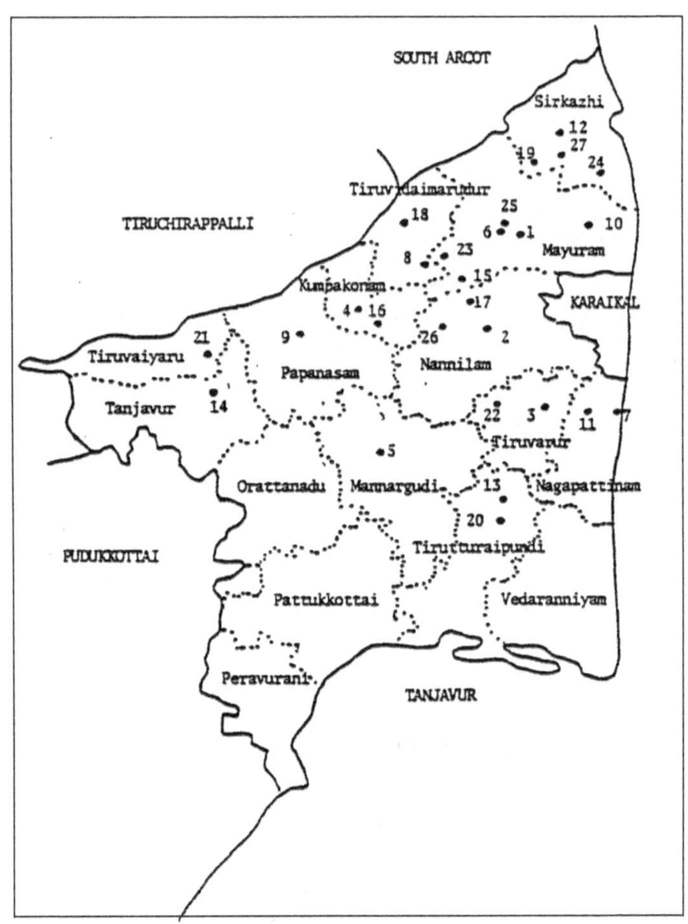

Key: ———————— District (*mavattam*) division
      ············· Sub-district (*taluk*) division
      TANJAVUR District name
      Tanjavur Sub-district name

1	Darumapuram	10	Sembonnarkoyil	19	Tiruppungur
2	Injikkudi	11	Sikkal	20	Tirutturaipundi
3	Kilvelur	12	Sirkazhi	21	Tiruvaiyaru
4	Kumbakonam	13	Tandaracheri	22	Tiruvarur
5	Mannargudi	14	Tanjavur	23	Tiruvavadudurai
6	Mayuram	15	Terirandur	24	Tiruvengadu
7	Nagapattinam	16	Tirucherai	25	Tiruvirandur
8	Narasinganpettai	17	Tiruppamburam	26	Tiruvizhimizhalai
9	Papanasam	18	Tiruppanandal	27	Vaidesvarankoyil

Map 3: Tanjavur District (Sub-District Locations)

[Administrative Divisions Based on 1981 Census of India]

Mēḷakkārar and barber musicians was established, this term was increasingly stigmatized for *Isai Vēḷāḷar* musicians because of the barbers' low social status. For this reason, a more prestigious term signifying music, *isai*,[265] was adopted to replace *mēḷam*, and to it was added *Vēḷāḷar*, the name for the high-ranking non-Brahman *jāti* whose members were prosperous land-holding agriculturalists.[266]

Some *Isai Vēḷāḷar* musicians claim that terms other than *Mēḷakkārar* were previously used as *jāti* names. A highly respected senior *nāgasvaram* musician, Chidambaram Radhakrishna Pillai (b. 1906), for example, recalled that the term *Isai Vēḷāḷar* replaced its predecessor Nagapasattar in the 1930s.[267] Darumapuram Govindarajan (b. 1933), another well-known musician, believes that people known as Nagapasattinar were predecessors of *Periya Mēḷam* musicians in Tanjavur, and traces the origin of the instrument's name (*nāgasvaram*) to these people (1987: 2).[268] The Nagapasam is mentioned as the designation of one of twenty-six sub-groups associated with the *Mēḷakkārar* in the Madras Census of 1891 (Stuart 1893 in A. Srinivasan 1984: 101), and possibly this term was in use in certain area, as Govindarajan seems to suggest. Nonetheless, Nagapasattar or its cognates are not mentioned in early ethnographic accounts including the comprehensive work by Thurston (1909).

At least two other names which were used prior to the *Isai Vēḷāḷar* have been reported from studies in other districts. Charlene Allison, based on her study in Tirunelveli district (southern Tamil Nadu) suggests that *Devadiya Pillaimar* was the *jāti* name before it was replaced by *Isai Vēḷāḷar*. She states that the *Isai Vēḷāḷar* is one of the three non-vegetarian *Vēḷāḷar* (Allison 1980: 77, 79). Yuko Nishimura, on the other hand, mentions yet another term, *Sengundar*, as its previous designation in the Pudukkottai district (1987: 27-8).[269] She estimates the time of the renaming to *Isai Vēḷāḷar* at around 1945, which roughly corresponds to the official adoption of the *Isai Vēḷāḷar* in Tanjavur district.[270] According to Thurston (1909, vol. 6: 361), a related term *Sengundam* is synonymous with *Kaikkōḷan* (*Kaikolan* in Thurston), a weaver *jāti* whose custom of donating girls provided the major recruiting pool of *dēvadāsis*.[271]

Apart from the *jāti* designations, the *nāgasvaram* musicians in the Tanjavur area are often called *nāgasvarakkārar* ('*nāgasvaram* player'), *nādasvarakkārar* ('*nādasvaram* player') or *nāyanakkārar* ('*nāyanam* player').[272] It is attached to the end of a *nāgasvaram* player's name as a kind of honorific title, especially when a respected musician is referred to by other *nāgasvaram* musicians. In a similar fashion, the *tavil* player is sometimes referred to as *tavilkkārar* or *tavildār*.[273] While the *ottu* musician was called *ottukkārar*, the player of *srutipeṭṭi* which has replaced the *ottu* is never addressed with the *kārar* suffix, signifying the lowering of the status of a drone player in the *Periya Mēḷam* ensemble.[274]

In addition, the extremely well-known *Isai Vēḷāḷar* musicians are sometimes addressed by the names of their ancestral localities without their given names. Rajarattinam Pillai, for instance, is sometimes referred to as Tiruvavaduduraiyar ('the one from Tiruvavadudurai') among his fellow musicians and patrons. Other examples include Tiruvengattar ('the one from Tiruvengadu') for Tiruvengadu Subramania Pillai (1906-86), a distinguished *nāgasvaram* musician who for some time performed with Rajarattinam Pillai, and Nidamangattar for Nidamangalam Minakshisundaram Pillai (1894-1949), probably the most influential *tavil* musician in the first half of the twentieth century.[275] The use of ancestral place names as address terms is based on the following logic, which also explains the prevalent use of initials for the same purpose not only for classical musicians but for many other public figures.[276] The musician referred to as such is so well-known that there is no need to mention his full name. Conversely, the musician himself becomes a kind of icon for his ancestral locality, and many small villages in the Tanjavur area are known only for *Periya Mēḷam* musicians hailing from them. Addressing the musician in this way, speakers publicly recognize and acknowledge his fame and popularity which allow the omission of his personal name. The above two ways of addressing *Periya Mēḷam* musicians are generally confined to the great *Isai Vēḷāḷar* musicians of the past (Cf. A. Srinivasan 1984: 163). In addition, from the patrons' point of view, the abbreviation of names functions as a type of linguistic code which marks the membership of a sub-culture of classical music lovers.

3. Social Organization

The most characteristic feature of the *Isai Vēḷāḷar jāti* is the professional division into *Periya Mēḷam* and *Ciṉṉa Mēḷam*. The *Isai Vēḷāḷar* is unique in that no other *jātis* whose members perform *Periya Mēḷam* music are associated with *Ciṉṉa Mēḷam*. Regardless of instrument specialization, *Periya Mēḷam* musicians stress their superiority over *Ciṉṉa Mēḷam* performers. The narrowest meaning of *mēḷam* is a double-headed drum, and by extension the term refers to an instrumental ensemble including drum/s and its music.[277] Its even broader meaning is any entertainment related to temple activities, as an offering to the deity.[278] Therefore, the instrumental ensemble accompanying temple rituals is called *Periya Mēḷam* ('big drum' referring to *tavil*, or 'big ensemble' containing *tavil*) whereas the ensemble which provides music to temple dance is known as *Ciṉṉa Mēḷam* ('small drum' referring to *mridaṅgam*, or 'small ensemble').[279]

a. Periya Mēḷam lineages

Many senior *Isai Vēḷāḷar nāgasvaram* musicians state that *nāgasvaram* and *tavil* players formed not totally exclusive, but largely separate, patrilineal lines until about fifty years ago. They claim that very few *tavil* players were found in the family of *nāgasvaram* musicians, and vice versa. According to them, there was a tacit understanding and expectation that the sons of a musician, particularly the eldest, would succeed to their father's musical specialization. To succeed the hereditary occupation (*toḻil*) of the family was thought of as a matter of course, rather than an occupational option. Though not a rule, marriage into a lineage of the same instrument specialization was preferred.

This was for both economic and musical reasons. It is common for a *nāgasvaram* musician to marry ('give') his daughter to one of his promising disciples. This practice not only ensures the economic well-being of his daughter, but also keeps the musical knowledge within his lineage (A. Srinivasan 1984: 217-8). When the *nāgasvaram* musician has no sons or brothers to play with, his son-in-law is a prime candidate to fill that position. When a *nāgasvaram* musician dies before his son is old enough to complete, or even initiate, training, it is also common for his son-in-law to become his own son's *guru*. An example is given from a lineage of the *nāgasvaram* musicians in Tiruvarur (Figure 5-1). It is true that well-known families of *nāgasvaram* musicians

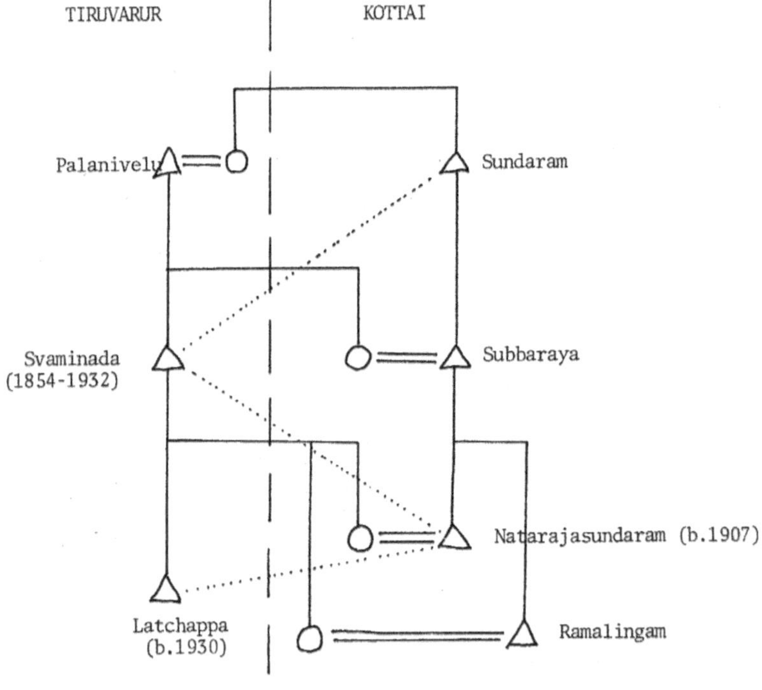

Figure 5-1: Mutual Transmission of Musical Knowledge
between Two Lineages of *Nāgasvaram* Musicians (Tiruvarur and Kottai)

have very few *tavil* players in their lineages even today,[280] but their claim of mutual exclusiveness between *nāgasvaram* and *tavil* lineages often appears exaggerated.

Although the existence of some families specializing in the *ottu* separate from those of *nāgasvaram* or *tavil* is acknowledged by contemporary musicians, the majority of the *ottu* players came from the lineages of *nāgasvaram* musicians. Some senior *nāgasvaram* musicians claim that playing the *ottu* was the prerequisite for *nāgasvaram* playing, and that only those who had not become proficient on *nāgasvaram* would remain as *ottu* players. However, only a few contemporary *nāgasvaram* players, including those who were trained when the use of the *ottu* was prevalent, either practised or performed on *ottu* before becoming a *nāgasvaram* musician. Others, in contrast, stress the status of the *ottu* as an independently sacred instrument and argue that most *ottu* players had no intention of becoming *nāgasvaram* players.[281]

b. *Ciṉṉa Mēḷam lineages*

Since the institution of *Ciṉṉa Mēḷam* was officially abolished in 1947 in Tamil Nadu (then Madras State), the following accounts relate to the situation before that time. *Ciṉṉa Mēḷam* practitioners can be divided into *naṭṭuvaṉārs* and *dēvadāsis* which were distinct from each other in occupational specialization and kinship organization. The *naṭṭuvaṉārs* referred to male dance masters who trained the *dēvadāsis*, and had their own patrilineal lineages through which the knowledge and skills pertinent to their occupation as well as material inheritance were transmitted.

Dēvadāsi refers to a class of women who through various ceremonies of 'marriage' dedicated themselves, or, more frequently, were given to the deities of temples (A. Srinivasan 1985: 1869). By marrying the deity, the *dēvadāsi* obtained the status of *nittiyasumaṅgali* ('ever-auspicious woman') which provided her with a rationale for serving in the temple as well as for being present at auspicious domestic functions, especially marriage ceremonies. Once becoming a *dēvadāsi*, she was not allowed to have a human husband, but her sexual partner was chosen by arrangement with the eldest female member of her family (*tāykkiṟavi*). Male issues from either type of lineages could become instrumentalists, but those from *dēvadāsi* lineage would become independent to form a patrilineal line, whenever it was economically feasible.

Periya Mēḷam musicians stress the existence of a clearly marked hierarchy among these four types of occupations and lineages associated with the *Isai Vēḷāḷars*, with the *nāgasvaram* at the top followed by the *tavil, naṭṭuvaṉār*, and *dēvadāsi*. Within the context of a *nāgasvaram* ensemble, the superior position of the *nāgasvaram* musician was evident in the various rights he held over his accompanists. The alleged fact that the *tavil* player customarily appeared at the performance prior to the *nāgasvaram* player, regardless of the former's musical attainments and popularity, publicly expressed the superiority of *nāgasvaram* players as a group over *tavil* players.[282]

The *dēvadāsis* were considered the lowest of the four because of their alleged association with prostitution. The social movement to abolish the dedication of young girls to temple and temple dancing (Anti-Nautch Movement), which started in earnest in the last decades of the nineteenth century placed a strong social stigma on *dēvadāsis* and their profession in particular and their *jāti* in general (Oddie 1979: 104; A. Srinivasan 1983: 74).[283] Since *Periya Mēḷam* musicians and *dēvadāsis* belonged to the same *jāti* in the Tanjavur area, the need to disassociate themselves from the increasingly stigmatized *dēvadāsis*, or more precisely the negative connotations they had come to assume, must have been strongly felt by the *Periya Mēḷam* musicians.

The inter-*jāti* difference and hierarchy which practitioners of *Periya Mēḷam* music emphasize is not nearly as well known as the notion of *Periya Mēḷam* musicians and *dēvadāsi* belonging to the same *jāti*. The social status of the entire *jāti* is often considered to have been degraded due to the increasing practice of prostitution among *dēvadāsis* (Visswanathan 1983: 86-7, et al.).

The men of the *Periya Mēḷam* and *naṭṭuvaṉār* lineages could and did marry undedicated girls from the *dēvadāsi* households, and many *Periya Mēḷam* musicians were sons of *dēvadāsis* themselves, as Rajarattinam Pillai might have been. However, the common statement by contemporary *Periya Mēḷam* musicians that they never 'gave' their girls to the male members of the *dēvadāsi* lineages is indicative of their desire to distance themselves away from such lineages.

The inferior position of the *naṭṭuvaṉārs*, as claimed by both *nāgasvaram* and *tavil* musicians, derived from their occupational association with the *dēvadāsis*. Despite the proclaimed avoidance of marital alliances and communal dining with them, the *naṭṭuvaṉārs were* occasionally subject to contemptuous statements and treatment both by *Periya Mēḷam* musicians and non-*Isai Vēḷāḷars*.[284] The assumed hierarchical order among the *jāti* and the competition within each professional group sometimes resulted in tragic incidents, which illustrate the magnitude of the phenomenon.[285]

Srinivasan (1983, 1985) discusses in detail the transformation of the stigmatized *dēvadāsi* dance into the respected art form known today as Bharata Natyam. She contends that the legislation banning the *dēvadāsi* institution facilitated Brahmans to take up, and eventually monopolize, the art themselves since the association of dancing and *dēvadāsis* was legally eliminated. In the process, the dance tradition of the *dēvadāsis* was 'Sanskritized' by Brahman journalists and scholars. Bharata Natyam has become a part of the marriage incentive to Brahman girls, superseding training in vocal music and *vīṇa* in popularity partly because of its lavishness. While *dēvadāsis*, deprived of their traditional livelihood, had great difficulty in the process of assimilation, a good number of *naṭṭuvaṉārs* found a respected status as dance teachers to Brahman girls in urban centres. This newly found status elevated the *naṭṭuvaṉārs'* standing within the *Isai Vēḷāḷars*, while *Periya Mēḷam* musicians' antipathy toward *naṭṭuvaṉārs* in some cases worsened due to jealousy of the fame and prosperity which some established *naṭṭuvaṉārs* have acquired as well as the frustration over what they perceive as the decreasing respect to their own profession.

c. *Hierarchy among Isai Vēḷāḷar Nāgasvaram musicians*

The relative decrease of temple salaries and the emergence of new performing contexts, such as radio programmes and concerts (see Chapter 4), has created a clearly delineated and newly defined hierarchy among the *nāgasvaram* musicians in Tanjavur district. Within one locality, a village or town, a group of musicians who depend upon temple services for their entire income is often contrasted with those who perform for social functions in addition to, or instead of, playing for the temple. It is usually implied that the temple musicians' inability to obtain 'outside (of the temple)' engagements is directly attributed to their poor performance skill, and a complex mixture of sympathy and contempt toward these musicians is expressed by those who do perform at social functions regularly. Since the salary for temple duty alone is often insufficient to maintain a good living standard, the dire economic and living conditions of such musicians is also insinuated.

The musicians who perform for social functions are divided into two categories: those who perform only within the village or town of their residence, and those who obtain engagements outside their immediate locality. Remuneration from 'outside (of the town)' performance (*veḷikkaccēri*) is substantially higher, since it compensates for necessary travel and these performances are sponsored only by wealthy patrons. Many musicians in the Tanjavur area travel as far as Madras and Coimbatore, or even to urban centres of North India with a large population of resident South Indians such as Bombay and New Delhi. They may travel for as much as two weeks per month during the auspicious months for marriage ceremonies.

Most, but not all, musicians who get 'outside (of the town)' engagements perform for AIR programmes. As was previously mentioned, although its remuneration is comparatively small, AIR performances are the most powerful means for public display of musicians' talent, which may lead to more lucrative engagements for domestic functions and temple festivals in the future. Higher AIR grades tend to provide the musician with the pretext to seek higher remuneration for their performance at domestic functions. Participation in the prestigious music festivals and titles given by *sabhās* and other music institutions are used for the same purpose.

The general acceptance of AIR ratings as the criterion of a musician's artistic merit has occasionally resulted in the neglect of some highly-talented musicians who for one reason or another did not pass, or refused to take, the audition. These musicians, including those from well-known lineages, are reconciled to less respect and lower remuneration from less discerning patrons while their talent may be recognized among musicians. The competitive nature of the profession makes *nāgasvaram* musicians well aware of the professional standings of others.

d. Prominent lineages of Nāgasvaram musicians

Among *Isai Vēḷāḷar nāgasvaram* musicians in the Tanjavur area, several families of musicians maintain a degree of prestige and fame considerably higher than others, on the basis of the number of well-known exponents in the past, and often on their musical specialization. At present, five such families are generally recognized, and they are known by their ancestral place (*sonda ūru*), as in the case of individual musicians. Each family has at least one extraordinary exponent of *nāgasvaram* playing within the last two generations who is known to have excelled in a certain repertoire or aspect of music, which tends to remain the expertise of the entire family. These prestigious families show a high degree of intermarriage, and are characterized by the absence, or small representations, of *tavil* players in their lineages.

Sembonnarkoyil Ramasami Pillai (1880-1923) is often considered to have been one of the three extraordinary musicians around the turn of the century, along with Tirumarugal Natesa Pillai (1874-1903), the step-father of Rajarattinam Pillai, and Mannargudi Chinna Pakkiri (1869-1915) (Sankaran 1961: 49, 1986a: 70). Ramasami Pillai is known especially for his superb rendition of *rakti mēḷam* and *pallavi*, which are believed to have been handed down through his family. Although several other musicians outside his lineage in the past were recognized for their mastery on *rakti mēlam*, such as Nagapattinam Verasami Pillai in the nineteenth century (B.M. Sundaram 1973: 66) and Chidambaram Vaittiyanada Pillai (1884-1937), this repertoire is today associated almost exclusively with musicians belonging to the Sembonnarkoyil lineage (Sankaran 1964). Ramasami's four sons were all known to be good players of *rakti mēlam*.[286] The current exponents of this otherwise disappearing repertoire are his two sets of grandsons.[287]

The fame of the Tiruvizhimizhalai family is based on the immense success of two brothers, Subramaniya Pillai (1893-1984) and Natarajasundaram Pillai (b. 1896), who played together as the Tiruvizhimizhalai Brothers. As mentioned earlier, they excelled in rendition of *kīrttanais*, and their popularity at domestic functions was responsible for the perpetuation of the ensemble format of two *nāgasvarams*, although they did not initiate this format. Before teaming up with his brother, Subramaniya Pillai studied with, and accompanied Sembonnarkoyil Ramasami Pillai, and later married his daughter. Natarajasundaram Pillai's son married Ramasami Pillai's granddaughter (Figure 5-2). Subramaniya Pillai was awarded the most prestigious *Sangīta Kalānidhi* title from the Music Academy in 1956, the first of only two awarded to *nāgasvaram* players.[288] The current representatives of this family are Subramaniya Pillai's two sons, Govindaraja Pillai and Dakshinamurthy Pillai.

One family of musicians in Injikkudi is known for their extended treatment of *rāgam* and *rāgamalika*.[289] Although oral history attests to six unbroken generations of Injikkudi *nāgasvaram* musicians, it was not until Injikkudi Pichaikannu (1904-75) and Kandasami (1933-88) that Injikkudi established its current fame. Kandasami held the prestigious position of *ādīṉa vittuvāṉ* at the Tiruvavadudurai Madam to which Rajarattinam Pillai was previously attached, from 1971 until his death in 1988.

A lineage associated with Tiruppamburam (Nannilam taluk)

is famous for its extended repertoire, and unique among the lineages discussed here in that it has produced a number of *Karnāṭak* musicians, especially vocalists. Musicians of this lineage are particularly known for carrying on the compositions by Muttu Tandavar (*Isai Vēḷāḷar* composer of the sixteenth century) and Muttusvami Diksitar, as their ancestors were direct disciples of these two composers (Arunachalam 1989: 134, 182-3).[290] The family enjoyed patronage from the royal family of Chettinad, and many of its members held positions at various music institutions. The first widely recognized musicians in this family were two brothers, Natarajasundaram Pillai (1869-1938) and Sivasubramania Pillai, who, as mentioned in Chapter 3, initiated the ensemble format including two *nāgasvarams*. Natarajasundaram's three sons all became well-known musicians.

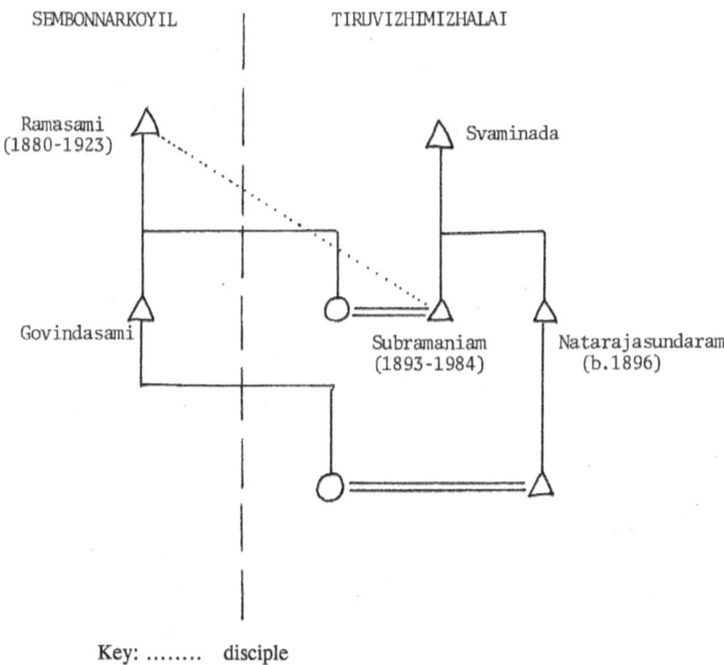

Figure 5-2: Relationship between Sembonnarkoyil and Tiruvizhimizhalai Lineages of *Nāgasvaram* Musicians

His first son, Swaminatha Pillai (b. 1900-61), was one of the best-known flute players in the twentieth century. While teaching at the Annamalai University and the Central College of Carnatic Music, he trained many disciples who later became distinguished musicians, such as Tiruvarur V. Namasivayam (vocal, 1926-70), Tanjore Viswanathan (flute, 1926-2002), and Sirkazhi S. Govindarajan (vocal, 1933-88). Natarajasundaram Pillai's second and third sons, T.N. Somasundaram Pillai (1904-71) and T.N. Sivasubramania Pillai, were both excellent *nāgasvaram* players and held teaching positions at the Palani Nagasvaram College (he was its first principal) and the Annamalai University respectively.[291] T.N. Somasundaram Pillai's son, T.N.S. Shanmukasundaram, is a vocalist and currently the head of the Government College of Music in Madurai, whereas T.N. Sivasubramaniam's son, T.N.S. Tirunavukkarasu, is also a vocalist and teaches at the *Tamiḻ Isai Kallūri* (Tamil Music College) in Madras (Sivasubramania Pillai 1979). Perhaps the most promising *nāgasvaram* players of the younger generation in the 1980s are performing as the Tiruppamburam Brothers (T.K.S. Swaminathan and T.K.S. Minakshisundaram). Although distantly related to Ramasami's lineage otherwise, their maternal grandfather was Injikkudi Pichaikannu Pillai, whose father-in-law was Tiruppamburam Sivasubramania Pillai.

Lastly, Tirucherai is another place with many well-known *nāgasvaram* musicians. Venkatrama Pillai (1871-1949) is said to have been an expert in *pallavi* (B.M. Sundaram 1977), and the first *nāgasvaram* musician to make gramophone recordings.[292] His second son, Subbaraya Pillai, was also a highly distinguished musician. He studied with Tiruppamburam Natarajasundaram Pillai, and eventually married his *guru's* daughter. Subbaraya Pillai's son, Sivasubramania Pillai (1927-94) also studied with Natarajasundaram Pillai as well as with his two brothers, and became a well-respected musician and teacher (The Tirupati Music College). Sivasubramaniam married a daughter of Swaminatha Pillai, a son of his own teacher, Natarajasundaram Pillai (Figure 5-3).

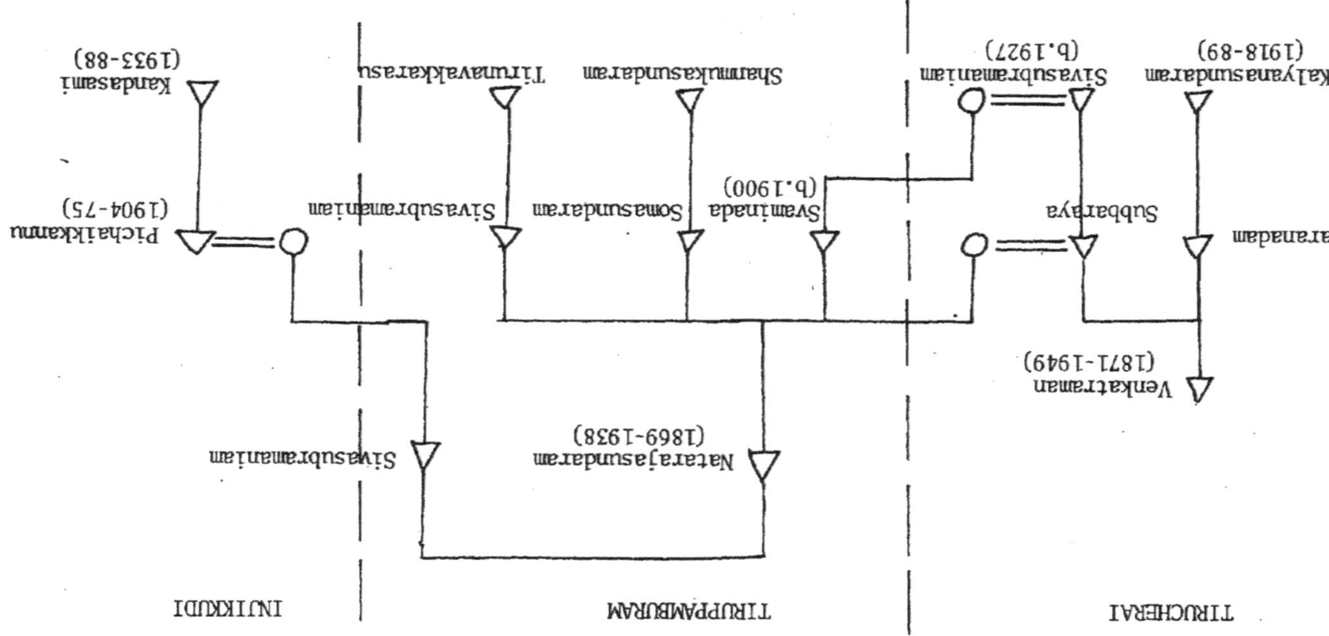

Figure 5-3: Lineage of *Nāgasvaram* Musicians Associated with Tiruppamburam, Tirucherai, and Injikkudi

All the five locations which these families are associated with are small villages in the north-eastern part of Tanjavur district (see Map 3). The existence of these villages is known outside their immediate areas only through the families of *nāgasvaram* musicians. However, many musicians belonging to these families now live in towns such as Mayiladuthurai, which are well connected to other urban centres by public transportation, or in cities to accept positions at music colleges as teachers, or at the temples as *dēvastāṉa vittuvāṉs*, or even simply to provide better educational opportunities for their children, rather than remaining at their ancestral villages. The continuing use of the name of ancestral villages may point to the pervasive notion that the traditional culture is deeply rooted in rural areas.

Although Rajarattinam Pillai was considered an extraordinary musician and was associated, professionally and by kinship, with so many distinguished musicians of his time, he did not become the fore-father of the lineage of Tiruvavadudurai *nāgasvaram* musicians, as Sembonnarkoyil Ramasami Pillai or Tiruppamburam Natarajasundaram Pillai did in their respective lineages. While the ultimate reason for this was Rajarattinam Pillai's inability to have male offspring, the absence of lineage enables Rajarattinam Pillai to become a public property of sorts, instead of his identity being firmly attached to a particular family of *nāgasvaram* musicians who would claim him as one of their founding fore-fathers. With no contemporary family of musicians to claim artistic inheritance through valued father-to-son transmission of musical knowledge, the symbol of Rajarattinam Pillai is easily co-opted by almost any interested party, and the range of interpretations of Rajarattinam Pillai is made substantially wider than otherwise.

4. Discourse of Declining Tradition

It is commonly believed that the quality of *nāgasvaram* playing at the time of my research is substantially inferior to that in the first half of the twentieth century.[293] Notably, this view, broadly taken, is accepted by a number of *Isai Vēḷāḷar Periya*

Mēḷam musicians themselves, as well as by other musicians and patrons. The sense of decline or disintegration of the whole tradition is generally expressed in terms of four interrelated phenomena: 1) the dwindling appreciation for the traditional music, 2) the decreasing temple support, 3) the disappearing or attenuated ritual performance practice, and 4) the decreasing number of distinguished musicians. The first two may be classified as perceived causes for the decline, and the last two as its manifestations. As the previous glory of *Periya Mēḷam* tradition is confined to the achievements of the *Isai Vēḷāḷars* in the Tanjavur area, the discourse of its decline is also directed, whether specified or not, to the situation in the same area. The absence of conflicting views even among non-*Isai Vēḷāḷar* musicians speaks to the continuing hegemony of *Isai Vēḷāḷar* in *Periya Mēḷam* music.

First, the changing taste of the masses for music is cited as a major reason for the increasingly less favourable climate for *Periya Mēḷam* music. There is a strong sense among *Periya Mēḷam* musicians that their music, played at such public performance contexts as temple rituals and festivals, is meant not only for a selected audience but for the masses (*janaṅgaḷ*) as well. The huge turnout and their attentive listening during the procession is often interpreted by musicians themselves and devoted *rasikars* as an indication of the higher musical knowledge of the mass audience in the past. Even when discounting the romanticized exaggeration as to the degree of musical conversance of the masses, it is probably true that the number of people who enjoyed listening to *Periya Mēḷam* music was once considerably larger than it is today.

Periya Mēḷam musicians unanimously blame film music for the decreasing interest in *Periya Mēḷam* music. Although film songs were based upon classical music and were performed by classically-trained musicians until about the 1930s, and thus a major portion of their audience overlapped, the clientele of these two genres has become almost completely separate. The decline of *rāgam* elaboration can be understood against this background. Since people began to prefer film songs, *nāgasvaram* musicians lost the context to play elaborate *rāgam* improvisation, still considered the most important repertoire of *nāgasvaram* music. Many musicians of the present generation claim to be capable of playing in such a manner, but rhetorically question the audience's interest. *Periya Mēḷam* musicians and their patrons often state the dilemma that even if contemporary musicians can play as skillfully as their predecessors did in the past there is no audience to appreciate the music.

Secondly, monthly salaries from the temples where musicians serve have become increasingly insufficient, and this economic depression has been the primary cause for the disintegration of hereditary *Periya Mēḷam* musicianship. As discussed in the previous chapter, the decline of the *Periya Mēḷam* tradition was connected to the non-Brahman movement and its religious reforms which instigated the discontinuation of hereditary trustees.

Apart from this overarching change, the heavy concentration of Brahmanical temples in Tanjavur district made the musicians in this district particularly vulnerable to the non-Brahman movement whose primary thrust was to 'deBrahmanise' South India. The Dravida Munnetra Kazhagam (DMK), which was formed in 1949, succeeding its two predecessors, the Dravida Kazhagam (DK) of 1944 and the Justice Party of the 1920s, formed the state government in Tamil Nadu in 1967. With their anti-Brahman, pro-Dravidian ideology, The DMK supported temples which housed Tamil (non-Brahmanical) deities, whereas those which enshrined Aryan (Brahmanical) deities became increasingly neglected. As a consequence, many Brahmanical temples in the Tanjavur area which had patronized *Isai Vēḷāḷar Periya Mēḷam* musicians suffered from revenue loss and inaccessibility to government funds, while wealthy temples of Tamil deities, such as the one for Meenakshi/Sundareswarar in Madurai and the one for Murugan in Palani, became even more prominent (Kennedy 1974).

Thirdly, the systematized performance practice of *Periya Mēḷam* music at temples, along with other associated temple musical traditions, is considered on the verge of extinction, if not already defunct, with only a handful of temples maintaining the simplified practices. As explained in the previous chapter, the system of time-*rāgam* correspondence has been increasingly violated or maintained in a much simplified manner, and certain repertoire associated with temple rituals and festivals survives only nominally. Furthermore, many musicians attached to temples of the present generation often have no heirs interested in succeeding to their family profession due to the unfavourable financial prospects and lower respect given to the profession of playing *Periya Mēḷam* music.[294]

Lastly, the decline of the tradition is described conversely by the previous existence of many great musicians whose musical ability and talent can be matched only by one or two contemporary counterparts, if any. The names of fifteen to twenty accomplished musicians who were actively performing during the first five decades of the twentieth century are given with ease by musicians and patrons, to depict the decline after that period. All the masterful musicians on the *nāgasvaram* belonged to the *Isai Vēḷāḷar jāti* from the Tanjavur area, the only exception being Madurai Ponnusami Pillai (1879-1929) who was also an *Isai Vēḷāḷar* but from Madurai. The depth of oral history of the previous musicians seldom goes beyond 1900, and is usually confined to the period after the 1920s, in spite of their argument for the antiquity of the tradition.[295]

II. BARBER MUSICIANS

The association of barbers with the musical ensemble featuring double-reed aerophones and drums is particularly strong in South India, though not totally peculiar to the region.[296] According to district gazetteers of the four southern states, *nāgasvaram* and *tavil* musicians belonging to the various barber castes are found in wide geographical areas, covering northern and central Tamil Nadu, southern and coastal Andhra Pradesh, and southern Karnataka states, whereas the barber musicians in the northern parts of Andhra Pradesh and Karnataka states play *shahnāī* and *ḍōlu* instead for various social functions.[297]

Recent anthropological work in South India not only agrees with the data gleaned from district gazetteers, but it also complements them in the districts where information is ambiguous or not provided. Based upon her field research in Karnataka conducted in 1966-7, Suzanne Hanchett reports that barbers played pipes and drums for Lakshmi rituals at a village in Hassan district (1988: 114). Chandrashekhar Bhat, from his fieldwork in 1969-71, mentions that barbers (*Hajama*) are invited to play music during weddings in Mysore district (1984: 133). For Tamil Nadu, Michael Moffatt speaks of barber *Periya Mēḷam* musicians in southern Chingleput district (northern Tamil Nadu), based on his 1970-2 field research (1979: 135-6).[298] Paul Hiebert, on the other hand, reports of the village ensembles, including barber musicians playing instruments known as *shahnāī* and *dōlu* at an unspecified location in central Andhra Pradesh at the time of his field research in 1963-5 (1971: 42).[299] The distribution of barber musicians in South India based on the evidence mentioned above is shown in Map 4.

Some researchers on music have falsely concluded that the players of *Periya Mēḷam* music all belong to the barber caste. This is probably because the areas where most of their research has been conducted include major urban centres such as Madras and Bangalore and the distinction between musicians belonging to a barber caste and *Isai Vēḷāḷar* musicians is blurred or non-existent, excepting those migrants from the Tanjavur area. For example, Captain C.R. Day mentions in his famous *The Music and Musical Instruments of Southern India and the Deccan* that *nāgasara* and *dhōl* players are mostly taken from a Telugu-speaking barber caste known as *Mangala-Vandlu* (1891: 95), who were probably the ancestors of the present-day barber *jāti* of *Mangala*. Although Day mentions the *Melakara jāti*, they were described as practitioners of the *Ciṉṉa Mēḷam* (*chinnamela* in Day) tradition, and not those of the *Periya Mēḷam* (*peryamēla* or *pathamēḷa*) (1891: 97).[300] More recently, Kathleen and Adrian L'Armand state that players of *Periya Mēḷam* before 1850 were males of the barber caste (1983: 412).

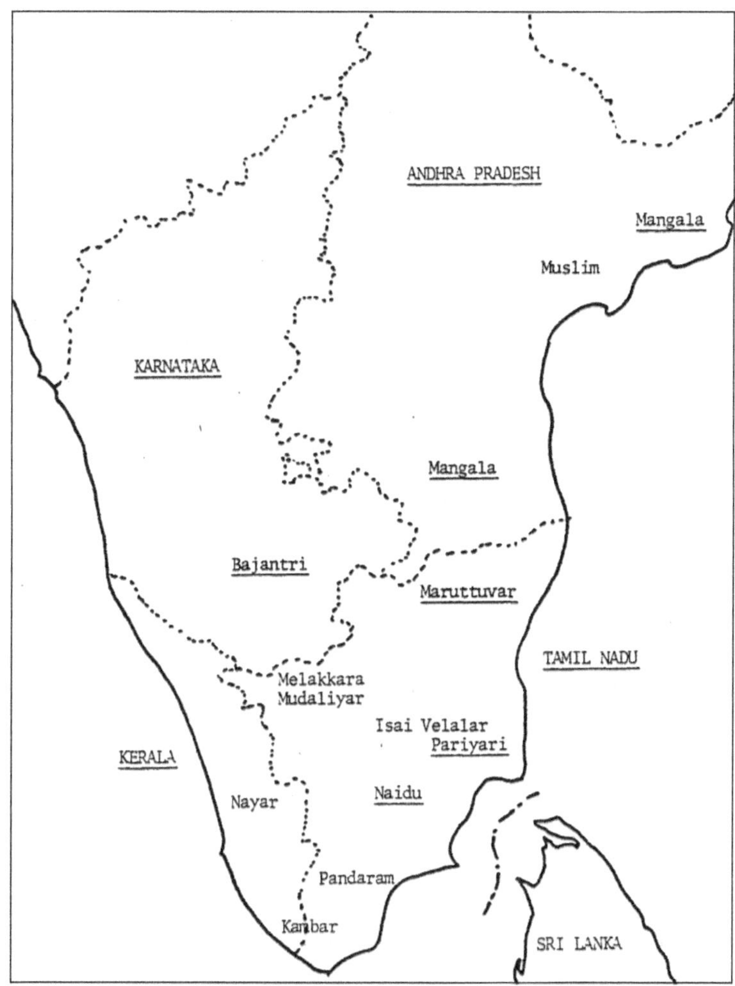

Key: Maruttuvar   Barber castes
      Isai Velalar   Other castes

Map 4: South India (Distribution of Castes of *Periya Mēḷam* Musicians)

On the other hand, scholars such as Nazir Jairazbhoy seem to ignore the existence of barber *Periya Mēḷam* musicians altogether (1980: 149).

Although epigraphical evidence, as mentioned in Chapter 4, points to the existence of *Periya Mēḷam* players in these areas from the end of the fifteenth century, their caste identity was not indicated. An important piece of evidence which suggests the association of barbers with music-making is a Telugu inscription (dated AD 1552) found at the Chennakesava Temple in Kamalapuram (Cuddapah district, Andhra Pradesh). It records the gift of land to a barber named Pumala Chinnaya for the employment of musicians in the temple. V. Rangacharya, chronicler of this evidence, interprets this inscription as indicating that barbers were musicians at the temples much as they are today (1985: 612).

Regardless of the validity of Rangacharya's interpretation, the tradition of members of barber castes playing *Periya Mēḷam* music can be traced with reasonable certainty at least for a couple of centuries, based on the oral history of musicians themselves, the wide distribution of barber musicians in South India today, and historical accounts by Europeans. As to the last source, Abbe Dubois (c. 1770-1848) stated that the performance of wind instruments was left exclusively to the barbers and *Paṟaiyars* (*Pariahs* in Dubois) (1986: 63-4).[301] A British writer and translator, Frederic Shoberl (1775-1853), compared barbers in Telinga (northern Karnataka) who officiated as musicians in the temples with those in the Malabar coastal areas (present-day Kerala state) who never played musical instruments at temples (1822: 35).[302] Nevertheless, the *jāti* names of barber castes whose members were musicians were not mentioned in European records until M. A. Sherring (1826-80) described the association of the barber *jātis* (*Nāyinda* or *Hajama* in Mysore and *Ambaṭṭaṉ* in Tamil Nadu) with music-making (1881: 124, 157).[303] C.D. Maclean also mentioned in his *Glossary of the Madras Presidency*, originally published in 1893, that the barber (*Ambaṭṭar*) was often a musician (1982: 25).

At present, the barbers in South India are known under various names, depending upon their mother tongues and areas of concentration. The following discussion is confined to barber musicians in the states of Tamil Nadu and Karnataka. The barber musicians known as *Mangala* ('auspicious') in Andhra Pradesh are not included here because of the lack of sufficient data, whereas the exclusion of Kerala state is simply due to the absence of a strong presence of barber *Periya Mēḷam* musicians.[304]

1. Barber Musicians in Tamil Nadu

Barber musicians in Tamil Nadu can be divided into two main groups based upon their mother tongues: Tamil-speaking and Telugu-speaking barbers. Tamil-speaking *Periya Mēḷam* musicians who belong to the barber *jātis* in Tamil Nadu are concentrated in its northern district, whereas Telugu-speaking musicians are prominent in its central districts.

a. Tamil-speaking Barber musicians

Ambaṭṭaṉ is the term most frequently used to refer to the Tamil-speaking barbers, and less frequently to their *jāti*, by non-*jāti* members. This term derives from two Sanskrit terms *amba* ('near') and *s'tha* ('to stand'), therefore meaning 'he who stands near to shave his clients, or treat his patients' as interpreted by Thurston (1909, vol. 1: 32).[305] The original occupation of this caste is believed to have been that of a surgeon for males and of a midwife for females, onto which barbering and playing music were later added. Since this term is often used today with derogatory connotations, the members of this *jāti*, especially among musicians, tend to prefer alternate names such as *Maruttuvar* ('medicine man'),[306] and *Paṇḍidar* ('doctor'). Although the term *Maruttuvar* was adopted as early as 1957 as the official designation in the state government record to refer to Tamil barbers, *Ambaṭṭaṉ* is still widely used today by those outside the *jāti*.[307]

Although *Ambaṭṭaṉ* may etymologically mean medicine man,

it is used primarily as a term of occupational designation for barbers in Madras and other urban centres where indigenous medicine has been largely replaced by a Western-style institutionalized health-care system.[308] In the scheme of analysing the Hindu social stratum based upon ritual purity and pollution, the low status of doctors and barbers can easily be traced, as in the case of washermen (*Vaṇṇaṉ*), to the inevitable contact with polluting bodily substance in their profession (Gough 1955: 24; Dumont 1970: 55). On the other hand, the choice by barbers and musicians of this term referring to doctors for their designation may be explained by the imported notion from the West of medical profession as being highly prestigious, along with Western medical technology.

Tamil-speaking barbers are also sometimes referred to as *Nāvidaṉ* or *Nāvisaṉ*. Both terms are derived from *napita*, signifying barber in Sanskrit. In the present work, the term *Maruttuvar* is used to refer to Tamil-speaking barbers and their *jāti* to follow the preference of the *jāti* members themselves, although the other two names, *Ambaṭṭaṉ* or *Nāvidan*, enjoy wider usage among non-*jāti* members.

With the decreasing demand for traditional health specialists, barbering and playing in a *Periya Mēḷam* ensemble have increasingly become two primary occupational options for the male members of this *jāti*. Although this tendency is found all over northern Tamil Nadu, it is particularly pronounced in Madras. Since becoming musician requires special talent and determination as well as physical aptitude, the decision to do so is generally left up to the individual at a young age, with a fair amount of encouragement given by a musician father to his sons.

Musicians and barbers are often found not only within the same lineage but also within the same household. It is commonly believed that all *Maruttuvar* musicians double as barbers (cf. Thurston 1909, vol. 1: 37). For this reason, they are looked down upon, and the assumption that their dedication to the art of playing *Periya Mēḷam* music and the standard of their musicianship are inferior is widely held by non-*Maruttuvar* musicians. This accusation is most often made by *Isai Vēḷāḷar nāgasvaram* players and their patrons.

Despite this popular belief, however, the *Maruttuvar* musicians who depend exclusively on playing *nāgasvaram* or *tavil* for their income exist in considerable number. They are referred to here, for the sake of discussion, as 'full-time' musicians as opposed to 'part-time' musicians, who have another profession, barbering or not, to supplement their income in addition to being a musician. Some established families have only full-time musicians in their extended households, and they tend to disassociate themselves from part-time musicians and barbers.

Although the categorical nouns corresponding to full-time and part-time musicians are absent, the division into these two groups constitutes one of the significant hierarchical criteria among *Maruttuvar* musicians themselves. Full-time musicians are thought to be better musicians, since they do not depend on non-musical activity to sustain their livelihood. As in the case of the Tanjavur area, the monthly salary for temple service in Madras covers only a small portion of musicians' necessary living expenses, even when they are lucky enough to be employed by temples. Obtaining sufficient engagements at social functions is a practical necessity for 'making it' as a full-time musician, and this is directly linked with the musical ability of the musicians. The contempt directed toward part-time musicians exists chiefly due to their implied musical incompetence.

However, the perception that all *Maruttuvar* musicians are part-time is widely held by people outside the *jāti*. This notion is often advanced to extend a lower artistic standard to all *Maruttuvar* musicians. In this case, not only is their musical competence questioned, but the degree of their dedication to the art form becomes a major criterion for criticism. Unjustly subsumed in this category, full-time *Maruttuvar* musicians need to disassociate themselves from part-time musicians and non-musicians of their *jāti*.

What makes the relationship between the *Isai Vēḷāḷar* musicians in the Tanjavur area and the *Maruttuvar* musicians in Madras peculiar is the presence of barber musicians in the Tanjavur area. In the Tanjavur area, the *jāti* which barber musicians belong to is most commonly known as *Pariyāri*, although they identify themselves as *Maruttuvars* in official records as in the case of their counterparts in northern districts.[309] The barber *jāti* in the Tanjavur area is referred to here as *Pariyāri* to distinguish them from their counterpart in northern Tamil Nadu. The chief patrons of *Pariyāri Periya Mēḷam* musicians are generally low-ranking non-Brahmans, for whom *Isai Vēḷāḷar* musicians usually refuse to perform. *Pariyāri* musicians are also sometimes found attached to non-Brahmanical temples, as *Isai Vēḷāḷar* musicians are to Brahmanical temples. The position of *Pariyāri* musicians makes a sharp contrast to *Maruttuvar* musicians who also perform for Brahmans and high caste non-Brahmans as well as at Brahmanical temples.

The mutually exclusive division of occupational territory among *Periya Mēḷam* musicians in the Tanjavur area has some important implications. When Brahmans and high-caste non-Brahmans of the Tanjavur area migrated to Madras, many of them preferred not to hire local barber (*Maruttuvar*) musicians, due to the strong occupational association of barber (*Pariyāri*) musicians with low-caste non-Brahmans in their home district. For this reason, many *Isai Vēḷāḷar* musicians were invited to perform in Madras, and the increasing demand acted as an incentive for some musicians to move to Madras themselves. For the visiting *Isai Vēḷāḷar Periya Mēḷam* musicians, a need to separate themselves decisively from barber musicians and thus to avoid the association with the low social status and negative stereotypes deriving from their traditional occupation of barbering instigated them to adopt the new *jāti* name.

b. *Telugu-speaking Barber musicians*

Apart from Tamil-speaking *Maruttuvars* and *Pariyāris*, there are many barber musicians who migrated from Andhra Pradesh to Tamil Nadu. Although originally Telugu-speaking people, they have extensively assimilated into Tamil culture and customs.

They often attach their *jāti* title of *Nāidu* to the end of their personal names.[310] *Nāidu* musicians are found all over Tamil Nadu, including areas such as Tanjavur and Madurai where *Isai Vēḷāḷar* musicians predominate.[311] They claim social and musical superiority to *Maruttuvar* musicians, with whom they do not generally intermarry.

Many *Nāidus* play clarinet in *Periya Mēḷam* ensemble format, replacing *nāgasvaram*. Although some musicians from other *jātis* also play clarinet, this instrument is most strongly identified with *Nāidu* musicians in Tamil Nadu today. Sometimes *nāgasvaram* and clarinet are found in the same ensemble.

The clarinet was introduced to South India by a Tanjavur king's penchant for Western culture. Sarabhoji II (1798-1832) is said to have organized an ensemble of Western instruments ('Tanjore Band') including clarinet (Seetha 1981: 111). Although this ensemble played only Western tunes, the clarinet was soon adopted for South Indian classical music. According to Sambamurthy, a *naṭṭuvaṉār* named Mahadeva of the nineteenth century is said to have been the first musician to play clarinet for *Ciṉṉa Mēḷam* (1971a: 26). Clarinet gained popularity in *Ciṉṉa Mēḷam* ensemble to replace *muhavīṉai* (a small double-reed aerophone), but it was later substituted with a flute.

Besides its use in *Ciṉṉa Mēḷam*, the clarinet was also featured in an ensemble consisting of Western instruments to play *Karnāṭak* compositions ('Band' or *bāṇḍu vāttiyam*).[312] *The Nadamuni Band* featuring a clarinet player, Balaraman, was the very first and best-known of such ensembles. This Madras-based group was extremely popular at marriage ceremonies in the 1920s and 1930s, toured extensively, performed for radio programmes, and made a number of disc recordings for *Columbia*.[313] Hiring both Rajarattinam Pillai's *Periya Mēḷam* ensemble and Balaraman's *Nadamuni Band* at the wedding was considered the most prestigious, and an eloquent indicator of the sponsors' cultured artistic taste as well as their wealth. Although very little is known about his life, Balaraman's music was greatly appreciated by many *Karnāṭak* and *Periya Mēḷam* musicians at that time.[314] Rajarattinam Pillai, for example, is said to have cancelled his own engagements to attend Balaraman's performance. Balaraman also played for dance recitals, as a guest musician to *Ciṉṉa Mēḷam* (Sankaran 1984a: 64). Although Balaraman's musical talent was considered extraordinary, no *Isai Vēḷāḷar nāgasvaram* musicians of repute could perform with him even if they wanted to, because of his low social status. A penalty would be imposed by the trustees of the temple or monastery against those who played for low-ranking *jātis* and non-Hindus, not to mention those who played with low-caste musicians.[315]

One clarinet musician who achieved fame after Balaraman was K.N. Radhakrishna Naidu (ca.1920-ca.1970), who was active in many different genres of performance including 'Band', Bharata Natyam, *Kālakshēpam*, and film music.[316] He is also believed to have proved the suitability of the clarinet for *Karnāṭak* music in the face of continuing skepticism among some orthodox *rasikars*,[317] by giving lecture-demonstration on clarinet music at the prestigious Music Academy. A firm request by the famous Brahman violin player Papa Venkataramaiyar to produce a radio programme with Radhakrishna Naidu engendered a heated controversy due to *Nāidu*'s low social status, but in the long run helped to increase the acceptance of clarinet into mainstream *Karnāṭak* music (Ellarvi 1970: 41).

The best-known and most successful *Nāidu* musician since the 1960s is A.K.C. Natarajan (b.1930). He first studied vocal music with Alathur Venkateswara Iyer (a Brahman), and then *nāgasvaram* with Iluppur Natesa Pillai (an *Isai Vēḷāḷar*). Severe competition among *nāgasvaram* musicians inspired him to take up clarinet under the guidance of his own father A.K. Chinnakrishna Naidu, a well-known clarinet player in Tiruchirappalli (Vasudevan 1965). Natarajan is credited with inventing a style for playing the clarinet much like that of the *nāgasvaram*, with abundant use of *gamakams*, and he became famous after switching to clarinet.[318] Natarajan is thought to be responsible for bringing the clarinet to the status of a concert instrument as Rajarattinam Pillai is believed to have done for the *nāgasvaram*. Natarajan sometimes performs with the typical *Karnāṭak* music accompaniment format of violin and *mridaṅgam*.

Although the association between *Nāidu* musicians and clarinet is very strong, some *Nāidu nāgasvaram* musicians have also achieved a considerable distinction, even in the early part of the twentieth century. It is said that Rangayya Naidu was a well-respected musician and a *dēvastāna vittuvāṉ* at the Konkannesvara Temple in Tanjavur (city) in the 1930s.[319] The *Isai Vēḷāḷar* students sometimes entered *gurukulavāsam* with distinguished *Nāidu* musicians. This tendency is especially evident in the areas where *Nāidu* musicians are prominent, such as Madurai. Many leading *Isai Vēḷāḷar nāgasvaram* musicians of the present generation in Madurai, including Madurai Alagusundaram (b. 1930), M.P.R. Ayyasamy (b. 1932), and Gurusami (b. 1930s), studied with G. Kuppusami Naidu, who played both *nāgasvaram* and clarinet.[320]

2. *Periya Mēḷam* Music in Madras

Since its founding in 1639, the city of Madras grew rapidly from a tiny fishing village into a political and commercial centre by the beginning of the nineteenth century, although no reliable statistical data were available until the first census of 1871. After about fifty years of relatively slow growth following the first Census, the rate of population growth intensified in the 1920s, and in the 1940s the population had increased more than 60 percent from since the previous decade. This fast growth is accountable partly to migration into the city from neighbouring areas and partly by the incorporation of surrounding areas into the city limits (Chandrasekhar 1964).

The emergence of Madras as a centre of musical activities is closely related to the cessation of royal patronage of music in many different locations in South India and, perhaps, more importantly, to the economic prosperity that is inseparable from its association with the East India Company. *Karnāṭak* musicians previously attached to the various courts gradually migrated in search of employment into Madras, where many early patrons of music and dance accumulated wealth as *dubāsh* (agents) to the Company (Raghavan 1958: 21).

Temples provided the major performance context both for music and dance, and many wealthy patrons were themselves hereditary trustees of temples. They patronized musicians and dancers by frequently organizing and sponsoring small gatherings specifically to enjoy music and dance during the temple festivals. This type of patronage was already established in the eighteenth century, and hence many musicians and composers migrated to Madras (Raghavan 1945, 1958; Sambamurthy 1982d).

Sambamurthy believes that many *nāgasvaram* musicians lived in Madras since the eighteenth century, though not revealing their *jāti* identity (1939: 435). Judging from the genealogies I collected, the majority of Madras *Maruttuvar* musicians moved to the city during the twentieth century from neighbouring districts, especially those of Chingleput, which Thurston described as the centre of the *Maruttuvar* community (1909, vol. 1: 36), and North Arcot. The migration to Madras grew to meet the increasing demand for engagements for social functions, as the city's population continued to rise. The parallel phenomenon is observed among many other service castes, including Brahman domestic ritual specialists known as *purōhidars* (K. Subramaniam 1974; Lewandowski 1975: 342).

Endowments were also given by these wealthy patrons to encourage musicians. Perhaps most important for *Periya Mēḷam* music was the annual music competition instituted at the Chennakesava Perumal Temple by Juttur Subramaniya Chetty of the nineteenth century.[321] The competition was held during its ten-day Periyalwar festival (Sambamurthy 1939: 434).[322] Participating musicians were not only handsomely remunerated, but the best performer was given an additional monetary award and gift.[323] This annual competition continues to provide aspiring musicians with a chance to exhibit their skill and acquire recognition, although increasing inflation has made the remuneration seem less lavish today (Sankaran 1986a: 72). An important consequence of this type of patronage is the increased frequency of visits to Madras by well-known *Isai Vēḷāḷar Periya Mēḷam* musicians which included Rajarattinam Pillai, therefore increasing chances of contact between them and local *Maruttuvar Periya Mēḷam* musicians. The Kapaleeswar Temple and the Sai Baba Temple in Mylapore and the Parthasarathy Temple in Triplicane also sponsor *Periya Mēḷam* performances by inviting a different *Periya Mēḷam* ensemble each day of the annual festival.[324]

3. Barber Musicians in Karnataka State

A barber *jāti* to which the practitioners of *Periya Mēḷam* ensembles in southern Karnataka state belong is known most commonly as *Nayinda*, a corrupted form of *napita* ('barber') in Sanskrit (Bhattacharya 1968: 243). The term *Hajām* or its cognates (*Hajjam, Hajāma*) is also frequently used to refer to barbers.[325] Barbering is believed to have been their original occupation, to which music-making was later added, and it continues to be the chief occupation of the majority of its members. Musicians of this *jāti* prefer to use *Bajantri*, which seems to derive from a Sanskrit *bāja* referring to music. *Mēlagāra*, meaning musicians, or *Balajiga* are also used, though less frequently, among musicians to refer to their *jāti* (Nanjundayya and Anantha Krishna Iyer 1931: 429-30, 434).

Unlike the *Maruttuvar* musicians in Tamil Nadu, a good number of prominent *Bajantri* musicians in Karnataka have been trained in the Tanjavur area in the traditional *gurukulavāsam* with *Isai Vēḷāḷar* musicians. The association of *Bajantri* musicians with the Tanjavur tradition dates back to at least the 1920s. One of the seniormost *nāgasvaram* musicians in Karnataka in the 1980s, A.V. Narayanappa (1912-94) of Bangalore, studied and eventually performed with Perambalur Angappa Pillai (1889-1966) in Tiruchirappalli in the early 1930s. Upon returning to Bangalore, Narayanappa became a popular musician and trained a number of students. In the late 1970s, he even established a *nāgasvaram* school in Srirangapattana near Mysore, where instruction is now provided by one of his senior disciples, P. Rajagopal, who studied, under Narayanappa's suggestion, in the Tanjavur area with Darumapuram Govindarajan (b. 1933) for several year.[326] Students who learned with Narayanappa and Rajagopal are proud of the Tanjavur style of playing *nāgasvaram*, although they have not themselves learned in the Tanjavur area.

Despite agreement on the recent deterioration of the Tanjavur tradition, training in the Tanjavur area is still generally believed to be essential to achieve high proficiency in *nāgasvaram* playing, as can be seen in the continuing presence of many *Bajantri* students in the Tanjavur area undergoing training in the traditional *gurukulavāsam*.[327] This is probably due to the professional success of contemporary players who have been trained in the Tanjavur area. The only *nāgasvaram* player with the highest grade (A) at All India Radio, Bangalore station, is M. Kodandaram, who studied for nine years in the Tanjavur area with two distinguished *Isai Vēḷāḷar* musicians: Tiruvengadu T.R. Jayarama Pillai and Mayuram Mamundiya Pillai. Similarly, the only *A* grade *nāgasvaram* player in Mysore station, N. Nagaraju, studied with another *Isai Vēḷāḷar* musician, Tiruvalaputtur Venu Pillai.[328]

Among the *Bajantri* musicians in the southern coastal area of Karnataka (Dakshin Kannada district), there is an increasing tendency to switch from *nāgasvaram* to saxophone. The saxophone is sometimes added to augment the regular *Periya Mēḷam* ensemble, featuring *nāgasvaram* and *tavil*. At other times, the saxophone replaces the *nāgasvaram* altogether. In recent years, some musicians began to play saxophone in the temple as part of daily rituals or calendrical festival, which were in the past exclusively the domain of *nāgasvaram* ensemble and other traditional instruments (Kassebaum 2004). Some musicians even predict the complete replacement of *nāgasvaram* by saxophones in this region in the near future.

The introduction of saxophones into Karnataka is attributed to Krishnaraja Wodeyar IV (1897-1940), the Maharaja of Mysore. As in the case of Sarabhoji II of Tanjavur, he was known for his enthusiasm for Western music and musical experiments.[329] He often ordered his court musicians to play compositions of *Karnāṭak* music on Western instruments, or vice versa. A well-known *vīṇa* player Seshanna (1852-1926) who was the chief court musician during Wodeyar's reign, for instance, was ordered to play *Karnāṭak* music on the piano, and Western compositions on *vīṇa*.[330] In the same fashion, a court *nāgasvaram* musician, Lakshminarasimayya, was ordered by the Maharaja to play *Karnāṭak* music on the saxophone. He taught many saxophone players of the succeeding generation, including Venkatappa Dogra who became very popular at marriage ceremonies around Mangalore in the 1960s.[331]

The existence of the saxophone tradition in Karnataka became known in other states mainly through the commercial success of Kadri Gopalnath (1949-2019). Hailing from a family belonging to the *Bajantri jāti*, he first practiced the *nāgasvaram*, but switched to the saxophone, inspired by his maternal uncle who was a saxophone player. While Gopalnath's popularity in coastal Karnataka grew rapidly with his participation in AIR programmes at the Mangalore station,[332] the nationwide and international recognition he enjoyed is largely indebted to his discipleship with and promotional assistance of T.V. Gopalakrishnan, a well-known Madras-based Brahman *mridaṅgam* player and vocalist.[333] Gopalakrishnan arranged a debut concert for Gopalnath in Madras, and accompanied him on the *mridaṅgam* himself. Gopalnath's popularity grew very quickly in Tamil Nadu, partly due to the novelty of the instrument, but mostly because of his artistic talent and achievement, which even rigidly orthodox *Karnāṭak* musicians acknowledge.[334] His enormous success can be seen in his active performance schedule in major music festivals all over India and his frequent foreign tours.[335]

Gopalnath has largely been taken into the mainstream of *Karnāṭak* music. Although occasionally playing in the *Periya Mēḷam* ensemble format, he performed more frequently to the accompaniment of violin and *mridaṅgam* at platform concerts or on radio programmes. Other saxophone players continue to perform with the *tavil* accompaniment, and performing contexts are confined by and large to marriage ceremonies in coastal Karnataka state.

A folk ensemble featuring *nāgasvaram*, locally known as *nāgasvara vādana* (*vādana*, Skt. 'sounding', 'instrumental music') is also very popular at weddings and other social functions in Dakshina Kannada district. This ensemble typically consists of one or two *nāgasvaram* (colloquially known as *wolaga* in Kannada), one *shruti* (a drone pipe), and one *dhōlak* (double-headed drum), with a possible addition of one *sammela* (a pair of small kettle-drum played with two bent sticks). Six such ensembles are registered at the AIR Mangalore station, and perform for a weekly programme on folk music primarily directed at agricultural labourers.[336] The relationship between this tradition and the *nāgasvaram* tradition developed in Tamil Nadu is unknown, and extensive research on this is in order.

III. NON-TRADITIONAL MUSICIANS

In the previous two sections, the two most important *jātis* associated with the *Periya Mēlam* have been discussed. The *Isai Vēlālar* musicians, of which Rajarattinam Pillai was one, are spread across a relatively small area in central Tamil Nadu at present, but are historically important, because of their alleged status as originators and trend-setters. In contrast, barber musicians are found in wide areas in northern and central Tamil Nadu as well as large parts of two neighbouring states, but their role in the history of South Indian music is less certain.

Apart from these two groups, there are several other groups associated with the *Periya Mēlam* today. Some are prominent only in certain geographical areas, whereas others belong to a *jāti* or gender previously unconnected to the *Periya Mēlam*, and, though small in number, their very existence may be socio-culturally significant. In this section, a brief description of seven such groups is provided. They are the Muslims in Andhra Pradesh, *Nāyars* in central Kerala, the *Paṇḍārams* in southern Tamil Nadu (Tirunelveli district) and southern Kerala, the *Mudaliyārs* in western Tamil Nadu (Salem and Coimbatore districts), the *Kambars* in Kanyakumari district, women, and Brahmans (Map 4). The players belonging to these groups are classified here as non-traditional musicians, since playing in the *Periya Mēḷam* ensemble is not their hereditary occupation over several generations and they came into this profession in recent years. The Muslim players in Andhra Pradesh are a possible exception in that their tradition allegedly originated in the seventeenth century, but the proportion of *Periya Mēḷam* musicians in the entire population is so small that they are included here as non-traditional musicians. Data used for the discussion of some groups derives primarily from secondary sources, and intensive field-research is to be conducted in the future.

1. Muslims

Despite its presumed origin in Hindu temples, *Periya Mēḷam* music is also performed by followers of Islam. In the Guntur district of Andhra Pradesh, Muslim musicians have been playing *Periya Mēḷam* music for at least a few generations.[337] While the Hindu *Periya Mēḷam* musicians belonging to a barber *jāti* known as *Mangala* are found in the southern and coastal districts of Andhra Pradesh, their Muslim counterparts are at present concentrated only at two locations in Guntur district: Chilakaluripet, a small town located about 50 kilometers southwest of the city of Guntur, and Karavadi in Ongole taluk (Jairazbhoy 1980: 149).[338] Though they are Muslims, these musicians have adopted Hindu customs and worship Hindu deities as well. They dress like Hindus, play for Hindu weddings, and some have even been attached to Hindu temples as *dēvastāṉa vittuvāṉs*.[339]

On the surface, the acceptance of Muslim musicians in Hindu temples and domestic rituals may appear contradictory to either religious doctrine, but it is not at all uncommon in India. The hereditary employment of Muslim musicians in Hindu temples in North India is an illustrative example.[340] In the case

of Tamil Nadu, the low level of communal friction may have
also contributed to the Hindu acceptance of Muslim musicians.
Nevertheless, resentment among some orthodox Hindus in the
Tanjavur area was apparent when a Muslim *nāgasvaram* player,
Sheik Chinna Moulana (1926-99),[341] and his ensemble were
invited to a temple festival in the early 1960s. The opposition
of the orthodox to this at that time may be discerned from a
newspaper editorial calling for the acceptance of artistically-
competent musicians, regardless of their religious affiliations.[342]

While the activity of most Muslim musicians has been
confined to their immediate locality in Andhra Pradesh, some
players achieved state-wide popularity, a few even in Tamil
Nadu, mainly through participation in AIR radio programmes.
The immense popularity which the afore-mentioned Chinna
Moulana enjoyed nationwide, however, is due partly to his
extended training in the Tanjavur area and his eventual migration
to Srirangam (Tiruchirappalli district, Tamil Nadu).[343] While
Moulana's musical talent is considered undebatable, the novelty
of a Muslim player in the Tanjavur area seems to have facilitated
his commercial success, at least in the initial stage of his career.
His fair complexion and sensitivity to Brahman customs are
also cited as contributing to the swift rise of his fame in Tamil
Nadu. His musical style is usually labelled as belonging to that
of Tanjavur,[344] although some senior *Isai Vēḷāḷar* musicians may
disagree.[345] The choice of Srirangam, an important religious
centre for Hindus, for his residence and a private *nāgasvaram*
school he ran there is symbolic of the acceptance and status he
possessed in Tamil Nadu.[346]

Jairazbhoy interprets the presence of Muslim *nāgasvaram*
musicians in southern Andhra Pradesh as supporting his
argument that the *nāgasvaram* may be an extension of North
Indian *sūrnay* tradition and that the instrument was introduced
into South India by wandering musicians (1980: 149). Jairazbhoy's
theory contrasts sharply with the unanimous belief by both
musicians and scholars in South India that *nāgasvaram* and *tavil*
are indigenous to the region, or more specifically to Tamil Nadu

(K. Ramachandran 1931; Arunachalam 1989: 89). Yet, given the morphological similarities between North Indian *sūrnay* and a type of *nāgasvaram* still played at the Tyagaraja Swamy Temple (*Tiruvārūr bāri nāgasvaram*), which is widely considered the older type of the presently-used instrument, his assertion deserves further investigation.[347]

2. Nāyars

In the central and southern parts of Kerala, temple music has been provided by musicians belonging to a *jāti* known as *Nāyar*. They often have the honorific caste title of Panicker to their names.[348] Among the instruments traditionally played by the *Nāyars*, a double-reed aerophone called *kuṟuṅkuḻal* is believed to be indigenous to the region.[349] The *kuṟuṅkuḻal* was once an essential part of daily temple worship and the *pañcavādyam* ('five instruments') ensemble, but it is on the verge of extinction with only a few competent exponents performing today. Unlike the *nāgasvaram*, the *kuṟuṅkuḻal* was never played for domestic ceremonies, and its exclusive use in temples has probably caused the decline of its tradition, as in the case of many other temple traditions.[350] The *nāgasvaram* has replaced the *kuṟuṅkuḻal* in many performing contexts traditionally associated with the latter, and most *kuṟuṅkuḻal* musicians double as *nāgasvaram* players. The introduction of *nāgasvaram* into Kerala is thought to be relatively recent, and a result of Tamil influence (L.S. Rajagopalan 1975, 1988).[351]

The *Nāyar* musicians themselves often admit that the *nāgasvaram* tradition in Kerala is insubstantial in terms of the overall artistic standard and the number of accomplished musicians when compared to that of Tamil Nadu in general and the Tanjavur area in particular. Many prominent musicians in Kerala have been trained in the Tanjavur area for this reason, and it is still commonly believed that extended musical training in Tanjavur is essential for serious musicianship.[352] Several *Nāyar* musicians became famous all over South India after discipleship with well-known *Isai Vēḷāḷar* musicians from Tanjavur district.

Ambalpuzha K. Sankaranarayana Panicker (1911-67), one of the best Kerala musicians of his time, became popular due to his training and probably more importantly to his association with Tiruvidaimarudur Virusami Pillai (1901-73) who was at one time attached to the Travancore court (Narayana Panicker 1968: 3-4; Pattabhiraman and Sankaran 1987: 37).[353] A popular *nāgasvaram* duo commonly known as the Haripad Brothers (Gopalakrishna Panicker b. 1919, and Chellappa Panicker b. 1924) also had an extended period of discipleship with him. Another popular *Nāyar nāgasvaram* player, Varkala Ramakrishna Panicker (b. 1923) studied with Kulikkarai Pichaiyappa Pillai, another famous *Isai Vēḷāḷar nāgasvaram* musician. A *Nāyar nāgasvaram* player, Thiruvizha Jayashankar (b. 1940), is also popular. Although not trained in Tanjavur, he achieved popularity through radio programmes and by teaming up with the well-known *Isai Vēḷāḷar tavil* player Valayapatti A.R. Subramaniam (b. 1941).

3. Women

Periya Mēḷam music has been the monopoly of male musicians with only a few notable exceptions.[354] Some older *nāgasvaram* musicians illustrate, by way of fantastic anecdotes, that women during their menstrual periods are ritually polluting to the instruments. According to these musicians, if a menstruating woman merely crosses a room where instruments are kept, the heads of the *tavil* will burst or the *nāgasvaram* will crack during the performance.[355] However, most male musicians positively assert that women are equally entitled to play *Periya Mēḷam* music given sufficient commitment and talent, and they tend to deduce the paucity of female players to the instruments themselves which are described physically demanding and therefore generally unsuitable for women.[356]

Whatever the reason, it has not prevented several talented women from entering this profession. The female *nāgasvaram* player who is best known and unanimously considered the most talented is Madurai S. Ponnuthayi (1929-2012). She studied with several teachers in Madurai including Madurai Natesa

Pillai, son of a famous musician Madurai Ponnusami Pillai (1879-1930), and became the first woman to be recognized as having led a *Periya Mēḷam* ensemble. The immediate inspiration for Ponnuthayi to take up the instrument came from two girls who were studying *nāgasvaram* with their father, Raju Pillai (*nāgasvaram*) in Tanjavur, although these girls did not acquire enough proficiency to lead their own ensemble.[357] The general disbelief of women's capability to play *nāgasvaram* at that time increased Ponnuthayi's struggle to establish herself as a professional musician at first, but with firm determination and the moral support of her family, she soon became popular at domestic functions and on radio programmes.[358] Ponnuthayi eventually performed for important and highly publicized political gatherings in the presence of such political dignitaries as Jawaharlal Nehru and S. Radhakrishnan.[359] She also became the role model for many other women who followed her path. M.A. Meera (b. 1946), for example, recollects the inspiration she received from observing the magnificent looking Ponnuthayi, with all her gold jewelry in a beautiful Kanchipuram *sari*, going off to a performance in which she led all male accompanists.[360] Since Ponnuthayi's debut in the 1940s, about two dozen female *nāgasvaram* players have achieved varying degrees of success, and hiring these musicians for marriage ceremonies was in vogue from the 1950s through the early 1970s.[361] Despite the increasing visibility of female players, Ponnuthayi was the only player who commanded respect from her male counterparts and other musicians of *Karnāṭak* music.[362] The popularity of female *nāgasvaram* musicians largely derives from the novelty of the phenomenon, and the presence of Ponnuthayi represented the potential ability of female musicians. There have also been some adept female *tavil* players such as Tanjavur Pakkiri Ammal and Tanjavur Kalyani, but their number was even smaller than that of *nāgasvaram* musicians, and none has achieved the status Ponnuthayi managed to obtain. Ponnuthayi and most other expert female *nāgasvaram* musicians never performed with women *tavil* players for this reason.[363]

Figure 5-4: A portrait of Madurai S. Ponnuthayi (Photo courtesy: Madurai Ponnuthayi)

A turning point of her career came abruptly when Ponnuthayi was given the opportunity to accompany Rajarattinam Pillai in 1944, when a death in the family prevented his second *nāgasvaram* player, Karukurichi Arunachalam, from attending a concert scheduled in Madurai where she lived. Her talent was observed by many who attended the concert and became widely recognized. The extent of Ponnuthayi's success at this occasion must be judged against the tremendous fear held by *nāgasvaram* musicians of accompanying Rajarattinam Pillai. Even established musicians with many years of experience were often hesitant to accompany Rajarattinam Pillai to avoid public humiliation.[364] The mere fact that a young girl of fifteen managed to accompany Rajarattinam Pillai was something to marvel at and greatly appreciated. Impressed by her talent, Rajarattinam Pillai himself later invited her to accompany him twice in Madras, which drew further attention to Ponnuthayi.[365]

Although the ritual pollution associated with female sexuality has not hindered the emergence of female *Periya Mēḷam* players altogether, it has posed significant limitations on them. While menstruating woman can be purified, as claimed by female musicians themselves, by taking an oil bath and performing a *puja* before playing music,[366] followers of more orthodox philosophy still resent the very existence of female players who periodically 'go out of doors' (a reference to the menstruation period). The aspect which affects female musicians most seriously, however, is related to the position of widows in Hindu society. The death of a husband prior to his wife is considered to be due

Figure 5-5: Madurai S. Ponnuthayi at a temple
procession (Photo courtesy: Madurai S. Ponnuthayi)

to the inauspiciousness which she inherently possesses, and a widow is not allowed to participate in any auspicious occasions which she will contaminate with her destructive quality.[367] Since the income of *Periya Mēḷam* musicians depends heavily on remuneration from auspicious domestic functions, the career of a female musician may be terminated at any given time by her husband's death over which she has no control. Ponnuthayi, for example, was virtually forced into retirement despite her capability and desire to perform, when her husband died in 1972, although she continued to perform occasionally for radio programmes until 1979.[368]

The best female *nāgasvaram* musician since the 1980s is generally agreed to be Kaleeshabi Mahaboob, a young Muslim woman who is a relative and a disciple of Sheik Chinna Moulana. Kaleeshabi was encouraged to practice *nāgasvaram* at early age by her parents, presumably because she had no male siblings. After marrying Sheik Mahaboob Subhani (b. 1951) who had learned *nāgasvaram* with her paternal uncle (Sheik John Saheb) and Sheik Chinna Moulana, she started to perform with her husband. Following their *guru* Chinna Moulana's path, they migrated from their native Chilakaluripet in Andhra Pradesh to Tamil Nadu (Tiruchirappalli) where they have performed widely as Chinna Moulana's best-known disciples.

4. Brahmans

Considering the extent to which other instruments originally associated with *Isai Vēḷāḷars* have been adopted by Brahman musicians, the virtual absence of Brahman *Periya Mēḷam* players even today appears peculiar at first glance. While the polluting quality of the instruments (the repeated contacts with saliva for the *nāgasvaram* and the use of animal hide for the *tavil*) is customarily given as the primary reason for their non-involvement in *Periya Mēḷam* music, many Brahmans have become prominent players of *kuḻal* (flute), *mridaṅgam*, *kañjirā*, and *mōrsing* (mouth harp) which pose the same problem of ritual pollution.

L'Armand and L'Armand report from their statistical sampling of musicians in Madras that the initial appearance of a Brahman *mridaṅgam* player in a public performance took place in the first decade of the twentieth century and that by the 1930s the cross-overs from one musical tradition to another such as that of Brahmans to *mridaṅgam* playing had become common (1983: 429-30, 434).[369] While the phenomenon of Brahmans taking up instruments previously inaccessible to them can be placed partly in the process of overall secularization during that time, in the virtual absence of such cross-over in *Periya Mēḷam* music seems to give an insight into the uniqueness it possesses.

The emergence of Brahman *kuḻal* and *mridaṅgam* players is

closely related to the new performance context toward the end of the nineteenth century. Previous to that time, both instruments were played only as part of *Ciṉṉa Mēḷam* or as accompaniment to *Kālakshēpam*. As the *kuḻal* and *mridaṅgam* were taken onto the concert stage, they ceased to have their original association with temple dance and its practitioners, thus facilitating Brahmans in playing these instruments in the *jāti* neutralized context.[370] On the other hand, no such contextual transformation occurred in *Periya Mēḷam* music. Although *Periya Mēḷam* has been played in a concert setting, its primary performance contexts firmly remain the temple and domestic rituals, with the initial *jāti* linkage still intact.[371]

The theological basis of *kuḻal* and *mridaṅgam* may have been effectively utilized to ease the transformation of these instruments into ones suitable for Brahmans. The *kuḻal* is the deity Krishna's indispensable attribute, and he is often depicted holding the instrument in playing position, whereas *mridaṅgam* is closely associated with Nandikesvara in literature and iconographical representations. The *kuḻal* and *mridaṅgam* along with *vīṇa* came to be considered the three most celebrated instruments on the basis of their frequent references in classical literature and close association with deities (Sambamurthy 1976: 15; Tumilan 1988: 53). This type of reasoning may be interpreted as an effort on the part of concerned Brahmans first to venture into new instruments, then to legitimize their new occupation. With the lack of references in literature and representations in iconography, it would have been considerably more difficult to establish a similar status for *nāgasvaram* or *tavil*.[372]

Palani Lakshminarasimhan, the first and so far only Brahman *nāgasvaram* player to lead his own ensemble, was trained at the *nāgasvaram* college in Palani (Madurai district) in the early 1960s, instead of the traditional *gurukulavāsam*.[373] Although, when he started out, he had struggle against the resistance and disapproval from his own *jāti* members, he eventually led his own ensemble and is widely known among musicians and patrons of classical music. In fact, Lakshminarasimhan's emergence and the existence of several Brahman disciples under training are often given by other musicians as examples of the social and cultural change in recent years which has affected music.[374] Additionally, as in the case of female musicians, no prominent Brahman professional *tavil* musician has yet emerged.

5. *Paṇḍārams, Mudaliyārs,* and *Kambars*

The existence of *Periya Mēḷam* musicians belonging to the *Paṇḍāram jāti* in Tirunelveli district (southern Tamil Nadu) is known outside of this area chiefly due to the enormous success of Karukurichi Arunachalam (1921-64). He became well-known as a regular accompanist to Rajarattinam Pillai, and after Rajarattinam Pillai's death in 1956, Arunachalam was generally considered the best player as well as Rajarattinam Pillai's artistic heir until his own premature death in 1964.[375]

According to Thurston, *Paṇḍāram* as an occupational term refers to any non-Brahman priest, and as a *jāti* name refers to a staunch Saivite group whose traditional occupation is to serve temples by supplying flowers and singing *tēvāram* (Saivite devotional) hymns (1909, vol. 6: 45-6).[376] For this occupational association, *Isai Vēḷāḷar* musicians often describe Arunachalam as a son of a garland-maker from Tirunelveli district.[377]

The Backward Classes Commission of 1970 in its Report mentions the *Mēḷakkāra Mudaliyār* as being a small community of *Periya Mēḷam* musicians in the Coimbatore district (1975: 172). Brenda Beck (1972) reports that temple musicians in western Tamil Nadu (districts of Salem and Coimbatore) belong to *Mēḷakkāra Mudaliyār*, a distinct sub-group of *Mudaliyār* which is the omnibus *jāti* in this region as in the case of the *Vēḷāḷar* in the Tanjavur area. According to Beck, *Mēḷakkāra Mudaliyārs* form matrilineal kinship (1972: 208), and this may suggest that this group was originally associated only with *Ciṉṉa Mēḷam*, and that some male members began to play *Periya Mēḷam* with the abolition of temple dancing. This theory may be supported by the name of its associated *jāti, Seṅgundam (Kaikkōḷan) Mudaliyār*, as given by Beck, since this group is known to have dedicated girls to temples,[378] and by the dominance of *Maruttuvars* as *Periya Mēḷam* musicians in this region.[379] One of the most popular *nāgasvaram* musicians in the second half of the twentieth century, Namagiripettai Krishnan (1924-2001), belonged to this *jāti*, although he neither attached the *Mudaliyār* title to his name nor voluntarily revealed his *jāti* identity, perhaps because of the strong association of barbers and musicians with this region.[380]

The *Kambar* is a very small *jāti* in the southern most districts of Kanyakumari and Tirunelveli in Tamil Nadu as well as in the Trivandrum district in Kerala, whose main traditional occupation is, as in the case of *Isai Vēḷāḷars*, to play *nāgasvaram* and *tavil* (Reiniche 1979).[381] The total population of this *jāti* was estimated at about two thousand in the 1970s, and according to the Commission Report most families suffered economically with their only income being the monthly salary from the temple, which figured between forty and fifty rupees a month.[382]

6. Implications of Non-*Isai Vēḷāḷar* Musicians

The emergence of non-traditional *Periya Mēḷam* musicians has several important implications. First of all, it has strengthened the *jāti* identity of *Isai Vēḷāḷar* musicians. Previously, the fiercely competitive nature of *Periya Mēḷam* music performance resulted in the fragmentation of the community of *Periya Mēḷam* musicians into many prominent families and their followers. Although generally courteous to each other, musicians accept and even cherish the high degree of competitiveness as part of their career. The performance of *Periya Mēḷam* music is often compared to a battlefield, as in the Tamil saying quoted by musicians themselves, '*pōrkkaḷattil oppāri eṉṉa*' (What is [the use of] crying on the battlefield?). While this type of competitive atmosphere maintained a high level of performance, some tragic incidents have also been triggered by excessive professional rivalry.[383]

While the performance tradition of barber musicians and Muslim musicians can be traced back at least for several generations, the *Isai Vēḷāḷar* musicians in Tanjavur tend to claim that they have entered into their profession more recently. Their insistence must be interpreted as a manifestation of their concern toward the increasing prominence of musicians from other *jātis* threatening the absolute superiority of Tanjavur-based musicians. While intense professional rivalry remains an important element of the Tanjavur *Periya Mēḷam* tradition, it appears far more genteel than before, probably because members now share the need to defend the superiority of their tradition as a group. Judgement of rival *Isai Vēḷāḷar* musicians tends to be reasonable and often appreciative, and the harshest criticism is almost always directed to, and reserved for, non-*Isai Vēḷāḷar* players.

Seen in this light, it may seem paradoxical that Tanjavur *Isai Vēḷāḷar* musicians have shown little reluctance to training students from other geographical areas or *jātis*. Their disciples from other areas are sometimes mentioned as proof of their popularity as individual musicians and teachers. Ironically, the musicians trained in the Tanjavur area are the ones who have achieved prominence, challenging the artistic dominance of *Periya Mēḷam* music by *Isai Vēḷāḷar* musicians. There are a few important exceptions to this observation, but the impact of Tanjavur trained non-*Isai Vēḷāḷar* musicians on recent trends has to be fully recognized. The non-*Isai Vēḷāḷar* musicians who acquired professional training from *Isai Vēḷāḷar* master musicians have in turn an enormous pride in their association with the Tanjavur tradition. They identify themselves artistically with *Isai Vēḷāḷar* musicians, and often deplore the inferior musical standard of those who have not learned the Tanjavur style.

Their general willingness to teach students from other areas contrasts sharply with the avoidance among Tanjavur *Isai Vēḷāḷar* musicians to perform with non-*Isai Vēḷāḷar* players. For example, a famous *tavil* musician, Nachiyarkoyil P. Ragava Pillai (1914-64) refused for many years to accompany Karukurichi Arunachalam (*Paṇḍāram*) even when he was at the zenith of his popularity and widely considered the best *nāgasvaram* musician. Such reluctance has eased since then, and some prominent non-*Isai Vēḷāḷar nāgasvaram* musicians do now perform with *Isai Vēḷāḷar tavil* musicians. Both Sheik Chinna Moulana (Muslim) and Namagiripettai Krishnan (*Mudaliyār*) have performed with many leading *Isai Vēḷāḷar tavil* musicians since the early stage of their careers in the 1960s, while Thiruvizha Jayashankar (*Nāyar*) became well-known performing regularly with Valayapatti Subramaniam (*Isai Vēḷāḷar*) on *tavil*. One exception to this recent tendency is the case of *Maruttuvar* musicians in Madras, and the peculiar relationship between *Isai Vēḷāḷar* musicians and *Maruttuvar* musicians will be analysed in the next chapter.

Lastly, in comparison with the emergence of a number of prominent non-*Isai Vēḷāḷar nāgasvaram* musicians since the 1950s, very few non-*Isai Vēḷāḷar tavil* musicians have achieved the similar status. The most successful non-*Isai Vēḷāḷar tavil* player today is Tanjavur T.R. Govindarajan (a *Pariyāri*, b. 1952), who teaches *tavil* at the Raja's College of Music in Tiruvaiyaru (Tanjavur district). Govindarajan is the only prominent non-*Isai Vēḷāḷar tavil* player who has accompanied many well-known *Isai Vēḷāḷar nāgasvaram* musicians as a *siṟappu tavil* player. His success as a musician, however, is often considered to be derived from his long professional association with Haridwaramangalam A. Palanivel (an *Isai Vēḷāḷar*, b.1948), who is considered one of the most popular, innovative, and musically influential *tavil* players at present.

As already mentioned, Rajarattinam Pillai was instrumental in the breakthrough of *Periya Mēḷam* musicians from other *jātis*, with his sustained encouragement of Karukurichi Arunachalam who became the first non-*Isai Vēḷāḷar nāgasvaram* player of considerable repute, and an ideal role model for all succeeding aspirants of *Periya Mēḷam* music. The period after Rajarattinam Pillai's death is best characterized by their increasing prominence at the expense of *Isai Vēḷāḷar* musicians. In the 1970s, this tendency was further accelerated, as many distinguished *Isai Vēḷāḷar nāgasvaram* musicians retired or passed away.[384] This shift is best exemplified by the fact that none of the three most prominent *nāgasvaram* players during the 1960s through the 1990s (Sheik Chinna Moulana, Namagiripettai Krishnan, and Thiruvizha Jayashankar) belong to the *Isai Vēḷāḷar jāti*.[385]

The absence of prominent *Isai Vēḷāḷar* musicians may be
traced to a combination of factors ranging from the complex
relations between them and their Brahman patrons to a shift in
tastes. It does not necessarily indicate a lowering of their musical
competence in relation to that of non-*Isai Vēḷāḷar* musicians.
Whatever the reasons may be, it undeniably has strengthened
the notion that the *Isai Vēḷāḷar* domination of *nāgasvaram* music is
on the verge of extinction, if not already completely superseded.

SIX

Multiple Interpretations of Rajarattinam Pillai

1. Attributes of T.N. Rajarattinam Pillai

The preceding chapters provide the background information on *Periya Mēḷam* music against which Rajarattinam Pillai as a polysemic symbol is to be analysed. They include the musical format in which he played, the contexts in which the music was performed, and the *jāti* of musicians he belonged to, played with, and influenced. The present chapter focuses upon Rajarattinam Pillai by discussing the attributes he is believed to have possessed.

If one follows Max Weber's general definition that charisma is 'a certain quality of an individual personality by virtue of which he is set apart from ordinary men and treated as endowed with supernatural, superhuman, or at least specially exceptional qualities' (1947: 358), both the written and oral accounts of those who knew Rajarattinam Pillai testify that he was undeniably charismatic. When Rajarattinam Pillai was alive, his extreme quality, both musical and personal, commanded attention from, and exerted tremendous influence over, other musicians and patrons. Musicians identified themselves with Rajarattinam Pillai by emulating a wide range of his perceived attributes, from playing style to physical appearance, and by discursively emphasizing their personal contacts with him, as if such contacts would transfer his charisma to them.

With his death in 1956, Rajarattinam Pillai's physical presence on which his charisma had been created was lost forever. But Rajarattinam Pillai, or rather the discourse on him, continued to influence others in many significant ways. Paradoxically, the absence of Rajarattinam Pillai in body enhanced his influence as a symbol. Any aspects of his life and music which were part of the discourse on him during his lifetime could now be exaggerated, distorted, omitted, or even created, according to the political motivations of various individuals and groups of individuals. To be sure, the use of any symbol can be viewed as intrinsically political, but as the passing of time made the immediate memory of Rajarattinam Pillai fade or become less homogeneous, it rather conveniently made room for interpretations which would otherwise have been difficult to make viable. What may be termed as the cult of Rajarattinam Pillai continues to thrive, involving primarily those who had little or no personal contact with him.

The musical and personal traits of Rajarattinam Pillai, as identified by contemporary musicians and patrons, are important attributes which contribute to the formation (social reproduction) of his charisma. Because of the reasons mentioned above, an attribute is considered here not as a static quality inherent in a charismatic person, but as a fluid complex of interpretations by other musicians and patrons. Therefore, the relationship between an attribute and the aspects found in either the *Karnāṭak* music tradition or that of *Periya Mēḷam* is contingent, both in terms of its nature and degree, on the individuals or the group of individuals who give it meaning as well as on the context in which the meaning is given. In this sense, charisma is assumed to emerge out of the dialectic interaction between these attributes and the perception by his followers of their own social and cultural situation.

1. Musical Attributes

a. Improvisation

Rajarattinam Pillai is best known for his mastery in extensive *rāgam* improvisation, an aspect considered by the *Isai Vēḷāḷar* the heart and soul of *nāgasvaram* music, rather than his renditions of compositions.[386] For this association, he was even nicknamed as *Rāga-rattinam* ('jewel of *rāgam* [playing]') after his given name Rajarattinam ('jewel among kings') by some patrons (Ellarvi 1967: 112). In his improvisatory performance, three aspects are identified as constituting Rajarattinam Pillai's excellence.

First, the ability to play extremely fast passages, known as *briga*, on *nāgasvaram* is an acknowledged hallmark of Rajarattinam Pillai's music (Pattabhiraman and Ramnarayan 1983; Venkatraman 1984: 27).[387] While those who lived through the first half of the twentieth century may point out the existence of musicians who could play the *nāgasvaram* at equal or even greater speed than Rajarattinam Pillai, the ability to render *briga* is mostly identified with him (Seshagopalan 1983: 35; T. R. Subramaniam 1985: 75). Moreover, *Karnāṭak* musicians, especially vocalists, who render such passages are now labelled as performing in *nāgasvaram* style (*nāgasvara bāṇi*), often contrasted to the slower *gamakam* (ornamentation) laden vocal or *vīṇa* style.

On the other hand, a style of playing in a slower tempo characterized by the abundant use of *gamakam* has also been important in *nāgasvaram* music. Vocal music is considered a prerequisite training for *nāgasvaram* music, and accordingly rudimentary lessons are learned vocally for a few years before starting on the instrument. Some performers, including Rajarattinam Pillai, are known for their ability to play the *nāgasvaram* exactly like a 'vocalist' would sing with their characteristic melodic inflections (Ellarvi 1967: 101),[388] while a few actually gave vocal concerts, as Rajarattinam Pillai did a number of times.

A second feature of Rajarattinam Pillai which separates him from others is his extraordinary musical creativity and imagination (*karpaṉai*, 'imagination'). The extended improvisation on a *rāgam*, a stronghold of *nāgasvaram* musicians, was performed at all night temple processions. It was common for a *nāgasvaram* player to spend several hours in elaborating a single *rāgam* on such an occasion, and his musicianship was measured, or at least described, by the duration of his improvisation without exhausting fresh ideas. Rajarattinam Pillai's ability to convey different aspects or shades of a *rāgam* at each of his performances evoked praise and envy from his colleagues.

Although Rajarattinam Pillai is believed to have excelled in any *rāgams* he chose to play, Todi is the *rāgam* with which he is by far most strongly associated.[389] Rajarattinam Pillai's identity as a musician became inseparable with Todi *rāgam* to the extent that, it is often stated, the audience would not be satisfied if he did not play this *rāgam*, and that his musical excellence is usually described as part of his performance in this *rāgam*. The association of Rajarattinam Pillai and Todi *rāgam* appears to have been established by the early 1930s (*The Hindu*, 21 March 1935; Tumilan 1988: 106). His renditions of *rāgam* (*ālāpaṉai*) and *pallavi* in Todi *rāgam* were released by Odeon in 1934 and 1935 respectively. The relationship between a performer and a specific *rāgam* appears stronger in the past, and many musicians are still known for their *rāgam* specialty. Some musicians are even known with the name of the *rāgam* attached to their name as a prefix, such as Kilvelur 'Saveri' Kandasami (B.M. Sundaram 1973: 66).

A third distinct characteristic of Rajarattinam Pillai's playing is the unmistakable tone quality he achieved on his instrument. While tone quality is a criterion upon which the identity of any individual *nāgasvaram* musician is based, that of Rajarattinam Pillai is always described as extraordinary or divine. Rajarattinam Pillai is also perceived as the inventor of the pitch-2 *nāgasvaram*, and his tone on this instrument serves as a model for many others.

As mentioned above, Rajarattinam Pillai is known mainly for his mastery in extensive *rāgam* improvisation rather than

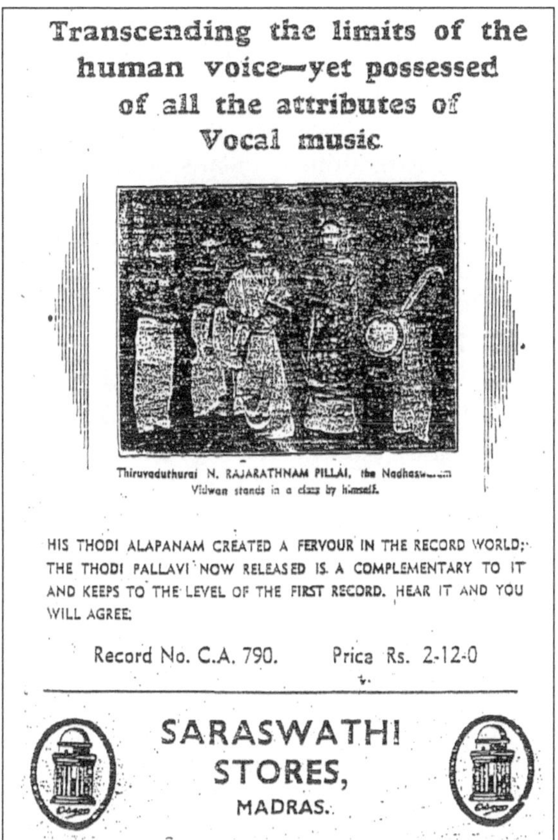

Figure 6-1: Newspaper Advertisement of
Rajarattinam Pillai's Disc Recording
(*The Hindu*, 18 March 1935)

for playing compositions. This is significant because the gradual shift of emphasis in repertoire from improvisation to compositions was underway during his lifetime. Rajarattinam Pillai is sometimes seen as the last luminary of the declining tradition, and in as much as Rajarattinam Pillai represents the greatness of *nāgasvaram* tradition, he symbolizes the end of the golden era of *nāgasvaram* playing in the Tanjavur area and of the musicians who nurtured it.

In contrast to the degree to which Rajarattinam Pillai

represented one important aspect of *nāgasvaram* music (*rāgam* elaboration), he was antithetical to other aspects of *nāgasvaram* tradition, namely the *mallāri* and *rakti*, the repertoire inseparably connected to temple contexts and exclusive to *Periya Mēḷam* music. Reportedly, Rajarattinam Pillai's negative evaluation of both forms derived from his dislike of excessive emphasis on rhythmic permutations at the expense of melodic beauty. He is even quoted to have said, 'I am proud of having taken the initiatives in driving the nail into the coffin of the *Rakti Mēḷam*.' (Sankaran 1981: 294).

Probably not unrelated to Rajarattinam Pillai's enormous interest in melodic improvisation and his dislike of an aspect of excessive mathematical permutation in music was his enthusiasm for North Indian *shahnāī* music by Ustad Bismillah Khan. Concert organizers and radio programme producers sometimes played Bismillah Khan's recordings, it is said, to pacify Rajarattinam Pillai in his precarious moods (Sankaran 1961: 50, 1981: 291; Tumilan 1988: 138).

b. Adaptation and innovation

Rajarattinam Pillai is known widely as an innovator par excellence. Many new performance practices are attributed to his invention. As mentioned in Chapter 3, Rajarattinam Pillai is believed to have invented the pitch-2 *nāgasvaram*, the type most frequently used today, and to be the first *nāgasvaram* musician to use the *srutipeṭṭi* replacing the *ottu* to provide the drone for the entire ensemble.

Rajarattinam Pillai is also credited with bringing *nāgasvaram* music into the concert hall. In this new context, he played *nāgasvaram* both in the regular *Periya Mēḷam* format with *tavil* accompaniment and with the typical accompanying instruments of *Karnāṭak* music (*tamburā sruti*), viz. violin, *mridaṅgam*, and *tamburā*. As the use of microphones became common in *Karnāṭak* music recitals in concert halls, Rajarattinam Pillai requested for them although they were not acoustically necessary.

Other new features that Rajarattinam Pillai is thought to have brought to *nāgasvaram* music concern the appearance of musicians during performance. As explained in Chapter 3, he was the first *nāgasvaram* player to adopt a Western hairstyle and to wear a Western-style silk shirt during performances. The *kuḍumi* and bare upper torso, considered important ways of expressing one's devotion and obeisance to God, have a strong spiritual and ritual connotation, and were strictly observed by *Periya Mēḷam* musicians prior to Rajarattinam Pillai's innovation. Off stage, he even wore Western trousers and shoes, unheard of among musicians at that time. He also insisted on sitting on a cart when playing for temple procession, instead of performing in the traditional standing position.[390]

Rajarattinam Pillai's decision to break away from these customs along with his insistence on the use of microphones was, in part, his way of challenging the conventional restriction placed on *Isai Vēḷālar* musicians by Brahmans, by explicitly adopting their performance practices or by negotiating with authorities for change.[391] In doing so, he also paved the way for *Periya Mēḷam* music to break away from its original ritual context by discarding the physical appearance and customs associated with it.

2. Personal Attributes

In sharp contrast to the high regards which Rajarattinam Pillai received as a musician, his personal life is given a colourful yet considerably negative assessment by other musicians and *rasikars*. I was often asked why I wanted to know about his personal life, which according to many was worthless, and possibly detrimental to his reputation as a musician. Yet, many versions of anecdotes illustrating his personal traits are common among musicians and patrons of classical music. As discussed in detail in the next section, Rajarattinam Pillai's personal traits, or their perception by others, has propelled *Isai Vēḷālar* musicians to have a highly ambivalent assessment of him. He symbolized the musical excellence of their tradition but also promoted and reinforced the abused notion of *Isai Vēḷāḷar Periya Mēḷam* musicians by categorically succumbing to moral corruption.

a. Polygamy and promiscuity

It is commonly known that Rajarattinam Pillai had five wives. His strong desire for and failure to have children is given as a reason, at least in written accounts, for his polygamy. It is said that his first wife, Sarada, was consulted for determining the suitability of subsequent wives (Tumilan 1988: 72-8). Although having multiple wives for want of offspring was not at all uncommon among *Periya Mēḷam* musicians, the discourse on Rajarattinam Pillai's polygamy insinuates, if not directly points to his sexual voracity. Furthermore, Rajarattinam Pillai's immorality associated with sexual promiscuity is illustrated by the unspecified number of mistresses he allegedly had all over South India in addition to his five wives. Many of Rajarattinam Pillai's mistresses and other more transient companions are believed to have been high-profile film and stage actresses. Anecdotes concerning Rajarattinam Pillai's inconsiderate behavior toward his wives, usually, excepting Sarada, have also been circulated.

Though embarrassed by Rajarattinam Pillai's reputation for excessive promiscuity, *Isai Vēḷāḷar* musicians shift the emphasis and point out, sometimes even with admiration, that it was his musical ability and resultant economic affluence which allowed him to sustain five wives and other extra-marital liaisons.

b. Heavy drinking and non-vegetarianism

Rajarattinam Pillai is said to have had a huge appetite for food and drinks and his dietary habits are often connected to his musical energy and personal tendencies. Heavy drinking and alcoholism are widely recognized social problems, commonly believed to be found mainly among male members of low-ranking *jāti* groups, although it is by no means absent among females or members of other *jātis*. Drinking alcohol is considered highly degrading among Brahmans (Padfield 1975: 140) who tend to connect low-caste members with the habit of heavy drinking, especially crudely brewed liquor known as *sārāyam*, and consequent rowdy behaviour.

Rajarattinam Pillai's habit of heavy drinking is well known. Although he mostly drank expensive Western-style liquor (whisky, brandy and wine), his habit is often linked to his untrustworthy disposition in general and to his frequent cancellation of performance engagements in particular (Tumilan 1988: 92-5).[392] It also strengthens the common belief among Brahmans that the vast majority of *Periya Mēḷam* musicians suffer from the same problem. Although some *Isai Vēḷāḷar* musicians show a tendency for heavy drinking, they are often criticized by other *Isai Vēḷāḷar* musicians who do not consume alcohol, for perpetuating the already widely held stereotypes.

Vegetarianism marks the diet of Brahmans in South India, although it is practiced in varying degrees, depending upon the definition of vegetarianism and different restrictions by sub-sects (Mandelbaum 1972: 455-6). While vegetarianism was originally adopted perhaps by the competition with Buddhists and Jains for ritual supremacy, it has achieved the status of the superior form of diet (Dumont 1970). For this reason, only vegetarian food is served on festive occasions even among most non-Brahman *jātis*, and the complete conversion of some non-Brahmans to vegetarianism for a higher ritual rank (Sanskritization) indicates the prevalence of this notion.[393]

Antithetic to the high value attached to being a vegetarian (*saiva*), Rajarattinam Pillai is believed to have eaten a large quantity of meat (mutton) every day, in addition to his voracious consumption of other items such as purified butter, buttermilk and yogurt (Tumilan 1988: 92). Although most *Isai Vēḷāḷars* are non-vegetarians (*asaiva*) except when they are in ritual observance, the amount and frequency of meat consumption separates Rajarattinam Pillai from others. This dietary habit is taken to be the primary reason for the tremendous stamina which sustained his music. Many Brahmans believe that non-vegetarianism is a necessity among *Periya Mēḷam* musicians to maintain the extreme physical strength for playing *nāgasvaram* and *tavil*, and often refer to the case of Rajarattinam Pillai to illustrate this point. Some even cite the connection between meat consumption and playing *Periya Mēḷam* music as a reason for the unsuitability of Brahmans as practitioners of this genre. The notion of *Periya Mēḷam* musicians as non-vegetarians is also inseparably connected to the stereotypical image of their physical stockiness. Rajarattinam Pillai often serves as an example, with his torso and neck described to be unusually stocky and strong.

A widely-held notion, related to conceptions about dietary habits, drinking, and carefree sexual lives, is that *Periya Mēḷam* musicians suffer premature deaths. Although some attribute early deaths among *Periya Mēḷam* musicians to the strenuous nature of playing *nāgasvaram* and *tavil*, many more trace the phenomenon to the *Periya Mēḷam* musicians' lifestyle.[394]

c. *Luxury and lack of economic sense*

Rajarattinam Pillai's predilection for luxury, extravagance and flamboyance is a frequent topic of conversation among musicians and patrons. The examples which are told to illustrate this range from a huge imported car, with unbelievably low gas mileage,[395] to travel, often involving a huge entourage in the first-class railway coach (Tumilan 1988: 62),[396] from giant-sized diamond earrings (*vairakkaḍukkaṉ*) and gold necklaces (*taṅgaccaṅgili*) to a letterhead with a large photograph of himself (Sankaran 1981; Tumilan 1988: 62).[397] Yet, the extravagant appearance is by no means limited to Rajarattinam Pillai. Many *Periya Mēḷam* musicians during Rajarattinam Pillai's lifetime wore gold necklaces, finger rings, earrings, silk *vēṭṭi* (dhoti), and *poṉṉāḍai*[398] which were all expensive items. These constituted a grand and auspiciousness-emanating appearance, which was appreciated at domestic functions. Because of the widely-held belief of their

Figure 6-2: The Letterhead Used by Rajarattinam Pillai
(ca. 1945)

extravagant appearance, the term *Mēḻakkārar* was even defined
as a 'dandy, pompous or showy man' in the Tamil Lexicon
(1934: 3360).

In contrast to his indulgence in luxury, or perhaps as a
concomitant of it, Rajarattinam Pillai had little sense of financial
management. He is said to have spent all his money from his
performances almost as soon as he received it, and he often
asked his friends for loans. He died literally penniless, although
he made an enormous sum of money during his lifetime,
estimated at 15 lakh rupees (Rs. 1,500,000) (Tumilan 1988: 153).[399]
Apart from his impulsive expenditure on luxurious items, one
anecdote effectively illustrates the notion of Rajarattinam Pillai's
lack of economic sense and what appeared to many as his
eccentric behaviour. Tiruvavadudurai, where he lived for most
of his life, was a small village with no railway station. When
returning from engagements at faraway places, such as Madras
for example, he, more than once, stopped the train by pulling the
emergency chain, so it braked at Narasinganpettai, the nearest
station to Tiruvavadudurai, and walked home after paying the
stiff fine for its illegitimate use.

Rajarattinam Pillai was by far the highest paid *nāgasvaram* player during the prime period of his career, which lasted from the mid-1930s to his death in 1956. The amount of remuneration is a tangible and direct measure of a patron's interest in a musician and of his musical skills. The greatness of a musician is often described by how much he received (succeeded in demanding) at a given performance. Once his reputation for high fees was established, Rajarattinam Pillai himself became an eloquent indicator of his patron's wealth. For this reason, Rajarattinam Pillai was invited to perform for domestic functions by many public figures and dignitaries.

Figure 6-3: The Picture of Rajarattinam Pillai
which Appeared in the Announcement of
His First Death Anniversary (1957)

d. Devotion to music and temperament

Rajarattinam Pillai's devotion to *nāgasvaram* music is best exemplified by his routine of strenuous practice even during his last years and his refusal to rest in spite of his doctor's warning. A chronic heart disorder caused him to suffer a series of collapses between performances and practices, but he refused to stop playing, maintaining with a pun, 'I am Raja-rattinam ('the king of gems') now since I have practised (hard). I am only *Karudai-rattinam* ('a donkey's gem') if I stop (playing) now' (Tumilan 1988: 154). This type of firm dedication and complete self-identification with *nāgasvaram* music, although romanticized by musicians and patrons alike, was not at all uncommon among contemporary musicians, and especially noticeable among those of the older generation.[400]

Rajarattinam Pillai took an enormous pride in his achievements and in the great tradition which he inherited and represented, and when it was disrespectfully violated, he made a point of protesting against it in his own fashion. Rajarattinam Pillai was known for his quick temper which resulted in the cancellation of a number of performance engagements (Sankaran 1981: 291), though his outbursts were not usually the result of a precarious disposition, as much as his reaction to a lack of respect toward him personally or for the *Periya Mēḷam* tradition.[401]

Perhaps, the personal trait of Rajarattinam Pillai that stands out most on the surface is his desire to imitate, and often outdo, customs and habits associated with Brahman musicians and patrons. However, his emulation of Brahman customs is not an individualized case of Sanskritization as defined by Srinivas (1971), since Brahman supremacy was not simply accepted as a norm to be emulated, but rather challenged by him as something to be decentred and redefined. It is with this perspective that Rajarattinam Pillai's self-identification as a *saṅgīta vittuvāṉ* (classical musician; the prestigious category with the strongest connotational associations with Brahmans) rather than as a mere *nāgasvara vittuvāṉ* (*nāgasvaram* musician) has to be seen. Rajarattinam Pillai's motivation in this case was not so much to seek an advantageous position for himself by somehow acquiring membership into Brahman musician brotherhood, as to challenge the definition of *saṅgīta vittuvāṉ* which allowed Brahman musicians more prestige and a position of dominance over non-Brahman musicians. Throughout his career, Rajarattinam Pillai tried to redefine the contour of dominant discourse by asserting his own definition of himself and music culture, although the effectiveness of his strategy was circumvented to a great degree by the characterization of Rajarattinam Pillai's self-identification and definition as his selfish drive for success at the expense of others. In the process, he was caught in a dilemma; while Rajarattinam Pillai was deeply frustrated over what he saw as the persistent discrimination towards *Isai Vēḷāḷars* by Brahmans, he suffered from the criticism of some of his fellow *Isai Vēḷāḷar* musicians for selling out.

If the imitation of Brahman customs and lifestyle could be Rajarattinam Pillai's way of subversion, this was because the superiority of *Karnāṭak* musicians (predominantly Brahmans) over *Periya Mēḷam* counterparts (all non-Brahmans) was expressed or marked most clearly on tangible difference (or discrimination) in performance practice. For example, in the annual festival to commemorate Tyagaraja's death in Tiruvaiyaru, only *Karnāṭak* musicians were allowed to perform on the stage while *Periya Mēḷam* musicians had no choice but to remain standing and dedicate their performance of Tyagaraja's compositions. This situation continued for many years until Rajarattinam Pillai acquired permission to sit and perform on the stage in 1939, after intense negotiation with festival organizers.

Within *Karnāṭak* music, Brahman musicians were always given superior position. It is customary to present musicians with a flower garland or shawl after a performance to express the appreciation of the sponsor of the event. When all musicians were Brahmans, the gift was always presented in the order of the hierarchy based on specialization: first to the soloist (vocalist or instrumentalist), then to the melodic accompanist (most frequently violin player), and finally to the rhythmic accompanist (*mridaṅgam* player) (Sankaran 1987: 38). This hierarchy was also faithfully manifested in the remuneration for each musician. However, when Brahman and non-Brahman musicians shared the stage, Brahmans were always given attention first even if the soloist was a non-Brahman. Rajarattinam Pillai is said to have preferred Brahman accompanists when he performed with *tamburā sruti*, either on *nāgasvaram* or vocal, and being presented with a gift first in the presence of Brahman accompanists was clearly a public display of his subversive intent.

3. Intensity of Attributes

Many of the attributes described above are in fact found among many practitioners of both *Karnāṭak* music and *Periya Mēḷam* music. What distinguishes Rajarattinam Pillai from others then is the intensity of those characteristics. Consider the example of Rajarattinam Pillai's excellence in improvisation. While extended improvisation has always been regarded as the essence, or aesthetic hallmark, of *nāgasvaram* music, and it is considered intrinsically desirable, Rajarattinam Pillai's ability to mesmerize the audience by playing one *rāgam* for four consecutive nights is considered extraordinary.

Edward Shils argues that extraordinariness is generated from the combination of centrality and intensity (1975: 258). If we follow Shils, Rajarattinam Pillai's charisma may be understood as deriving from a combination of what he specialized in (centrality) and the manner in which he executed it (intensity). Although Shils' centrality refers to some feature central to man's existence and often conceived as God, *rāgam* in music is in quality no different, if we consider that, in South India, the music, best presented in *rāgam* elaboration, is conceptualized as the manifestation of, or a path to, the highest being.

Furthermore, the intense state of his allegedly negative personal aspects also creates a sense of 'outsiderness' in Rajarattinam Pillai, since it is normally absent in, thus not the part of, routinized everyday life. The social importance of having male offspring encouraged many *Periya Mēḷam* musicians to seek a second and even third marriage, but having five wives is considered extreme, and this extremeness suggests the possibility of other dubious motives.

Once the notion of Rajarattinam Pillai's excessive behaviour is established, the extent of that excessiveness is often exaggerated as well. Some Brahman patrons state that Rajarattinam Pillai had a big glittering ring on each of his ten fingers, with the reflection of lights on them flying in all directions as his fingers moved in a dazzling speed, while Rajarattinam Pillai's accompanists and other close associates all agree that he had only two rings on each hand (last two fingers) during performances. Diamond earrings were an emblem of well-respected musicians of the past, but the size of those worn by Rajarattinam Pillai was regarded as being extreme, reminding one observer of 'a pair of automobile headlights' (Sankaran 1981: 292).

II. MULTIPLE INTERPRETATIONS OF RAJARATTINAM PILLAI

I have described Rajarattinam Pillai's musical and personal attributes which are potentially responsible for symbolic formation. These attributes are separately described in the form of a list of features without analysing the ways in which the attributes are, individually or collectively, utilized or manipulated by different groups of musicians and patrons. In this last section, I discuss the socially constructed interpretations or knowledge (social memory) about Rajarattinam Pillai of three distinct *jāti* groups of musicians and patrons: Brahmans, *Isai Vēḷāḷars*, and *Maruttuvars*. The selection of these three groups over others is based upon their importance in the contemporary *Periya Mēḷam* tradition. Brahmans not only constitute the vast majority of *Karnāṭak* musicians and patrons, but they are as a group the most important patrons of *Periya Mēḷam* music as well, though they themselves are not its practitioners.[402] Their artistic predilection for and patronage of *Periya Mēḷam* music have been largely responsible for its survival. *Isai Vēḷāḷars*, in contrast, are admittedly the originators and authentic practitioners of the *Periya Mēḷam* tradition. Rajarattinam Pillai and virtually all other well-known musicians of the past generations belonged to this *jāti*. Furthermore, with the exception of Madurai Ponnusami Pillai, all were from Tanjavur district. The third group represents *Periya Mēḷam* musicians who belong to the *Maruttuvar jāti* whose predominant professional association is barbering. The *Maruttuvar* musicians are numerically significant in northern Tamil Nadu, and their strong presence in Madras has not only caused a conflict with *Isai Vēḷāḷar* musicians but it may also result in their increasing prominence in the future.

The individuals in these groups are not regarded as passively interpreting symbols but actively utilizing them for the maintenance and enhancement of their social standing (Firth 1973; Bynum 1986: 10). Therefore, a symbol becomes a site of the complex, active and ongoing process in which different interpretations of the symbol engage each other and struggle for dominance. The musical and personal characteristics of Rajarattinam Pillai described in the previous section are manipulated in different sets and combinations to gain the maximum benefits, depending upon the varying motives and socio-economic background of each group and the imposed perceptions of each other. What follows is an analysis of the discursive strategies which each group employs to achieve their goal and the motives for such manipulation, as well as a description of the multi-faceted attributes Rajarattinam Pillai is believed to have possessed, which allowed such strategies to be successful.

Jāti affiliation is the most widely practised and the broadest epistemological level of distinction by which musicians and patrons are identified and recognized by themselves, while other factors such as economic standing, level of education, and artistic competence generally assume importance within this primary level of distinction. It seems reasonable, therefore, to adopt this category as the broadest analytical units, from which other factors can be considered.

Two related limitations surrounding the use of this broad formation for an analytical framework must be pointed out. The first, and the most obvious, is the danger of according the *jāti* with the status of the only determining factor, thus unjustifiably neglecting other variables in the analysis. Another limitation is that inter-*jāti* interactions and mutual influences will be overlooked, if one succumbs to the rigidity with which the difference in perceptions between *jātis* may be conceptualized. Such inter-*jāti* interactions are manifest in the individual or factional alliances which may affect the interpretation of a given individual. A person may be forced to, or in some cases be willing to, interpret in a way contradicting the general tendency found among her/his own group, or may alter interpretations in certain contexts to protect her/his individual position. The perspectives within the same *jāti* or sub-*jāti* in different geographical locations may also significantly differ. In short, the heterogeneity of interpretations within each group in consideration as well as the temporal changeability of an interpretation may be overlooked. In this study, neither the absolute homogeneity of perception within a given *jāti* nor the static nature of a given perception are suggested. The division by *jātis* is adopted here only to serve as a guidepost from which the complexity of the power relations in South Indian music culture is to be approached.

1. Brahmans

The dominant majority of musicians and patrons of *Karnāṭak* music are Brahmans.[403] L'Armand and L'Armand report that Brahman musicians constituted between 60 and 70 percent of all musicians in their samplings between 1928/29 and 1976/77 (1983: 427).[404] Although no statistical data is available for the caste distribution of patrons, I believe the percentage of Brahman concert-goers is even higher than the figure for musicians. Regardless of the validity of Brahmans' factual numerical dominance, importantly, the notion that *Karnāṭak* music is a primarily Brahman activity is widely held by non-Brahmans.[405]

Regarded as manifesting Brahman sensibility and ideology, *Karnāṭak* music is an important means by which Brahmans' cultural and social identity is expressed and maintained (Reck 1984: 215-6; Nettl 1985: 41). The need for a powerful symbol for assuring their identity was strengthened by the non-Brahman movement which started in the late nineteenth century. This political movement articulated the division between Brahmans and non-Brahmans and advanced criticism against Brahman dominance of South Indian society and culture in general by questioning the validity of their ideology (Irschick 1969; Karashima 1988). While it may be argued that the political aspect of the non-Brahman movement was in essence a power struggle of 'have-nots' against the 'haves' in the disguise of caste conflict (Baker 1976; Awaya 1988: 83), it is undeniable that the division between Brahmans and non-Brahmans became a dominant typological criterion in the everyday consciousness of musicians and their patrons. Although the first non-Brahman political organization (Justice Party) came into existence only in 1916, non-Brahmans had already voiced their concern in the 1880s and 1890s regarding the disproportionate number of Brahmans in the legislature, public service, and higher education (Irschick 1969: 351). The penetration of the capitalist economy and Western modernism since the nineteenth century altered the traditional sense of the caste system characterized by hierarchy based on ritual purity of the designated profession. The conflict between Brahmans and non-Brahmans became most drastic in the urban centres where traditional caste ideology was challenged to the greatest extent (Karashima 1988: 162-3).

E.V. Ramaswamy Naicker (1879-1973), perhaps the most important figure in the non-Brahman movement,[406] made a public statement in 1930 to protest against the monopoly of classical music by Brahmans. His statement was made as part of his speech condemning the Brahman domination of South Indian society in general. Ramaswamy Naicker encouraged non-Brahmans to patronize non-Brahman musicians who, according to him, were denied due recognition by Brahmans, and sponsored a series of concerts by non-Brahman musicians in the same year (Mangalamurugesan 1979: 98; Nambi Arooran 1980: 255). Ironically, however, public criticism against Brahman dominance of music resulted in the heightened sense of its 'Brahmanness' which further alienated non-Brahmans from classical music.

Given the Brahman orientation of *Karnāṭak* music, it is not a mere coincidence that its ideological and aesthetic ideal of *Karnāṭak* music is enmeshed in the image of the three Brahman saint-composers of the early nineteenth century, collectively known as the Trinity (*mummūrttihal* or *mummaṇihal*). The lives of these three saint-composers (Tyagaraja, Muttusvami Diksitar, and Syama Sastri) are characterized by total and intense devotion to the deity in all aspects of life, avoidance of secular patronage, and indifference to worldly affairs. The concept of music as a devotional path, exemplified in the Trinity's personal relations and commitment to music, serves as the ideological ideal of music-making in general.[407]

The projection of these three composers as the culmination of South Indian music not only belittles the significance of others, including a number of non-Brahman composers, but it also serves to authenticate the Brahmans' *raison d'être* and legitimates their dominance. Admittedly, many non-Brahman musicians, particularly *Isai Vēḷāḷars*, trace their artistic heritage to one of the Trinity through an unbroken series of discipleship, as in the case of most Brahman musicians.

It is important to remember that the modern music profession dependent upon contractual performances at concert halls and at domestic functions is viewed as preventing musicians from living a life close to this ideal. The projection of themselves as artistic descendants of one of these three saint-composers, by allying themselves to their lineages, compensates for the lack of saintliness in contemporary musicianship, thereby easing the tension between the projected ideal and the reality. For Brahman musicians, it provides legitimacy for occupying a central place in the *Karnāṭak* music tradition, while it also functions as a kind of behavioural and emotional code for musicians. The spiritual and devotional ideal of music exemplified in the discourse on the Trinity is also shared by non-Brahman musicians. Yet, the Brahmans' historical roles in classical music was underscored, thus legitimized, by establishing the omnipotent status of the three Brahman composers and accentuating their caste affiliations against the background of the heightened schism between Brahmans and non-Brahmans in the political sphere.[408]

Although Rajarattinam Pillai's *nāgasvaram* playing is unanimously appreciated by Brahmans, his musical excellence on the instrument is often connected to and explained by his strong background in vocal music, the backbone of *Karnāṭak* music. In *Karnāṭak* music, vocal music is considered superior to instrumental music, not only because texts of compositions can be verbally rendered, but because the *gamakams* (ornamental techniques) available in vocal music are regarded as most suitable to bring out the aesthetic essence of music. On the basis of the paramountcy of vocal music in *Karnāṭak* music and Rajarattinam Pillai's strong credentials in vocal music, the musical aspect of Rajarattinam Pillai is incorporated into and identified with the *Karnāṭak* music tradition, despite the fact that he was essentially a *nāgasvaram* musician. Closely related to this incorporation is the accentuated descriptions of his discipleship with two Brahman musicians at the expense of *Isai Vēḷāḷar* teachers. Especially, it is widely believed by Brahmans that Rajarattinam Pillai's primary *guru* was Tirukkodikaval Krishna Iyer, one of the most distinguished Brahman musicians in the early decades of the twentieth century. Although Rajarattinam Pillai was also sent to study with Ammachathiram Kannusvami Pillai (1876-1927), a well-known *tavil* musician, but also considered by many *Isai Vēḷāḷars* an excellent vocalist, his discipleship with Kannusami is, if mentioned at all, seldom emphasized. What is at issue is not with whom Rajarattinam Pillai actually learned the intricacy of music most, but the manner in which the connection between his musical excellence and his discipleship with Brahman teachers is often made. Put differently, Rajarattinam Pillai as a musician is depicted by Brahmans as belonging to the overarching *Karnāṭak* music tradition rather than to the *Periya Mēḷam* tradition, which is, in this case, conveniently interpreted by them as a subordinate or less significant sphere of *Karnāṭak* music. Rajarattinam Pillai's own self-projection as a *saṅgīta vittuvāṉ* rather than a *nāgasvara vittuvāṉ* also facilitated this interpretation by Brahman patrons, though for Rajarattinam Pillai it may well have been his own way of protesting against the Brahmans' characterization of *Karnāṭak* music as their own.[409]

Although Rajarattinam Pillai's exceptional talent in vocal music and his many vocal performances both at concert halls and for radio programmes is stressed by Brahman patrons, his interest in vocal music is by no means exceptional among *nāgasvaram* musicians. On the contrary, vocal music is an integral part of learning *nāgasvaram*. Rudimentary lessons in vocal music are considered indispensable for playing *nāgasvaram*, and students usually spend a few years in vocal lessons before they start practicing on the *nāgasvaram*. In fact, a number of *nāgasvaram* players have been competent vocalists, although they may not have performed publicly as Rajarattinam Pillai did. However, the ideational importance of vocal music and the actual prevalence of vocal training among *nāgasvaram* musicians is left, though usually very subtly, out of the context in which Rajarattinam Pillai's background in vocal music is stressed by Brahmans.

Apart from his potent affiliation with vocal music tradition, the general acceptance of Rajarattinam Pillai was further facilitated, or rationalized, by the artistic approval of his music by several top-ranking *Karnāṭak* musicians. Particularly, Rajarattinam Pillai's music received wider acceptance among Brahmans through the filter of G.N. Balasubramaniam (1910-65), a distinguished Brahman vocalist with immense popularity, who is widely regarded to have been influenced and inspired by *nāgasvaram* music, particularly that of Rajarattinam Pillai.[410] Balasubramaniam's *briga,* in a style previously possible only by instrumentalist, was considered an enormous achievement.[411]

Because of his immense popularity, the notion of *briga* as the representative feature of *nāgasvaram* music was also solidified (Cf. S. Ramachandran 1985: 23; T.R. Subramaniam 1985). The general indebtedness of vocalists to *nāgasvaram* players of the past is also expressed by several senior vocalists, including, and most notably, the senior most vocalist Semmangudi Srinivasa Iyer (1908-2003), who, speaking for his generation, publicly admitted the great influence of *nāgasvaram* music on vocal music.[412]

In contrast to their praise of his performance skill, both vocal and on the *nāgasvaram*, Brahmans disapprovingly refer to Rajarattinam Pillai's personal attributes which appear to be diametrically opposed to the image of ideal musicianship embodied by the Trinity.[413] Importantly, these attributes are construed as part of the general tendencies of *Periya Mēḷam* musicians as a whole. By means of colourful anecdotes surrounding Rajarattinam Pillai (see Section 1), Brahmans characterize the entire *Periya Mēḷam* community with immoral qualities, warrant their own moral superiority, and distance themselves from the *Periya Mēḷam* tradition and Rajarattinam Pillai who hails from it. In other words, Rajarattinam Pillai's greatness is attributed to the circumstantial benefit from *Karnāṭak* music received through his vocal training with two Brahman teachers, while his *Periya Mēḷam* background is seen only as the source of his undesirable lifestyle and corrupt habits.

For many Brahman musicians, then, Rajarattinam Pillai as a musician is not merely the best *nāgasvaram* player, but has become a symbol representing the entire *Karnāṭak* music tradition. This rationalization was achieved by carefully separating the symbol of Rajarattinam Pillai into two distinct sets of aspects. The musical aspects that Rajarattinam Pillai symbolizes are incorporated into *Karnāṭak* music, which is an integral part of Brahmanic music culture and identity, while his personal attributes are possibly overemphasized to maintain the negative characterization of the *Periya Mēḷam* tradition. Moreover, even the seemingly positive interpretation of Rajarattinam Pillai's musical attributes is not unequivocal. The praise of Rajarattinam Pillai and other past *nāgasvaram* musicians by Brahman patrons often insinuates a lowered artistic standard among the present generation of musicians, and thus justifies the disadvantageous situations in which they are placed today, no matter how genuine their appraisal of the past musicians may be.

2. *Isai Vēḷāḷar* Musicians in Tanjavur

Isai Vēḷāḷars, who claim to have been the originators and authentic carriers of *Periya Mēḷam* music tradition, are concentrated in the Tanjavur area and Rajarattinam Pillai belonged to this *jāti*. The interpretation of Rajarattinam Pillai by *Isai Vēḷāḷars* as a subordinate group exists inevitably in relation to the all-pervasive dominant discourses, not apart from them or by itself (Bommes and Wright 1982: 255; Alonso 1988a: 49).

With tremendous artistic and material achievements, Rajarattinam Pillai serves as a role model for *Isai Vēḷāḷar* musicians of the following generations. He excelled in *rāgam* elaboration which they consider by far the most important aspect of *nāgasvaram* playing (or music in general, they are likely to add), and many musicians idolize him as the leader of their tradition. The high visibility of Rajarattinam Pillai at prestigious festivals, highly publicized political meetings, and marriage functions of wealthy patrons, as well as the Brahmans' enthusiastic approval of his music gave them a sense of power and self-confidence.

Rajarattinam Pillai's popularity as a musical leader of *Isai Vēḷāḷars* is not unrelated to the state of *Periya Mēḷam* music in the twentieth century, which is often characterized by the gradual decline in the original context, performance standard, and social standing of its practitioners. As described in Chapter 4, the two most significant reasons for this change are believed to be decreasing economic support from temples and the increasing popularity of film songs in place of *Periya Mēḷam* music. Nevertheless, a host of virtuoso musicians, including Rajarattinam Pillai, emerged during the first half of the twentieth century, against this background of general decline. In fact, this period is sometimes regarded both by *Isai Vēḷāḷar Periya Mēḷam* musicians and by Brahman musicians and patrons as a golden era of *nāgasvaram* music due to the large number of accomplished musicians and the high level of artistic achievement. Put differently, it was an era in which the gap between a small group of fortunate musicians and the rest had significantly widened. Almost certainly the hierarchy among *nāgasvaram* musicians existed before, but a phenomenon peculiar to the twentieth century is the occupational disintegration of their community with more families leaving their hereditary profession.

Although Rajarattinam Pillai's insistence on adopting some *Karnāṭak* music performance practices is considered by Brahmans to be childish and a result of a lack of formal education and behavioural sophistication,[414] the simulation of practices previously confined to *Karnāṭak* musicians is often interpreted by *Isai Vēḷāḷars* to have been Rajarattinam Pillai's overt challenge to the Brahman domination of music culture and the discrimination against them. The inability of the Brahmans to curb his adoption of these practices is appreciatively interpreted as an indication of the status and power that Rajarattinam Pillai achieved.

It is true that *Isai Vēḷāḷar* musicians frown upon Rajarattinam Pillai's idiosyncratic habits and lifestyle and that their criticism of him is often harsher than that by Brahmans. Rajarattinam Pillai's sharp tongue and derogatory manners also generated enmity among some of his fellow *Periya Mēḷam* musicians.[415] Nevertheless, *Isai Vēḷāḷar* musicians object to the exaggeration by Brahmans of Rajarattinam Pillai's personal attributes and their extension of such attributes to the entire *Isai Vēḷāḷar jāti*. This sentiment is evident in the comment by a *nāgasvaram* musician, 'If one of us drinks, it is our inescapable urge for alcohol, and if one of them (Brahmans) drinks, it's a personal matter, even if they admit they do.' A comparison with the discourses on another charismatic musician T.R. Mahalingam (1926-86) will shed additional light on this issue. Mahalingam was a Brahman flute player, considered an unparalleled genius but eccentric, and in fact many of his alleged features are identical to those of Rajarattinam Pillai. Although Mahalingam was known for his precarious moods and undesirable habits including continuous drinking, these features are considered the mere whims of a genius, and never extended to the Brahman community in general or to the sub-sect to which he belonged. This interpretation in dominant discourse may not seem all too surprising, given the pervasiveness of the Brahman perspective, and it exacerbates the *Isai Vēḷāḷars'* frustration over what they regard as hypocritical tendencies among Brahmans.

Isai Vēḷāḷar musicians also detest the Brahman characterization of themselves as the authoritative practitioners of *Karnāṭak* music, exploiting the image of ideal musicianship which was 'fabricated' by Brahmans into the image of the Trinity. Furthermore, the description of the Trinity itself is considered selective by many *Isai Vēḷāḷar* musicians. While it is well known that Muttusvami Diksitar one of the Trinity, had a number of non-Brahman disciples at the Tyagaraja Swamy Temple in Tiruvarur (Raghavan 1975b), the musical influence of these musicians on Diksitar, to which some *Isai Vēḷāḷar* musicians emphatically point, is virtually ignored by Brahmans. A similar disparity can be found in the case of Tyagaraja, another member of the Trinity. While the musical source of Tyagaraja's compositions is usually traced to other Brahman composers of the preceding era, especially Purandaradasa (1484-1564) and Kshetrayya (seventeenth century), some *Isai Vēḷāḷar* musicians argue that Tyagaraja learned music mostly or exclusively from *nāgasvaram* musicians, as Rajarattinam Pillai is believed to have done.[416]

A serious dilemma exists among *Isai Vēḷāḷar* musicians who must face the negative characterization of Rajarattinam Pillai and its extension to their entire group while they remain dependent on Brahman patrons for both economic stability and artistic appreciation. As the number of non-Brahman patrons for *Periya Mēḷam* music has decreased in recent years, the *Isai Vēḷāḷars'* dependence on Brahmans has become even more prominent.

The *Isai Vēḷāḷars* have enormous pride in their own tradition of *nāgusvuram* music and its contribution to the enhancement of musical taste among the masses as well as to the formation of present-day *Karnāṭak* music, none of which, from their point of view, is appropriately acknowledged by Brahmans. Despite the strong sense among *Isai Vēḷāḷar* musicians of maltreatment and exploitation by Brahmans over the years, the loss of Brahman patronage by open challenge on the individual level would be suicidal for them. Since Brahmans do not play *nāgasvaram* music, they depend on non-Brahman *nāgasvaram* musicians for temple and domestic rituals calling for *nāgasvaram* music. There have been a few concerted subversive demonstrations against Brahman discrimination,[417] but an open attack by an individual musician has been virtually non-existent because he can be easily replaced by another.[418]

3. *Maruttuvar* Musicians in Madras

Periya Mēḷam musicians belonging to the barber *jātis* are found today in wide geographical areas in South India, covering northern Tamil Nadu, including Madras as well as southern parts of its two neighbouring states of Karnataka and Andhra Pradesh. The Tamil barber musicians in Madras, known as *Maruttuvar*, began to have direct contact with visiting *Isai Vēḷāḷar* musicians at least by the last decades of the nineteenth century as the city grew into a metropolitan centre which lavishly patronized not only *Karnāṭak* music but also *Periya Mēḷam* music through temple festivals and privately endowed performances (See Chapter 5, Section 2).

Because of the widely held notion of the *Maruttuvar* musicians' status as 'newcomers' to the profession of playing *Periya Mēḷam*, and thus of their inferior musical competence, aspiring *Maruttuvar* musicians have had to struggle against this notion, and that has affected the manner in which they exhibit their connection to Rajarattinam Pillai. For these *Maruttuvar* musicians, Rajarattinam Pillai's extended stays in and eventual migration to Madras provided them opportunities to have contact with him both as listeners and accompanists. Rajarattinam Pillai's arbitrary selection of accompanists and the virtual absence of *Isai Vēḷāḷar* disciples in *gurukulavāsam* (traditional method of transmitting musical knowledge) also contributed to the relative ease with which *Maruttuvar* musicians claim their close connection to him.[419] Excepting the second *nāgasvaram* player, Rajarattinam Pillai was not selective of accompanists, sometimes employing *Maruttuvar* musicians in sharp contrast to other traditional *Isai Vēḷāḷar* musicians of repute who refused to play with musicians of *jātis* other than their own.[420]

The *Maruttuvar* musicians characterize Rajarattinam Pillai as the best musician in *nāgasvaram* music in general, not only of the Tanjavur area to which most *Isai Vēḷāḷar* musicians belong, but of all South India, which includes Madras. They deny the common assertion, maintained particularly by *Isai Vēḷāḷar* musicians, that performance standard and style vary according to *jāti* affiliations or geographical areas. Rajarattinam Pillai is portrayed by the *Maruttuvars* as the foremost exponent of *nāgasvaram* music, while his *jāti* affiliation is deliberately ignored or played down. Although *Maruttuvar* musicians recognize the existence of great players from the Tanjavur area during Rajarattinam Pillai's lifetime, they emphatically point to the recent corruption of the Tanjavur tradition and the uniformity in performance standard throughout Tamil Nadu today. By departicularising Rajarattinam Pillai's *jāti* affiliation, the *Maruttuvars* incorporate themselves into a single entity of *nāgasvaram* tradition, thus legitimizing their existence as its practitioners.

The increasing prominence of *Maruttuvar nāgasvaram* musicians since Rajarattinam Pillai's death has affected the interpretation of Rajarattinam Pillai by *Isai Vēḷāḷar* musicians. First, as in the case of the prominence of other non-*Isai Vēḷāḷar* musicians, it has induced a higher degree of professional solidarity among previously fragmented *Isai Vēḷāḷar Periya Mēḷam* musicians, who needed to distance themselves as a group from *Maruttuvar* musicians, regarded as having considerably lower social status.[421] As a consequence, Rajarattinam Pillai's *jāti* identity is now emphasized in order to reduce the potential effectiveness of the Rajarattinam Pillai symbol to represent the entire *Periya Mēḷam* tradition, which includes *Maruttuvar* musicians.

Secondly, it has propelled *Isai Vēḷāḷar* musicians to emphasize the superiority of the musical tradition developed in the Tanjavur area, to which many leading *Karnāṭak* musicians belong in terms of musical style. Tanjavur serves as a common denominator for *Isai Vēḷāḷar Periya Mēḷam* musicians and Brahman *Karnāṭak* musicians, and the authority and prestige associated with *Karnāṭak* music, which *Isai Vēḷāḷars* otherwise struggle against, is utilized against *Maruttuvar* musicians. Furthermore, the *Maruttuvar* musicians are often criticized for their lack of training in vocal music which, to *Isai Vēḷāḷars*, explains their inferior performing ability, and Rajarattinam Pillai, who professionally performed as a vocalist, is cited as an illustrating example of the importance of vocal music for *nāgasvaram* playing. The logic used by *Karnāṭak* musicians to incorporate Rajarattinam Pillai into their own artistic territory is used hereby *Isai Vēḷāḷars* against *Maruttuvar* musicians.

4. Social Memory and Identity Maintenance

The analysis of the social memory of Rajarattinam Pillai has not only revealed the existence of incongruent interpretations of the past and present, each reflecting the socio-cultural position of a group in opposition to others, but has also demonstrated how the past is represented for ideological contestation and for securing identity. Fredrik Barth (1969) points out in his classic study of ethnic groups the importance of social boundary for maintaining the identity of a group in multi-ethnic society. While the formation of Barth's assertion appears to assume the *a priori* existence of ethnic groups as mutually discernible entities, Michel de Certeau emphasizes that the very existence of a group identity hinges on the creation of others/strangers, only against whom the concrete sense of its identity is realized.

The most concise statement of de Certeau's position is given in the introduction to his *L'étranger ou L'union dans la différence.*

> (T)oute société se définit par ce qu'elle exclut. Elle se constitue en se différenciant. *Former un groupe, c'est créer des étrangers.* Une structure bipolaire, essentelle a toute société, pose un 'dehors' pour qu'existe un 'entre nous'; des frontieres, pour que se dessine un pays intérieur; des 'autres', pour qu'un 'nous' prenne corps. (de Certeau 1969: 10; italics mine)[422]

From this vantage point, one may characterize the position of the *Isai Vēḷāḷar Periya Mēḷam* musicians as cultural 'others' which have helped define the Brahman identity.

Under a continuous and trenchant attack on their cultural and religious ideology, Brahmans have found in music a relatively stable ground for the maintenance of their identity, by characterizing *Isai Vēḷāḷar* musicians as polar opposite to the ideal image of musicianship symbolized by the Trinity. The characterization of *Isai Vēḷāḷars* as corrupted, uneducated and unsophisticated, which is epitomized in the case of Rajarattinam Pillai, has served as an effective pretext for not giving them due public recognition. In this sense, *Isai Vēḷāḷar* musicians have been effectively set aside from the power structure of South Indian music.

The emergence of an extraordinary musician like Rajarattinam Pillai who had the potential of transcending the boundary could have upset the projected image of social and cultural hierarchy to the Brahmans' advantage. Since Rajarattinam Pillai's musical attainments were undisputable, what is attempted is not the denial of Rajarattinam Pillai's musical competence, but instead a subtle yet tactful refusal to recognize the artistic excellence of the entire *nāgasvaram* tradition which he belonged to and inherited.

On the other hand, the extent of Rajarattinam Pillai's popularity as a leader of *Isai Vēḷāḷar* musicians is best understood when it is seen against the dominant discourse on the state of *nāgasvaram* music in the twentieth century. The gradual decline in its performance standard, the number of dexterous exponents, and social standing of its practitioners, which characterize *nāgasvaram* music of this period, are believed to have been caused by the decreasing economic support from temples and the increasing popularity of film songs in place of *nāgasvaram* music. It is important that Brahmans are largely responsible for the formation and dissemination of these notions.

Ironically, both of these two phenomena were by-products of the non-Brahman movement, many of whose active proponents were themselves members of the *Isai Vēḷāḷar jāti* (A. Srinivasan 1984: 14-6). Given the pervasive notion of decline in the dominant discourse, the impact of Rajarattinam Pillai as a powerful symbol is perhaps greater at present to the *Isai Vēḷāḷar* musicians. This is because he represents the essence and identity of their tradition (extended *rāgam* improvisation) when it is given a decreasing value and appreciation, and because he was able to transcend the unfair boundaries set by the Brahmans to achieve unprecedented fame at a time when an increasing number of non-*Isai Vēḷāḷar* musicians have gained popularity and recognition previously unavailable to them, therefore seriously eroding the *Isai Vēḷāḷars'* previous domination of the *nāgasvaram* tradition.

One consequence of the non-Brahman movement was the increasing urge of the non-Brahmans for their own music tradition separate from the one now identified with Brahmans. This sentiment, a reaction to Brahman domination of classical music, was one of the major driving forces operating toward the advent of the Tamil Music movement (*Tamiḻ Isai Iyakkam*) in 1935.[423] One of the major criticism of Brahman dominated classical music was the neglect of Tamil compositions. Given the symbolic implications of the Trinity whose compositions were mostly written in Sanskrit or Telugu, very few Tamil compositions were performed at concerts.

However, to characterize the Tamil Music movement an entirely non-Brahman activity is misleading. Many Brahman musicians and patrons participated in the movement, though their views as to the desirable position of Tamil songs within the classical music tradition varied considerably. The original thrust of this movement was not specifically sectarian and rather derived from the frustration over the dominance of Sanskrit and Telugu language in music.[424] In its initial stage, the primary aim of the movement was the propagation of Tamil songs with an eye to the democratization of music. However, as more radical views such as the eliminations of Telugu and Sanskrit compositions began to appear, the movement itself came to be regarded by many Brahmans as anti-Brahman and resulted in the alienation of many Brahman supporters of the movement. As Nambi Arooran points out, the Tamil Music movement acquired considerable support from the leaders of the non-Brahman movement and the Justice Party, while opposition came mainly from Brahman musicians and Brahman-oriented organizations such as the Music Academy (1980: 265).

Nevertheless, the impact of the Tamil Music movement on *Periya Mēḷam* musicians is not unequivocal. The attempt to propagate Tamil compositions placed many *Isai Vēḷāḷar* musicians and composers in the limelight since these compositions were transmitted primarily through families of *Isai Vēḷāḷar* musicians.[425] The Tamil Isai Sangam, the organizational manifestation of the movement, has patronized *Periya Mēḷam* music more than any other organizations, most of which were Brahman-controlled. Yet, the disproportionate attention to the language issue in music in a way de-emphasized the improvisational aspect of music, a stronghold of *Periya Mēḷam* music, and perhaps helped accelerate the shift of emphasis in repertoire from extended improvisation to compositions.

In short, the non-Brahman movement crystalized the ambiguity of *Isai Vēḷāḷar*'s position in South Indian music culture. While *Isai Vēḷāḷars* are non-Brahmans themselves, they depend for their livelihood on part of the culture which increasingly assumed a Brahmanical identity. As the Brahmanical culture was condemned by non-Brahmans in the political arena, they unwittingly criticized the part of the musical tradition in which *Isai Vēḷāḷar Periya Mēḷam* musicians specialized. As Amy Catlin reports, for example, the *pallavi*, the highly technical and improvisational form cultivated particularly by *Periya Mēḷam* musicians, was rejected by non-Brahmans as a musical manifestation of the elitist incomprehensibleness associated with the arcane Brahman scholar (1980: 41). This characterization of the *pallavi* was a double blow to *Isai Vēḷāḷar Periya Mēḷam* musicians. It reduced the popularity of the form, while the contribution of *Isai Vēḷāḷar* musicians to the development of this form remained unacknowledged.

5. Dimensions of Brahman Hegemony in Music

From the point of view of non-Brahmans, the history of South Indian music in the twentieth century can be seen as the Brahmans' continuous, and largely successful, effort to project themselves as authoritative practitioners of the entire tradition to the exclusion of non-Brahman musicians. They attempted to assert their centrality in *Karnāṭak* music by consolidating political power to build a system most beneficial to them, as well as by portraying non-Brahman musicians as a group as secondary and peripheral.

This process involved gradual and subtle manipulation due to the prominence of non-Brahman musicians in the formation of present-day *Karnāṭak* music. Two of the three important historical sources of *Karnāṭak* music were maintained by musicians belonging to a non-Brahman *jāti* of *Isai Vēḷāḷar*, and many of the playing techniques of accompaniment instruments used in *Karnāṭak* music were developed by them. *Mridaṅgam* musicians who played for *Karnāṭak* music concerts, for example, were mostly non-Brahmans before 1910 (L'Armand and L'Armand 1983: 429-30). The increasing prominence in the 1920s of Brahman players of instruments (*mridaṅgam, kañjirā, flute, morsing,* etc.) previously considered unfit for them due to their ritually polluting quality is usually explained as part of an overall process of secularization among Brahmans, but the attenuation of the stigma attached to learning such instruments by the increasing sense of *Karnāṭak* music as being an activity of Brahman dominance should not be forgotten.

By no means am I suggesting here the conscious attempt by individual Brahmans to eliminate non-Brahman musicians from music-making. As I mentioned before, Brahmans have been the most important group responsible for the survival of the *Periya Mēlam* tradition. Many *Isai Vēlālar* musicians were respected, admired, and patronized for their individual expertise by Brahman connoisseurs. Importantly, however, the audience for *Periya Mēlam* performances, either during the temple festival or at concert halls, is often mutually exclusive to that for *Karnāṭak* music: those who are concert goers of *Karnāṭak* music tend not to attend *Periya Mēlam* recitals, and vice versa, although exceptions apply to this observation. There are many Brahmans, particularly of the older generation, who have special affection toward *Periya Mēlam* music. Several Brahman connoisseurs confessed that they enjoyed *Periya Mēlam* music so much that they would have become *Periya Mēlam* players themselves if the customary inhibition had not prevented them from doing so.[426] The audience for *Periya Mēlam* recitals at concert halls is comprised of these Brahman *rasikars* and members of *jātis* associated with *Periya Mēlam* music. These Brahman connoisseurs often established personal acquaintance and friendship with *Periya Mēlam* musicians.

In addition, there also existed a number of progressive Brahmans who wholeheartedly fought against social inequality based on caste. In the realm of *Periya Mēlam* music, it was Brahmans who were instrumental in establishing the associations for *nāgasvaram* musicians, who could not organize themselves for the improvement of their threatened profession.[427] A well-known film director K. Subramanyam (1904-71) was an enthusiastic patron of *Periya Mēlam* music, and in the 1950s he established the South Indian Nadhaswara Artists' Association (*Teṉṉindiyā Nāadasvarak Kalaiñarhaḷ Sangam*) to improve their professional condition (health benefits, transportation concessions, and pension from the state government) and social prestige.[428] This organization ceased to function with the death of Subramanyam in 1971, since its activity was almost solely due to his individual efforts. Another organization, Sri Nagasvaravali, was established in 1981 by Tanjavur Upendran, a well-known *Isai Vēḷāḷar mridaṅgam* musician, and N. Sivaramakrishnan, a Brahman banker and dedicated patron of *Periya Mēḷam* music. Frustrated by the neglect of *Periya Mēḷam* music, they primarily aimed to gain *Periya Mēḷam* the 'right place' in South Indian music and to raise consciousness of its high artistic merit by providing deserving musicians with performance opportunities and conducting felicitous functions.[429] More than two hundred *Periya Mēḷam* musicians were its honorary members.[430]

Nevertheless, these dedicated individuals often received stiff resistance from the orthodox section of the Brahman community for what was thought of as a threat to the latter's social and religious position. The severity of the resistance can be detected in the case of Subramanyam. He was excommunicated from the Brahman community for the radicalism he expressed in his controversial film, *Thyagabhoomi* ('The Land of Sacrifice'), in which the traditional prohibition against Adi Dravidas (*dalits*) entering temples was criticized (Baskaran 1981: 116-8).[431] Although Subramanyam's plight was triggered by what his film symbolized and not directly related to his stance on non-Brahman musicians, his involvement in *Periya Mēḷam* musicians and other non-Brahman performing artists was also considered a part of his larger effort to breach the previous social order. Sivaramakrishnan also recollects the slanderous criticism and lack of support for his involvement from his own community.

The position of *Isai Vēḷāḷar* musicians in *Karnāṭak* music further illuminates the nature of Brahman hegemony. A number of *Isai Vēḷāḷar* soloists and accompanists are actively involved in performing *Karnāṭak* music, often sharing the stage with Brahman musicians, and some have been honoured with prestigious titles from Brahman-controlled organizations. On the surface, non-Brahman musicians seem to enjoy a healthy representation and prestige. Yet, their talent has been tactfully appropriated and manipulated in such a way that Brahman dominance would remain not only unchallenged but reinforced.

Even those who have achieved the highest honour remain in effect under the supervision of their Brahman *gurus* or primary patrons as to their professional conduct, and they themselves are unable to develop sufficient influence to change the pattern of domination, no matter the degree to which their musical talent is appreciated by Brahman patrons. Other non-Brahman musicians without such connections may have to struggle against the lack of opportunities for prestigious performances and public recognition in the form of titles and grades, or have to develop their professional career outside the Brahman-controlled music associations altogether.

Self-identification with and emulation of Brahmans on the part of *Isai Vēḷāḷar Karnāṭak* musicians also facilitated Brahman manipulation of symbols to their benefit. A prime example of seemingly conscious self-Brahmanisation can be seen in the case of M.S. Subbulakshmi, perhaps the best-known South Indian musician of all time. Although a thorough analysis of the discourse on this internationally-famed musician requires a separate study, a brief observation will be provided here in relation to the case of Rajarattinam Pillai. Although hailing from a *dēvadāsi* lineage in Madurai, Subbulakshmi married a Brahman, acted and spoke like a Brahman, and in many ways even generated the image of the ideal Brahman woman and musician. In addition to her presumed musical excellence, Subbulakshmi was often praised for her quality of saintliness, including her indifference to material rewards, belief in charity, and total devotion to her Brahman husband (Venkataraman 1986; Gangadhar 2002). For these qualities, she was sometimes compared to, or even considered, a contemporary reincarnation of female saints of the past, such as Mirabai of the sixteenth century.[432] Her *dēvadāsi* heritage was markedly de-emphasized in dominant discourse, though it is common knowledge among patrons of music. Subbulakshmi became the epitome of class and elegance for Brahman women in general, and her appearance and paraphernalia was imitated by them (George 2004: 222-3).[433]

Although her musical talent is unanimously acknowledged,

both by Brahmans and by *Isai Vēḷāḷars*, the extent of her fame and the status she enjoyed might well have been considerably less without this type of complete self-identification with Brahman values and customs. While saintly figures with positive attributes characterizing Subbulakshmi could be found among *Isai Vēḷāḷars*, herself being a prime example, her saintliness and musical talent were both attributed in a considerable degree to the Brahman environment which, with utmost care, nurtured these qualities in her to the extent she commanded her elevated status. At the same time that the social stigma attached to *dēvadāsi* heritage was almost completely eliminated by the process of wholesale Brahmanisation, Subbulakshmi's artistic heritage was effectively appropriated to reinforce Brahman hegemony of music.

Seen this way, the difference and similarity in the Brahman discursive strategy to characterize Subbulakshmi and Rajarattinam Pillai is clear. Hailing from what was characterized by Brahmans as a peripheral tradition (*Periya Mēḷam* music), Rajarattinam Pillai achieved a level of musical attainment which Brahman *Karnāṭak* musicians and patrons could not deny. Since *Karnāṭak* music had maintained the image of centrality partly by portraying the *Periya Mēḷam* tradition as a musically secondary and socially inferior subculture, the emergence of an extraordinary musician like Rajarattinam Pillai who had the potential of transcending the boundary could have upset the projected image of their artistic superiority. In other words, Rajarattinam Pillai was a dangerous anomaly in the hierarchical structure Brahmans managed to project in that he belonged to neither group, and thus was a threat to the existing hierarchy. Two complementary discursive strategies were taken simultaneously to neutralize Rajarattinam Pillai's prominence which could threaten the Brahman monopoly of *Karnāṭak* music: incorporation and alienation. Rajarattinam Pillai's musical self was incorporated into *Karnāṭak* music tradition as part of its representative feature, therefore even strengthening the merit of the tradition, whereas his non-musical self was defined as belonging only to the *Periya Mēḷam* music tradition.

III. CONCLUDING REMARKS

The present chapter is based upon my desire to evaluate the extent to which an analysis of the discourse on a charismatic individual musician can contribute to the understanding of the music culture to which s/he belongs. The basic premise here is that a charismatic musician not only draws considerable attention from the constituting members of music culture, but the discourse on this individual is also dialectically connected to their socio-cultural situation. With this perspective, I have chosen to inquire how the discourse on Rajarattinam Pillai is socially and politically significant in South Indian music culture, instead of yielding to the notion that the genius is a self-complete unit for analysis and asking only what musical features make this particular individual a genius.

Multiple interpretations of Rajarattinam Pillai by three caste groups of musicians and patrons (Brahmans, *Isai Vēḷāḷars*, and *Maruttuvars*) have been analysed. The socio-cultural situation surrounding each group and the changing position of each group in the social and music hierarchy can be identified as affecting and reflecting the interpretation of Rajarattinam Pillai on the general level. For Brahmans, the trenchant attack on Brahmanical culture in the non-Brahman movement generated the need for establishing a cultural arena in which to assert their identity. In contrast, *Isai Vēḷāḷars* needed a powerful symbol to prevent their previously hegemonic domination of *Periya Mēḷam* music from further erosion, against the widely-held notion of the decline of their artistic competence and the increasing prominence of *Periya Mēḷam* musicians belonging to other *jāti* groups. *Maruttuvars*, on the other hand, are forced to utilize anything to establish their niche in *Periya Mēḷam* music in light of their low social status and assumed inferior artistic competence.

Analysis of Rajarattinam Pillai as a polysemic symbol has suggested that the discursive strategies adopted by different groups of musicians and patrons are not only the manifestation or reflection of the power relations existing in South Indian music culture, but themselves are the sites of continuing political maneuver for reinforcing desired ideology and identity maintenance. A wide variety of aspects or issues surrounding music and musicians—from the position of vocal music to extended improvisation, from the ideal of saintly musicianship to the habit of heavy drinking—is contested through Rajarattinam Pillai's presumed attributes.

The *Isai Vēḷāḷars* find in Rajarattinam Pillai a means of symbolic cultural resistance or the refusal of complete subjugation to Brahmans. Although their interpretations (subordinate discourse) are rarely advanced face-to-face with Brahmans to avoid retaliation, *Isai Vēḷāḷars* can maintain pride in their own musical heritage and even the sense of musical superiority by maintaining the image of Rajarattinam Pillai as a musician with unprecedented talent who fought against Brahman hegemony. The discourse on Rajarattinam Pillai also functions as a plausible explanation or legitimation of the drastic changes in *Periya Mēḷam* music during his lifetime and its alienation from the original ritual setting.

Analysis of the differences in interpretation of Rajarattinam Pillai between *Isai Vēḷāḷars* and *Mamttuvars* has also revealed the complex interplay between dominant and subordinate discourses. The appropriation of the primacy of vocal music by *Isai Vēḷāḷars* for establishing a position superior to the *Maruttuvar* musicians has the effect of reinforcing Brahman appropriation of the same aspect of music against *Isai Vēḷāḷars* themselves. This unwitting endorsement and reinforcement of the dominant discourse by the subordinate groups is also common in what Gramsci calls 'contradictory consciousness' (1971: 333). While the non-Brahman musicians criticize the tendency for preferential treatment of Brahman musicians by Brahman-controlled organizations, once they are individually given benefits, such as performance opportunities and titles, from the same organizations, the prestige associated with organizations is often utilized to establish their superior position against other members.

Admittedly, the theme of Brahman hegemony advanced in

this study requires further elaboration with additional separate studies on the different aspects of South Indian music culture, and the analysis of Rajarattinam Pillai in this work only serves as an introduction to a comprehensive inquiry on this complex issue. It may be argued that the present study attempts to integrate subordinate discourses on one level, while ignoring, if not being unaware of, those on others, and that such omission will lead us to oversimplify the enormous complexity found in South Indian music culture as a whole. I cannot, and do not pretend to, examine all the possible layers which could be analysed in South Indian music culture, for practical reasons. Here I will simply point to potential areas of investigation for the refinement of the thesis of power relations and Brahman hegemony advanced in this study.

The discussion in the present study is confined largely to music culture in the city of Madras and the district of Tanjavur (central Tamil Nadu), where most of my research was conducted. Focusing on these two geographical areas is ironic in its political implications, since the intention of the present study is to integrate the hitherto neglected perspectives of the subordinate groups into an analysis of music culture in general, and yet this irony itself manifests the multiple layers of power relations in South Indian music. As explained in Chapters 4 and 5, while Tanjavur and Madras are described in existing literature (read dominance discourse) as present artistic centres for *Periya Mēḷam* and *Karnāṭak* music traditions respectively, the authentication of the musical supremacy of these locations and musicians associated with them has encountered disapproval within each tradition.

Another limitation of the present study concerns the omission of the *Ciṉṉa Mēḷam* tradition from the discussion. *Periya Mēḷam* and *Ciṉṉa Mēḷam* were the two musico-ritual performance traditions among the *Isai Vēḷāḷars*, until the latter's transformation into a Brahman-oriented concert art form known today as Bharata Natyam and consequent disassociation from the *Isai Vēḷāḷars* in the early decades of the twentieth century. The process of this transformation, which itself reveals an aspect of the Brahman/non-Brahman relationship, has been ably analysed by Amrit Srinivasan (1984). Although her insightful findings on the relationship between these two traditions among the *Isai Vēḷāḷars* is incorporated into the present study whenever considered relevant, the discussion of this aspect in relation to the theme of Brahman hegemony is preliminary.

Detailed discursive analysis on charismatic musicians and composers other than Rajarattinam Pillai will provide more insights into the nature of the power relations. In addition to M.S. Subbulakshmi and T.R. Mahalingam, who I briefly discussed earlier, a few other individuals are important candidates for such an inquiry. To give just two examples, I mention Papanasam Sivan (1890-1973) and Veena Dhanammal (1867-1938). A discursive analysis on Papanasam Sivan, the most celebrated Brahman composer of Tamil songs in the twentieth century, will further illuminate aspects of the Brahmans' relationship to the highly politicized *Tamiḻ Isai* movement. I speculate that the elevation of Sivan to the status of a saint-composer, reminiscent, not surprisingly, of that of the Trinity,[434] is the Brahmans' reactive strategy to the non-Brahman attempt to co-opt Tamil compositions or language, in an effort to establish their own music culture to the exclusion of Brahmans, and thereby to push forward Dravidian nationalism. Here we may find an example of a dominant group who seeks 'to absorb victories by subordinate groups in order to reestablish cultural hegemony' (O'Brien and Roseberry 1991: 14).

The discourse on a legendary *dēvadāsi vīṇa* player Dhanammal and her descendants must also be analysed for their unique position in *Karnāṭak* music. Their musical influence has been enormous, and three family members, T. Brinda (1912-96), T. Balasaraswati (1918-84), T. Viswanathan (1927-2002), have been given the most prestigious award of *Saṅgīta Kalānidhi* from the Brahman-controlled Music Academy. They are often considered musicians' musicians, and enjoy a cult-like following in probably one of the most elitist sections of Brahman patronage.[435] In my judgement, the careful discursive analysis of Dhanammal, along with that of Subbulakshmi, will generate more nuanced insights into the process of the Brahmanisation of the *dēvadāsi* heritage in general.

Additionally, a detailed analysis of historical change in the discourse on the Trinity, particularly Tyagaraja, is crucial in determining the process in which the current Brahman hegemony, based heavily upon what they are made to symbolize, was established.

As Hobsbawm and Ranger's important study (1983) continues to remind us, the past is used for the manipulation of the present. In order to account for the present, to justify it, understand it, and criticize it, the past is used, selectively appropriated, remembered, forgotten, or invented (also Kajiwara 1984; Tonkin et al. 1989).[436] Social memory of Rajarattinam Pillai reflects and embodies the situation in which South Indian music culture is placed today, as the polysemy of his charisma derives from, and corresponds to, the conflicting yet oddly synergetic relationship between Brahmans and non-Brahmans. Rajarattinam Pillai serves as a site of contestation where a multitude of interpretations, or 'accents' (Volosinov 1973), are accorded to his attributes for the legitimation of one's desired position and for securing one's identity. Finally, and perhaps most fundamentally, the very existence of subordinate discourses on Rajarattinam Pillai by *Isai Vēḷāḷars* and other non-Brahmans indicates the Brahman dominance of South Indian classical music itself.

(Originally submitted to the University of Washington
in 1992 as a doctoral dissertation.)

Glossary

The following conventions are used in the glossary. An alternate term is indicated in parenthesis ( ) immediately after each entry. The etymological explanation of the entry is given in brackets [ ], if applicable, after the alternate terms. The definition of each entry is given immediately after the colon. When the spelling generally accepted in the literature (such as *mridangam*) is used, the spelling based on the transliteration system employed in the present study is given in //. Tamil, Sanskrit and Urdu are abbreviated as Tm., Sk., and Ur.

Āccāmaram ஆச்சாமரம்: a type of ebony used to make the body of the *nāgasvaram* (*diospyros ebenaster*)

Āccāri ஆச்சாரி: a caste name for *nāgasvaram* and *tavil* makers

ādīṇakarttar ஆதீன கர்த்தர்: the head of the *ādīṇam*; spiritual leader of non-Brahman Saivites

ādīṇam ஆதீனம்: primary monastery which controls smaller monasteries (*maḍams*)

ādīṇa mēḷam ஆதீனமேளம்: *Periya Mēḷam* ensemble attached to *ādīṇam*

ādīṇa vittuvāṉ ஆதீனவித்துவான்: musician attached to *ādīṇam*

āhamam ஆகமம் [Sk. *Agama*]: sacred text of ritual procedure and artifact

ahāram அகாரம்: a blowing technique used for *nāgasvaram*

Ahila Ulaha Nādasura Cakkaravartti அகில உலக நாதசுர சக்கரவர்த்தி: 'World Renowned Emperor of *Nāgasvaram*'; the best-known title given to Rajarattinam Pillai

alaṅkāram அலங்காரம் [Tm. decoration]: one of the rudimentary music exercises for beginning students

ālāpaṉai ஆலாபனை: melodic improvisation prior to rendering the composition

alārippu அலாரிப்பு: a short rhythmic improvisation on *tavil* at the commencement of a temple ritual

āḻvār ஆழ்வார்: Vaishnavite saint-poet

Ambaṭṭaṉ அம்பட்டன்: a caste name for Tamil barbers, often considered derogatory

aṉaisu அனைசு (*aṉusu, aṉasu*): the bell attached to the distal end of the main body of the *nāgasvaram*

āṉandam ஆனந்தம் [Tm. bliss]: a composition played immediately after the consecration of marriage

aṉbaḷippu அன்பளிப்பு [Tm. gift]: gift to musicians as an appreciation of their performance

aṉulōma அனுலோம: a performance technique in which a composition is played twice as fast while the *tāḷam* is kept constant

aṉupallavi அனுபல்லவி: the second section of several compositional forms used in South Indian classical music

aptapūrtti அப்தபூர்த்தி: ritual to commemorate the first birthday of a child

araiyar அரையர்: a professional reciter of hymns at Vaishnavite temple

asaivam அசைவம்: non-vegetarianism

āstāṉa vittuvāṉ ஆஸ்தானவித்துவான்: a musician attached to a court, state or temple

aṭcarāppiyāsam அட்சராப்பியாசம்: a ritual to mark the beginning of Vedic study

Bajantri: a caste name for barber musicians in Karnataka

bāṇḍuvāttiyam பாண்டுவாத்தியம் [English, band]: a Western-style ensemble of brass and wood wind instruments and drums

bāṇi பாணி: style

bāri nāgasvaram பாரிநாகஸ்வரம் [*bha'rī*, Ur. *big, weighty*]: bigger sized, lower-pitched *nāgasvaram*

bhajaṉa/bajaṉai/ பஜனை: congregational singing of devotional songs

bhakti /bakti/ பக்தி: devotion

Bharata Natyam/*baratanāṭṭiyam*/பரதநாட்டியம்: a classical dance of South India *briga* (*brikka*): extremely fast melodic passages most typically found in *nāgasvaram* music

caraṇam சரணம்: the third section of the most commonly performed compositional types such as *kīrttaṉai*

Cheṭṭiār/Cheṭṭiyār/ செட்டியார்: a caste name for Tamil traders and merchants

Chola/Chōḻa/ சோழ: South Indian kingdom between ninth and thirteenth centuries

Ciṉṉa Mēḷam சின்னமேளம்: temple dance and its accompaniment

darsan/*darisaṉam*/ தரிசனம்: having a glimpse (of a deity, saint, etc.)

dēvadāsi (*dāsi*) தேவதாசி (தாசி): a generic term for female dancers attached to, or associated with, Hindu temples and royal courts

dēvastāṉa vittuvāṉ தேவஸ்தான வித்துவான்: musicians who are on the payrolls of temples for their service

dīpārādaṉai தீபாராதனை: a ritual to offer light by waving it before the deity

dubāsh /*dubāsi*/துபாசி: literally, 'two languages'; translater or agent (to the East India Company)

eccil எச்சில்: saliva

eḍuppu எடுப்பு [Tm. taking]: the beginning point of the text of a composition

emperumāṉaḍiyār எம்பெருமானடியார்: a term referring to temple dancers in medieval documents

gamakam கமகம்: ornamental devices

gambīram கம்பீரம்: majesty

gauravasambaḷam கவுரவசம்பளம் [*gauravam*, Tm. honor]: honorary salary

geṭṭimēḷam கெட்டிமேளம் [*geṭṭi*, Tm. loudness]: a type of fanfare played by *Periya Mēḷam* ensemble

gītam கீதம்: a short composition for beginning students

gōpuram கோபுரம்: a gate tower of a temple

gōshṭi கோஷ்டி [Tm. group]: musical ensemble

grhapravēsa கிரஹப்ரவேச: a ritual to mark the initial entry into the bridegroom's house *guru* குரு: preceptor, teacher

gurukkaḷ குருக்கள்: priests who perform *pūja* at Saivite temples

gurukulavāsam குருகுலவாசம்: traditional method of knowledge transmission

iḍai bāri இடை பாரி [*iḍai*, Tm. middle]: medium sized (instrument)

iḍantalai [*iḍam*, Tm. left side; *talai*, Tm. head]: lower-pitched head of *tavil* played by a wooden stick

iṇippu இனிப்பு: sweetness (often used to describe good music)

Isai Vēḷāḷar இசைவேளாளர்: a caste name for *Periya Mēḷam* musicians in central Tamil Nadu

īṭṭimaram ஈட்டிமரம்: a type of rosewood (Dalbergia latifolia) used to make the *aṇaisu* (bell) of *nāgasvaram*

jamīndār ஜமீன்தார்: landlord

janaṅgaḷ ஜனங்கள் (*makkaḷ* மக்கள்): the masses, ordinary people

jāṇavāsam ஜானவாசம்: same as *māppiḷḷai aḻaippu* (Brahman usage)

jāru ஜாரு: a type of musical ornamentation; portamento

jāvaḷi ஜாவளி: a compositional type characterized by erotic and devotional texts

kaccēri கச்சேரி [Ur. *kachahri*]: performance, concert

kaḍukkaṇ கடுக்கன் [Tm. a type of stud worn by males for ornamentation]: a stud worn by *Periya Mēḷam* musicians and Brahmans; often with diamond (*vairam*)

kādukuttudal காதுகுத்துதல் [Tm. piercing of ears]: the ritual in which a child's ears are pierced; a *Periya Mēḷam* ensemble is sometimes engaged for this ritual

Kaikkōḷan கைக்கோளன்: a caste name for Tamil weavers

Kalaimāmaṇi கலைமாமணி: a title given to musicians by the Tamil Nadu Government

Kālakshēpam காலகேஷபம்: a form of recitation and song with musical accompaniment, also known as *Katakalakshepam* or *Harikata*

kālam காலம்: time, speed

kaḻi கழி [Tm. stick]: a wooden stick used to play the *tavil*

kal nāgasvaram கல் நாகஸ்வரம் [kal, Tm. stone]: *nāgasvaram* made of soap stone *kalyāṇa kaccēri* கல்யாண கச்சேரி: musical performance at wedding ceremony

kalyāṇam கல்யாணம்: marriage

kalyāṇa maṇḍapam கல்யாண மண்டபம்: a hall where marriage ceremony takes place

Kambar கம்பர்: a caste name for *Periya Mēḷam* musicians in Kanyakumari and Tirunelveli districts of Tamil Nadu and southern Kerala state

Kambu கம்பு [Tm. stick]: same as *kaḻi*

kanjira கஞ்சிரா: tambourine used in *Karnāṭak* music

karpaṉai கற்பனை [Tm. imagination]: musical imagination or creativity

karumādi கருமாதி: funeral ritual

kāsiyāttirai காசியாத்திரை: a marriage ritual in which the bridegroom sets out for a mock pilgrimage to Banaras

kaṭṭai கட்டை [Tm. reed in a harmonium]: a term to indicate the pitch of instruments and voice, e.g. 2-*kaṭṭai*

kayaṟu கயறு [Tm. string]: a string connecting the two different body parts of the *nāgasvaram* together

kēḷviñāṉam கேள்விஞானம்: musical knowledge obtained by repeated listening

keṇḍai கெண்டை (*kaṇḍai* கண்டை): a copper staple on which the reed of the *nāgasvaram* is placed

kīrttaṉai கீர்த்தனை: the most frequently performed compositional form in South Indian classical music

koḍukoṭṭi கொடுகொட்டி (*kiḍikeṭṭi* கிடிக்கெட்டி): a pair of kettle drums used to accompany *nāgasvaram* in Tiruvarur area

Koñjum Salaṅgai கொஞ்சும் சலங்கை: a Tamil film made in 1962

kōyil கோயில் (*kōvil* கோவில்): temple

kōyil kaccēri கோயில் கச்சேரி: music recitals at temples, often as part of their annual festivals

kōyil sampradāyam கோயில் சம்ப்ரதாயம்: temple tradition; performance practice at temples

kucci குச்சி [Tm. stick]: an ivory or plastic stick used to adjust the opening of the *nāgasvaram* reed *kuḍamuḻā* குடமுழா: a Tamil term for *pañjamuhavāttiyam*

kūḍu கூடு [Tm. receptacle]: small thimbles *tavil* players wear on their fingers during performance

kuḍumi குடுமி: a traditional hair style with the front part of the head shaved and a tuft on the back part

kuḻal குழல்: pipe, flute

Kumbakōṇamtimiri கும்பகோணம்திமிரி: a small-sized *nāgasvaram* used in Kumbakonam, in contrast to *Tiruvārūr bāri*, a larger *nāgasvaram*

kuṅgumam குங்குமம்: vermilion powder worn on forehead

kūṛai aṇidal கூறை அணிதல்: a ritual in which the bridegroom gives the marriage *sari* (*poḍavai*) to thebride

kūṛaipoḍavai கூறைபுடவை: expensive *sari* given to the bride as a symbol of marriage

kuṛuṅkuḻal குறுங்குழல்: a short double-reed aerophone in Kerala

kūṭṭu கூட்டு: ensemble

lāli லாலி: a type of marriage song sung and played on *nāgasvaram*

liṅgam லிங்கம்: phallic symbol of Siva

Madam மடம்: monastery

maḍattu mēlam மடத்து மேளம்: *Periya Mēḷam* ensemble attached to the Madam

mahārājā மகாராஜா: king

mahuḍi மகுடி: a single reed aerophone used by snake charmers

mālai மாலை: garland

mālaimaṛṛal மாலை மாற்றல்: a ritual during the wedding ceremony in which garlands are exchanged by bride and bridegroom

mallāri மல்லாரி: instrumental composition played by *Periya Mēḷam* ensemble at the outset of a procession

maṇamēḍai மணமேடை: a platform on which marriage consecration ritual is performed

maṅgaḷam மங்களம்: auspiciousness; a short composition to conclude a performance

maṅgaḷavāttiyam மங்களவாத்தியம்: auspicious instrument, such as *nāgasvaram*and *tavil*

manōdharma saṅgītam மனோதர்மசங்கீதம்: improvisational music, as opposed to *kalpita saṅgīita* or composed music

māppiḷḷai aḻaippu மாப்பிள்ளை அழைப்பு [*māppiḷḷai* Tm. bridegroom, *aḻaippu* Tm. invitation]: a ritual inwhich bridegroom and his family are invited to bride's house or weddinghall

Maruttuvar மருத்துவர் [Tm. doctor]: a caste name by which Madras Tamil barber musicians prefer to refer to themselves

mattaḷam மத்தளம்: a double-headed drum resembling *mridaṅgam*

māvaṭṭam மாவட்டம்: district; same as *jillā*

Mēḷakkāra Mudaliyār மேளக்கார முதலியார்: a caste name for *Periya Mēḷam* musicians in western Tamil Nadu

Mēḷakkārar மேளக்காரர்: the former caste name for *Isai Vēḷāḷars* in Tanjavur area

mēḷam மேளம்: 1) drum; 2) (*Periya Mēḷam*) ensemble; 3) *nāgasvaram*; 4) parental mode; 5) *rāgam*

mēḷanaisu [*mēḷ*, Tm. up, above]: upper part of the body of *nāgasvaram* which was formerly made of a separate piece of wood

mirāsudār மிராசுதார்: landlord

mōrsing/*mōrsiṅ* மோர்சிங்: mouth harp used in *Karnāṭak* music

mridaṅgam மிருதங்கம்: double headed drum; the primary rhythmic accompaniment instrument in *Karnāṭak* music

muhavīṇai முகவீணை [*muham*, Tm. face]: a small double-reed aerophone used in some temples and *terukkūttu* dance drama; previously used in *Ciṉṉa Mēḷam*

muhūrttam முஹூர்த்தம் [Sk. *muhūrtah*]: auspicious time; marriage consecration ceremony

mūlamūrtti மூலமூர்த்தி [*mūlam*, Tm. root]: image of the deity permanently placed in sanctum sanctorum (*mūlasthānam*) of temple

mūlasthānam மூலஸ்தானம்: sanctum sanctorum of the temple

mummūrttihaḷ மும்மூர்த்திகள்: The Trinity; three Brahman saint-composers of the early nineteenth century, Tyagaraja, Muttusvami Diksitar, and Syama Sastri

muṉpaṇam முன்பணம்: advance money

Muttamiḻ Pēravai முத்தமிழ்பேரவை: a cultural organization sponsored by the DMK party.

Muttukkārar முத்துக்காரர்: term used in the medieval documents to refer to time-keeper for dance performance

naḍai நடை: subdivision of beat

nādam: (musical) sound

Nādār நாடார்: a name of the Tamil caste associated with toddy-tapping

nādasvaram நாதஸ்வரம் (*nādasuram*): an alternate term for *nāgasvaram*

nāgasvarabāṇi நாகஸ்வரபாணி: musical style peculiar to *nāgasvaram*, usually in contrast to that of vocal music

nāgasvarakkārar நாகஸ்வரக்காரர்: *nāgasvaram* musician (often honorific)

nāgasvaram நாகஸ்வரம் (*nāgasuram* நாகசுரம்): double-reed aerophone used in *Periya Mēḷam* music

nāgasvaravādana: an instrumental ensemble featuring *nāgasvaram* in Karnataka

nāgasvara vittuvāṉ நாகஸ்வரவித்துவான்: *nāgasvaram* musician (often in contrast to *saṅgīta vittuvāṉ*)

Nāidu நாய்டு: a caste name/title for Telugu speaking barber musicians in Tamil Nadu

naivēttiyam நைவேத்தியம் (*neyvēttiyam* நெய்வேத்தியம்): a temple ritual to offer food to the deity

naiyāṇḍi mēḷam நையாண்டி மேளம் [*naiyāṇḍi*, Tm. joke, satire]: folk *nāgasvaram* ensemble accompanying various dance forms

nalaṅgu நலங்கு [Tm. anointing]: a ritual during wedding ceremony in which the couple smeared the saffron and turmeric paste onto each other's legs

namasivāya நமசிவாய: five sacred syllables of Siva

nāṇaltaṭṭai நாணல்தட்டை: a dried stalk of a plant used to make reed for *nāgasvaram*

ñāṉam ஞானம் [Tm. knowledge]: knowledge, musical knowledge

naṭṭuvaṉār நட்டுவானார்: dance master

Nāvidar நாவிதர்: a caste name for Tamil barbers; also see *Maruttuvar* and *Ambaṭṭaṉ*

nāyaṉakkārar நாயனக்காரர்: a *nāgasvaram* musician (often honorific)

nāyaṉam நாயனம்: a colloquial Tamil term for *nāgasvaram*; used most frequently by *Periya Mēḷam* musicians themselves

nāyaṉār நாயனார்: Saivite saint-poets

Nāyar நாயர்: a cast name for *Periya Mēḷam* musicians in central and southern Kerala

Nayinda: a caste name for Kannada barbers

Nī நீ: you (casual, intimate, and less respectful)

niccaya tāmbūlam நிச்சய தாம்பூலம் [*niccayam* நிச்சயம் Tm. assurance; *tāmbūlam* தாம்பூலம் Tm. betel-leaf]: betrothal ritual

nīṅga நீங்கள்: you (formal, respectful)

noṭṭu நோட்டு [English, note]: compositions influenced by western band music

ōḍal: a double-headed barrel-shaped drum used in some temples to augment the *Periya Mēḷam* ensemble

ōḍam ஓடம் [Tm. barge]: compositions played on *nāgasvaram* during the *Teppotsavam* (Floating Festival) when the deity is taken on a raft in the tank of the temple

ōduvār ஒதுவார்: professional reciters of *tēvāram* hymns at Siva temples

oli ஒலி: sound

ottu ஒத்து: a double-reed instrument used to provide drone to *nāgasvaram*

ottukkārar ஒத்துக்காரர்: *ottu* player

paccaippiḍi பச்சைப்பிடி: ball-shaped preparation made from rice; used during the *ūñjal* ritual

packāvaj: a double-headed barrel-shaped drum used in *dhrupad* style of Hindustani music

padakkam பதக்கம்: a medal or coin (given to *Periya Mēḷam* musicians as a token of appreciation for their performance

padam பதம்: a type of composition derived from the repertoire of music accompanying dance and characterized by romantic and devotional texts

paḍi: a composition played by *Periya Mēḷam* ensemble at Vaishnavite temples when the deity returns to the temple from procession

pai பை [Tm. bag]: cloth bag in which *nāgasvaram* is kept and transported

pakkavāttiyam பக்கவாத்தியம் [*pakkam*, Tm. side]: accompaniment instrument *pallavi* பல்லவி [Tm. refrain]: 1) the first section of most commonly performed compositional types; 2) improvisational form specialized in by *Periya Mēḷam* musicians

paḷḷiyaraisēvai பள்ளியறைசேவை: a temple ritual in which the deity is lulled to sleep with music

paṇ பண்: melodic mode used in ancient South India

Paṇḍāram பண்டாரம்: a caste name of non-Brahman priests; some members play *Periya Mēḷam* music in Tirunelveli district of Tamil Nadu state

*Pandithar/Paṇḍidar/*பண்டிதர்/: a caste name for Tamil barbers; same as *Maruttuvar*

paṅgu பங்கு [Tm. share]: prescribed share of remuneration in the *Periya Mēḷam* ensemble

Panicker/*Paṇikkar/*பணிக்கர்/: an honorific title used by *Nayar Periya Mēḷam* musicians

Pañjamuhavāttiyam பஞ்சமுகவாத்தியம் [Sk.*pañcan* five; Tm. *muham* face; Sk.*vādyam* musical instrument]:

Paṟaiyar பறையர்: a caste name for Tamil dalits; players of *naiyāṇḍi mēḷam*

Pariyāri பரியாரி: a caste name for barber musicians in Tanjavur area

pāṭṭi பாட்டி [English, party]: musical ensemble

pāṭṭu பாட்டு: *song*

peṇ aḻaippu பெண் அழைப்பு [Tm. invitation of the bride]: a ritual which takes place the night before the *muhūrttam* among some non-Brahman *jātis*

periyamallāri பெரிய மல்லாரி: a type of *mallāri* played at the commencement of the temple procession; often simply called *mallāri*

Periya Mēḷam பெரிய மேளம்: a musical tradition featuring *nāgasvaram* and *tavil* which provides music at temple and domestic rituals

peruvaṅgiyam பெருவங்கியம்: a type of aerophone mentioned in Tamil classical literature

poṉṉāḍai பொன்னாடை: a braided shawl presented to musicians

prabandam பிரபந்தம்: *Vaishnavite hymns*

prakāram பிரகாரம்: inner concentric enclosure of South Indian temples *prasādam* பிரசாதம்: food offering to the deity

pratilōma பிரதிலோம: a performance technique in which a composition is twice asslow while the *tāḷam* is kept constant

pūja/pūjai பூஜை: ritual, offering

pullānkuḷal புல்லாங்குழல்: transverse flute

puṅgi புங்கி: a single-reed aerophone used by snake charmers

pūṇūlkalyāṇam பூணூல் கல்யாணம்: a Tamil term for *upanayanam*

purōhidar ப்ரோஹிதர் [Sk. *purokita*]: a priest to officiate domestic rituals

rāga ālāpaṇai ராகஆலாபனை: improvisation on *rāgam* without the confines of *tālam*

rāgam ராகம் [Sk. *rag*] 1) melodic modal system on which Indian music is based; 2) improvisation on a *rāgam*

rāgamālika ராகமாளிகை: a form in which a number of different *rāgams* are performed in succession

rakti mēḷam ரக்தி மேளம் (*rattimēḷam*) [*rakti*, Tm. charm]: highly improvisational instrumental compositions played only by *Periya Mēḷam* ensembles

rasa: aesthetic principle permeating Indian culture

sabhā சபா/*sabai*/சபை [Sk. *sabhā*]: association, organization

sādaham சாதகம் [Sk. *sadhaka*]: practice

sādarā [Ur. *cādara*]: same as *poṉṉāḍai*

sahōdararhaḷ சகோதரர்கள்: brother

saivam சைவம்: vegetarian, vegetarianism

sakti சக்தி: power, creative force

sambaḷam சம்பளம் [Tm. salary]: monthly salary for the musicians attached to temples or monasteries

sāmipuṟappāḍu சாமிபுறப்பாடு: beginning of the procession of a deity

sammela: a pair of kettle drum used in conjunction with *nāgasvaram* in Dakshin Kanara district of Karnataka state

Saṅgīta Kalānidhi சங்கீதகலாநிதி: the musical title annually given by the Music Academy, Madras since 1942

saṅgītam சங்கீதம்: *music*

saṅgītasabhā சங்கீதசபா: an association that sponsors music recitals *saṅgīta vittuvāṉ* சங்கீதவித்துவான்: musician (particularly of *Karnāṭak* music)

sanniyāsi சந்நியாசி: ascetic

sārāyam சாராயம்: crudely brewed alcoholic beverage

sari [Hindi; Tm. *poḍavai* புடவை]: a wrapped garment of cotton, silk, or synthetic material worn by women

sāyaraccai சாயரச்சை (*sāyaraṭcai* சாயரட்சை): one of the six daily temple rituals, conducted in the early evening

Seṅgundar செங்குந்தர்: a caste name for Tamil weavers

shahnāī: a double-reed aerophone used widely in North India

Silappadikāram சிலப்பதிகாரம்: Tamil epic composed between the second and fifth centuries AD

Sīmandam சீமந்தம் (Sk. *simanta*): domestic ritual conducted at the sixth or eighth month of pregnancy

siṟappu mēḷam சிறப்பு மேளம்: *Periya Mēḷam* ensemble invited for special occasions

siṟappu tavil சிறப்பு தவில்: guest *tavil* players who have emerged since the late 1950s; often replaced by the half English phrase, 'special *tavil*'

sīvāḷi சீவாளி: reed, or mouthpiece with reed, used for *nāgasvaram* and *muhavīṇai*

sōham சோகம்: sorrow

sondaūru சொந்தஊர்: ancestral place

sruti சுருதி: tonic pitch, drone

srutipeṭṭi சுருதி பெட்டி [*peṭṭi*, Tm. box]: a bellows-pumped reed organ which provides drone in the *Periya Mēḷam* music

sutta matyamam சுத்தமத்யமம்: perfect fourth

svarakalpaṉā சுவரகல்பனா: improvised passages within the confines of *tāḷam*

svaram ஸ்வரம்: pitch level

tablā: a pair of kettle drums widely used in *Hindustani* music

tāḷam தாளம்: 1) rhythmic cycle; 2) a pair of hand cymbals used in *Periya Mēḷam* ensemble

taḷihaimallāri தளிகை மல்லாரி: a type of *mallāri* played during the *neivēttiyam* ritual *tālikaṭṭudal* தாலிகட்டுதல்: a ritual during the marriage ceremony in which the *tāli* (marriage necklace) is tied around the bride's neck to consecrate the marriage

taluk/*tāluka* தாலுகா: subdivision of a district

tamburā தம்புரா: a long-necked lute without frets which provides the drone in *Karnāṭak* music

tamburā śruti தம்புரா சுருதி: accompaniment format used in *Karnāṭak* music consisting typically of violin, *mridaṅgam* and *tamburā*

tandan āgasvaram தந்தநாகஸ்வரம்: *nāgasvaram* made of ivory

taṅgaccaṅgili தங்கச்சங்கிலி: gold chain, traditional paraphernalia of *Periya Mēḷam* musicians

taṅgan āgasvaram தங்க நாகஸ்வரம்: *nāgasvaram* covered with gold foil

taṇi āvarttaṇam தனிஆவர்த்தனம்: a solo by rhythmic accompanist

taṉṉakkāram தன்னக்காரம்: a blowing technique which combines *ahāram* and *tuttukkāram*

tavil தவில்: a barrel-shaped double-headed drum used in *Periya Mēḷam* ensemble

tavildār தவில்தார்: *tavil* player (honorific)

tavilkkārar தவில்க்காரர்: *tavil* player

tavul (*davul*) தவுல்: a colloquial termof *tavil*

tāyattu தாயத்து [Ur. *ta'it*]: a talisman worn by musicians

tāykkiḻavi தாய்க்கிழவி: the eldest female member of the *dēvadāsi* household

tēr தேர் (*radam*): temple car

terukkūttu தெருக்கூத்து: a dance drama in Tamil Nadu in which *muhaviṇai* is used as an accompaniment instrument

tēvāram தேவாரம்: Tamil devotional hymns by the three Saivite saint-poets: Tirunanasambandar, Tirunavukkarasar, and Sundaramurtti

tillāṉā தில்லானா: a type of technical and abstract composition derived from dance repertoire

Tillāṉā Mōhaṉāmbāḷ தில்லானா மோகனாம்பாள்: a Tamil film made in 1968 with a *nāgasvaram* musician as the main character

Timiri nāgasvaram திமிரி நாகஸ்வரம்: shorter and higher-pitched *nāgasvaram*

tirumaṇaalaippu திருமண அழைப்பு: marriage invitation

tirumaṇam திருமணம்: marriage

tirumāṉam தீருமானம்: conclusion, decision

tiruppaḷḷiyeḻucci திருப்பள்ளியெழுச்சி: a temple ritual in which *nāgasvaram* is played to wake up the deity

tiruppugaḻ திருப்புகழ்: compositions by the fifteenth century composer Arunagirinattar

Tiruvārūr bāri திருவாரூர்பாரி: a type of *nāgasvaram* used at the Tyagarajasvami Temple in Tiruvarur, often contrasted to *Kumbakōṇam timiri*

tiruviḻā திருவிழா: festival

toppi தொப்பி [Tm. hat]: lower-pitched head of *tavil* and *mridaṅgam*; same as *iḍantalai*

toḻil தொழில்: occupation, profession

tuttukkāram துத்துக்காரம்: a blowing technique used for *nāgasvaram*, tonguing

uḻavu உழவு: the main body (pipe) of *nāgasvaram*

uḷḷūr vittuvāṉ உள்ளூர்வித்துவான்: local musicians

ūñjal ஊஞ்சல் [Tm. swing]: a ritual during the marriage ceremony in which the couple sit on a swing; songs sung during the ritual, same as *ūñjal pāṭṭu*

ūñjalpāṭṭu ஊஞ்சல் பாட்டு [*pāṭṭu*, Tm. song]: songs sung during the *ūñjal* ritual

upanayaṇam உபநயனம்: initiation ritual for male Brahmans which requires the *Periya Mēḷam* ensemble

uṟsavam உற்சவம் (*utsavam*, Sk. *utsava*): temple festival; also *tiruviḻā*

uṟsavamūrtti உற்சவமூர்த்தி: a movable image of the deity used in temple procession

uṟumimēḷam உறுமிமேளம்: a folk ensemble featuring *nāgasvaram* and *uṟumi* (drum)

uruppaḍi உருப்படி: compositions, often used in contrast to the improvisational part of music

uruṭṭuccol உருட்டுச்சொல் [Tm. jolling syllables]: *tavil* accompaniment to *rāgam* elaboration on *nāgasvaram ūrvalam* ஊர்வலம்: procession

vāhaṉam வாஹனம்: vehicle for the deity

vairakkaḍukkaṉ வைரக்கடுக்கன்: diamond ear ornament

vaḷaikkāppu வளைகாப்பு: A domestic ritual held after the fifth month of pregnancy

valantalai வலந்தலை [*valam*, Tm. right side, *talai*, Tm. head]: higher-pitched head of *tavil*

vaṅgiyam வங்கியம் [Sk. vamsa, bamboo]: aerophone mentioned in classical Tamil literature

Vaṇṇāṉ வண்ணான்: a caste name for Tamil washermen

varavēṟpu வரவேற்பு [Tm. welcome]: reception at marriage ceremony

vāttiyam வாத்தியம் [Sk. *vadya*]: musical instrument

Vēḷāḷar வேளாளர்: a general term for high-ranking non-Brahman castes in Tamil Nadu

veḷikkaccēri வெளிக்கச்சேரி [*veḷi* வெளி, Tm. outside]: 1) performance for domestic rituals, 2) performance outside the locality of residence

vēṭṭi வேட்டி [Sk. *veshti*]: lower garment for men, *dhoti*

vibūti விபூதி: Sacred ash smeared on forehead and other parts of the body

vīṇa/vīṇai வீணை/: a primary plucked lute in South India

viralaḍi விரலடி [*viral* விரல், Tm. finger, *aḍi* அடி, Tm. to hit]: A fingering technique on *nāgasvaram* which involves quick closings and openings of fingerholes

wolaga: a Kannada term for *nāgasvara*

APPENDIX 1

Key Musicians Consulted

The following list only includes the musicians with whom I conducted extended ethnographic interviews. The other musicians I have consulted on casual basis are not included here. Following the full name of the musicians, each entry provides 1) date and place of birth (and death if applicable), 2) *jāti* and gender affiliations, 3) primary teachers, 4) date/s and location/s of interviews, and 5) institutional affiliation (temple, *ādīnam*, school etc.) and its location, wherever the information is availble. Some information is intentionally excluded from the list either upon the request by musicians themselves, or wherever else I judge the revelation might jeopardize their interest.

Nāgasvaram Musicians

1. Alagusundaram (Arahusundaram), Madurai N.
    1) 1930; 2) *Isai Vēḷāḷar*/male; 3) Madurai G. Kuppusami Naidu, Mannargudi Gurusami; 4) January 1989, Madurai; 5) Minakshi Temple (Madurai)
2. Ayyasamy (Ayyaccami), Madurai M.P.R.
    1) 1932; 2) *Isai Vēḷāḷar*/male; 3) G. Kuppusami Naidu, Mannargudi Gurusami; 4) January 1989, Madurai; 5) Sri Prasanna Venkatesa Perumal Temple (Madurai)
3. Balaraju, G.C.
    1) c. 1935; 2) *Naidu*/male; 3) G. Kuppusami Naidu (father); 4) January 1989, Madurai
4. Balu, Tiruvalaputtur
    1) 1936; 2) *Isai Vēḷāḷar*/male; 3) Tiruvalaputtur Venu Pillai; 4) January 1989, Madras; 5) Kapalisvara Temple (Mylapore, Madras)

5. Dakshnamoorthi (Dekshnamurtti), Pinnaimanagar K.M.
   1) 1953; 2) *Isai Vēḷāḷar*/male; 3) Parudiyappakoyil P.K. Saundirajan (d.1985); 4) August 1986, Thanjavur
6. Ellappa Mudaliyar, C.K.
   1) 1922, Kanchipuram; 2) male; 3) Gangadaram Pillai, Sembonnarkoyil Govindasami Pillai; 4) November 1986, Kanchipuram (Chingelput district); 5) Kamakshi Temple (Kanchipuam)
7. Ganesh, M.N.
   1) 1954; 2) *Bajantri*/male; 3) P. Rajagopal, A.V. Narayanappa; 4) May 1987, Melkote (Mandya district, Karnataka)
8. Ganesan, N.G.
   1) 1942, Nedunamangalam; 2) *Isai Vēḷāḷar*/male; 3) Govindasami (father), Sikkal Kandasami, Tiruppamburam Somasundaram; 4) June 1987, Kilvelur (Tanjavur district); 5) Akshayalingasvami Temple (Kilvelur)
9. Gangadaram, V.
   1) 1898; 2) male; 3) Gurusami (father-in-law); 4) January 1987, Kanchipuram (Chingleput district); 5) Kamakshi Temple (Kanchipuram)
10. Godandapani, Tanjavur
    1) 1935, Tanjavur; 2) *Isai Vēḷāḷar*/male; 3) Vallam V.A. Krishnan, T.N. Rajarattinam Pillai; 4) August 1986, January 1989, Tanjavur
11. Godandaram, M.
    1) c. 1940; 2) *Bajantri*/male; 3) Tiruvengadu Jayarama Pillai, Mayuram Mamundiya Pillai; 4) August 1987, Bangalore
12. Govindaraja Pillai, T.
    1) 1914; 2) *Isai Vēḷāḷar*/male; 3) Varuvul Virasami Pillai; 4) September 1986, Mayuram (Tanjavur district); 5) Mayuranada Temple (Mayuram)
13. Govindarajan, Darumapuram A.
    1) 1933; 2) *Isai Vēḷāḷar*/male; 3) Darumapuram Abiramasundaram (father, 1912-62); 4) January 1989, Madurai; 5) Lecturer, Government College of Music (Madurai)
14. Kaleeshabi Mahaboob (Kalishabi Mehabub)
    2) Muslim/female; 3) Chinna Meera Saheb (father), Sheik Chinna Moulana; 4) October 1986, Tiruchirappalli

15. Kalyana, Nagapattinam P.L.N.

  1) 1922; 2) *Isai Vēḷāḷar*/male; 3) Velupalayam Rattina Pillai; 4) June 1987, Nagapattinam (Tanjavur district); 5) Soundaraja Perumal Temple (Nagapattinam)

16. Kalyanasundaram Pillai, Tirucherai

  1) 1918-89; 2) *Isai Vēḷāḷar*/male; 3) Tirucherai Saranadam (father), Tirucherai Subbaraya (paternal uncle); 4) September 1987, Tandaracheri (Tanjavur district)

17. Kandasami Pillai, Injikkudi E.P.

  1) 1932-1988; 2) *Isai Vēḷāḷar*/male; 3) Injikkudi Pichaikannu (father, 1904-75); 4) September 1987, Mayiladuthurai (Tanjavur district); 5) Tiruvavadudurai Madam (Tiruvavadudurai)

18. Kuttikrishnan Nayar, P.

  1) 1920s; 2) *Nāyar*/male; 3) Kumbakonam D.G. Natesa Pillai; 4) February 1987, Guruvayur (Trichur district, Kerala); 5) Krishna Temple (Guruvayur)

19. Latchappa Pillai, Tiruvarur S.

  1) 1930-2013; 2) *Isai Vēḷāḷar*/male; 3) Sikkal Natarajasundaram Pillai, Kulikkarai Pichaiyappa Pillai (1913-79), T.N. Rajarattinam Pillai (1898-1956); 4) continuous (1986-1987, 1989-1990), Madras; 5) Lecturer, Government College of Music (Madras)

20. Mani, Paruttiyappakoyil K.V.

  1) 1944; 2) *Isai Vēḷāḷar*/male; 3) Arudurai Perumarukoil Gaurisami; 4) August Tanjavur; 5) Raja Rama Temple (Tanjavur)

21. Mathurai (Madurai), P.K.

  1) 1925-97, Madras; 2) *Maruttuvar*/male; 3) Mylapore Masulamani (b. 1914); 4) December 1988, Madras; 5) Balasubramaniam Temple (Teynampet, Madras)

22. Meera (Mira), Madurai M.A.

  1) 1946, Madurai; 2) *Isai Vēḷāḷar*/female; 3) M.P.N. Sethuraman (brother-in-law, 1928-2000); 4) October 1986, Madurai

23. Muthukumaraswami (Muttukkumarasami), Sembonnarkoyil S.R.D.

  1) 1929; 2) *Isai Vēḷāḷar*/male; 3) Tiruvirandur A.K. Ganesan, S.R. Dakshinamurtti (father, 1904-76); 4) September 1987, Mayuram (Tanjavur district)

24. Narayanappa, A.V.

  1) 1912-94, Arkalagur (Hassan district); 2) *Bajantri*/male; 3) Perambalur Angappa Pillai (1890-1964), Thanjavur Rangayya Naidu; 4) July 1987, Bangalore

25. Nataraja Kambar
    1) c. 1930; 2) *Kambar*/male; 3) Nagerkoyil A. Ganesa Kambar;
    4) February 1987, Trivandrum; 5) Padmanabhaswamy Temple
    (Trivandrum)

26. Natarajasundaram, Sikkal
    1) 1907, Chidambaram; 2) *Isai Vēḷāḷar*/male; 3) Kottai Subbaraya
    Pillai (father, 1843-1919), Tiruvarur Svaminada Pillai (1854-
    1925); 4) June 1987, Sikkal (Tanjavur district); 5) Dandapani
    Temple (Poravacheri, Tanjavur district)

27. Natarajasundaram, Tiruvuzhimizhalai S.
    1) 1896; 2) *Isai Vēḷāḷar*/male; 3) Svaminada Pillai (father),
    Konerirajapuram Vaidyanatha Iyer; 4) September 1986, Madras

28. Palani, P.L.G.M.T.
    1) 1959, Nagapattinam; 2) *Isai Vēḷāḷar*/male; 3) Injikkudi
    Pichaikannu (maternal grandfather, 1904-75); 4) June 1987,
    Nagapattinam (Tanjavur district); 5) Krishnan Temple
    (Nagapattinam)

29. Palaniswamy, Mambalam M.K.S.
    1) 1945, Madras; 2) *Maruttuvar*/male; 3) M.K. Swaminatham
    (father), Kalakkadu Ramanarayana Iyer (1910-92); 4) continuous,
    Madras; 5) Siva Vishnu Temple (Madras)

30. Paramasivan, Kasanadu K.V.
    1) 1928, Kasanadu; 2) *Isai Vēḷāḷar*/male; 3) Pandanallur
    Kandasami, Tiruvaiyaru Krishna; 4) August 1986, Tanjavur

31. Ponnuttay, Madurai M.S.
    1) 1929-2012, Madurai; 2) *Isai Vēḷāḷar*/female; 3) M.P. Natesa
    Pillai; 4) January 1989 & February 1993, Madurai

32. Premalata, Mambalam K.R. & Mambalam K.R. Sarasvati
    1) 1960s; 2) *Maruttuvar*/female; 3) Tiruvarur Latchappa Pillai,
    M.K.S. Siva; 4) January 1989, Madras

33. Radhakrishna Pillai, Chidambaram S.
    1) 1906, Nalladai (Tanjavur district); 2) *Isai Vēḷāḷar*/male;
    3) Chidambaram Vaittiyanada Pillai (1884-1937); 4) July 1986,
    January 1989, Chidambaram (South Arcot district); 5) Nataraja
    Temple (Chidambaram)

34. Rajarattinam Pillai, Injikkudi
    1) 1944, Injikkudi; 2) *Isai Vēḷāḷar*/male; 3) Tiruppamburam T.N.
    Somasundaram (1904-71), Tirukkarukavul Subbramaniyam,
    Andankoyil Selvarattinam; 4) June 1987, Nagapattinam

(Tanjavur district); 5) Soundaraja Perumal Temple (Nagapattinam)

35. Rajarattinam Pillai, Kottur

1) 1932-87; 2) *Isai Vēḷāḷar*/male; 3) Tiruvidaimarudur P.S. Virusami Pillai (1896-1973), Tiruvengadu T.P. Subramaniya Pillai (1906-86); 4) November 1986, Madras

36. Ramasami, Tanjavur

1) 1913-90; 2) *Isai Vēḷāḷar*/male; 3) Tiruvidaimarudur Virasami Pillai (1896-1973), T.N. Rajarattinam Pillai; 4) January 1989, Tanjavur; 5) Kamakshiamman Temple (Tanjavur)

37. Ramadasappa, B.

1) 1930s; 2) *Bajantri*/male; 3) Chikkamuniswamappa (father), Munivenkatappa (paternal uncle); 4) August 1987, Bangalore

38. Renganathan (Renganadan), V.

1) 1932; 2) *Isai Vēḷāḷar*/male; 3) Poraiyur Kumarasami, Vaduvur Raju Pillai; 4) August 1986, Kumbakonam (Tanjavur district); 5) Ranganathasamy Temple (Tirukadupirai)

39. Selvaganapathy, Tiruvarur K.

1) c. 1935; 2) *Isai Vēḷāḷar*/male; 3) Tiruvarur Kuppusami (father) 4) May 1986, June 1987, Tiruvarur (Tanjavur district); 5) Tyagarajasvami Temple (Tiruvarur)

40. Selvambal, Vaidesvarankoyil V.R.

1) 1920; 2) *Isai Vēḷāḷar*/female; 3) Narayanasami (paternal uncle); 4) September 1987, Vaidesvarankoyil (Tanjavur district)

41. Sethuraman (Seduraman), Madurai M.P.N.

1) 1928-2000, Madurai; 2) *Isai Vēḷāḷar*/male; 3) M.P. Natesa Pillai (father); 4) October 1986, Madurai; 5) Minakshi Temple (Madurai)

42. Sivasubramanya (Sivasubramaniya) Pillai, Tirucherai T.V.S.

1) 1927-94, Tiruvizhimizhalai; 2) *Isai Vēḷāḷar*/male; 3) Tirucherai Subbaraya Pillai (father), Tiruppamburam Natarajasundaram Pillai (maternal grandfather, 1869-1938); 4) August 1987, Madras

43. Subhani (Subani), Sheik Mehabub (Shaik Mahaboob)

1) 1951; 2) Muslim/male; 3) Chekrapadu John Saheb, Sheik Chinna Moulana; 4) October 1986, Tiruchirappalli

44. Vaidyanathan (Vaittiyanadan), S.R.D.

1) 1929-2013; 2) *Isai Vēḷāḷar*/male; 4) July 1986, Chidambaram (South Arcot district); 5) Lecturer, Annamalai University (Chidambaram)

45. Venkatesan, Nagapattinam G.
　　1) 1947, Nagapattinam; 2) *Isai Vēḷāḷar*/male; 3) N.G. Ganesan, K. Kandasami (paternal uncle); 4) June 1987, Nagapattinam (Tanjavur district); 5) Kayarohanaswarar Neelayadakshi Temple (Nagapattinam)

Other Musicians (*tavil*, vocal, etc.), Musicologists, and Connoisseurs of Music

1. Balakrishna, S. (film director)
　　2) Brahman/male; 4) January 1989, Madras
2. Balasundaram, Tiruvottiyur A. (*tavil*)
　　2) *Maruttuvar*/male; 3) Valangaiman Shanmukasundaram Pillai; 4) February 1987, Tiruvottiyur
3. Brinda, Tanjavur (vocal, *vīṇa*)
　　1) 1912-96; 2) female; 3) Nayana Pillai; 4) continuous, Madras
4. Dakshinamurtti Pillai, V.N.G (*tavil*)
　　1) 1931; 2) *Isai Vēḷāḷar*/male; 4) September 1986, Madras;
　　5) Government College of Music (lecturer)
5. Ganesan, G (*ottu*)
　　1) male; 3) Gurusamy (father); 4) January 1987, Kanchipuram (Chingleput district); 5) Kamakshiamman Temple (Kanchipuram)
6. Gopalakrishna Sarma, U. (connoisseur)
　　2) male; 4) October 1986, Madras
7. Gopalnath, Kadri (saxophone)
　　1) 1950-2019; 2) *Bajantri*/male; 3) T.V. Gopalakrishnan; 4) August 1987, Mangalore (Dakshin Kannada district, Karnataka)
8. Isaac, L. (musicologist)
　　Christian/female; 3) P. Sambamurthy; 4) 1987, Trivandrum;
　　5) University of Madras (professor), retired
9. Karthikeyan, V. (son of AyyampettaiVenugopala Pillai)
　　2) *Isai Vēḷāḷar*/male; 4) 1986-1987, Madras; 5) State Bank of India
10. Mani, Madurai G.S. (vocal)
　　1) 1934; 2) Brahman/male; 3) Ayyampettai Venugopala Pillai (*nāgasvaram*, 1904-65); 4) March-April 1987, Madras
11. Natarajasundaram, S. (*sīvāḷi* maker)
　　2) *Isai Vēḷāḷar*/male; 4) August 1986, Tiruvavadudurai
12. Nayar, M.K.K. (connoisseur)
　　1) 1920-87; 2) *Nāyar*/male; 4) 1987, Trivandrum; 5) Kerala Kalamandalam (former chairman)

13. Parthasarathy, S.V. (*vīṇa*)
    1) 1917-2007; 2) male; 4) July 1986, Chidambaram (South Arcot district); 5) Annamalai University, Department of Music (dean)
14. Parthasarathy, T.S. (musicologist, critic)
    1) 1912-2006; 2) Brahman/male; 4) continuous, Madras; 5) Music Academy, Madras (secretary)
15. Rajagopalan, L.S. (independent scholar)
    1) 1922-2008; 2) Brahman/male; 4) 1987, Trichur; written communications (1987-1991)
16. Rajam Iyer, B. (vocal)
    1) 1922-2009, near Karaikkudi (Ramanadapuram district); 2) Brahman/male; 3) Ariyakkudi Ramanuja Ayyanger; 4) April 1987, Madras; 5) The Teachers' College of Music, Music Academy (principal)
17. Rajapur Kassebaum, Gayatri (*gottuvadyam*, vocal)
    1) 1938-2020; 2) Brahman/female; 3) Budalur Krishnamurthy Sastri (1894-1978), Musiri Subramaniam(1899-1975)
18. Rajasekar Iyer
    2) Brahman/male; 4) August 1987, Mangalore; 5) All India Radio, Mangalore station (farm radio officer)
19. Ramamurthy, S.R. (connoisseur)
    2) Brahman/male; 4) June 1986, Madras
20. Ramu, K.P. (*tavil*)
    2) *Maruttuvar*/male; 4) January 1989, Madras
21. Renganada Āccāri (*nāgasvaram* maker)
    1) 1917; 2) Āccāri/male; 4) August 1986, Narasinganpettai (Tanjavur district)
22. Sankaran, T.
    1) 1906-2000; 2) *Isai Vēḷāḷar*/male; 4) continuous (1986-1987), Madras; written communications (1987-1992); 5) *Tamiḻ Isai Kalluri* (principal), All India Radio, retired
23. Sastri, B.V.K. (musicologist, critic)
    1) 1916-2003: 2) Brahman/male; 4) May 1987, Bangalore
24. Sivananda Bekal
    2) male; 4) August 1987, Mangalore; 5) All India Radio, Mangalore station
25. Sivaramakrishnan, N. (connoisseur)
    1) 1951; 2) Brahman/male; 4) 1986-87, Nagapattinam and Tanjavur; written communications (1986-1992); 5) Sri Nagasvaravali (co-founder and secretary)

26. Subramaniam, Padma (Bharata Natyam dancer)
     1) 1943; 2) Brahman/female; 4) January 1989, Madras
27. Subramaniyam, V. (*vīṇa*, critic)
     2) male; 4) May 1987, Bangalore
28. Sundaram, B.M. (musicologist, composer)
     1) 1935; 2) *Isai Vēḷāḷar*/male; 3) M. Balamuralikrishna;
     4) November 1986, May 1987, Pondicherry; written
     communications; 5) All India Radio, Pondicherry station
29. Upendran, Tanjavur (*mridaṅgam*)
     1) 1934-1991; 2) *Isai Vēḷāḷar*/male; 3) Thanjavur RajamIyer;
     4) 1986-87, Madras and Chidambaram; 5) Nagasvaraveli (co-
     founder and secretary)
30. L. Venkataraman (connoisseur)
     1) male; 4) 1986, Tiruchirappalli; 5) Rasika Ranjana Sabha
     (secretary)

Recordings of T.N. Rajarattinam Pillai

I. 78 Rpm Discs

1. Odeon CA-720   (Columbia 720-2) (released in August, 1934)
   Side A/B   Rāgam (Todi)   MD1814
       MD1815

2. Columbia CA-731   (November, 1934)
   Side A   Yochanakamala (Durbar)   MD1721
   Side B   NiravadhiSugadha (Ravichandrika)   MD1750

3. Columbia CA-790   (March, 1935)
   Side A/B   Pallavi (Todi-Rāgamalika)   MD1816
       MD1817

4. Columbia CA-916   (July, 1935)
   Side A   Alapana (Shanmugapriya)   MD2604
   Side B   Vallinayaka (Shanmugapriya)   MD2605

5. Odeon CA-917-2   (July, 1935)
   Side A/B   Alapana (Bhairavi)   MD2614
       MD2615

6. Columbia CA-918-2   (Odeon CA-918) (July, 1935)
   Side A/B   Pallavi (Bhairavi)   MD2616
       MD2617

7. *Columbia   (Odeon CA-919-2) (July, 1935)
   Side A   Rāgam (Malkos)   MD2648
   Side B   Rāgam (Behag)   MD2649

8. *Columbia CA-920   (July, 1935)
   Side A   Nannuvidachi (Reetigowla)   MD2608
   Side B   Miscellany-Mangalam   MD2650

9. Odeon CA-1001
   Side A   Alapana (Saveri)   MD1819
   Side B   Pallavi (Varali, Begada, Kambhoji)   MD2641

10. Odeon CA-1002
    Side A   Mariyadakadayya (Bhairavi)   MD1775
    Side B   Nanupalimpa (Mohana)   MD1788

11. Odeon CA-1003
    Side A   Alapana (Kambhoji)   MD2621
    Side B   Alapana (Kalyani)   MD2622

12. Odeon CA-1004
    Side A/B   Pallavi (Kalyani, Rāgamalika)   MD2623
                                                      MD2632

13. Odeon CA-1005
    Side A   Alapana (Sindhbhairavi)   MD1792
    Side B   Alapana with tambura (Kapi)   MD1839

14. Odeon CA-1148
    Side A/B   Alapana (Natabhairavi)   MD3105
                                                      MD3106

15. Odeon CA-1169
    Side A/B   Alapana (Simendramadhyamam)   MD3119
                                                      MD3120

16. Odeon CA-1196
    Side A   Samajavaragamana (Hindolam)   MD2640
    Side B   Ninnujuchi (Sourasgtram)   MD2651

17. Odeon CA-1234-2
    Side A/B   Alapana (Vachaspati)   MD3103
                                                      MD3104

18. Columbia CA-1465
    Side A/B   Raga Alapana (Panthuvarali)   MD3928
                                                      MD3929

19. Columbia GE-6043-2
    Side A   Pallavi (Pantuvarali)   MD3930
    Side B   Pallavi (Rāgamalika)   MD3931

20. ♦Columbia GE-6348-2
    Side A/B   Alapana (Subhapantuvarali)   CEI19723
                                                      CEI19724

21. Columbia GE-6349-2
    Side A   Pallavi (Sibhapantuvarali)   CEI19727
    Side B   Pallavi (Rāgamalika)   CEI19728

22. ◆Columbia GE-6390
    Side A/B   Alapana (Kharaharapriya)   CEI19725
                                                           CEI19726

23. ◆Columbia GE-6472
    Side A/B   Sivaguruparane (Kalyani)   CEI19732
                                                           CEI19733

24. Columbia GE-22090
    Side A   Alapana (Kanada)   CEI90859
    Side B   Konjum Kiligal (Kanada)   CEI90860

25. Columbia GE-22108
    Side A/B   Alapana (Anandabhairavi)   CEI90855
                                                           CEI90856

26. Columbia GE-22119-2
    Side A/B   Alapana (Vageeswari)   CEI90853
                                                           CEI90854

27. Columbia GE-22121
    Side A   Karunakarane (Kokilapriya)   CEI90857
    Side B   OlamittaSurumbu   CEI90858

28. ^Columbia GE-22222
    Side A/B   Alapana (Kambhoji)   MD3932
                                                            MD3933

29. *Columbia GE-22223
    Side A/B   Alapana (Charukesi)   CEI19721
                                                           CEI19722

Out of this list, I have obtained only fourteen recordings (#1-4, 6-8, 10, 20, 22-24, 28-29).

II. Cassette and CD Releases and Reissues

1. *Nadhaswaram (HMV STHV56894, 1977)*

Side A   1. Marugelara (Jayanthasri)
             2. Raghuvara Nannu (Pantuvarali)
             3. Raaga Aalapana (Kambhoji)

*The other seven items are by other *nagasvaram* musicians. This recording was reissued in CD with the same title by Saregama India (CDNF 157094, 2005)

2. *Nadhaswara Chakravarthi T.N. Rajaratnam Pillai*
(AVM: MEI-SR 1088, 1983)

Side A 1. Janakiramana (Suddha Seemantini)
     2. Mariyatha (Bhairavam)
     3. Raghu Vara (Pantuvarali)
Side B 1. Jesinadella (Todi)

*This recording was reissued in CD as *Nadaswara Chakravarthi Thiruvaduthurai T. N. Rajarathinam Pillai* by Kosmik (KMDA 081, 2008) with the addition of one more item, Samajarasah.

3. *Live Concert: Nadhaswara Chakravarthi Thiruvaduthurai T. N. Rajarathinam Pillai & Party (Echo: 6ECIC 2502)*

Side A 1. Jaanaki Ramana (Suddha Seemandhini)
     2. Mariyaatha Kaathaya (Bhairavam)
     3. Sivaguruparane (Kalyani)
Side B 1. Rāgam-Pallavi-Rāgamalika (Shanmugapriya)

4. *The Great Tradition: Masters of Music*
(HMV: EALP-1453/54, 1986)

Side 4 1. Rāgam Todi

5. *T.N. Rajarathnam Pillai: Camatic-Nadhaswaram*
(HMV: STC 03B 6790, 1988)

This is a collection of previously released 78 rpm disc recordings. The items included in this cassette are indicated with * in the previous section.

Side A 1. Sivaguruparane (Kalyani)
     2. Rāgam (Kambhoji)
     3. Rāgam (Charukesi)
     4. Rāgam (Karaharapriya)
Side B 1. Rāgam-Pallavi-Rāgamalika (Subhapantuvarali)
     2. Rāgam (Malkauns)
     3. Rāgam (Behag)
     4. NannuVidachi (Reethigowla)
     5. Mangalam

*This recording was reissued in CD as *T.N. Rajarathnam Pillai: Nadhaswaramby Saregama India (CDNF 157080, 2005)*.

6. *Gems from the Carnatic Classical, Volume I*
(*HMV: STCS 03B 6763, 1989*)

The two selections included in this anthology were originally released in 1934 from Clolumbia (CA 731). See #2 in the previous section for detail

Side B 4. Yochana
     5. Niravathi Sukhada

7. *T.N. Rajaratnam Pillai's Nadhaswaram (Classical)*
(*Sirco: 6 SRC 5016, c. 1989*)

Side A 1. Karunai Saivai (Kalyani) TNR
     2. Sarasa Samadana (Kapinarayani) Tyagaraja
     3. Rama Nipaitanaku (Kedaram) Tyagaraja
Side B 1. Rāgam-Tanam-Pallavi (Kiravani), Rāgamalika
       (Kamboji-Kanada-Varali)
     2. Devotional kirttana (Sindhubhairavi)
     3. Mangalam (Sri)

8. (*AVM: 60B 9053, 1991*)

Side A 1. Raguvara Nannu (Panthuvarali)
     2. Upacharamu (Bhairavi)
     3. Nannuchuda (Chakravaham)
Side B 1. Samajavarah (Hindolam)
     2. Sivaguru (Kalyani)

*This recording was reissued in CD as *Scintillating Sound of Nadaswaram: T.N. Rajarathnam Pillai* (Kosmik: KMDA018, 2008). Kosmic also released a CD in the same year with the same title (KM580029) in which the third item Nannu Chuda (Chakravaham *rāgam*) was replaced by Ninnu Joochi (Saurashtra *rāgam*).

9. *T.N. Rajaratham Pillai Birth Centenary: Concert Recorded from the Archives of the Music Academy, Madras (1998)*

     1. Raghuvara (Pantuvarali)
     2. Aragimpave (Todi)
     3. Pallavi (Shanmukhapriya & Ragamalika)

10. *Akashvani Sangeet T.N. Rajaratnam Pillai Nagaswaram*
(*AIR(C-ARCH) C-23, 2005*)

     1. Ninnu Juchi (Raga: Saurashtram)
     2. Upacharamu Jesevaru (Raga: Bhairavi)
     3. Alapana and Pallavi (Raga: Shanmukhapriya)

Effects of Nostalgia: The Discourse of Decline in *Periya Mēḷam* Music of South India

I. INTRODUCTION

Anthropologist Renato Rosaldo refutes the often-assumed notion of nostalgia as a personal, pure, and therefore innocent yearning for the past. In his essay, Rosaldo describes nostalgia as 'a particularly appropriate emotion to invoke in attempting to establish one's innocence and at the same time talk about what one has destroyed' (Rosaldo 1989: 108), which he calls imperialist nostalgia. He then argues that the pose of innocent yearning in this type of nostalgia not only captures people's imagination but it also conceals its complicity with domination. Although Rosaldo's observation pertains most immediately to the kind of nostalgia which agents of (Western) imperialism embrace toward the very forms of life they intentionally altered or destroyed, the effect of nostalgia in drawing attention away from the fundamental asymmetry of power, or rendering them less visible, seems to have much wider application.[436]

In this article, I wish to examine an aspect of nostalgic reflection directed toward the first half of this century in contemporary South Indian music culture. For this purpose, I will focus upon an important musical tradition within it known as *Periya Mēḷam*. One of the two major traditions of classical music in South India today, *Periya Mēḷam* refers to a genre of instrumental music which accompanies temple and domestic rituals and festivities. The ensemble includes *nāgasvaram* (double-reed aerophone), *tavil* (double-headed drum), *tāḷam* (a pair of hand cymbals) and *sruti* box (*srutipeṭṭi*, free reed instrument for drone). The other classical tradition, *Karnāṭak* music, centres around vocal music, and is performed most prominently in concert hall recitals today. The vocalist is commonly accompanied by violin, *mridaṅgam* (double-headed drum) and *tamburā* (plucked lute for drone).[437] Roughly put, these two traditions are based upon the same fundamental melodic (*rāgam*) and rhythmic (*tāḷam*) principles and share much of repertoire, yet they are separated from each other in performance media and contexts. In existing literature, *Karnāṭak* music is often equated with the generic category of South Indian classical music. In such cases, *Periya Mēḷam* music is considered its specialized sub-tradition. In this article, *Karnāṭak* music refers to the classical music of South India to the exclusion of *Periya Mēḷam* music for clear differentiation in discussion.

Periya Mēḷam music and *Karnāṭak* music have distinct geographic centers. *Karnāṭak* music has been primarily an urban phenomenon ever since the source of patronage began to shift from royal courts and wealthy landlord classes to secular voluntary organizations in the last half of the nineteenth century (Higgins 1976). It is produced and consumed most profusely in metropolitan centres such as Madras and Bangalore. In contrast, the functional and economic base of *Periya Mēḷam* music remains rural with many practitioners attached to temples located all over Tamil Nadu and parts of its neighbouring states (Andhra Pradesh, Karnataka, and Kerala). Although many established musicians travel frequently to urban centres for performances, the majority of *Periya Mēḷam* musicians reside in rural areas.

Another aspect decisively separating these two traditions is the caste affiliations of their practitioners. The vast majority of both musicians and patrons of *Karnāṭak* tradition are Brahmans, and activities relating to *Karnāṭak* music (teaching, learning, performing, and attending concerts) are dominated by Brahmans. In contrast, *Periya Mēḷam* musicians are virtually all non-Brahmans while their patrons and most enthusiastic connoisseurs (excepting themselves) are Brahmans. The most influential among practitioners of *Periya Mēḷam* music are those belonging to the non-Brahman caste of *Isai Vēḷāḷar*, who virtually monopolized *Periya Mēḷam* music until musicians belonging to other caste groups became prominent in the second half of the twentieth century. *Isai Vēḷāḷars* are concentrated in Tanjavur and its surrounding districts in central Tamil Nadu state, and *Periya Mēḷam* musicians referred to in this article are confined to this particular group of musicians.[438]

Dominant discourse concerning South Indian music culture consists predominantly of perspectives advanced by Brahmans. Aided by their domination of scholarship and music journalism and by *Isai Vēḷāḷar* musicians' economic dependence on Brahman patronage, Brahmans have established their perspective on South Indian music as the authoritative voice to the exclusion of *Isai Vēḷāḷar* interpretation.[439] I take a position that Brahmans' nostalgic gaze into the idealized past has served as a pervasive rhetorical mode of articulation on which dominant discourse is predicated, and my primary aim in this article is to delineate how it has confined *Periya Mēḷam* music to the past, and contributed to the widely-held notion of its artistic decline after the middle of the twentieth century. In doing so, I will also suggest that nostalgia with its potent ability to make asymmetrical power relations appear natural and innocent is an effective means of subjugating non-Brahman practitioners of South Indian music.

II. THE PERIOD OF MAJOR TRANSFORMATION: 1900-1950

Throughout this article, the first half of the twentieth century is referred to as the period toward which nostalgic reflection is directed. In *Periya Mēḷam* music, memory about the past rarely goes beyond the beginning of the twentieth century. As described later, reflections of the past are often expressed with references to specific players. Few *Periya Mēḷam* musicians from the previous centuries are remembered, and those who are remembered seldom serve, in sharp contrast to some past composers of *Karnāṭak* music, as symbols to represent the entire genre. Within many distinguished families of *Periya Mēḷam* musicians, the genealogies can be established for more than five generations. Yet, even in such cases, only the members of the particular lineage remember the musicians of the past centuries.[440]

The first half of the twentieth century, especially after around 1920, may be described as that of major transformation in the history of *Periya Mēḷam* music. Many new performance practices and contexts which remain intact today came into existence during this period, while older practices were either discontinued altogether or considerably attenuated. The changes which occurred during this period were drastic and pervasive, and were found in many aspects of the *Periya Mēḷam* tradition, including the size and pitch of the instruments, the instrumentation of the ensemble, playing techniques, repertoire, intergroup hierarchy, and physical appearance of its practitioners. These changes were intimately connected with the introduction of new performance contexts and media for *Periya Mēḷam* music such as disc recordings (by the early 1920s), concert hall performances (by the early 1930s), and radio programmes (starting in 1938)[441] which were added to the traditional contexts of temple rituals and festivals as well as domestic life cycle rituals such as *kalyāṇam* (wedding) and *upanayaṇam* (initiation ritual for male Brahmans) (Terada 1992: 155-73).

Of these new performance media, the existence of sound recordings since the early 1920s provide the musicians of the first half of the century with a special edge as the object of contemporary nostalgic reflection, over those who played before the advent of this technology. Elder connoisseurs and patrons of music had firsthand experience with the music and its practitioners during the first half of the twentieth century. Through their anecdotes and stories, younger musicians and patrons hear of the past time they themselves could not experience. The reissues of the 78rpm disc recordings and the private recordings of live performances by the past *Periya Mēḷam* masters have been available on commercial cassette tapes since the 1980s. While the emergence of such recordings may in itself be evidence by which a degree of nostalgia is measured, it has enabled younger musicians and patrons to affirm what they have heard from their elders, and thereby in some ways to internalize their nostalgic reflection. Many musicians and patrons speak of the great *Periya Mēḷam* musicians of this period as if they themselves had seen and heard them.

Particularly pertinent to the analysis of *Periya Mēḷam* music as an object of nostalgia is the continuing popularity of the Tamil film *Tillana Mohanambal*. Released in 1968, this film was based on a popular magazine serial novel with the same title.[442] While the story revolves around the romantic relationship between a *nāgasvaram* musician and a temple dancer (*dēvadāsi*), the popularity of this film, according to Randor Guy, a well-known film historian, hinges upon its successful retention of 'the aroma, flavour and taste of a bygone period' (Guy 1991: 37) with a detailed depiction of the world of the *Periya Mēḷam* and temple dance, 'two pillars' of Tamil traditional culture (*The Hindu* 1968). The protagonist of the story is believed to have been modelled after T.N. Rajarattinam Pillai (1898-1956), a controversial and highly charismatic *nāgasvaram* player whose performing career extended from the late 1910s to 1956. This is one reason for general agreement among musicians and patrons that the film faithfully depicts the customs and sentiments of the music culture in the first half of the twentieth century, although it contains some factual contradictions and its temporal setting is unspecified.

III. NOSTALGIA AND THE DISCOURSE OF DECLINE IN SOUTH INDIAN MUSIC

The separation of time between the present and the past is a necessary condition for nostalgia. Since nostalgia hinges upon the sense of irretrievable loss, this separated past as an object of nostalgia also has to be perceived as more favourable in some ways than the present (Chase and Shaw 1989: 2-4). Importantly, the ability to feel nostalgia for the past has to do with the way we make the past contrast with the present (Davis 1979: 11-12). Because of its reliance on our perception (constructed image) of the present and the past, nostalgia is by no means natural. It is socially formulated and transmitted.

Nostalgia may be regarded as intensely personal when individually experienced, but this very notion conceals an aspect of nostalgia that can be politicized and manipulated. Brahmans construct their visions of a golden past in effect to legitimate their privileged position at present and to neutralize the potential criticism from *Isai Vēḷāḷar* musicians. Nostalgia as a socially constructed phenomenon is, in short, 'not just a sentiment but also a rhetorical practice' (Doane and Hodges 1987: 3). In this article, nostalgia is conceptualized as being constituted by two types of discursively constructed image: the glorious past (how it was) and the decline since that time (why it is not). It is in their description that the dominant discourse and counter interpretations of the practitioners of the *Periya Mēḷam* music differ significantly.[443]

On the general level, a notion that the artistic standard of *Periya Mēḷam* music today is substantially inferior to that in the first half of the present century is seldom questioned by connoisseurs, patrons, and even practitioners of *Periya Mēḷam* music themselves. While expressed most frequently in oral discourse, this notion has also been advanced in academic literature and popular journals (Isaac 1964: 384; Mahadevan 1988; Orr 1990). I will describe the two aspects of the imagery surrounding the decline from 'the golden past' by which nostalgia is expressed: 1) deritualization, by which I mean the decrease of ritualistic association, and 2) the close interaction with *Karnāṭak* music. I will then analyze the reasons given in the dominant discourse to account for the decline or disintegration of the *Periya Mēḷam* tradition.

1. Deritualization of *Periya Mēḷam* Music

Periya Mēḷam music is believed to be invested with auspiciousness (*maṅgaḷam*) and majesty (*gambīram*). This belief stems from its strong contextual association with temple and domestic rituals, in which the participation of *Periya Mēḷam* musicians is considered indispensable. The all-night temple procession which marked the climax of annual temple festivals was the ideal performance context for extended improvisation, the artistic hallmark of *Periya Mēḷam* music. It is in the imagery of such procession as well as daily temple rituals that the connection between the music and its auspicious quality is expressed. The image of the idealized past of *Periya Mēḷam* music is evoked most eloquently in the description of these performance contexts.

Figure 1: Chidambaram Vaidyanathan (1884-1937), one of the star *nāgasvaram* musicians of the past

Frequently, *Periya Mēḷam* music at temple rituals and festivals acts as a symbol to induce intense nostalgia about the early decades of this century, the period characterized by a leisurely pace of life and the piety of the masses who spent ample time in ritual activities. I will quote two observers for illustration. In the first example, a historian recollects the *Periya Mēḷam* music played during the annual festival at the famous Nataraja Temple in Chidambaram, where he spent his youth, while in the second the author speaks of the daily rituals at temples presumably in Tanjavur district.

> During the festival nights of Ani Tirumanjanam and Arudra Darsanam, I have lingered for hours at a stretch at the corners of the main car streets, in the thrall of *Nadasvaram* music of Chidambaram Vaidyanathan of revered memory...Ever since my boyhood, when I heard it first, nothing has stirred me to the depths of my being as much as Chidambaram Vaidyanathan's *Mallari* in the raga, Nattai played traditionally when Nataraja and Sivakama Sundari are taken out in procession during the festivals (Natarajan 1974: 137).[444]

> Two hundred temples studded the delta region [in Tanjavur district]. From Viswaroopa in the small hours of breaking dawn to Ardhajama of dead of night, echo of Timiri Nāgasvaram and Tavil kept up a symphony of stirring, soulful music everywhere (Rangaramanuja Ayyangar 1977: 3).

Three points made in these quotations are common in the nostalgic description of *Periya Mēḷam* music; 1) the inherent ability of the music to induce religious emotion, 2) the repertoire exclusive to the context of temple procession and *Periya Mēḷam* music, and 3) the presence of virtuosic musicians. First, the sound of *Periya Mēḷam* music is considered to evoke intense religious emotions. Many worshippers claim that they feel the presence of the deity in the sound of *Periya Mēḷam* music. Listening to extended improvisation by *Periya Mēḷam* ensembles, to quote Semmangudi Srinivasa Iyer (b. 1908), the most respected senior vocalist today, 'even atheists would feel overwhelmed by bhakti (devotion)' (Srinivasa Iyer 1986: 19). Furthermore, the notion that *Periya Mēḷam* music is able to evoke religious emotions is closely connected to the sound of the higher-pitched *timiri nāgasvaram* whose carrying power is regarded as the majesty of the instrument. The association with the power to affect or incite religious emotions is considered much stronger for the *timiri nāgasvaram* than for the lower-pitched *nāgasvaram* (*bāri nāgasvaram*) used today.[445]

The positive reference to the higher-pitched *nāgasvaram* is an indirect criticism of the lowering of the pitch of the instrument during the first half of this century and *Periya Mēḷam* music's apparent loss of majesty or immediate identification with the sacred context. One critic even describes the sound of the lower-pitched *nāgasvaram* as an 'unmusical frog-croak' (Mahadevan 1988: 35; also see Rangaramanuja Ayyangar 1977: 3, 8).[446] The criticism directed toward the lower-pitched and longer *bāri nāgasvaram* is not limited to the tonal register of the instrument. The elongation of the instrument is said to have made the attainment of a certain pitch (*sutta mattiyamam*, perfect fourth above the tonic) difficult, and this technical difficulty has contributed to the downgraded performance standard. Some even claim that, because of this difficulty, many less competent *nāgasvaram* musicians avoided playing *ragams* including this pitch, causing the selection of *ragams* in a given performance to be unbalanced (Sankaran 1990: 39).

Strongly associated with temple procession in the past is the repertoire confined to this performance context and exclusive to *Periya Mēḷam* music. *Mallāri*, mentioned in the first quotation, is a type of highly technical composition which requires precise renderings of a relatively short composed melody in different speeds within a constant rhythmic cycle. Many structurally complex *mallāris* were played to accompany various ritual activities in the past, but only a small number of simple *mallāris* are played rather perfunctorily today in one particular context (the commencement of a procession). Another repertoire exclusive to *Periya Mēḷam* music which evokes strong nostalgia is *rakti*, a highly improvisational form based on a particular rhythmic formula, which was once a prominent feature in temple procession in the Tanjavur area. The performance tradition of the *rakti* is on the verge of extinction, and the grandiose and competitive performances of *rakti* in the past are missed by many old connoisseurs of *Periya Mēḷam* music.

Another aspect of the image of temple procession is the presence of virtuosi. The performances at processions during the first half of the twentieth century are often remembered by the participation of particular musicians of repute, such as Chidambaram Vaidyanathan (1884-1937) in the first quotation. The decline of the *Periya Mēḷam* tradition since that time is indicated conversely by the previous existence of many virtuosic and often charismatic musicians whose musical caliber can be matched by few contemporary counterparts. The names of one to two dozen accomplished musicians during the first half of this century are given with ease by contemporary musicians and patrons, in effect to depict the decline after that period.[447] Some even go further to assert that the participation of accomplished *Periya Mēḷam* musicians was more important than the presence of the image (*mūrtti*) of the deity, the normally presumed focus of the festival. The participation of well-known *Periya Mēḷam* musicians is often stated by Brahmans and non-Brahmans alike to have been essential to ensure a large turnout, an indicator of success at temple festivals.

Apart from the changes in temple procession, the decline of the *Periya Mēḷam* tradition is also described in its performance practice during daily rituals at temples. In archetypal practice, rituals were offered six times a day, each ritual accompanied by a *Periya Mēḷam* ensemble playing *rāgams* prescribed for that. Viswarupa and Ardhajama in the second quotation correspond to the first and last of these six daily rituals. It is generally agreed that *Periya Mēḷam* musicians observed the system of playing *rāgams* prescribed for particular ritual times and activities until the early decades of the twentieth century. According to Rangaramanuja Ayyangar, the author of the second quotation, this system of music-context correspondence deteriorated during the second quarter of this century (Rangaramanuja Ayyangar 1972: xii-xiii).

Yet another aspect of the deritualization of *Periya Mēḷam* music is the change in the physical appearance of its players. The traditional appearance of musicians, which was considered auspicious and suitable for its ritual performance context, consisted most prominently of *kuḍumi* (shaved front part of the head with a tuft on the crown) and bare upper torso which were replaced by western hairstyle ('crop') and Western-style shirt. The *kuḍumi* and bare upper torso, both indicators of one's devotion and obeisance to the god, have strong spiritual and ritual connotations. Gold necklaces (*taṅgaccaṅgili*) and diamond earrings (*vairakkaḍukkaṇ*), which contributed to the aura of auspiciousness are worn by few contemporary musicians. Many Brahman patrons deplore the loss of the grand appearance which characterized *Periya Mēḷam* musicians in the past.

Important to my discussion is a strong correlation established between artistic debasement and moral corruption derived from deritualization. *Periya Mēḷam* musicians are largely considered 'a decadent fraternity,' although they were '[o]nce the custodians of expansive Ragam and Pallavi,' to quote Rangaramanuja Ayyangar again (1977: 34). The evocation of the idealized image of *Periya Mēḷam* musicians of the past has the effect of producing a sharper contrast between musicians in the past and their contemporary counterparts. One Brahman connoisseur of *Periya Mēḷam* music emphasized the total devotion of musicians in previous times toward their art, saying 'If they had nothing to eat, they drank water and kept on playing music (for the god). They had that much devotion.' The image of the past *Periya Mēḷam* musicians as single-mindedly devoted to their music is often juxtaposed with what is seen as such widespread social practices as heavy drinking and promiscuity at present.

2. Close Interaction with *Karnāṭak* Music

Another aspect of the 'golden past' imagery of *Periya Mēḷam* music is its close association with *Karnāṭak* music during the first half of the twentieth century. A high degree of interaction between these two traditions is mentioned by Brahman musicians and patrons. According to them, *nāgasvaram* musicians expanded their compositional repertoire by learning from Brahman practitioners of *Karnāṭak* music. Many compositions identified as representative of *Karnāṭak* music, most notably those by the famed three 'saint-composers' of the early nineteenth century (Tyagaraja, Muttusvami Diksitar, and Syama Sastri), figure prominently in the repertoire of *Periya Mēḷam* music today. The Tiruvizhimizhalai Brothers (Subramania Pillai 1893-1984, Natarajasundaram Pillai b. 1896) are mentioned as a prime example of the influence of *Karnāṭak* music on *Periya Mēḷam* tradition. An extremely influential *nāgasvaram* duo during the 1920s through 1950s, they are considered to have popularized the performance of compositions (particularly *kirttanais*) by *Periya Mēḷam* ensembles as well as the typical ensemble format at present including two *nāgasvaram*.[448] It is widely believed among Brahmans that the Tiruvizhimizhalai Brothers learned many compositions from Konerirajapuram Vaidyanatha Iyer (1878-1920), one of the most influential Brahman vocalists of his day.

Conversely, *Karnāṭak* musicians received inspiration from the extended improvisation that was the specialty of *nāgasvaram* musicians. For example, Semmangudi Srinivasa Iyer whom I quoted earlier, recollects,

I used to sit on the Kaveri bridge during festival time at Tiruvaiyaru and lose myself in the deep and powerful music of the nadaswaram. This listening experience helped me to sing (Srinivasa Iyer 1986: 20).[449]

Srinivasa Iyer's vocal improvisation is, in fact, believed to have been heavily influenced by *nāgasvaram* music, at least at the initial stage of his career (Menon 1989: 35; Parthasarathy 1989: 16; Pattabhi Raman 1993: 5-6).[450]

Importantly, the interaction between the two traditions, regardless of its actual prevalence, is seen as the primary reason for the achievement of high artistic standards in classical music in general. Yet, although the loss of active interaction with *Karnāṭak* music is considered by Brahmans to have contributed to the artistic stagnation of *Periya Mēḷam* music today, the opposite case is rarely made (Mahadevan 1988). Equally important is that the image invoked in these descriptions tends to be one of a harmonious relationship between Brahmans and *Isai Vēḷāḷars* during this period despite the heightened communal tension created by social movements with an anti-Brahman orientation. Brahmans describe their relationship with *Isai Vēḷāḷar* musicians mainly by expressing their affection and respect for *Periya Mēḷam* music, and by individual cases of friendship (Tumilan 1988).

3. Discourse of Decline and Institutional Patronage

One area in which the nostalgic mode of reflection can be observed with tangible effects is in the discourse concerning the institutional patronage of *Periya Mēḷam* music, particularly in the way in which nostalgic evocation is utilized to help legitimize the indifference of music associations to *Periya Mēḷam* music. The concert hall recital sponsored by voluntary associations of music lovers has been the most prestigious, though not the most numerous, performance context for *Karnāṭak* music since the early decades of the twentieth century. These associations, known as *saṅgīta sabhās*, filled the void created by the cessation of princely patronage. Though much later than *Karnāṭak* music, *Periya Mēḷam* music also began to be played in this setting in the 1930s.

In the programmes sponsored by the music associations today, *Periya Mēḷam* music is, if not completely neglected, given a mere ceremonial role. During the annual music festival, the most prominent and (for musicians) prestigious activity of a music association, a *Periya*

Mēḷam ensemble is engaged most typically at its commencement, often immediately preceding the official opening ceremony, to ensure the success of the event with auspicious music.[451] In such contexts, *Periya Mēḷam* music merely provides the sonorous background for the occasion, and very few people listen to the music attentively. In contrast, *Periya Mēḷam* music was heard in the 1930s and 1940s (and even through the 1950s) as part of the main programme, often occupying the prestigious time slots instead of simply fulfilling a ceremonial function.[452]

The officials of music associations provide several reasons for the current scarcity of *Periya Mēḷam* recitals. Their most frequent explanation is the absence of master musicians like those of earlier years. Deploring the decline of artistic standards today, some officials claim that they would be willing to sponsor more *Periya Mēḷam* concerts if such musicians were available. Their nostalgic reference to the past *Periya Mēḷam* musicians of repute affirms their appreciation of the genre, thus protect themselves from the potential charge of categorical neglect or discrimination for not sponsoring *Periya Mēḷam* recitals. For *Periya Mēḷam* musicians, this reasoning is only a pretext for not giving them an opportunity to prove their ability, because most music associations encourage young performers of *Karnāṭak* music by sponsoring concerts and competitions while similar events for upcoming *Periya Mēḷam* musicians are virtually non-existent.

The indifference to *Periya Mēḷam* music among concert-goers is claimed to be another major reason for the music associations' reluctance to sponsor more recitals. Music associations are dependent for their existence upon membership fees and donations from individual patrons and supporting organizations, whose preference inevitably reflects the selection of the genre and musicians. Many associations are forced to include dramas and comedy shows in their programmes, even if the officials themselves are devoted exclusively to classical music (Subramania Iyer 1966: 145), and it is all the more difficult under such circumstances to find a rationale for sponsoring *Periya Mēḷam* recitals for which attendance is considered invariably low. The image that is often contrasted to the lack of interest today is the huge turnout at *Periya Mēḷam* performances in the past. The interest and knowledge among the masses in classical music in general is firmly believed to have been cultivated by *Periya Mēḷam* music (Subramania Iyer 1962), Elder patrons and musicians including *sabha* (music organization) officials deplore the passing of an era in which even a lowly rickshaw driver was not only interested in listening to elaborate improvisation but also musically conversant enough to identify the *rāgams* (modes) used in it (Mahadevan 1990).

Although (and because) officials admire the greatness of *Periya Mēḷam* music in temple procession context in the past, they claim that *Periya Mēḷam* music is meant for outdoor performances and that its volume is unsuitable for performances inside concert halls. *Periya Mēḷam* musicians discredit this claim by pointing out the loudness of current *Karnāṭak* music concerts due to amplification.[453] *Periya Mēḷam* musicians often express their frustration that Brahmans characterize *Periya Mēḷam* music as music meant for outdoor performance while not sufficiently patronizing such performances.

Periya Mēḷam musicians tend to interpret the reluctance of music associations in sponsoring their music as a manifestation of the categorical neglect of the genre (cf. Orr 1990). It is sometimes spoken of as an example of the discrimination by Brahmans, who constitute the majority of concert organizers and patrons, against *Periya Mēḷam* musicians, who are virtually all non-Brahmans. In this context, *Periya Mēḷam* musicians' remarks on the generosity of devoted patrons and connoisseurs in the past are not so much the sentimental yearning for a lost past as their critical judgment against the (to them) un-justifiable lack of patronage and appreciation at present.

IV. COUNTER INTERPRETATIONS OF *PERIYA MĒḶAM* MUSICIANS

Perspectives of *Periya Mēḷam* musicians on their artistic tradition differ significantly from the dominant discourse I have so far described. For the majority of *Periya Mēḷam* musicians, the changing musical taste of the masses was a primary reason for the increasingly hostile economic and social environment for *Periya Mēḷam* musicians. As in the case of Brahman patrons, *Periya Mēḷam* musicians themselves idealize the first half of the century as a period in which the pace of the temple procession was leisurely and musicians could indulge themselves in extended improvisation which was listened to with acute attention and admiration by the thousands of people in attendance. However, *Periya Mēḷam* musicians single out two factors external to their control to explain the dwindling interest in their music: the increasing popularity of film music and the lack of promotion from music associations, which are controlled almost invariably by Brahmans and have become the most prestigious source of patronage for *Karnāṭak* music during the twentieth century.

The increasing popularity of film songs since the 1930s paralleled the shift of interest in *Periya Mēḷam* music from the improvisation-centered repertoire to that of composed music. The predilection toward composed music gradually reduced the attendance at all-night processions featuring extended improvisation. With this tendency, *Periya Mēḷam* musicians began to lose the performance context for the repertoire most strongly identified with, and most valued by, themselves. The dilemma of many contemporary *Periya Mēḷam* musicians lies in the gap between their professed ability to play extended improvisation as much as their predecessors did and the absence of the audience to appreciate and patronize such music.

The first half of the twentieth century is also remembered by *Periya Mēḷam* musicians for many devoted and extremely generous patrons of their music. The generosity of wealthy patrons, both Brahmans and high caste non-Brahmans alike, is illustrated by expensive gifts they presented as well as the frequency of gift-giving. Expensive and valued items such as gold coins (*padakkam*) and silk shawls (*poṉṉāḍai*) were frequently presented to *Periya Mēḷam* musicians as tokens of appreciation of their achievements. Anecdotes concerning gifts of such extraordinary items as automobiles and elephants to star players of the past are also circulated among *Periya Mēḷam* musicians (B.M. Sundaram 1992). The story of a wealthy patron during this period who died penniless because of his excessive habit of gift-giving to musicians is also known to many musicians.

Related to the presence of generous patrons in the past was the sufficient financial and moral support to *Periya Mēḷam* musicians from temple administrations. At many temples, monthly salaries for musicians have become inadequate, and the lack of financial support has weakened the foundation of their entire community with an increasing number of musicians forced out of their hereditary profession. While the occupational option for the sons of *Periya Mēḷam* musicians widened considerably by the weakening traditional code on hereditary professions and the increase of urban clerical jobs, *Periya Mēḷam* musicians mainly blame the lack of patronage for the discontinuation of the profession in many lineages.

For *Periya Mēḷam* musicians, the decline of their tradition is connected to financial and administrative changes in the temples. The financial status of many temples in the Tanjavur area was intimately intertwined with governmental politics in Tamil Nadu state. The DMK (Dravida Munnetra Kazhagam, Dravidian Progressive Federation), formed in 1949 to succeed the two earlier non-Brahman political parties, came into power in 1967. With their anti-Brahmanical and pro-Dravidian ideology, the DMK supported temples which housed Tamil (non-Brahmanical) deities, whereas those which enshrined Sanskritic (Brahmanical) deities became increasingly neglected. As a consequence, many Brahmanical temples in the Tanjavur area which had generously patronized *Periya Mēḷam* musicians suffered from the revenue loss and inaccessibility to government funds, while wealthy temples of Tamil deities, such as those for Minakshi in Madurai and for Murugan in Palani, became even more prominent (Kennedy 1974).

According to *Periya Mēḷam* musicians, it is the indifference of contemporary trustees, who have the administrative authority over temple servants including *Periya Mēḷam* musicians, that is more damaging than the general decline of wealth in Tanjavur temples. Hereditary temple trustees of the past were themselves often enthusiastic connoisseurs and patrons of music as well as other performing and literary arts (Raghavan 1945, 1958: 21-39). *Periya Mēḷam* musicians remember many trustees who, due to their knowledge of music, acted as overseers of the traditional performance practice at their temples.[454] Contemporary trustees tend to be members of lower non-Brahman castes appointed by the non-Brahman oriented state government, and they often have, according to *Periya Mēḷam* musicians, neither knowledge nor interest in temple rituals and the music associated with them.[455]

To counteract the lack of support from individual trustees, *Periya Mēḷam* musicians have repeatedly requested the state government to regulate the salary of temple musicians as well as to institute pension, health benefits and travel concessions (Virusvami Pillai 1962: 17-18). The organizations that represent the castes of *Periya Mēḷam* musicians such as the South Indian Nadhaswara Artists' Association have also requested the state government to help alleviate the economic predicament of musicians.[456]

Images of past glory are evoked by *Periya Mēḷam* musicians as proof of the intrinsic artistic merit of their music and its continuation to the present. They would argue that it was not artistic decline but rather various social changes that caused a decline in popularity and respect for *Periya Mēḷam* music, and that the tradition still maintains high artistic standards today, if not exactly comparable to those in the past. In addition, while generally recollecting the past as a better time than the present, *Periya Mēḷam* musicians refer to widespread tension and rivalry between Brahmans and non-Brahman musicians, and Brahmans' discriminatory practices and patronizing attitudes toward them.

V. CONCLUDING REMARKS

If nostalgia is predicated on the decisive separation of the past and present, that separation is maintained, reinforced, or stabilized by the repeated evocations of nostalgia itself. Furthermore, the past and the present are not simply separated but are also opposed to one another in dominant discourse concerning South Indian music. The positive appraisal of *Periya Mēḷam* music is revealed to its fullest extent only when projected against the notion of the present deterioration, which, in turn, is strengthened by the repeated telling of such appraisal.

Within this system of opposition, Brahmans' nostalgic glorification of *Periya Mēḷam* music has an effect of imprisoning the music and its practitioners in the past, and thus denying their contemporaneity, while providing Brahmans with an air of innocence in justifying such denial. More specifically, the high estimation of *Periya Mēḷam* music, epitomized in the description of performance at temple contexts, has two types of damaging effects for its musicians. First, the emphasis on the inseparable connection between the artistic merit of *Periya Mēḷam* music and the rural ritual context has made it difficult for *Periya Mēḷam* to discard the widely accepted image that it is the music principally for rituals and to be transformed into an urban concert art form for which most present-day patronage is available. Second, the notion of moral corruption among contemporary *Periya Mēḷam* musicians is solidified by the causal link, which is rhetorically highlighted, between the sacred nature of *Periya Mēḷam* music, its artistic excellence, and the degree of devotion among its practitioners in the past. By this type of narrative strategy, *Periya Mēḷam* musicians are rendered susceptible to criticism about their moral conduct, which in turn is utilized as the explanation for artistic disintegration.

While nostalgic reflection among *Periya Mēḷam* musicians is also based on the separation of time, the present and the past are not completely opposed. Instead, it expresses their yearning for artistic continuity which has been threatened by the lack of patronage and other adverse social changes as well as a strong sense of dislocation. However, *Periya Mēḷam* musicians' perception of the continuity of artistic merit from the past is incompatible with the system of opposition in dominant discourse. Even so, the act of remembering the past provides *Periya Mēḷam* musicians with a positive sense of subjective identity which has been increasingly vulnerable in recent years.

The images invoked in nostalgia toward the first half of this century not only indicate the asymmetry of power, but also provide a site of ensuing struggle between competing discourses although nostalgia engenders the most compelling consequences when used by a dominant group. While nostalgic articulation of the golden past of *Periya Mēḷam* music, which supports Brahman domination, is one small segment within the dominant discourse on South Indian music, that mode of articulation appears pervasive and prevalent in such discourse. An analysis of nostalgia is, then, an attempt to expose critically the ideological underpinning which has determined the contour of the dominant discourse.

ACKNOWLEDGMENTS

An earlier version of this article was presented at the 1992 annual conference of the Society for Ethnomusicology (Bellevue, Washington). I acknowledge with gratitude the funding for the research in South India (1986-87) provided by the American Institute of Indian Studies. I also thank Edward Henry, Daniel Neuman, Yoshio Sugimoto and Shigeharu Tanabe for insightful comments from which I benefitted greatly. Any remaining shortcomings are mine.

(Originally published in 1996 in the *Bulletin of the National Museum of Ethnology* (21/4: 921-939). Republished here with permission from the National Museum of Ethnology.)

Tamiḻ Isai as a Challenge to Brahmanical Music Culture in South India

TWO OVERLAPPING TERMS refer to classical music in South India. By far the better known of the two is *Karnāṭaka Saṅgīta* (or *Karnāṭak* music), which is for many synonymous with South Indian classical music. The other term, *Tamiḻ Isai,* is relatively unknown outside the state of Tamil Nadu where Tamil is the state language and spoken by most of the people. These two terms do not necessarily refer to two decisively separate musical systems, but rather point to different modes of historical interpretation and competing ideologies based on language and caste. The contrastive use of *saṅgīta* (Sanskrit) and *isai* (Tamil), which have both been translated into English as 'music,' is an eloquent testimony to the different linguistic and caste orientations. Schematically put, *Karnāṭaka Saṅgīta* refers to the culture of classical music based on compositions in Telugu and Sanskrit and performed and patronized primarily by members of the Brahman caste, whereas *Tamiḻ Isai,* music in the Tamil language and/or a musical tradition nurtured by Tamils, has been advanced mostly by non-Brahmans.

The relationship between caste and language has long been intricate, ambivalent and contentious in the culture of South Indian classical music. This essay is a preliminary exploration of an aspect of this relationship as manifested in the controversial events relating to the issues of *Tamiḻ Isai* (music). In particular, I will focus on the methods of popularizing Tamil songs used by different organizations, and their role in promoting or maintaining differing perspectives on music history. Music organizations such as the Music Academy, Madras, and the Tamil Isai Sangam symbolize and actively promote competing ideologies based on caste and language in South Indian classical music. My primary aim in this essay is to gauge to what extent the Music Academy has contributed to the maintenance of Brahmanical dominance based on its continual authorization of Brahman-centred history, and the degree to which the non-Brahman organizations have represented the oppressed perspectives to form counter forces to the Music Academy.

Music Academy as a Citadel of Brahmanical Music Culture

The Music Academy (hereafter 'Academy') was established in 1928 to develop and disseminate classical music and dance. The plan to establish the Academy was adopted at the session of the Indian National Congress in Chennai (then Madras) in 1927. This beginning indicates that the surging nationalism behind the National Congress meeting and the desire to create 'Indian music' as being just as honourable as, yet distinct from, 'Western music,' formed the backdrop for the establishment of the Academy.

What is known as classical music today lost its previous royal patronage due to the cessation of princely courts in South India in the middle of the 19th century, and needed to find new patrons if it was to survive. Many musicians migrated to Madras in search of individual patrons who acquired wealth from the city's bourgeoning economy and by working with the British as *dubāshs*, agents who mediated between the colonial government and the local society. For such music to find a wider audience, however, it needed to be reformulated (or 'revived') to make it attractive to the emerging urban middle classes, and the Academy was instrumental in such reformulation both by providing academic legitimacy, which rendered music a respectable profession and leisure activity, and by broadening the audience base through education (Subramanian 1999).

The Academy became the centre of musical performance and research early on, and it has been since then the most influential and prestigious organization for South Indian classical music. The Academy confers the *Saṅgīta Kalānidhi*, the most coveted musical title, which is presented to a musician each year at its annual music festival in December. The opportunity to perform at this festival is often considered the emblem of 'making it' as a professional musician. It has become a yardstick by which to measure the degree of success and rank in the hierarchy among musicians. For this reason, the Academy has been the site of intense lobbying by aspiring musicians and their supporting patrons (Figure 1).

Figure 1: The main building of the Music Academy (Chennai, 1998)

The Academy was also a source of inspiration for other music organizations (known as *saṅgīta sabhās*) which were established in great number throughout the twentieth century. Modelling themselves after the Academy, they started organizing annual music and dance festivals, increasing performance opportunities for musicians. Despite the proliferation of *sabhās*, the Academy has maintained its uniqueness among such organizations for its academic activities. At the scholarly sessions during its annual festival, musicologists and musicians gather to discuss a wide range of topics relating to music and dance. The content of the session is reported daily in *The Hindu*. Prominent musicologists at the Academy, including P. Sambamurthy (1901-73) and V. Raghavan (1908-79), were also affiliated with the Department of Indian Music at Madras University. Because the Academy provided a prestigious venue for scholarly discussion via its annual conference and journal, it became the centre of research activities. The Academy, along with Madras University, has provided both physical space and institutional support for Brahman musicians, patrons, critics, and journalists who form a rather exclusive network for mutual support and encouragement.

Deification of the Musical Trinity

What type of history has been collectively projected by Brahman scholars and musicians, and how have musical organizations such as the Academy helped maintain or fortify the history portrayed in this way? The most important historical figure in this issue is Tyagaraja, the 19th-century composer whose name has been equated with the essence of South Indian classical music. Tyagaraja is one of the three Brahman composers collectively known as the *saṅgīta mummūrtti* or Musical Trinity, who are said to represent the pinnacle of South Indian music history. The contributions of these composers are regarded with such high esteem that the history of South Indian music is often divided into three eras: the Trinity era, which is often described as the 'Golden Age' of South Indian music (Venkatarama Iyer 1979; Music Academy 1988: 170), and two eras preceding and following this period. All three composers are described as 'saint composers' and their lives characterized by their passionate devotion to the deity and avoidance of worldly affairs. The power of their music is said to have been so potent that it caused miracles such as opening temple gates, inducing rainfall, lighting lamps or even reviving the dead (Srinivasan 1962: 42-3; Sambamurthy 1970: 169-70). Moreover, writings on music history almost unanimously agree that the Trinity composers were born in the same time period (the late 18th century) and in the same locality (the famous temple town of Tiruvarur) (Jackson 1991: 30). This narrative suggests the work of the higher being who sent them to the human world for some divine purpose, thereby enhancing their status as extraordinary beings (Srinivasan 1962: 94).

The image of the Trinity (especially Tyagaraja) as saintly figures has been advanced through the activities of the Academy, which include publishing articles on the Trinity in the *Journal of the Music Academy* (started in 1930), teaching their compositions at its Teachers' College of Music (opened in 1931), conducting commemorative festivals and music competitions highlighting their work, and celebrating their achievements at the annual music conference. Their auditorium is adorned with portraits of the Trinity, as is the case of performance venues for many other Brahman-controlled music associations (Figure 2). With all these activities, the image of the Trinity as saint composers who define South Indian classical music has been repeatedly evoked and confirmed.

Figure 2: The portrait of the Music Trinity decorates the concert hall of a music organization (Chennai, 1999).

The narrative accounts of Tyagaraja are numerous, and virtually all writings on him impress readers with his saintly attributes. P. Sambamurthy, who was a professor of music at Madras University for twenty-five years (1937-61) and an active participant in the Academy's academic conferences, states, 'Tyagaraja, the poet, saint and composer is the greatest name in the history of South Indian Music. He is one of those minstrels of god, who came to this world to contribute to human happiness and uplift' (1970: 1). S. Seetha, Sambamurthy's student and successor at Madras University, depicts Tyagaraja as 'both a saint and a great composer whose compositions breathe the highest spiritual truths' (1981: 201). H. Narayanaswami describes his eminence as 'If Carnatic Music could be imagined as a living thing. Saint Tyagaraja will be its heart; the rest of the Composers will form the other parts' (1989: 2). Hundreds of other writings reconfirm and perpetuate the centrality of Tyagaraja in South Indian music by repeatedly projecting his saintly image.

Paramount to my argument is the discourse on the Trinity's caste affiliation and the line of artistic transmission: they were not only all Brahmans, but were also described as having inherited music that had been passed down by a string of Brahman composers. In Tyagaraja's case, frequently mentioned composers include Purandara Dasa (16th century), Kshetrayya (17th century), and Sonti Venkataramanayya, with whom Tyagaraja is believed to have studied in person (Sambamurthy 1970; Raghavan 1979, 1983). Within this dominant narrative, one is easily led to conclude that Brahman musicians have inherited a musical tradition of their own that saw its highest manifestation in Tyagaraja. Focusing upon the narrative construction, my aim here is not to belittle Tyagaraja's tremendous contribution, but simply to bring to the foreground the power of such narrative to create an illusion of unmediated reality that Ana Maria Alonso calls 'effects of truth' (1988). As I later discuss, it was this construction of narrative that became a focal point of contention for non-Brahmans, both individuals and organizations, who denounced Brahman dominance in music.

Tyagaraja was a Telugu Brahman, and composed almost all his songs in Telugu. The other two composers of the Trinity, Muttusvami Diksitar and Syama Sastri, were both Tamil Brahmans, who, nevertheless, composed their songs primarily in Sanskrit and Telugu. The prominence of these two languages in their compositions requires a historical explanation. Tanjavur, where the Trinity lived, had been ruled by Telugu-speaking Nayak kings between 1544 and 1673. Because of their generous patronage toward the performing arts and because Telugu was the official language, they attracted scholars, poets and musicians from Telugu-speaking areas.[457] Sanskrit, on the other hand, has been the sacred language of religious scriptures and rituals, and historically Brahmans have been its primary custodians.

Within the context of a performance, the hierarchy of languages in music was evident: the Telugu and Sanskrit compositions by the Trinity and other Brahman composers are played as main items whereas a few short pieces in Tamil are played at the end of the performance as *tukkaḍā* (miscellaneous, minor, or insignificant pieces). With the increasing awareness of the antiquity of Tamil language around the turn of the century, many non-Brahmans began to ask a deceptively simple question: why are Tamil songs given little importance in Tamil-speaking areas?

Tamil Isai Movement

It was out of frustration at what was perceived to be the denigration of Tamil songs (and by extension Tamil language and culture) in predominantly Tamil-speaking areas that the *Tamiḻ Isai* movement (*Tamiḻ Isai Iyakkam*) emerged. It proposed to propagate Tamil songs to oppose the domination of Telugu and Sanskrit compositions in which Brahman musicians historically specialized. The first concerted effort to popularize Tamil songs was made by Annamalai Chettiar (1881-1948), a prominent patron of Tamil culture. In 1935 he made a substantial donation to Annamalai University, which he had himself established earlier.

As its promoters were dissatisfied with the slow rate of progress, many *Tamiḻ Isai* conferences were held in the first half of the 1940s. In 1941, Annamalai Chettiar organized the first *Tamiḻ Isai* conference at Annamalai University, and stated in his inaugural speech, 'Music performances should begin with Tamil songs and end too with Tamil songs. The lion's share of the performance should be in Tamil. Songs from other languages can also form part of the concert,' and his insistence was passed as a resolution of the conference (Ramanathan Chettiar 1992: 24).[458] This resolution jolted the classical music world 'like a clap of thunder,' to quote Anandhi Ramachandran (1983: 4), and similar public statements that followed it became a source of controversy, generating a series of heated debates regarding the issue of language in music at conferences, public gatherings, and mass media.

Criticism from the Music Academy

The most trenchant (and often indignant) criticism of the *Tamiḻ Isai* movement came from the Academy and individual Brahmans closely associated with it, while supporters of the movement were by and large non-Brahmans (Nambi Arooran 1980: 265; Rajadurai 1997: 3-28). The major points of contention may be summarized in the following four areas.

First, many Brahman musicians and scholars emphasized the primacy of music over language. Reacting against the 1941 resolution at the Annamalai conference, a prominent Brahman performer and scholar, Mudikondan Venkatrama Iyer (1897-1975), stated, 'Music in its highest form did not require the help of language' (Music Academy 1942: 17). Venkatrama Iyer served later as the principal of the Teacher's College of Music for twenty-five years (1948-72) and was a frequent speaker at the Academy. Many other speakers stressed that the essence of classical music is *rāgam*, and language is secondary in importance (Music Academy 1942: 17; 1945: 8-9; 1946: 3, 6-7).[459] Similarly, T.T. Krishnamachari (1899-1974), a major patron of the Academy, claimed that 'Music was a wordless search for beauty in sound' (in A. Ramachandran 1983: 6).[460] During its annual conference, the Academy passed the resolution that 'it should be the aim of all musicians and lovers of music to preserve and maintain the highest standard of classical Carnatic music and that no consideration of language should be imported so as to lower or impair that standard' (Music Academy 1941: 17).

The second criticism concerned the artistic freedom of musicians. Some Brahman musicians opposed the 1941 resolution as a rude intrusion into their inherent right to choose compositions for their performance. Opposing the method, rather than the intent, of popularizing Tamil songs, Musiri Subramaniya Iyer (1899-1975) stated during the annual Music Academy conference in the same year that musicians have the right to choose what they play. Semmangudi Srinivasa Iyer (1908-2003) added that the masses cannot define good music and that 'democracy in music is [an] evil' (Music Academy 1944; Nambi Arooran 1975: 57, 1980: 261).

Their objection was intensified when another resolution was passed at the *Tamiḻ Isai* conference in 1943. This resolution requested radio stations to enforce the 'fair' representation of Tamil songs, with 80 per cent of songs in Tamil and 20 per cent in other languages on radio programmes from the Tiruchirapalli station, and 40 per cent in Tamil and 40 per cent in Telugu from the Madras station (Ramanathan Chettiar 1993: 15-6).[461] Reflecting the views of influential Brahman musicians such as those quoted above, a unanimously passed resolution during the conference declared, 'in the interest of classical music it is not desirable to prescribe any percentage of songs in any language in the recitals, in public concerts, radio programmes or in university syllabuses' (Music Academy 1944: 11-2).

Another common criticism of the *Tamiḻ Isai* movement concerns the supposed dearth of Tamil compositions of high order. Many musicians expressed the view that the great composers of classical music wrote lyrics in Telugu and Sanskrit, and that it is wrong to popularize Tamil songs at the expense of worthy songs in other languages.[462] Behind this criticism is the widely accepted characterization of Telugu as the most suitable language for music, often hailed as the 'Italian of the East.' The common view at the Academy then was that '(t)he inclusion of greater

number of Tamil songs would lower the quality of Carnatic music'
(A. Ramachandran 1983: 6).

In response to such criticism, proponents of the movement stressed
that there were many worthy compositions in Tamil but that these
were simply neglected by musicians. They quoted the recollection of
U.V. Swaminatha Iyer (1885-1942), a highly respected Brahman scholar
of Tamil language and literature, of the custom of singing Tamil songs
in the past and of their fall into oblivion (A. Ramachandran 1983: 6).
Other proponents of the movement maintained that songs by non-
Brahman composers such as Muttutandavar 'exercised great influence
over 'Carnatic' [*Karnāṭak*] musicians till about 1900 A.D. that is until the
craze of Telugu songs got hold of them' (Arunachalam 1989: 139).[463] At
the same time as these counter-arguments were advanced, proponents
of the movement responded to this particular criticism by making efforts
to enlarge the repertoire of Tamil songs of high calibre. Competitions
with cash awards for singing Tamil songs were instituted at Annamalai
University, which also published the notations of more than 1,300 Tamil
songs in multiple volumes, starting in 1943 (Chelladurai 1996).

Lastly, yet another criticism was advanced from the Academy that
the *Tamil Isai* movement was a political movement in disguise, based on
language and caste prejudice. According to them, the movement was
not about music, but rather was essentially an outlet for a non-Brahman
political party (Justice Party) to circumvent Brahman ideology and
authority. The proponents of the movement negated this criticism by
pointing to the existence of many Brahman supporters, including highly
prominent public figures such as C. Rajagopalacharia (1878-1972)[464] and
Kalki Krishnamurthy (1897-1968).[465] Even E. Krishna Iyer (1897-1968),
secretary of the Academy for the first ten years of its existence, called
in 1929 for more Tamil songs to be performed (Nambi Arooran 1980:
254; Music Academy 1997: 22-3), but his support for Tamil songs was an
exception at the Academy, and was not reflected in its 1941 resolution
to denounce the *Tamil Isai* movement. His proposal for a resolution that
would reconcile the both sides of argument was flatly rejected by the
all-Brahman Experts Committee (Music Academy 1941: 17, 1997: 22-3).

Tamil Isai Sangam

The Tamil Isai Sangam (Tamil Music Association, hereafter 'Sangam')
was established in 1943 at the peak of this controversy over *Tamil
Isai*. Faced with stiff resistance from the Academy, protagonists of

the movement realized the need to establish an organization of their own that would embody their beliefs. The Sangam started organizing an annual festival in December to challenge the dominance of the Academy by sponsoring many performances of Tamil songs. While the Sangam sponsored both Brahman and non-Brahman musicians, the ratio of participating non-Brahman musicians was much higher here than at the Academy. It also held academic conferences on *Tamiḻ Isai*, to give a sense of official authorization to their activities and to assess the continuity between ancient Tamil music and present practice.

A music school (*Tamiḻ Isai Kallūri* or Tamil Music College) was established in 1944 in Madras and later at a few other places to popularize Tamil songs. Songs in other languages are excluded from the curricula. Instruction is given mostly in vocal music, while a course on *Periya Mēḷam* music was also recently created (Figure 3).[466] Annual competitions with cash awards were instituted by the Sangam to popularize Tamil songs and to encourage *Periya Mēḷam* music.

Figure 3: A vocal music class at *Tamiḻ Isai Kallūri* (Chennai, 1999)

Because non-Brahman musicians were the primary purveyors of Tamil compositions, the Sangam became the single most important patron of non-Brahman musicians and their repertoire, as opposed to the Academy and other Brahman controlled organizations which, according to many non-Brahmans, provided preferential patronage to Brahman musicians.[467]

Are Tamil Songs More Popular Today?

Many Brahmans believe that the *Tamil Isai* movement's intent to popularize Tamil songs has gradually been accepted by mainstream classical music. It is true that many Brahman opponents of the movement eventually performed at the Sangam's annual festival. Prominent Brahman musicians such as Musiri Subramaniya Iyer and Semmangudi Srinivasa Iyer who, as mentioned earlier, initially criticized the *Tamil Isai* movement, eventually sang Tamil songs at the Sangam, and both were awarded the musical title of *Isai Pērariñar* in 1963 and 1969 respectively.[468]

On the other hand, the dominance of Trinity compositions in Telugu and Sanskrit remains intact at the Academy and other Brahman-controlled *sabhās*. For example, during the 1998 festival, 470 compositions were presented at the Academy, of which 143 (33 per cent) were songs by Tyagaraja. The total number of Trinity compositions was 228, comprising 49 per cent of the whole. A rough estimate of Tamil songs would be about 5 per cent. While these figures may be read either as improvement or as stagnation, depending on who interprets them, the representation of Tamil songs at Brahman-controlled organizations continues to appear far from the objectives initially set some sixty years ago by the movement.[469]

Public music education has also become a site of negotiation for popularizing Tamil songs. For example, Telugu and Sanskrit songs had been predominant in the curriculum of the Tamil Nadu Government Music College (*Tamil Nāḍu Arasu Isai Kallūri*), a performing arts college run by the state since 1949.[470] When Tiruppamburam Shanmugasundaram (b.1937) was appointed as the principal of the college in 1988 as the first non-Brahman to assume the post, he managed to overhaul its Telugu- and Sanskrit-dominated curriculum to one with predominantly Tamil songs (approximately 70 per cent according to the teachers) and hired many young non-Brahman musicians as instructors. Shanmugasundaram is a non-Brahman (of the *Isai Vēḷāḷar* caste) vocalist from an illustrious family of musicians who has a long association with the *Tamil Isai* movement. One of his uncles, Tiruppamburam Swaminatha Pillai (1900-61), was not only a famous flute player but was also considered one of the most prominent supporters of the movement.[471] However, when Shanmugasundaram retired in 1999 and a Brahman succeeded to his position as principal, the Telugu- and Sanskrit-oriented syllabus was restored and the representation of Tamil songs became marginalized once again, as virtually all non-Brahman teachers at the college had predicted.

Moreover, the state of Tamil Nadu, led by Chief Minister M. Karunanidhi, declared in the mid-1990s that it would open a state-run music school (*Tamil Nāḍu Arasu Isaippalli*) to teach *Tamil Isai* in each of the 30 districts of the state. This programme began in 1997 with the opening of ten schools, and seventeen schools were in operation as of 2001 offering courses in classical vocal music (Tamil songs), *Periya Mēḷam*, *tēvāram* (Tamil hymns on the deity Siva) and Bharata Natyam.[472] As the practitioners of these forms are mostly non-Brahmans, these government schools provide them with more employment opportunities.

Even the Department of Indian Music at Madras University, another centre of Brahman music scholarship, has been under pressure from the university administration to modify the Telugu- and Sanskrit-centred curriculum. During the tenure of a non-Brahman vice-chancellor, the decision to gradually Tamilise the syllabus was made through laborious negotiations and careful lobbying.[473] As of 2004, the curriculum of the corresponding course was largely Tamil-based, and a plan to expand it to the regular courses is underway. In addition to placing emphasis on teaching Tamil songs, the Tamilization of Sanskrit-derived musical terminology has been proposed, and some changes have already been made.

New Radicalism against Brahmanical Music Culture

The Sangam claims to have spearheaded the movement to propagate Tamil songs, but the evaluation of its success has not gone unchallenged: several organizations have been established out of frustration with the Sangam's moderate stance toward caste-based discrimination in music and/or its inability to fight it. Two of the most radical, and thus controversial, organizations to have appeared in the 1990s are *Makkaḷ Kalai Illakiya Kaḷaham* and *Tandai Periyār Tamil Isai Maṉṟam*. The existence of these organizations is rarely documented in music scholarship and journalism, as these tacitly assume a kind of spiritualist universalism in which music stands beyond mundane human activities; attempts to refocus music-making as a social phenomenon (not to mention a 'caste' issue that has already been stigmatized) are consequently shunned as distasteful or even blasphemous.

Nothing but Tamil Songs

I have already discussed the image manipulation of Tyagaraja in Brahmanical music culture. Apart from the activities of the Academy, one of the most potent venues for conjuring up Tyagaraja's saintly image is Tyagaraja Aradhana, a musical tribute on his death anniversary in Tiruvaiyaru, a small town on the Kaveri River near the city of Tanjavur, where he is believed to have died (attained *samādi* or eternal bliss).[474] The function in Tiruvaiyaru, the oldest of its kind, started in 1908, but for the past twenty-five years or so, it has spread not only to other parts of India, but also to many locations outside India (North America, Europe, and Australia) where South Indians have migrated (Hansen 1996; Ravi 1999: 449-51). Musicians of all grades and fans gather to pay homage to Tyagaraja by singing his compositions in Telugu. In recent years, it has also become a media event as portions of the festival are broadcast on TV and radio.

A scandal erupted during the Tyagaraja Aradhana in Tiruvaiyaru in 1997, which marked the 150th anniversary of Tyagaraja's death. The members of a left-wing organization called *Makkaḷ Kalai Illakiya Kaḷaham* (hereafter MKIK; People's Association for Arts and Literature) disrupted the festival by shouting pro-Tamil slogans and raising a banner that read 'Sing in Tamil' (*Tamiḻil Pāḍu*). They requested that only Tamil songs be sung in Tamil Nadu, and that Tyagaraja's Telugu lyrics be translated into Tamil (Kaliyappan 1999: 46; Pudiya Kalaccaram 2002). The protesters were quickly taken away from the site (and reportedly beaten afterwards) by the police.[475] Although it attracted media attention, as the MKIK had hoped, this incident has furthered Brahmans' exasperation toward what they often refer to as 'Tamil chauvinists.' During the festival in 1998 and 1999, the organizers appealed to the audience for the issue of language and caste not to be a factor at the festival for the saint, who transcended human or worldly divisions such as caste and language (*The Hindu*, 3 January 1999), but the police security was so heavy that it spoiled the reverential atmosphere the organizers had striven to create. Even a few participating musicians were not allowed inside the site.

The event in 1997 was by no means the first clash of interests at the Tyagaraja Aradhana festival. Ever since its inception, it has been plagued with communal tension between Brahman and non-Brahman musicians, despite its portrayal of universal humanism and comradeship based on the sacred art of music.[476] For many non-Brahman musicians, the festival has long been a site of negotiation to eliminate discriminatory practices, including the separation of places for eating and performance at the festival site, and more generally to challenge Brahmans' condescending attitude and treatment toward non-Brahmans. For example, it was during the 1939 festival that the performers of *Periya Mēḷam* (all non-Brahmans) were allowed for the first time to play onstage in sitting positions, as their Brahman counterparts had always done. This change was achieved only after intense negotiation by a charismatic and influential *nāgasvaram* musician, T.N. Rajarattinam Pillai (1898-1956) (B.M. Sundaram 1998: 9). This practice became gradually accepted in the 1940s outside this performance context after the age-old practice was broken in Tiruvaiyaru. More recently, many posters were placed around the town in 1971 during the festival, condemning the Brahman domination of music (*The Hindu*, 17 January 1971), and a group of *Periya Mēḷam* musicians attempted, though unsuccessfully, to boycott a performance for the procession during the festival, allegedly to humiliate the organizers.

At least for the past ten years, pro-*Tamiḻ Isai* slogans have been written on the walls around Tiruvaiyaru at the time of the festival, offending Brahmans and alienating moderate non-Brahmans (Srinivasan 1999). In 1999, anti-Tyagaraja Aradhana slogans were written on the walls on the road connecting Tiruvaiyaru and Tanjavur (Figures 4 and 5).

Figures 4-5: The MKIK slogans on the wall (near Tiruvaiyaru, 1999)

The text of two such slogans reads:

Karnataka music is a stolen music.
Sing in Tamil or we will make you sing [in Tamil].

Demand a public apology from the Tyagaraja Festival Committee, which disgraced the *Tamiḻ Isai* artist Dandapani Desikar for his singing in Tamil.[477]

The supporters of *Tamil Isai* often cite anecdotes illustrating the ill-treatment of non-Brahman musicians and the contempt toward the Tamil language felt by Brahmans. M.M. Dandapani Desikar (1908-72) was a famous vocalist and a prominent supporter of the movement (Figure 6).[478] When he sang at the Tyagaraja Aradhana in 1952, he gave a performance mostly of Tyagaraja compositions, but started and ended his performance with Tamil songs as was his custom at any public concert. After his performance, the stage where he was sitting was purified with water, because the sanctity of Tyagaraja had been rudely violated by the singing of Tamil songs (Kaliyappan 1999: 39; Irankumaran 1993: 38).[479] Articles critical of his insertion of Tamil songs also appeared in newspapers and magazines. For non-Brahmans, this is one of the most widely distributed anecdotes, often told to illustrate not only the Brahman suppression of Tamil songs but also the Brahman discrimination against non-Brahman musicians.[480]

Figure 6: M.M. Dandapani Desikar

According to K. Kaliyappan, the secretary of the MKIK's Tanjavur branch, they are not opposed to Tyagaraja's music since they regard it as deriving from *Tamil Isai*. Their objective is the complete elimination of songs written in any languages but Tamil from Tamil-speaking areas. While uncomfortable with the MKIK's confrontational method of protest, many moderate non-Brahmans sympathize with their thesis of Brahman domination of music.[481]

In Pursuit of Non-Devotional Tamil Songs

The *Tandai Periyār Tamil Isai Manṟam* (Periyar Tamil Music Association, hereafter TPTIM) was established in 1993 by a wealthy Chennai-based entrepreneur, N. Arunachalam. The name of the organization derives from Periyar or E.V. Ramasamy Naicker (1879-1973), who was the central figure in the non-Brahman movement. Periyar's vehement criticism of caste-based discrimination was extended to the Brahman monopoly of music and their suppression of non-Brahman musicians (Rajadurai 1997; Geetha and Rajadurai 1998: 318). Through his writings and speeches, he encouraged non-Brahmans to support their fellow musicians and himself organized a music festival for non-Brahman musicians in 1930 (Nambi Arooran 1983: 255).[482]

A staunch supporter of Periyar, Arunachalam aimed to realize his philosophy (known as *Periyār kolgai*, or Periyar's principle) by establishing the organization. Arunachalam was disillusioned not only with the Brahman monopoly of music, which he considers the manifestation of Brahman cultural hegemony, but also with what he describes as the 'Brahman takeover of the Tamil Isai Sangam' and its consequent inability to promote *Tamil Isai* and non-Brahman musicians.[483] According to Arunachalam, Brahmans tactfully positioned themselves into the organization through personal friendship and networking, and began influencing the organization in their favour. Although the heads of the organization remain descendants of Annamalai Chettiar, the founder of the organization, many Brahmans have in fact become officers of the Sangam.

Many supporters of the TPTIM point to the strong presence of Brahman musicians at the Sangam's music festival which, from their perspective, should patronize primarily non-Brahman musicians. They believe that the Sangam was providing more patronage to Brahman musicians than to non-Brahman counterparts. For the festival for 1998-99, for example, 11 (35 per cent) out of 32 music recitals were headed by

Brahman soloists; and at least 43 (47 per cent) out of 92 accompanists were Brahmans. These figures include the performers of *nagasvaram* (double-reed aerophone) who invariably belong to non-Brahman castes, and if these are excluded, the figure for Brahman musicians will be even higher. The supporters of the TPTIM emphatically comment on Sangam's 'excessive' support of Brahman musicians at the expense of non-Brahman counterparts.

The primary activity of the TPTIM is its annual festival in Chennai. One would hear none of the compositions performed either at the Academy or at the Sangam. Participating musicians are exclusively non-Brahman, and only Tamil songs are allowed to be part of the programme. Restrictions are placed not only on language, but also on the content of the song text. Reflecting Periyar's atheistic philosophy, the TPTIM does not endorse compositions in praise of deities, and this policy excludes virtually all compositions patronized by the Sangam. Not even compositions in Tamil are spared. Instead, the compositions performed at this festival are songs to praise the beauty of the Tamil language and culture, or songs that criticize what they consider anti-Tamil practices.

One frequently sung composition, *Tamiḷā! Nī Pēsuvadu Tamiḷā?* (Tamil! Is it Tamil that you are speaking?), is a good example of this. The first verse of this composition reads:

> Tamil! Is it Tamil that you are speaking?
> You are calling a beautiful child 'Baby'
> What the heck? You are calling your father 'Daddy'
> You are killing the life of Tamil
> Does English eat up this beautiful Tamil?
> Is it okay if your mother tongue dies in front of your eyes?
> Tamil! Is it Tamil that you are speaking?[484]

The song may appear on the surface as a straightforward warning toward Tamilians in general against the excessive use of English, but the non-Brahman audience at the festival tended to interpret it as a criticism of the Brahman custom to make heavy use of English words and expressions in their daily conversation. Many even assert that English is so much a part of Brahman speech that they cannot speak Tamil properly. According to Ramaswamy, Brahmans were already seen by the 1920s as destroying the Tamil language with their excessive use of English and Sanskrit (1997: 28, 194-7).

The TPTIM makes no claim of direct affiliation with the Dravida Kazhagam (DK), a political party that Periyar led, but many supporters in fact belong to the party. In addition, Arunachalam is known to be a supporter of the LTTE (Liberation Tigers for Tamil Elam) which has been engaged in the militant separatist movement for minority Tamils against the Sri Lankan government since the 1980s. In his office in Chennai, a portrait of a tiger, the symbol of the LTTE, is hung prominently behind his desk. Arunachalam is also a close ally and generous patron of Kasi Anandan (b. 1938), a Sri Lankan poet, who has provided lyrics for many of the songs performed at the TPTIM music festival. Arunachalam has published Anandan's poems from his own printing house (Anandan 1998), and released cassette recordings of Tamil compositions, including Anandan's songs.[485]

The TPTIM strives for the complete Tamilization of the Tamil language, which they regard as having been polluted with the intrusion of other languages—a fact for which they hold Brahmans responsible. They have replaced many Sanskrit-derived technical terms in music with Tamil equivalents. For example, *isai vaḷaṅgiyavar* has replaced *saṅgīta vittuvāṉ*, a common term for a musician. The Tamilization of language is not restricted to musical terms, and is a part of their effort to eliminate foreign words from the Tamil language in general. Even for a foreign item such as the telephone they use a coined Tamil term (*tolaipēsi*, literally 'distance talk').

Because of the TPTIM's overt anti-Brahmanism and Tamilization of music, many non-Brahman musicians shy away from performing at this festival for fear of being branded as 'Brahman haters' and as a consequence losing Brahman patronage. Even those who perform for this festival do not necessarily share the organization's objectives. Such musicians will perform at other venues, including Brahman-controlled *sabhās*, if given the opportunity, and in such cases they mostly perform the repertoire of classical music that the TPTIM aspires to eliminate. Most non-Brahman musicians I have talked to are critical of Brahman preferential treatment to their fellow musicians, and the reluctance on the part of the Academy and other Brahman music organizations to patronize non-Brahman musicians. Yet they are ambivalent about the TPTIM's radical anti-Brahman stance: while grateful for the performance opportunities, they are hesitant to identify themselves with it completely to avoid being ostracized by other performance venues (Figure 7).

Figure 7: A concert at the TPTIM's annual music festival (Chennai, 1999).
Note the portrait of Periyar prominently displayed on stage right.

Moreover, the musicians' ambivalence derives not only from
ideological reasons but also from musical considerations. Since the
TPTIM endorses no classical repertoire, musicians are obliged to learn
compositions that are suggested for their performances. Consequently,
many are seen performing with texts and/or notation in front of them.
Apart from the frequently expressed criticism against the TPTIM's
overtly anti-Brahman rhetoric, one of the major problems for the TPTIM
is a lack of compositions that would not contradict their ideology, and
one would frequently hear the same songs performed repeatedly, such
as the work that can be identified as their theme song, *Tamilē Uyirē
Vaṇakkam.* In order to break the monotony of playing the same songs
repeatedly, some musicians re-set this composition to different *rāgams*
(melodic modes).[486]

Rewriting the History

Many proponents of the *Tamil Isai* movement claim that what is known
as *Karnāṭaka Saṅgīta* is in fact *Tamil Isai*, renamed with a Sanskrit-derived
designation to make it appear to be a tradition created and transmitted
by Brahmans (Arunachalam 1989: 10). They have no disagreement with
the notion that Tyagaraja was one of the most significant musicians

that South India has ever produced, and do not generally question his saintly disposition. In fact, many non-Brahmans, musicians and patrons alike, including the founder of the *Tamil Isai* movement, Annamalai Chettiar, have expressed their adoration for his music.

Many musicians who belong to the non-Brahman caste of *Isai Vēḷāḷar* believe that Tyagaraja's main musical influence came from their own ancestors during his lifetime. For example, some question Tyagaraja's discipleship with Sonti Venkataramanayya, a theme unanimously accepted in the dominant discourse, asserting instead that Tyagaraja learned music mostly from *nāgasvaram* musicians in Tiruvaiyaru.[487] They 'are prepared to honour him [Tyagaraja] as the greatest musician of *Tamil Isai*' who simply used the language medium of Telugu with the music nurtured by Tamils (Arunachalam 1989; Ilankumaran 1993: 37).[488] Similarly, while Muttusvami Diksitar is known to have taught a number of non-Brahman disciples, their musical influence on this esteemed composer—on which many non-Brahman musicians emphatically remark—is virtually absent from the writings of Academy-affiliated scholars such as T.L. Venkatarama Iyer (1968, 1979) and V. Raghavan (1975a, 1975b) (Terada 2000: 479).

The proponents of the *Tamil Isai* movement challenge the absolute position of the Trinity in Brahman discourse by highlighting the presence of non-Brahman composers of Tamil songs. M. Arunachalam, for example, characterizes three prominent non-Brahman composers of the 16th to 18th centuries as the Elder Trinity or Sirkari Trinity.[489] By describing Tyagaraja and two other Brahman composers of the 18th century as the Tiruvarur Trinity (instead of the one and only Trinity) and juxtaposing them with the Sirkari Trinity, they aim to challenge the monopoly of Brahman composers (and by extension of Telugu and Sanskrit compositions) in South Indian classical music. The portraits of these non-Brahman composers are prominently displayed in the auditorium of the Sangam, in sharp contrast to the Academy and other Brahman-controlled organizations where the portraits of the Tiruvarur Trinity adorn their interior to the exclusion of the non-Brahman Trinity.

In so doing, the proponents of the *Tamil Isai* movement have attempted to relativize the position of the Trinity as the pinnacle of South Indian music, and insist that they are only one set of the Trinities that have appeared in the history of South Indian music. Few supporters of *Tamil Isai* aim to belittle the contribution of Tyagaraja, and they only criticize the manner in which Tyagaraja has been made into a potent cultural icon to symbolize Brahman music culture exclusively.

Concluding Remarks

I have discussed the role of the Academy in maintaining Brahman-centred music culture, and various forms of resistance manifested in the activities of non-Brahman organizations. By the various means described above (such as publications, speeches, conference resolutions, portraits, festivals, and establishing music colleges), these organizations each try to create and disseminate a particular sense of history.

For Brahmans, creating and maintaining a music culture of their own where they alone have the privileged position for self-definition is crucial for maintaining their cultural identity, which has been threatened throughout the twentieth century by socio-political movements against Brahmans.[490] For many non-Brahmans, the *Tamiḻ Isai* movement manifests their desire to reclaim their history, which according to them has been 'stolen' (*kalavāḍiya*) or denied by Brahmans. They assert that Brahman scholars have fabricated an image of South Indian music around a succession of Brahman composers, largely to the exclusion of non-Brahman contributions. While the methods of popularizing *Tamiḻ Isai* vary from the moderate and reconciliatory strategies by the Tamil Isai Sangam to the more radical and confrontational tactics adopted by the MKIK and TPTIM, they appear to share the perception that Brahmans have appropriated the music and dance tradition that non-Brahmans created and nurtured.

Lastly, investigating the issues concerning *Tamiḻ Isai* will enable us (as outside researchers) to break away from the constriction of the powerful dominant discourse. The Academy, along with Madras University, has been one of the best-known music organizations outside South India, serving as a gateway for foreign students and scholars interested in South Indian music. Their accessibility and use of English in their writings have made Brahman scholars and musicians the favoured collaborators for non-Indian researchers who might have internalized Brahman perspectives, thereby unwittingly becoming instrumental in perpetuating the 'Trinity myth' and the Brahman interpretations of history.[491]

(Originally published in 2008 in *Music and Society in South Asia: Perspectives from Japan* (203-226). Republished here with permission from the National Museum of Ethnology.)

The Circular Flow of South Indian Music and Dance

THROUGH HIS ANALYSIS of Indian popular culture such as film and fashion, social anthropologist Sugimoto Yoshio argues that Indian culture does not exclusively emanate from India. He believes that the presence and activities of Indians living abroad also has a significant affect on their culture in India. The *sari*, the quintessential female dress in India, is one such example. Whereas the traditional *sari* has a design, motif, colour combination, and a tying method which identify its region of origin, the new type of *sari*, produced for Indians living abroad (non-resident Indians or 'NRI'), cannot be traced to any particular region. This type of de-territorialized *sari* is now marketed in India and enjoys considerable popularity under the name of 'NRI *saris*'. Similarly, films have been produced in India with NRI themes (with NRI characters portrayed by India-based actors and/or shot in location in North America and Europe where they reside in large numbers) and have been successful not only in the diaspora communities, but in India as well. Sugimoto has advanced the concept of 'circular flow' (*kanryū* in Japanese) to describe and analyze this phenomenon (Sugimoto 2009).[492]

Three Vignettes

My research indicates that the concept of circular flow between India and its diaspora can also be observed in music and dance. I begin my discourse with three vignettes in order to illustrate how South Indian music is currently learned, performed and supported. They present three practitioners of *Karnāṭak* music, two currently home-based in the United Kingdom and the third in Chennai.

The first artist is a professional performer of *mridaṅgam*—the double- headed drum which is the primary instrument used in rhythmic accompaniment in South Indian music and dance. He immigrated to the UK from Chennai—the stronghold of *Karnāṭak* music—where he was trained. Although he performs frequently in the UK, half his time is spent in Europe where he is either a guest performer at concerts or joins musicians on tour from India. He only returns to Chennai in the music season of December-January, when he performs and takes advanced lessons from his *guru* (teacher/mentor) who lives there. He sometimes manages to find performance opportunities in the UK and Europe for his *guru* and his *guru*'s disciples.

The second artist is a young flute player living in London, where he was born. His parents are Sri Lankan Tamils who had to flee their homeland to escape the violent Tamil-Sinhala ethnic conflict. He studied South Indian classical music in the UK and completed his debut performance (described later) in 2004. When he performed in Chennai during its prestigious music season in 2007, his performance was prominently publicized in the local Tamil community magazine in London (Figure 1). A Canada-based Indian musician who happened to attend the concert in Chennai was so impressed with his performance that he invited the young flautist to perform in North America.[493]

The third artist is a vocalist and composer based in Chennai. He and his wife—also a vocalist—run a private music school for young, local students, and recently he began teaching *Karnāṭak* music to young Sri Lankan Tamil children living in Norway using Skype. Although he and his students live thousands of kilometres apart from each other (thus in different time zones), they sit down in front of their respective computers at prearranged times and have weekly lessons. He conducts his classes exclusively in the Tamil language and the children's parents are very happy that their children are learning both the music and the language (Figure 2).

These three vignettes, in all, represent a microcosm of the environment in which South Indian classical music is practised today. What is expressed here is not only the increased mobility of people involved in music, but also the continually widening options of music instruction, study, and performance. The first vignette is representative of the increasing number of India-trained musicians who have emigrated from India or who have multiple residencies in response to the growing demand for performance and teaching abroad. These musicians still maintain strong ties with India, and move constantly between various sites of performance and instruction.

Figure 1: A young Tamil musician featured in the London Tamil Community Magazine (2008).

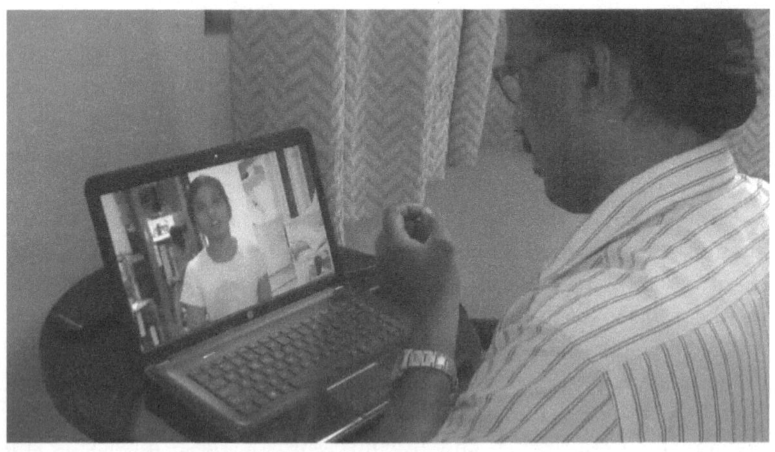

Figure 2: A Chennai-based vocalist giving a Skype lesson to a student in Norway (2013).

The second vignette demonstrates that an increasing number of young musicians who were born and trained outside of India are now making their presence felt in India, and that the city of Chennai has become a global hub where performers and fans of South Indian music and dance gather from all over the world and interact. Those from distant places (e.g. the UK and Canada in the vignette) make fortuitous connections in Chennai, resulting in performance opportunities both in and outside of India.

The third vignette relates the early stages of internet use for online instruction of Indian music, a practice which has since become a mainstay. I will discuss later in more detail how the use of this technology has rapidly grown and expanded.

The three vignettes show that people and music do not move only in the one direction; i.e. originating in India and flowing out to Indian communities abroad (or for that matter, from Chennai to other Indian cities), as previously conceptualized. Rather, the musical culture of India circulates or flows between various music-making centers around the world in a complex, multidirectional manner.

Amongst the many places where South Indian music and dance are practised, both the USA and the UK have become highly influential centers of activity. In the remaining portion of this essay, I will discuss the circular flow of South Indian music and dance in and out of the two countries where the differences in socio-cultural backgrounds of their practitioners and the patrons/supporters affect the performance practice and artistic content.

Indian Communities in the USA

South Indian music is studied and performed at an unprecedented level of activity in the USA today. At least two factors are behind this increase in music making; one is the growth of the Indian economy, and the other is the change in the US immigration laws. India has made major strides in its economic outlook since the liberalization of its economy in 1991, particularly in the IT industry.[494] This domestic economic growth has been responsible for producing a great number of highly trained IT professionals, of whom many were attracted to the opportunity of accumulating a level of wealth not attainable in India. They migrated in large numbers, and the USA has been by far the most popular destination (Fuller and Narasimhan 2007).

The second factor was an amendment to the American immigration law in 1965 which allowed large-scale movement of Indian people to the USA. The abolishment of the national origin quota system saw a dramatic increase in the number of immigrants, especially those from Asia, with South Asians being no exception. According to the government census, the population of Indians shot up from 0.8 million in 1990 to 1.7 million in 2000 and 2.8 million in 2010. In addition to the numerical growth of the population, the class and caste affiliations of immigrants were markedly different from pre-1965 immigrants. Those who came after 1965 tended to be highly-educated professionals, and came from all over India—including from four of the southern states; whereas earlier immigrants were usually labourers from North India. The majority of post-1965 immigrants were high-salaried professionals, and Indian Americans constitute the wealthiest ethnic group in the USA (Khagram, Desai and Varughese 2001).

Despite their wealth, their prominence in professional occupations and increasing political clout, Indian Americans have suffered from prejudice and racially-motivated violence. Very few consider themselves fully assimilated, or indeed integrated into mainstream society, since Americans place people of Indian descent in a relatively low social status (Leonard 1997; Fuller and Narasimhan 2007). Many women refrained from wearing a *sari* or from putting a bindi on their foreheads outside of their homes to prevent being easily identified as Indians.

Classical Indian music and dance is patronized by the Indian communities which have formed in many large cities, supported by their economic prosperity. For first-generation immigrants, Indian music and dance fulfills both a nostalgic desire for their homeland and also serves as an important medium to teach their American-born children the 'culture back home' in a less didactic manner. Since the mid-1970s, non-profit membership music associations (known as saṅgītasabhās in South India) have been established in many large cities to organize concerts aid offer courses on music and dance. The first such association, Carnatic Music Association of North America (CMANA), was established in New York (1976), followed by Cincinnati (1979), Minneapolis (1980), Seattle (1981), Chicago (1983), Freemont, California (1985), Portland, Oregon (1987), Austin (1991); and many others. As the number of associations increased, a few individuals assumed the role of coordinating North American tours by visiting Indian musicians.

Initially, Indian classical music was popularized by Ravi Shankar

(1920-2012) with his widely-publicized association with the Beatles; consequently, Northern Indian classical (*Hindustani*) music—of which Shankar was an exponent and world-famous icon—was promoted heavily by music associations in their early years. The situation changed when IT engineers from the four southern states of India (Tamil Nadu, Andhra Pradesh, Karnataka and Kerala) began to migrate in large numbers to the USA. These immigrants tended to come from high-caste backgrounds, particularly Brahmans, who are the primary supporters of South Indian music and dance (Singer 1972; Chuyen 2004; Fuller and Narasimhan 2007). Today, South Indian music and dance are practised at least as actively and vibrantly as, if not more than, their North Indian counterparts.[495]

Many schools teaching South Indian classical dance began to appear in the 1970s. They were established not only by well-known dancers but also by the wives and daughters of immigrant engineers to North America, who had only received limited training in India (O'Shea 2007: 3).[496]

Today, the largest and most important event of South Indian music and dance in North America is undoubtedly the Cleveland Thyagaraja Festival. Held annually in Cleveland, Ohio, since 1978, this music festival commemorates the achievements of Tyagaraja (1767-1847)—the best known and most frequently performed composer in South Indian music. The anniversary of his death has been celebrated annually for one-and-a-half centuries in the small town of Tiruvaiyaru in the Tanjavur district where he attained his 'eternal bliss' (*samādi*). Similar festivals have been organized in Chennai and many other cities in India.

In the spirit of the celebration in Tiruvaiyaru, commemorative music festivals are organized in South Indian communities all across North America; Katherine Hansen reported that it was already celebrated in more than 100 places at the time of her writing (Hansen 1996). By far the most famous and grandly executed today is the Cleveland festival. In 2010, the festival ran for twelve days and attracted about 8,000 people; many top-ranking musicians were invited from India to perform and to serve as judges at competitions held in conjunction with the festival. They often give workshops, providing opportunities for North America-based students to learn directly from established musicians from India. The festival was broadcasted on Indian TV and an invitation to perform at the festival has become a status symbol for visiting musicians.

NRI Influences on India

The increasingly vibrant activities in music and dance outside of India have simultaneously increased movement of musicians from India to diaspora communities, and at the same time seen a dramatic movement of people in the opposite direction from diaspora communities to Chennai. Musicians travel from India to perform in concert tours, take up extended residency in teaching posts, participate in workshops, and even relocate altogether or take up multiple residencies. On the other hand, the flow back into India of people arises from NRI children wishing to study Indian dance and music at source, the desire to visit Chennai, to study with teachers there, or simply to watch their favourite stars perform during the music season.

The music associations and musicians in Chennai tend to be receptive to requests from people abroad since they are perceived as potential sponsors of foreign tours. The music associations depend on corporate sponsors to conduct their annual festival and year-long regular activities. The degree of their dependence is greater now because the fees for star performers have inflated ('skyrocketed' according to some) mainly due to their exposure to remunerations from foreign tours and the teaching of students outside of India. Corporate sponsorship is prominently displayed on banners at performance venues, and in advertisements in newspapers and concert programmes (Figure 3). Sponsors include major banks and financial services as well as

Figure 3: The banners of corporate sponsors for the
Chennai music festival (2012).

developers of expensive residential projects who target the wealthy NRIs who wish to invest or retire in India.

For aspiring NRI artists, a performance during the prestigious music season in Chennai is a lifetime aspiration and a primary means to raise their status as artists, especially for those who wish to be professionals (O'Shea 2007: 155). Responding to the surging demand, many music associations invite NRI artists for the music festival and a few even organize a festival specifically for NRI artists. While the artistic intention of organizers in supporting NRI artists may not be questioned, the prospect of acquiring corporate sponsorship is also a factor that should not to be forgotten.

The pioneering music association in Chennai which supports NRI artists is Hamsadvani, which has conducted music festivals specifically for them since 1995. The association was established by a well-known patron of music, R. Ramachandran, and since his death in 2007, his son, R. Sundar has been running the organization. When I visited his house in south Chennai one evening in 2008, our conversation was interrupted many times by phone calls from different continents inquiring about performance opportunities for the upcoming music season (Figure 4).

Figure 4: The head of music association in Chennai
receiving a phone call from abroad (2008).

Other music associations began to sponsor musicians from abroad as well; the name of the musician's country of residence (such as USA, Canada, and Singapore) is added in parenthesis, indicating that they are still treated separately, as a group apart from local musicians.

Sri Lankan Tamil Communities in the UK

Although South Indian music and dance are as actively practised in the UK as in the USA, the patronage in these two countries is vastly different from one another. South Indian communities are the primary supporters in the USA; however, the large Sri Lankan Tamil community is the most enthusiastic patron of South Indian music and dance in the UK.

Triggered by the massacre of Tamils in 1983, the ethnic conflict between the Sinhalese majority and the Tamil minority turned into an armed struggle between the Sri Lankan Government Army and the LTTE (Liberation Tigers of Tamil Elam), a separatist military group seeking to build a Tamil nation. When the escalation of the armed conflict led to increased civilian casualties, many Tamils left their homeland, escaping to the UK, Europe, Canada and Australia and settling in these countries as refugees in the late 1980s to early 1990s. The strict immigration policies for refugees resulted in a relatively small number of Sri Lankan Tamils in the USA.

The majority of Tamils in the UK are refugees from Sri Lanka and their descendants, who decisively outnumber Tamils from India.[497] Tamils from these two countries have not formed a cohesive, single community based on ethnicity and language. Generally, they do not even mingle socially, since they come from significantly different backgrounds, class and, caste in addition to having emigrated for vastly different reasons. While Sri Lankan Tamils still harbor a desire to return to their homeland, it has become a distant reality as the foundations of their life have been established in the host society and their children, having grown up in the West, are reluctant to move to Sri Lanka with their parents. For this reason, the transmission of Tamil culture to the second generation is regarded as one of the most urgent and important agendas for the Sri Lankan Tamil community.

Venues for Learning Music and Dance

It is a widely observed phenomenon that immigrant communities tend to establish supplementary schools to teach their children their parent's language. Around the world, diaspora communities of the Tamil have established what is known as Tamil schools—tamiḻpāḍasālai—where music and dance are also taught.[498] Although not compulsory, most students learn music and/or dance alongside the Tamil language. Tamil schools are only open during weekends and they use local elementary and middle school facilities. Local schools welcome such utilization as they are under pressure to put these public facilities to effective use, and if they do, funds from the government are obtainable for such efforts.

Apart from Tamil schools, generally managed by Sri Lankan Tamils, some schools were established by musicians and dancers from India and specifically offer classes in the performing arts. The Trinities School of Music is such an example. It was founded in 1995 by Thiruvarur L. Kothandapani, a violin player from an established family of musicians in Tamil Nadu, who immigrated to the UK in 1990. Virtually all the students at this school are Tamil children of Sri Lankan descent (Figure 5). Known to have very high artistic standards, the classes by Indian teachers attract students who have previously developed a serious interest in music and dance in a Tamil school.

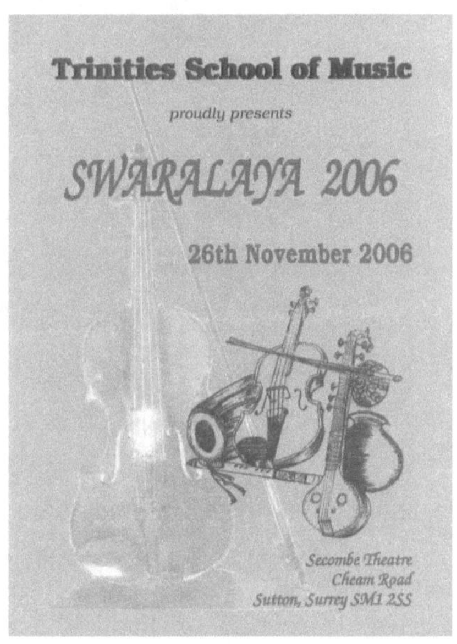

Figure 5: The concert programme of the Trinities School of Music in London (2006).

South Indian music and dance can also be learned through the Bharatiya Vidya Bhavan, an organization established in 1938 in Mumbai, India, to promote Hindu-based Indian culture. It now has more than one hundred branches in India and abroad, and the London Centre, established in 1972, is the largest and most active outside of India. The Centre offers classes during weekends in Indian classical music and dance genres. A variety of styles and instruments are taught, including those of North India (such as sitar, tabla and kathak); however, most students are Tamil, and learn—especially those of Sri Lankan descent—South Indian music (vocal, *vīṇa*, violin, flute) and dance—Bharata Natyam (Figure 6). The Centre's building is a refurbished Christian church; the chapel has been converted into a performance hall seating 300 people, and more than one hundred concerts are performed there annually. Included amongst those who have performed there are illustrious musicians such as Ravi Shankar.

Figure 6: Students studying *vīṇa* in London (2009).

The popularity of Tamil schools, performing arts schools, and cultural organizations such as the Bharatiya Vidya Bhavan, is derived from a strong desire and determination by parents to have their children learn the Tamil culture through music and dance. For Sri Lankan Tamils, Tamil culture is an important element of Tamil nationalism.

Araṅgētram

A kind of debut performance, the *araṅgētram*, a prominent social phenomenon in the Sri Lankan Tamil community, has an influence on

South Indian music and dance. The *araṅgētram* is a significant social event in Indian Tamil diaspora communities as well, but those in Sri Lankan Tamil communities have a greater impact on music making due to the size of their communities and the lavish nature of their *araṅgētram*s.

Historically, the *araṅgētram* goes back to the time when dance was offered to the deity at Hindu temples. Until the early decades of the twentieth century, women known as *dēvadāsis* were assigned to dance for the deity as an offering. They were then symbolically married to the deity, and therefore could not have secular marriages. Instead, they formed a semi-permanent relationship with wealthy patrons, usually from higher castes. Their daughters succeeded their *dēvadāsi* mothers, while their sons often became musicians to accompany dance. The *araṅgētram* was an event presenting a girl when she was ready to artistically to serve at the temple and sexually to future patrons (Gaston 1997; Narayana Murthy 2005: 55).

However, British colonial officers with their Victorian morals regarding sex, and Indian activists who internalized their doctrines, began to criticize the institution of temple dance and its practice by *dēvadāsis* as a feudal and immoral custom which must be abolished. Toward the end of the nineteenth century, they began a campaign for its legal abolishment. In those days, it was a coveted privilege for social dignitaries to invite famous *dēvadāsis* to perform at weddings and other social events, and the activists openly named and criticized those who patronized *dēvadāsis* in newspapers and other print media.

In 1947, temple dancing was officially banned in the Madras Presidency, which includes present-day Tamil Nadu. By then, however, it was already virtually extinct due to the staunch campaign. Inspired by surging nationalism, the *dēvadāsi* dance was 'revived' in the 1930s and 40s with a newly created designation of Bharata Natyam ('Indian dance') and in this process of revival, it became a stigma-free art form in which young girls from 'respectable' high caste families (particularly Brahmans) could safely participate.

With the 'revival' of South Indian dance, the *araṅgētram* evolved into an event to showcase a girl who had completed her training and was ready to pursue a career as a dancer. Eventually, vocalists and instrumentalists also began having *araṅgētram* ceremonies for the same purpose.

In Sri Lankan Tamil communities in the UK, the *araṅgētram* is changing its face again. A 15-year-old, Abbesega Anathavarathan, for example, began her dance training at the age of six at a local Tamil school; at her young age, she already had about ten years of experience in dance when I attended her *arangētram* in 2009. To further continue her training, she became a student of Usha Raghavan, a Bharata Natyam dancer from Chennai, who runs a dance school (Kalasagara, UK) in London.[499] On the back cover of the glossy programme booklet distributed at the *arangētram*, she salutes the guests with the traditional namaskāram (with her hands put together in front of her chest) in a striking blue dance costume (Figure 7). The list of invited guests is prominently printed in the programme, and the main guest and special guests each made a speech between pieces, including her father's friends of high social status and famous musicians from India, among others. The teachers often have artistic reservations about excessive speeches that interrupt the flow of the performance, but they also understand the parents' social needs.[500]

Figure 7: The programme booklet for an *arangētram* in London (2009).

The booklet includes a written programme of the recital with a brief explanation of each piece. In India, the identity of the composition and raga is not usually provided; the educated like to guess the identity of raga and the composition, it is part of their enjoyment when attending a concert. However, this custom is changing gradually due to the presence of NRIs and Sri Lankan Tamils in the audience; in the UK, in addition to the written programme, a professional M.C. (master of ceremonies) especially hired for the occasion, describes the pieces before each rendition. A comment from the school teacher emphasizes the girl's particular abilities in her school studies and in dance. A congratulatory message from Nithyasree Mahadevan, a famous female singer in Chennai, adds more status to the event. Finally, the booklet carries a message from the Tamil association in Sri Lanka, demonstrating her family's status in, and continuing connection to, the homeland.

After the performance, the dancer presented a gift to her *guru* and then to each of her accompanists, and then gave a speech thanking her *guru* and her parents. She demonstrated to the audience that she has not only completed her training but also excels in academic studies and social and public skills. The overall message conveyed is that she understands and respects her traditional culture and its values, yet simultaneously is fully capable of living in the West.

After the programme, it is customary for the guests to congratulate the dancer and her parents on the successful completion of the *araṅgētram*, and present a gift (usually cash). A professional photographer takes a photo of the dancer with each guest, keeping track of who came to the event. This post-performance ceremony of public acknowledgment is strikingly similar to that of wedding receptions.

As expected, to organize an event such as this requires a large sum of money. As of 2009, it was generally agreed that a minimum of 10,000 pounds was in order for a relatively simple *araṅgētram*, and if one invites musicians from India, the expense will be considerably more. The gifts from guests will partially defray the cost, but it is still a heavy burden for the dancer's parents. Because it has become a venue to show off wealth and to raise social status within the community, enormous pressure is imposed on parents to outdo the previous *araṅgētram*.[501]

Although essentially a dance event, the *araṅgētram* has gained importance for musicians as well, since it has created a need for live accompaniment and is therefore becoming a major source of their income (Gorringe 2005: 96, 102). Usually one week of intense rehearsals with musicians is necessary prior to the *araṅgētram* (Figure 8). Responding to the growing demand, some Indian musicians have migrated to the UK, while those trained in the UK have also become professional or semi- professional. Occasionally, Indian dance teachers invite an entire ensemble of musicians from India for the duration of *araṅgētram* if the parents are willing to cover the expenses.[502]

The *araṅgētram* phenomenon further connects India and the diaspora communities. As the interest in organizing an *araṅgētram* in a grand manner has escalated, it has become common for a dancer to change costumes frequently within a recital, sometimes between every

Figure 8: A rehearsal for the *araṅgētram* in London (2009).

few pieces performed. Several sets of dance costumes and ornaments are required. The dancer's parents (usually the mother) visit Chennai to purchase the necessary costumes and ornaments as well as order invitation cards and printed programmes. Certain shops in Chennai have become the mainstay of such trade.

Language Factor

The diaspora Tamils of Sri Lanka have become major players in the global network of South Indian music and dance. As previously mentioned, they are passionate about maintaining Tamil culture and language, and reflecting this predilection, first-generation immigrants have an overwhelming preference for Tamil compositions as opposed to those in other languages. The majority of Sri Lankan Tamil *araṅgētrams* consist predominantly—and often exclusively—of Tamil compositions. Most Indian dance teachers in the UK are willing to select Tamil compositions to satisfy Sri Lankan parents, although the training they provide is usually based on a repertoire consisting primarily of Telugu and Sanskrit compositions. These types of Tamil language-based dance *araṅgētrams* are slowly increasing in India too; partly because Sri Lankan dancers—after finishing an *arangētram* in the UK—then go on to pursue higher training with Chennai-based teachers, and consequently conduct a second *arangētram* there, in India.

The movement to promote Tamil compositions in *Karnāṭak* music has a long history in Tamil-speaking South India. Known as the Tamil music movement (*Tamiḻ Isai iyakkam*), it called for a fair share of Tamil songs in Tamil speaking areas and became a source of contentious negotiations based on caste, language and identity (Terada 2008).

The increasing presence of Sri Lankan Tamils, who may well be potential sponsors for musicians' overseas tours and residencies, is also having an influence on the repertoire of compositions presented in music concerts as well. As the majority of Sri Lankan Tamils prefer compositions in the Tamil language, the musicians present Tamil-oriented programmes to meet their audiences' liking, although they may be reluctant to admit that they make adjustments. This tendency is particularly strong when Indian musicians perform in the UK, where chances of being criticized by music aficionados from India are smaller. They often select relatively simple and catchy pieces, including those used in Tamil films such as *Alaipāyudē* (2000), which Sri Lankan Tamils tend to prefer. Because they show little interest in extensive improvisation and the performance is much shorter than in India, the 'heavy rāgas' such as Todi and Bhairavi, which require considerable time for satisfactory delineation, are performed less frequently.[503]

Internet Guru

A great deal of attention has been paid to the use of Skype and other online technologies to transmit music knowledge in music education in recent years. Musicians and students, in both India and the diaspora communities, utilize the technology extensively. I have already mentioned one-to-one music instruction on the internet, but the Cleveland Thyagaraja Festival conducted an experiment in 2007 to test the wider application of this new technology. They selected thirty eager young students from different locations across North America to perform at the Festival. They were tutored by the same Chennai-based teachers via Skype for a period of several weeks, and right before the festival they had in-person rehearsals together in Cleveland. The same teacher taught several students simultaneously, using the multi-screen system. Although there was a great deal of skepticism as to its effect and relevance as compared with the traditional method, the performance was regarded as a great success as many in the audience felt the students had progressed remarkably (Figure 9) (Rao and Ramachandran 2007). This attempt was widely publicized within music circles, and its success demonstrated the relevance of internet instruction, which will probably have a lasting impact on South Indian music-making. Since then, many music schools in Chennai, such as the MS Academy of World Music and Camatica.com, have begun using this medium for long-distance instruction.[504]

Figure 9: The Chennai-based master musician giving an
internet lesson to students in North America (2011).

Internet instruction began as an alternative teaching method for students who live far away from teachers. It was originally conceived as a supplementary teaching method to the traditional teacher-disciple relationship. For students abroad, the internet provided an opportunity to study with a famous teacher in Chennai without moving to India. The personal liaison with an established musician also serves as symbolic capital, which is almost as important as acquiring technical skills, to survive and thrive in the highly competitive world of classical music. Although skepticism still lingers among traditionalists in India, use of the internet has already become a widely practised mode of instruction. Some students in Chennai have also started using Skype to learn music with their teachers who live in different parts of the city. As this new teaching technology method invades a space traditionally reserved exclusively for domestic instruction, the nature of the *guru*-disciple relationship will be called into question.

Changing Perceptions

It is common to hear narratives that NRI (and to a lesser extent Sri Lankan Tamil) parents muscle into prestigious music associations with their monetary might to secure performance slots for their children, depriving talented local artists of performance opportunities (cf. O'Shea 2007: 153-57). This does not mean, however, that the practice of offering donations to secure a performance slot did not exist prior to the arrival of NRI dancers. On the contrary, it was customary for a dancer to voluntarily donate what is known as 'advertisement' (money) in order to dance at established venues. Local performers and patrons, however, often presume that an enormous sum of money has been paid by NRI dancers to perform regardless of their (inferior) artistic standard. Due to the actual frequency of such practice to 'buy out' a slot, some accomplished musicians who live outside of India are hesitant to perform in Chennai to avoid such characterizations being applied to them, as well as the less respectful treatment by sabhā officials (Satish 2007). A senior musician based in London relates her story of going to Chennai around 2005 to perform at several concerts during its music season, which her teachers had organized for her: 'Everyone saw (the announcements in) the paper and wherever I went, they would say to me 'Oh, you are performing in many places. So how much money are you giving?' I felt so sick. From that year on, I thought no way am I singing in Chennai.'[505]

To promote and encourage NRI and Sri Lankan Tamil students, a few organizations from outside of India began sponsoring concerts in Chennai during the music season. The Singapore Fine Arts Society, for example, has recently started to organize a festival of its own during the season in Chennai, featuring artists from Singapore. The above-mentioned Cleveland Thyagaraja Festival also conducts an unassuming festival of its own in Chennai to provide more performance opportunities for North America-based artists during the season. Sundaram stresses that the young musicians and dancers from North America are now as talented and well trained as their counterparts in India, aided by Skype instruction and frequent visits.[506] Even in concerts sponsored by other organizations 'it is not uncommon (in Chennai) to see Detroit so and so and New York so and so', following the custom among the South Indian musicians to affix the name of the place which they are originally from to their names.[507]

As some musicians and dancers from outside of India have acquired a reputation as solid performers, their undesirable image in India has finally begun to change for the better. Some musicians and dancers who were born and trained in the UK and North America now live in India as aspiring performers. Mythili Prakash, frequently mentioned as an example of this group of NRI artists, is the daughter of the accomplished Bharata Natyam dancer Viji Prakash, who migrated to the USA in 1976. She has made a name in Chennai as a solid performer and shares her time between Chennai and Los Angeles. Another success story revolves around Bhavajan Kumar, a Sri Lankan Tamil from Toronto (Canada), who now resides in Chennai as a professional BharataNatyam dancer.

Conclusion

The concept of 'circular flow' indicates that in order to carry out a study on Indian music and dance today it is not sufficient to study them as practised in India alone. They are an inseparable part of a globalized network of people, money and information, and thus it is not viable to conceptualize them as moving one way from India to its diaspora. It is much closer to reality to think of the flow as being circular between multiple centers of South Indian music and dance (Figures 10a and 10b).

The concept of circular flow is also problematic regarding the trope that connects place and authenticity uncritically. It is generally thought that music has an origin and develops in a particular place, be it a nation, area or community, and is given an aura of authenticity based on its connection to the place, buttressed by real or imaginary historical depth. Although the tenet that Indian music in India is the most authentic is upheld both in and outside of India, this concept should not become a tacit assumption for our academic analysis.

One may argue that the concept of 'circular flow' is specific to the case of Indian classical music and dance, and thus has limited applicability. However, many other music cultures have multiple centers of music

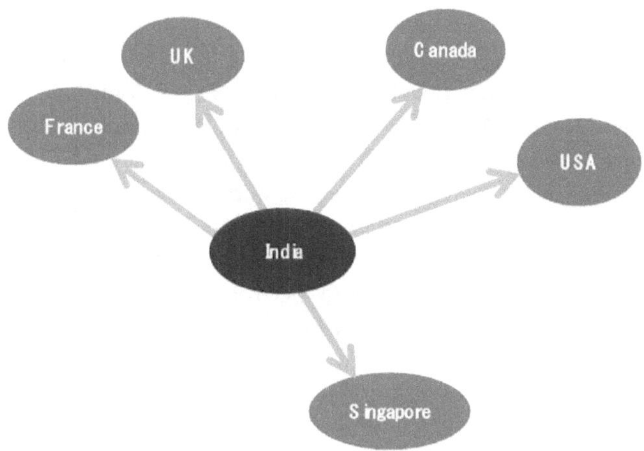

Figure 10a: Uni-directional flow model

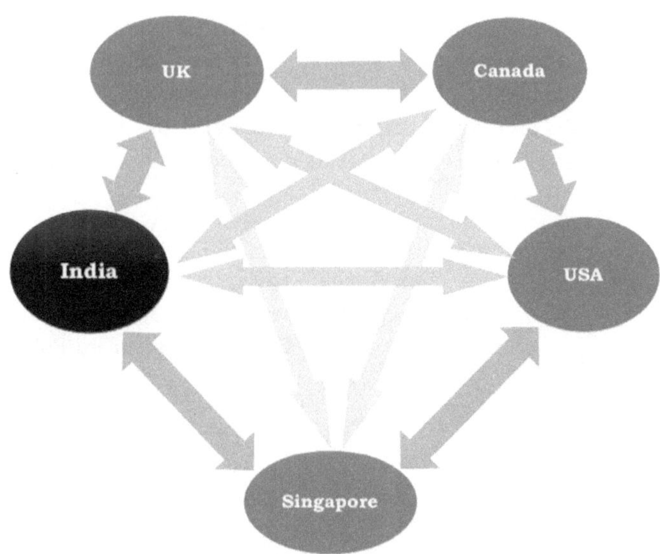

Figure 10b: Circular flow model

making. Just to give two examples, Jane Sugarman states 'Albanian homeland areas and the diaspora have come to comprise a single sphere or network of musical activities with multiple points of production and consumption' (Sugarman 2004: 25), stressing the need to document how moving (or migrating) people and music intersect. John Baily analyses the flow between Afghanistan and Afghan diaspora communities in the West, and observes 'a lot of circulation between various sites in the periphery' (Baily 2010: 169). As the effects of globalization deepen, more musical traditions will face a similar situation in which multiple centers of musical production and consumption are connected through physical movements of people and electronic means.

Finally, what are the implications of the 'circular flow' model of musical production in the study of music and minorities? While a great number of scholars continue to study minority groups or individuals as defined in a particular locality, as more people move, relocate, and have multiple residencies, the same group or individuals who are the majority in one locality can become a minority as they are placed in different majority-minority axes.

The scholars of music and minorities have struggled to study the intersection of multiple identities (such as gender and ethnicity) in a given locality, but the increased mobility of people, along with the 'circular flow' of culture discussed here further complicates the way we conduct our research and problematizes the concept of minority as defined in one locality. It remains an intricate challenge to investigate multiple layers of minority and majority identities in various shades and hues, and how they are manifest in the production and consumption of music and dance.

> (Originally published in 2014, in *Music and Minorities from Around the World: Research, Documentation and Interdisciplinary Study* (47-71). Republished here with permission from Cambridge Scholars Publishing.)

Notes

1   Rajarattinam Pillai is often referred to by musicians and patrons as TNR, as many well-known South Indian musicians are known by their initials. Pillai is a caste suffix which was used widely by various non-Brahman *jātis* (caste groups) including that of musicians, therefore it is not included in his abbreviated name. This practice of abbreviation is partly due to the economy of words, but also an act of acknowledging any musician's fame and popularity making the use of his or her full name unnecessary for identification.

2   The conventional history of Western classical music is characterized by the abundant documentation of individual composers, who are considered the trend-setters of their style periods. Despite increasing interest in the sociocultural aspects of music making, Western music history is still conceived and practised as the study of a diachronic succession of mostly great composers, who are linked in terms of musical style. Works on individual composers explicitly aim to provide biographical accounts, records of musical innovations and their influence on those who followed them.

3   The conflation of the notion of art with the achievements of autonomous individuals (or a concept of individual ownership) in Western musicology has been criticized within the discipline (Subotnik 1991).

4   For example, Frank Mitchell embodied the qualities of Navaho religion, for Charlotte Frisbie and David McAllester who edited his detailed autobiography (1978). Charles Keil (1979) includes biographical accounts of seven Tiv composers to illustrate the typical condition of becoming a composer and the motives of composing. More recently, Judith Vander describes five Shoshone female composers and musicians.

She notes the distinct repertoires of these women and calls them their respective song prints, but she believes that they are something larger than themselves as individuals (1988). As Stephen Slawek (1991: 161) argues, the studies of Indian classical musics may be an exception to the general rarity of works centered around the individual in ethnomusicology. Yet, a majority of such previous studies are based on the musical knowledge acquired from authors' gurus who are assumed to be representative samples of the musical tradition, or sub-tradition, to which they belong, and do not take on the cultural analysis of individual musicians themselves. Many previous studies found particular individual musicians as primary sources of specialized musical knowledge which could be obtained only through extended discipleship with them. For prime examples of this, see the works by Brown (1965) and Berberich (1974).

5   The discussion in the present study is confined to the traditions of South Indian classical music. For the sake of brevity, the term classical is omitted except when a distinction from other musical traditions (folk, film, North Indian, etc.) is necessary. There exist numerous traditions in South India of folk instrumental ensemble featuring *nāgasvaram* and other related double-reed aerophones. Although these music traditions are at present not based upon the musical system associated with the classical tradition, and therefore share very little with *Periya Mēḷam* music, some practitioners of the latter tradition trace their lineages to those associated with folk ensembles. However, a comprehensive comparison is difficult due to the lack of existing documentation on these traditions.

6   The survey of existing literature has revealed a lack of full-fledged studies on *Periya Mēḷam* music, despite repeated acknowledgement of its sociocultural and religious, if not musical, importance. To my knowledge, there are only two thesis-length works on the subject. K. Malarvizhi's 'Nagaswaram' (n.d.), a Master's thesis submitted to Madurai Kamaraj University, provides the descriptive accounts of the history, construction, playing techniques, and temple repertoire of the *nāgasvaram* as well as biographical notes on thirty-two eminent *nāgasvaram* and *tavil* players. Malarvizhi is

a granddaughter of the two well-known *nāgasvaram* players, Ayyampettai Venugopala Pillai (1904-65) and Kulikkarai Pichaiyappa Pillai (1913-79), and much of her data was gleaned from interviews with a number of prominent musicians. Unfortunately, despite her favourable 'insider' background, most of her otherwise intriguing findings are of lesser value due to the lack of scholastic consistency. Frank Berberich's 'The Tavil: Construction, Technique and Context in Present-day Jaffna' (1974), a Master's thesis submitted to the University of Hawaii, is based on the author's discipleship with a well-known *tavil* musician K. Ganesha Pillai in Jaffna, and provides useful factual information about the topics indicated in the subtitle. Although there are several articles on *Periya Mēḷam* music, they are all very short and the aim of each article is either a general introduction to the genre (Parthasarathy 1981; Sankaran 1986a; B.M. Sundaram 1986), a descriptive account of a specific occasion (Skelton 1971), or the historical evidence concerning the *nāgasvaram* (Raghavan 1949, 1955).

7   J. Pandian, for example, observes that Milton Singer's extended and sustained association and research among Brahmans may have contributed to developing a Brahmanical framework (1987: 29).

8   Referring to *Hindustani* (North Indian classical) music, Qureshi emphasizes the need for a systematic inquiry into the nature and content of oral source (1991).

9   For representative examples, see Deva (1974), Rangaramanuja Ayyangar (1972, 1977), Powers (1980), and Sambamurthy (1982d).

10   For examples of non-Brahman scholarship, see Ponnusami (1930), Kuppusami (1965), Pandither (1984), and Arunachalam (1989). For examples of Brahman counterparts, see the works of Sambamurthy, Raghavan, and Seetha.

11   For examples, see Hardgrave (1965), Irschick (1969), Saraswathi (1974), Barnett (1976a), Mangalamurugesan (1979), Nambi Arooran (1980), Rajagopal (1985), Karashima (1988), and Washbrook (1989).

12   For example, in 1912, 55 per cent of Deputy Collectors, 83.3 per cent of Sub-Judges, and 72.6 per cent of District Munsifs were Brahmans when they constituted merely 3.2 per cent of

the total male population in the Madras Presidency (Nambi Arooran 1980: 37).

13　Division and conflict between Brahmans and non-Brahmans is subject to regional variations. Within the state of Tamil Nadu, for example, the western districts have very few Brahmans and the social bifurcation into Brahmans and non-Brahmans is irrelevant.

14　Scott divides subordinate discourse into two arenas: 'public transcript' which is the discourse in the presence of the dominant, and 'hidden transcript', the discourse carried on 'off-stage' without the presence of the dominant group, and argues that the analysis of discrepancy between these two types of transcripts is crucial in understanding the impact of domination on public discourse (Scott 1990: 5).

15　The internalization of the oppression by the oppressed is described or analyzed by scholars in various disciplines, including history (Lears 1985: 573), psychoanalysis (Memmi 1965, 1984; Fanon 1967; Nandy 1983), education (Freire 1970: 27-56; 1985: 185), African-American feminism (hooks 1989: 112-9), and political science (Scott 1990).

16　Rajarattinam Pillai as a unit of analysis is considered a polysemic symbol in this study. According to Abner Cohen, symbols 'stand ambiguously for a multiplicity of disparate meanings, evoke sentiments and emotions, and impel men to action' (1974: ix). What is crucial in this definition is not only that a symbol has a capacity of carrying a number of disparate meanings (polysemy), but that the connection of a symbol to any meaning(s) is arbitrary, that is, culturally defined. The ambiguity inherent in the relationship between a symbol and a meaning which it stands for is to be emphasized to stay away from the rigidly static notion of the relationship.

17　The authorship of Volosinov's work has been in dispute. Some believe that Volosinov's primary work, *Marxism and the Philosophy of Language*, was written by Mikhail Bakhtin, but published under Volosinov's name. For different viewpoints on this controversy, see Matejka and Titunik (1986: ix-xi), Clark and Holquist (1984: 146-70), and Morson and Emerson (1989: 31-49).

18　See Volosinov (1973: 22-3) for a concept of multiaccentuality.

19 For similar arguments, see Williams (1977: 108-14) and Hall (1986: 22).

20 The relevance of investigating everyday forms of resistance is discussed in detail by Scott (1985, 1990).

21 See Alonso (1988a: 47-8) and Brow (1990: 3). For the intrinsic connection between history and politics, see Johnson et al. (1982), Poster (1982) and de Certeau (1988: 6-11).

22 For discussion of the relationship between discursive practice and hegemony, see Gramsci (1971), Laclau and Mouffe (1982), and Alonso (1988b).

23 The interview was reprinted in *Shanmukha* (Bhuvarahan 1987: 57-60), to which references are made here.

24 Ellarvi is a pen name for and a composite of the initials of L. R. Viswanatha Sarma (L.R.V.) who is a popular Brahman novelist as well as author of many biographies of musicians.

25 Tumilan is the pen name used by N. Ramasami Aiyar, a Brahman journalist, who contributed a number of articles on musicians in Tamil magazines such as *Dinamani Kadir*. Also see Muthiah (1989: 159-67).

26 In a newspaper article which reported his death, the time and place of Rajarattinam Pillai's birth is given as 1902 and Tirumarugal respectively (*The Hindu*, 13 December 1956).

27 According to one source, Rajarattinam Pillai was born into a family in which playing *nāgasvaram* was the occupation for the previous four generations (*Dinamani*, 13 December 1956).

28 Bhuvarahan (1987: 61). Tumilan states that Rajarattinam Pillai's grandfather's name was Sivarama Pillai instead of Sivanana Pillai (1988: 12).

29 The name of *Isai Vēḷāḷar* musician consisted of four parts; name of ancestral place, the initial of his father, his own given name, and caste title of Pillai (or Mudaliyar in some areas outside the Tanjavur district). The initials of his grandfather and even great-grandfather are sometimes added, especially when they were well-recognized musicians.

30 Tiruvavadudurai Madam is one of the three Saiva Madams in Tanjavur area, the other two located in Tiruppanandal and Darumapuram. All three Madams have been patronizing *Periya Mēḷam* musicians both by appointing *ādīna vittuvāṉs* and by honouring musicians with awards and gifts (Malarvizhi

n.d.: 28-9). See Chapter 4 (Section 1) for a description of *ādīṇa vittuvāṉ*.

31 This information is not directly mentioned in written literature.

32 Tumilan (1988: 15) maintains that Rajarattinam Pillai's initial vocal training was given by his paternal uncle, Kadiresam Pillai, while Sankaran (1981: 294) believes that Kadiresam Pillai, as well as one Rangasvami Pillai of Perumullai, gave *nāgasvaram* lessons to Rajarattinam Pillai.

33 One of Krishna Iyer's teachers was a *nāgasvaram* musician, Tiruppamburam Natarajasundaram Pillai (Rajagopalan and Sankaran 1987: 31). Aside from Rajarattinam Pillai, Krishna Iyer also taught another distinguished *nāgasvaram* musician, Tiruvidaimarudur Sivakorandu Pillai (B.M. Sundaram 2001: 73). These may indicate the high level of cross feeding of musical knowledge between Brahman and *Isai Veḷāḷar* musicians. Krishna Iyer is said to have been a strict teacher, like many other musicians at that time. This is illustrated by an anecdote that Rajarattinam Pillai once received a bloody nose after being hit by Krishna Iyer's bow when he could not meet the latter's expectation (Sankaran 1981: 294; Tumilan 1988: 22-3). Jayaraman gives Krishna Iyer's biographical dates as 1854-1912 (1986: 29).

34 Vaidyanatha Iyer's musical style has been described as being akin to that peculiar to *nāgasvaram* (Srinivasa Iyer 1978: 41). Rajarattinam Pillai believes that his own stepfather, Tirumarugal Natesa Pillai was Vaidyanatha Iyer's teacher for some time. He also recollects that the time of his training with Vaidyanatha Iyer was in 1909 (Bhuvarahan 1987). Both Venkataramayyar (1970) and Visuvanadayyar (1980) state that Vaidyanatha Iyer studied with a *nāgasvaram* musician in Konerirajapuram, although they disagree on who Vaidyanatha Iyer studied with.

35 N. Rajagopalan gave Kannusami Pillai's birth and death years as 1869-1923 (1990: 106).

36 Sankaran believes that Rajarattinam Pillai was initiated into *nāgasvaram* by his own paternal uncle, Kudiresan Pillai, then by Rangaswami Pillai of Perumulai before he studied with Markkanda Pillai (1981: 294). B.M. Sundaram estimates Rajarattinam Pillai's training under Kannusami Pillai was around 1910 (Interview, 1986).

37 Kiranur Ramasami Pillai was the very first instructor in *nāgasvaram* at the Government College of Music in Madras.

38 Ammachattiram Kannusami Pillai accompanied Rajarattinam Pillai for this occasion.

39 According to Tumian (1988: 48), Saminada Pillai was so impressed with Rajarattinam Pillai's playing at the wedding of Nidamangalam Minakshisundaram Pillai, a famous *tavil* musician, that he suggested his daughter's marriage to Rajarattinam Pillai.

40 Her father, Tirupparankunram Avadainayagam Pillai, and brother, T.A. Pichaiya Pillai, were both well-known *nāgasvaram* musicians (Tumilan 1988: 75-6).

41 *The Hindu*, 18 September and 2 October, 1936 (See Figure 2-1). Also see Tumilan (1988: 145).

42 After Rajarattinam Pillai's death, a woman who claimed to be his daughter appeared. She said her mother was Rajarattinam Pillai's third wife, who left him due to maltreatment. Regardless of the validity of her claim, there is no indication that Rajarattinam Pillai knew of her existence.

43 See Figures 6-2 and 6-3 for examples.

44 According to B.M. Sundaram, Nagapattinam Venugopala Pillai (1861-1917) was the very first *nāgasvaram* musician to perform abroad (Singapore) (1973: 67). While Rajarattinam Pillai is said to have boasted of a trip to Japan to his fellow musicians and patrons, there is no evidence that the trip actually took place.

45 For example, M.R. Radha, a leading stage actor of his time, donated the proceeds from his performance to Rajarattinam Pillai. The owner and manager of the Dasaprakash Hotel offered him a comfortable room at the hotel, free of charge (Sankaran 1961: 53; Tumilan 1988: 153).

46 Rajarattinam Pillai's immense popularity was evident in the way his death was reported. An influential Tamil newspaper, *Dinamani*, carried a long article on Rajarattinam Pillai's death and lifetime achievements on its first page with his photograph (13 December 1956). *The Hindu*, a leading English newspaper, also carried an article with his photograph. The President of India also sent a message of condolence to the Government of Madras (*The Hindu*, 29 December 1956).

47 The funeral procession is often described as accompanied by a

number of mourning film actresses who were associated with Rajarattinam Pillai.

48 To attach a *sīvāḷi*, the string is tied around the *keṇḍai* between the two coconut shell rings. The other string which wraps around the bottom part of the reed is then tied to the former string so that the reed will not be lost if it is accidentally detached from the *keṇḍai*.

49 The combination of these two techniques in scale practice is sometimes called *taṉṉakāram*.

50 Only two other families in Therizhandur, near Kuthalam, (Mayiladuthurai district) make *nāgasvarams* for *Periya Mēḷam nāgasvaram* musicians in Tamil Nadu.

51 A few *nāgasvaram* players make their own *sīvāḷis* and sell them to others, but they are not considered to be serious musicians by other *nāgasvaram* musicians.

52 In 1987, he charged Rs. 225 for a dozen *sīvāḷis*, as opposed to the average price of Rs. 150 per dozen.

53 *Kūḍus* are placed both on the fingertip and the second joint of each finger. They are used only for performances.

54 Berberich uses the term *kambu* for the wooden stick instead of *kaṟi* (1974: 40).

55 Valivur Muttuviru Pillai (1888-1923) is said to have introduced the practice of using *kūḍus* (B.M. Sundaram 2001: 271).

56 The *mridangam*, a double-headed barrel-shaped drum played with the hands, is the primary instrument to provide rhythmic accompaniment in *Karnāṭak* music.

57 The detail of tuning process is provided by Berberich (1974: 42-60).

58 The hand cymbals used for *Kālakshēpam* and *Bhajaṉa* are referred to as *jarla* (Premeela 1984: 60; Simon 1984: 79). *Kālakshēpam*, also known as *Katakālakshēpam*, *Harikata*, or *Harikatakālakshēpam*, is a form of recitation and song with musical accompaniment. The present form of *Kālakshēpam* was developed in Tanjavur through adaptation of a Maharashtrian form (Singer 1972: 167). See Premeela (1984) for a detailed discussion of this form. *Bhajaṉa* is a form of communal singing of devotional hymns.

59 *Sruti* is a Sanskrit term that refers to the tonic pitch or the drone which includes the tonic pitch (*Sa* in Indian sol-fa syllables). By extension, it also refers to the drone instrument

in some folk ensembles consisting of double-reed aerophones and drums.

60 Several terms including *mēḷam, gōshṭi, kūṭṭu,* and *pāṭṭi* (from English 'party') are used to refer to the ensemble.

61 Some *Karnāṭak* soloists perform with the same accompanists of their choice on a regular basis.

62 The *tāḷam* here refers to a rhythmic cycle in which a composition is set, and the *eḍuppu* is the beginning point of the text of the composition in the *tāḷam.*

63 In *Karnāṭak* music, the term *ālāpaṇai* (or more formally *rāga ālāpaṇai*) is used to refer to this melodic improvisation prior to composition, with the exception of *rāgam-tanam-pallavi,* an extensive improvisatory form in which the section of *rāgam* elaboration is called *rāgam.* Here I am following the convention in *Periya Mēḷam* music in which melodic improvisation is simply called *rāgam.*

64 On rare occasions, two players with no close kinship relationship have formed a fraternal duo. The best-known example of this was the Kiranur Brothers (Kannappa, 1896-1944, and Chinnatambi, 1897-1942) who were very popular in the 1930s (B.M. Sundaram 2001: 155-60).

65 The *kīrttaṇai* or *kriti* is the most frequently performed compositional form in classical music. Historical studies often describe the *kīrttaṇai* as a form which preceded the *kriti,* and as having more emphasis on text than the *kriti.* Yet, these two terms are used interchangeably among musicians, although *kriti*is used most often in *Karnāṭak* music and *Periya Mēḷam* musicians prefer the *kīrttaṇai.*

66 *Pallavi* here refers to a highly improvisational form, not to be confused with *pallavi* as the first section of compositional forms such as *kīrttaṇai.* See Chapter 4 for more information.

67 The same arrangement is made in *Karnāṭak* music when a left-handed *mridaṅgam* player switches places with a violin player. He sits to the soloist's left, and the violin player, who usually sits to the soloist's left, sits to his/her right.

68 All the musicians I interviewed agree on this point. Also see T.R. Subramaniam (1985: 77).

69 See K. Ramachandran (1931) and Subrahmanya Aiyar (1962: 68-9). Semmangudi Srinivasa Iyer (1908-2003) expressed his

indebtedness to the past *nāgasvaram* musicians at the Music Conference in Madras in 1986. The best internationally known Karnāṭak vocalist, M.S. Subbulakshmi (1916-2004), was also inspired by *nāgasvaram* music for her *rāgam* elaboration (Ramnarayan 1987). Also personal communication with Madurai G.S. Mani (1987). The influence of instrumental idioms developed by *nāgasvaram* players on vocal music is a worthy topic of inquiry in order to carefully modify the common notion that all spheres of *Karnāṭak* music are based on vocal music.

70   See Chapter 4 (Section 3) for details.

71   Interview with Tiruvarur Latchappa Pillai (1986). When four *nāgasvaram* players performed together, they played the compositions written exclusively for the annual festival.

72   They were initially called the Tiruvizhimizhalai Payyangal (Boys) because of their young age (Venkataramaiyar 1956: 33; Sankaran 1983: 18). Their dashing appearance also contributed to their popularity because it was thought to add a sense of auspiciousness and exuberance to the occasion (Rangaramanuja Iyengar 1972: xiii).

73   *The Hindu* (8 November 1932; 18 March 1935; 10 October 1936).

74   Sambamurthy reports that the practice of two vocalists singing together principally in unison and occasionally in octave apart was already found during the lifetime of Tyagaraja (1767-1817), who grouped his disciples into pairs and trained them to sing his compositions (1983: 316-7).

75   'Pitch-n' is a translation of 'n-*kaṭṭai*' in this study. The *kaṭṭais* refer to the reeds of the harmonium. The integral numbers correspond to the white keys of the harmonium, and are used to indicate the *sruti* (tonic pitch) of voice and instruments, in an ascending order, with 1 indicating c. A half step is indicated by ½ (*arai*). Thus, for example, 2½ *kaṭṭai* corresponds to d#.

76   Tiruvengadu Subramania Pillai is usually credited for having successfully performed the pitch-1 *nāgasvaram*.

77   According to *Tamil Lexicon*, *bāri* is a derivative of Urdu *bhari* and is defined as 'that which is heavy or big' (1932: 2623). Similarly, Jairazbhoy suggests that *bāri* may be related to Hindi *bhari* which signifies big, long, and heavy (1980: 149). The etymology of *timiri* is unknown.

78 For a similar example, see K. Ramachandran (1931).

79 *Tiruvārūr bāri* is often mentioned in a pair with *Kumbakōṇam timiri*, referring to a small *nāgasvaram* used in Kumbakonam in the past, although little about this instrument is known. Apart from this, there is a great deal of disagreement as to the usage of these two terms. Sambamurthy (1971a: 107) and Parthasarathy (1981) believe that only the pitch-5 *nāgasvaram*, is *timiri*, whereas *nāgasvaram* is which have pitches between 2 and 3 are *bāri*. Govindarajan, on the other hand, asserts that only the pitch-2 *nāgasvaram* is called *bāri*, the one of pitch-2½ *iḍaibāri* (middle *bāri*), and the one of pitch-4½ *timiri* (1987: 4). B.M. Sundaram advances yet another theory that *bāri* only refers to the instrument in Tyagaraja Swamy Temple, whereas pitch-2 and pitch-2½ *nāgasvarams* which were introduced by Rajarattinam Pillai are called *iḍaibāri* (Surya Prasad 1988). Malarvizhi believes that *timiri* refers only to the pitch-5 *nāgasvaram*, *bāri* to pitch-2 or pitch-2½ *nāgasvaram*, and *iḍaibāri* to *nāgasvarams* which have pitches between those two (pitch-3 to pitch-4½) (n.d.: 26).

80 This is evident in the disc recordings Rajarattinam Pillai made, starting in 1934.

81 Rajarattinam Pillai's sound on *nāgasvaram* is often described as sweet (*iṉippu*). The metaphor of taste to describe a favourable sound quality here is similar to that in English usage.

82 Higher-pitched wind instruments generally need more air than their lower-pitched counterparts.

83 Flora suggests the possibility of *ottu* and *oottu* (a toy instrument in Kerala) as cognates (1983: 31). L.S. Rajagopalan also describes a toy reed-aerophone in Kerala, but no name is given (1975: 145).

84 Although virtually all the musicians I contacted believed that there were no *ottu* players left, I located one player attached to Kamakshiamman Temple in Kanchipuram in 1987. However, his performance was restricted to the temple ritual context (Figure 3-6).

85 While B.M. Sundaram (2001: 111) reports that a *nāgasvaram* musician named Pandanainallur Ayyakkannu Pillai (1868-1944) used circular breathing for his performance, but this musician appears to be a rare exception.

86 An ensemble which accompanies various forms of folk

dances such as *Karagāṭṭam* and *Kāvaḍi*. It typically consists of *nāgasvarams, tavils, tāḷam*, and various other drums (*pambai* and *dōlak*).

87   An ensemble featuring the double-headed drum known as *uṟumi*.

88   A folk ensemble mainly found in Dakshin Kanara district, featuring 1 or 2 *wolaga* (*nāgasvaram*), *sruti* (drone pipe), and *dholak*. Sometimes, a pair of kettle-drums called *sammela* is added to the ensemble. *Nagasvara vādana* is played at life-cycle ceremonies and social functions.

89   The average share of the *nāgasvaram* player was approximately 60 percent of the whole remuneration.

90   The *tablā* is a pair of kettle-drum played with the hands. It is the primary rhythmic accompaniment instrument in *Hindustani* music. The only major exception is the older style known as *dhrupad* in which a double-headed barrel-shaped drum called *packavaj* is used.

91   James Kippen also provides anecdotes concerning *tablā* players in Lucknow who sometimes engaged in plots to make the soloist lose face by preparing complex materials prior to performance (1988: 59-62).

92   The front part of the head is shaved with a tuft remaining at the crown.

93   Beneath this has been the weakening correlation between a caste and its hereditary profession and the concomitant increase of caste neutral white-collar jobs in urban centers.

94   Arunachalam belonged to a *jāti* known as *Paṇḍāram*. See Chapter 5 (Section 3) for details.

95   Interview with Balakrishnan, 1990; see Chapter 6, Section 2 for Subramanyam's other activities. The call for establishing a *Periya Mēḷam* course at music schools was made as early as the 1930s (*The Hindu*, 23 July 1935).

96   Annamalai University was established with an endowment from Raja Annamalai Chettiar in 1929.

97   Although established by the funds endowed by a Maratha ruler of Tanjavur, Serfoji, the college is now affiliated with the government run Bharatidasan University in Tiruchirappalli.

98   These two, along with other wealthy temples, are also important patrons of *Periya Mēḷam* music who invite a number of ensembles for their annual festivals.

99 These schools include the one in Srirangam (Tiruchirappalli district) by Sheik Chinna Moulana, and the one in Srirangapattana (Mandya district, Karnataka) by A.V. Narayanappa. Darumapuram Govindarajan also had a school in Mayiladuthurai from 1959 until he took a position at the Government College in Madurai in 1979.

100 The incorporation of music learning into the curriculum of higher education was first made in 1929 when Raja Annamalai Music College was established. The Department of Indian Music at Madras University, which later became a major centre of music scholarship, was started in 1932 (1980: 254-5).

101 During these morning sessions, only basic exercises are practised. Practice of compositions and *rāgam* elaboration is typically done in the evening.

102 For example, the syllabus used in the Government College of Music in Madurai indicates that 8 *varṇams*, 30 *kīrttaṇais* in as many *rāgams*, 8 *pallavis*, and 5 *mallāris* (see Chapter 4) should be taught in three years.

103 At the time of research, students were given a monthly stipend of Rs. 100 at the government institutions.

104 It is also true that the extent of physical punishment varied from one *guru* to the next and that some students switched to a different *guru* because of the severity of the environment.

105 In schools in Palani and Tiruvaiyar, students and teachers live in the same dormitory, in an attempt to maintain the close personal connection between them.

106 For other similar examples of European reactions to temple music in South India, see Loti (1906: 26, 106),'The Civilian' (1921: 53), and Dubois (1986: 587).

107 The drums known under various names such as *dholak* and *dhole* in North India come in enormous morphological variety. The only common feature is that they are all double-headed drums, like the *tavil* (Deva 1977: 40).

108 *Tirumalai-Tirupati Devasthanam Epigraphical Series, Vol. II* (1933: 318-24).

109 *Tirumalai-Tirupati Devasthanam Epigraphical Series, Vol. V* (1937: 396-406).

110 *South Indian Inscriptions, Vol. IX* (1986: 643).

111 *South Indian Temple Inscriptions, Vol. I* (1982: 42-3). This evidence is quoted in Raghavan (1955) and Isaac (1964: 368).

112 Krishnadeva Raya is described to have had in his court thousands of women who served as palanquin bearers, doorkeepers, dancing-girls, warriors, wrestlers, and musicians including those who played 'pipes' (Sewell 1980: 249).

113 The *tēr* (or *radam*), which is often translated as a temple car, is a chariot-like vehicle on which the image of the deity is placed during the procession.

114 However, Nijenhuis and Gupta report that a priest used to dance in front of the deity to the accompaniment of the *nāgasvaram* in some Siva temples (1987: 197).

115 V.P.K. Sundaram (1985: 137) and Dick (1984b), however, equate *vangiyam* with *kuḻal* or *pullāṅkuḻal* (transverse flute).

116 For a detailed analysis of literary and iconographical evidence concerning wind instruments in North India, see Flora (1983).

117 At the Tyagaraja Swamy Temple in Tiruvarur, there are paintings containing valuable information on music. On the ceiling of the Devasriyan Mandapam, which is located in the third inner corridor (*prakāram*) of the temple, the exploits of the mythical Chola king Mucukunda are depicted in painted scenes. In one scene, the procession is accompanied by a number of musical instruments including those which resemble the type of *nāgasvaram* used in present-day temple rituals in Tiruvarur.

118 See *South Indian Inscriptions, Volume II/1* (1983: 3).

119 The *pañjamuhavāttiyam* has the large brass vessel as its body on top of which five tubular projections are attached. Each projection is covered with a skin. It is believed that Nandi (sacred bull) played this instrument when Siva danced (Das 1964), and these five 'faces' (*muham*) of the instrument correspond to the five 'faces' or manifestations of Siva, after which they are named. They are tuned in five different pitches. Six iconographical representations of this instrument are reported by Kuppuswamy and Hariharan (1985: 22, 23, 38, 41, 43, 60). In all examples, the instrument is depicted accompanying Nataraja's dance. In addition to these, Sambamurthy reports a bronze statue of Nataraja with a figure of a *pañjamuhavāttiyam* player (Banugopan) at His right foot at the Sivalokanatha Temple in Tiruppungur (Sirkazhi taluk, Tanjavur district) (1982b: 214). The only surviving player of

pañjamuhavāttiyam, Sankaramurtti (b. 1912), is attached to the Tyagaraja Swamy Temple in Tiruvarur. He is a descendent of Tambiyappa, a disciple of Muttusvami Diksitar. Sankaramurtti is in his seventies at present, without any capable successors. The instrument was discovered in the Marundeeswarar Temple in Thiruthuraipoondi (Thiruthuraipoondi taluk, Tanjavur district) (*The Hindu,* 1 October 1975), but its performance tradition has been discontinued. The term *pañjamuhavāttiyam* is of recent origin, and the instrument is referred to with its Tamil name, *kuḍavila* or *kuḍamula* in inscriptions and *tēvāram* hymns (Alavandar 1981: 103-5; Rangacharya 1985: 1434; Peterson 1989: 139).

120 The name Tyagaraja replaced its predecessor Vidivitankan in Tamil or Aruradhipadi m Sanskrit during the fifteenth and sixteenth centuries (Ponnusamy 1972: 24). See Ponnusamy for the history of the Tyagaraja Swamy Temple (1972: 28-45). Tyagaraja, the best known South Indian saint-composer, was named after this deity (Raghavan 1983: 36).

121 The badly damaged manuscript is in the possession of the families of T. S. Minakshisundaram Pillai (1916-88) and his younger brother T. S. Latchappa Pillai (1930-2013).

122 Music was, and still is, believed to have power to induce rain. Many anecdotes relating to the miracle evocation of rain by means of music are found in the Mahabharata, Puranams, and Jataka stories. Some *paṇs* (melodic modes used in ancient South India) and *rāgams,* such as Megaragakuranji, Megaranjani and Amrita Varshini are also known to be particularly effective for this purpose. See Sambamurthy (1982c: 246-52) for some of such anecdotes. Rain inducing *rāgas* have been also reported in *Hindustani* music (Neuman 1980: 67).

123 Interview with T.S. Latchappa Pillai (1986). Also see B.M. Sundaram (n.d.) and Krishnan and Latchappa (1988: 72). One of the two ivory *nāgasvarams* is displayed semi-permanently at the Tamil Isai Sangam Library in the Raja Annamalai Hall in Madras, whereas the other instrument is in the possession of the family of T.S. Latchappa Pillai.

124 The association of *rāgams* with certain times of the day is already mentioned in works such as Sangita Makaranda by Narada (c. 12th century), in which a certain number of correlations

with presently used *ragams* are found (Sambamurthy 1982c: 141-78). The tradition before Ramasami Diksitar's codification or what he based his system on is unknown.

125 Raghavan mentions the name of a *nagasvaram* player who was presumably Muttusvami Diksitar's disciple (1975b: 36), but his connection to contemporary musicians attached to Tyagaraja Swamy Temple is unknown.

126 Nijenhuis and Gupta report, more specifically, that a *nagasvaram* musician from Tanjavur named Rudra Paspati is said to have been responsible for the dissemination of some of Diksitar's compositions in Tanjavur during Diksitar's lifetime (1987: 102). Arunachalam, on the other hand, emphasizes the role of *nagasvaram* players in Tiruppamburam in preserving Diksitar's compositions (1989: 134). While the geographical association of Rudra Paspati is possibly Tiruppamburam, I could trace no musician by that name in the lineage of Tiruppamburam *nagasvaram* musicians during Diksitar's lifetime.

127 Some of the other important rites of adoration include *abisēkam* (bathing), *nēivettiyam* (feeding), *alaṅkāram* (decoration), and *dīpārādaṉai* (offering of light). Cf. Diehl (1956: 90).

128 The songs sung at *tiruppaḷḷiyaraiyerḷucci* are called *mēlukoluppu*. Kersenboom-Story provides the text of a *mēlukoluppu* she collected from P. Ranganayaki, former *dēvadāsi* from Tiruttani in North Arcot district (1987: 153-4). S. Ramanathan provides the notation and the text of two *mēlukoluppus* composed by Tyagaraja (1984: 114-7).

129 Rangaramanuja Ayyangar states that this system deteriorated in the second quarter of the twentieth century. He also relates his earliest personal experience of observing this system being violated in 1919 (1972: xii-xiii).

130 Neelayadakshi Kayarohaneshwarar Temple in Nagapattinam is an example of this (Interview with Nagapattinam G. Venkatesan, the *dēvastāṉa vittuvāṉ* of the temple, 1987).

131 In many small temples, the *Periya Mēḷam* is performed only during the *Sāyaraccai* ritual.

132 The music recital held as part of festivals is called *kōyil kaccēri*, distinguished from *kalyāṇa kaccēri* at wedding receptions and *sabhā kaccēri* is sponsored by cultural associations (*sabhās*). See Chapter 3 for more discussion on different types of *kaccēri*.

133 Interview with Tiruvalaputtur Balu (1989).

134 While some *vāhaṉams* are clearly related to the mythology of the deity, the significance of others is less certain. *Sesha* (snake), *Garuda* (bird), *Simha* (lion), and *Hanuman* (monkey king) are the common vehicles for the deity during the procession, but the pattern of assigning vehicles during the festival differs from temple to temple.

135 The time of commencing the procession seems to vary from one temple to the next. See B.M. Sundaram (1986: 87), and Ramanathan (1986: 11) for variations.

136 The first item performed by Bharata Natyam dancers is also known as *alārippu*, but there seems no apparent relation between these two. See Higgins (1973: 53-72) for a description of the *alārippu* in Bharata Natyam.

137 Sankaran believes that the term *mallāri* is related to *mallam* (wrestling), based on the importance of martial arts at previous temple festivals and the musicians' view of *mallāri* as 'wrestling with god' to make the deity set out for procession (Kersenboom-Story 1987: 77-8). It can be seen in the Manasollasa, an encyclopedia compiled in the twelfth century, that wrestling was an important form of entertainment in court life, along with music and dance. Kamat (1980: 68-72) also describes the popularity of wrestling in the social life of medieval Karnataka. In addition, a Portuguese trader, Domingo Paes, mentions dancing women who wrestled in the court of Krishnadevaraya (Sewell 1980: 268). Given the strong association of reed instruments with athletic activities in various parts of the world (Bryant 1990: 154), Sankaran's theory deserves further investigation. Jairazbhoy, on the other hand, suggests the connection between *mallāri* and *rāg* Malhar in North Indian music, based on linguistic similarity (1980: 155).

138 Berberich states that Adi (4+2+2), Misra Chapu (3+2+2), Sankirna Jati Triputa (9+2+2), Catrasra Jati Ata (4+4+2+2), and Kanda Chapu (2+3) are the commonly employed *tāḷams* for the *mallāri* (1974: 124).

139 Three speeds can be obtaining by doubling and halving the original speed. The technique of rendering a composition in faster or slower speeds is most commonly known as *aṉulōma* ('with the current'; the composition is played twice as fast

while the *tāḷam* is kept constant) and *pratilōma* ('against the current'; the composition is played twice as slow while the *tāḷam* is kept constant) respectively. However, some scholars define these two terms differently. Powers states that, *pratilōma* also refers to the doubling of the tempo of the rhythmic cycle while a composition is rendered in the same speed, in addition to the meaning given above (1980: 110). Others maintain that *aṉulōma* refers to the rendering of a melody in different speeds, whether faster or slower, whereas *pratilōma* is the rhythmic cycle itself rendered in different speeds while the melody is played in the same tempo (Sambamurthy 1982a: 33; Shankar 1985: 190, 206).

140 The first deviation occurred when a popular violin player Kunnakudi Vaidyanathan recorded a *mallāri* with *tavil* accompaniment on one of his commercial cassette tapes in the 1970s (Sankaran n.d.: 3). A well-known Bharata Natyam dancer, V.P. Dhananjayan, has also used a *mallāri* for a dance piece (Personal communication with Michael Nixon, 1990). As far as I know, however, no *mallāri* has ever been played in ritual context of temple procession on any other solo instruments but the *nāgasvaram*.

141 In fact, the type described here was called *periya mallāri*, to be distinguished from the other types of *mallāris* such as *taḷigai mallāri* which was performed during the *neyvēttiyam* ritual. Since the type played at the commencement of the procession is the only one practised in most temples at present, it is simply called *mallāri* in this study.

142 Rangaramanuja Iyengar, for example, remembers that Chinna Pakkiri played Begada *rāgam* for six hours (1977: 2).

143 The *eḍuppu* is the starting point of the text in rhythmic cycle.

144 For the connection of *pallavi* and *nāgasvaram* musicians, see Sangeeta Vimarsaka (1931) and B.M. Sundaram (1977).

145 *Tamil Lexicon* (1982: 3417).

146 Sankaran mentions elsewhere that Natakurinji is the most suitable of all *rāgams* for playing the *rakti mēḷam* (1976: 19). It is probable that the *rakti mēḷam* derived its name from *rakti rāgam* which refers to a type of *rāgam* best suited for elaboration in slow tempo, such as those mentioned above for *rakti mēḷam*. In this case, the *rakti rāgam* is contrasted to *ghana rāgam*,

those suitable for medium-tempo performance. However, the use of these two terms is not consistent. For example, the *ghana* ('heavy') *rāgam* is also considered ideal for extensive improvisation, and refers to the same *rāgams* categorized under the *rakti rāgam* in the above definition (Sambamurthy 1983: 16-7). In addition, the term *rakti* is also said to be the acronym of *rāgam, kaṇḍanam* ('five'), and *tīrumāṉam* ('conclusion'), which describes the musical characteristics of the *rakti mēḷam* (Interview with B.M. Sundaram, 1986; also see Sankaran 1986a: 73).

147 Sembonnarkoyil Ramasami Pillai (1880-1923) is said to have been its great exponent. See Chapter 5, Section 1 for more discussion. Musicians in Tiruvarur claim that the *rakti mēḷam* originated in the Tyagaraja Swamy Temple, and that only from the time of Ramasami this genre became strongly associated with Sembonnarkoyil *nāgasvaram* musicians.

148 One example of this is Parimala Ranganatha Temple in Tiruvirandur (Mayiladuthurai taluk, Tanjavur district) (Radhakrishna Pillai 1985).

149 *Padam* is a composition derived from the repertoire of music accompanying dance and characterized by romantic and devotional texts.

150 *Jāvaḷi* is another form of composition derived from dance repertoire, often with a textual theme of passionate or erotic love.

151 *Tiruppugaḷs* refer to compositions by Arunagirinada (15th century) characterized by the use of many unusual *tāḷams.*

152 Interview with T.S. Latchappa Pillai (1987). S. Ramanathan maintains that Heccarikka is played to welcome Rama when he arrives at the marriage hall (*kalyāṇa maṇḍapam*) in the temple (1984: 5).

153 Interview with Madurai M.P.R. Ayyasamy, the *dēvastāṉa vittuvāṉ* at the Sri Prasanna Venkatesa Perumal Temple in Madurai (1989).

154 Interviews with Madurai G.S. Mani (1987), N. Sivaramakrishnan (1987), and Balakrishnan (1989).

155 The custom of providing these privileges to temple musicians and dancers was recorded in a number of inscriptions from the Chola period onwards. See *South Indian Inscriptions, Volume II/2* (1984: 259-303) for example.

156 There are several musicians in the past who never skipped the temple duty for other engagements (Cf. Tanihai 1990).

157 A similar arrangement for temple priests (*gurukkal*) is reported by Singer (1972: 111-2).

158 As early as 1961, a well-known *nāgasvaram* musician, Tiruvidaimarudur Virusami Pillai (1901-73), made such a public plea as part of his presidential address at the annual Music Academy conference (1962: 15). The Report of the Backward Classes Commission, Tamil Nadu, also recommended that the minimum monthly remuneration be fixed at Rs. 200 per person (vol. 2, 1975: 24).

159 The retiring musician's recommendation often creates hard feeling among those who are not recommended against their expectation.

160 See Oddie (1984) and Nambi Arooran (1984) for the relationship between the *ādīnams* and Madams.

161 The other two are located in Darumapuram (Mayiladuthurai taluk) and Tiruppanandal (Kumbakonam taluk). See Nilakanta Sastri (1963: 116-9) for general description of the *ādīnam*, and Nambi Arooran (1981: 12/77-85) for the origin of these three *ādīnams*.

162 Interview with Injikkudi Kandasami Pillai (1987), who was the *ādīna vittuvāṉ* at Tiruvavadudurai Ādīnam from 1971 until his death in 1988.

163 A figure of Ponnusami Pillai is depicted in the wall-drawing inside the Marriage Hall in the Mysore court palace.

164 The Saivite saints whose hymns are sung at the temples by the *ōduvār* are known as *nāyaṉmār* (sing. *nāyaṉār*). The hymns of three most prominent *nāyaṉmār* are collectively called *tēvāram*, and they constitute the important vocal musical tradition in Saiva temples. See Peterson (1980) for a discussion on the significance of pilgrimage on *tēvāram* songs of Tamil Saivism. Vaishnava poet-saints (*āḻvārs*) composed hymns known as *prabandam*.

165 It is believed that when Diksitar composed and sang this *kīrttaṉai*, the closed temple door swung open and he had *darshan* (a glimpse) of the deity (Venkatarama Aiyar 1968: 40; Sambamurthy 1985b: 132-3).

166 Interview with Kilvelur N.G. Ganesan, the *dēvastāṉa vittuvāṉ* of the Akshayalinga Swamy Temple (1987). This composition, however, may be sung at concert hall recitals.

167 Interview with Nataraja Kambar (1987).

168 All the other instruments played in this temple are kept in the same room, and similarly are not to be taken outside of the temple.

169 Interview with Darumapuram A. Govindarajan (1989). Aghoramurthy is described as the furious aspect of Siva (Jagadisa Ayyar 1982: 262).

170 While a stone *nāgasvaram* is believe to have been played in several other temples as well, it is found only in Kumbeswarar Temple (Raghavan 1978). The origin and mythical explanation of this instrument is not known.

171 For the use of the *muhavīṇai* in *terukkūttu*, see Frasca (1990: 28-9).

172 The last player on *muhavīṇai*, Kudavasal Govindaraj, was replaced by his brother Ramamurtti, who played the regular 2-*kaṭṭai nāgasvaram*.

173 A similar observation is made by A. Srinivasan (1985: 1871).

174 While the sound produced by the entire ensemble is considered auspicious, the association of the *nāgasvaram* with auspiciousness appears particularly strong. The *tavil* is also described as an auspicious instrument (*maṅgala vāttiyam*) occasionally, whereas the *tāḷam* and *srutipeṭṭi* are never characterized as auspicious individually. The *ottu*, the predecessor of the *srutipeṭṭi*, was considered to exert auspiciousness as much as *nāgasvaram*. See Chapter 3 for discussion on the transition from the *ottu* to the *srutipeṭṭi*.

175 The four main categories used in the list is adopted from Pandey (1969: ix). This list is by no means exhaustive, and only a handful of important rituals of our immediate concern are listed in order to avoid the enormous detail necessary for the description. For details, see Pandey (1969), Kane (1968) and Chatteqee (1978). See Pandian (1987: 126-8) for an example of non-Brahman customs.

176 Rangaramanuja Ayyangar suggests that the four-day wedding was a norm before 1930 (1977: 5). Though referring to the custom in the Telugu-speaking areas, Padfield gives no hint of aberration from the five-day marriage ceremony (1975: 94-118). A one-day marriage ceremony was already noticeable in the 1950s, as reported in *Tanjore District Handbook* (1957: 140).

177 The wedding scene in films is ubiquitously accompanied by the music of *Periya Mēḷam* music, whether musicians appear on the screen or not. Also see Figure 4-5 for some visual representations of this association.

178 The invitation card is called *tirumaṇa aḷaippu* or more formerly *vivāha suba mūhurttap pattirihāi.* Two different sets of invitation cards are made, one for bride's side and the other for bridegroom's guests. The bride's family is responsible for making both sets. Each card is inserted into an envelope, four comers of which are often smeared with turmeric symbolizing the auspicious occasion.

179 The bridegroom used to get an expensive *vēṭṭi* (lower garment for men) in the past, but it is usually a Western-style suit that is presented today.

180 The red sports car appears to be a modern adaptation of the wedding cart with a red-curtained dome shaped top which was used in the past (Stevenson 1971: 66-7).

181 In some lavishly organized marriage ceremonies, a truck is hired for the musicians who sit on the back side and perform facing the bridegroom throughout the procession.

182 'English Note' or 'Note' (*nōṭṭu*) refers to pre-existing English brass band compositions to which Sanskrit text is added, or compositions inspired by them. They are composed in Sankarabharanam *rāgam* which is explained as corresponding to the Western major scale (Sambamurthy 1971a: 37; Raghavan 1977: iv), or in its derivatives such as Kundalavarali *rāgam.* The first to create 'Note' by setting Sanskrit text to brass band airs is said to have been Muttusvami Diksitar who was taken by his admirer and patron, Manali Venkatakrishna Mudaliar, to St. George Fort where he heard English bands (Venkatarama Aiyar 1968: 7-8; also interview with L.S. Rajagopalan, 1987). Diksitar even set the Sanskrit text for 'God Save the Queen'. Tyagaraja wrote a few compositions influenced by 'Note', two example being Sarasarasamaraikasura in Kundalavarali *rāgam,* and Ramimchuvarevaru in Subhoshini *rāgam.* Raghavan states that many performers of the last generation, especially instrumentalists, used to end their performances with a Note (1977: iv). Wolf, providing a concrete example to Raghavan's statement, reports that Karaikkudi Sambasiva Iyer (1888-

1958), a well-known *vīṇa* player, performed 'Notes' he himself composed at concerts (1989: 73). Sankaran further reports that Karur Chinna Devudu composed 'Notes' which were performed by Sanjeeva Rao (flute) and Madurai Mani Iyer (1987: 77). Particularly, Madurai Mani Iyer (1912-68) was known for his vocal renditions of 'Notes', and today his disciple T.V. Sankaranarayanan sometimes sings them. At present, however, 'Notes' are played almost exclusively by *Periya Mēḷam* musicians.

183 *Tamil Lexicon* (1982: 3232).

184 The description is based upon the author's observation of ten Brahman *muhūrttams* in 1986-7.

185 There is also a tendency among wealthy families to perform the marriage ceremony in a Western-style hotel.

186 Only those who cannot afford renting a hall have the ceremony at their house. I have witnessed only one such marriage ceremony in the quarter preserved for Scheduled Castes in south Madras. As explained later, marriage halls are in high demand in the marriage season, and if a ceremony has to take place in a short time, a hall may not be available.

187 Another *kīrttaṉai* which is sometimes played at this stage of the wedding is Janakirama by Tyagaraja in Suddasimantini *rāgam* (Interview with T.V.S. Sivasubramanya Pillai, 1987). However, although the use of these compositions during the *kāsiyāttirai* ritual is prevalent today, this performance practice may be of recent origin. Some older musicians believe that only Natakurinji *rāgam* was played during marriage ceremony.

188 However, some musicians consider Asaveri *rāgam* one of several *rāgams* not appropriate for auspicious occasions, and oppose its use at marriage ceremony (Interviews with S.R.D. Muthukumaraswami Pillai, 1987, et al.).

189 The text of this composition reads: 'Oh Raghuvira! Tyagaraja's Blessedness! Pray, come to my house; I bow to you. Bless me. I cannot bear the separation any longer. Till now, with unfulfilled desire, I have been in long and vexatious search for you. Pray, do come today at least, in your glory. My purpose in seeking you is to implore you every morning to teach me, to have the privilege of the Darsan of your enchanting face, to stand by your side and worship you every day, and thus be

blessed. Believing that you alone are my refuge, I have allowed myself to be in your grip. Why do you forget this and why do you not come to me promptly?' (Ramanujachari 1966: 303). Also see Jackson (1988: 25).

190 When the child marriage was prevalent, a young bridegroom and bride were placed on the shoulders of their respective maternal uncles during this ritual (Jagadisa Ayyar 1925: 55-7).

191 The exchange of garlands symbolizes the wish for a prosperous life based on mutual care and dependence (Sujatha 1987: 110).

192 The movement of the swing is representative of the disturbances likely to occur in the course of life ahead. The swing ritual is meant to caution the couple and advise them to remain steadfast to each other (Sasivalli 1985: 223; Sujatha 1987: 110).

193 Both *ūñjal* and *lāli* songs used to be an important part of *dēvadāsis'* repertoire. These songs were sung by them at *paḷḷiyarai sēvai*, the last of the daily rituals in which the deity is placed in the bed chamber (*paḷḷiyarai*) and lulled to sleep (Kersenboom-Story 1987). It is unknown whether Brahman women took over the *dēvadāsi*s tradition of singing these songs when the institution of *dēvadāsi*s were abolished. Thurston reports that Brahman women learned the marriage songs from childhood (1909, vol. 1: 290). At present, only older Brahman women know them.

194 The categories are determined by the context rather than musical structure or content.

195 Tyagaraja has composed several songs for this category. Seven of his compositions have been published with notation by S. Ramanathan (1984: 21-41). The most commonly heard *ūñjal* song today, however, is a Tamil composition, Kannunjaladiirundal, in Ananda Bhairavi *rāgam*. This *rāgam* is believed to lift the listener to a state of bliss (*ānandam*) (Rajam 1988: 41-3, et al.). Thyagarajan states that Suruti, Kurinji, Navaroj, Kapi, and Kanada *rāgams* are suited for marriage songs in addition to Ananda Bhairavi *rāgam* (1968: 24-5).

196 It is said that women used to be accompanied by *nāgasvaram* when they sang marriage songs (Personal communication with Michael Nixon, 1989). The descent of the pitch of *nāgasvaram* may be a reason for the discontinuation of this custom. As explained in Chapter 3, the tonic pitch of *nāgasvaram* was 4 or

5 (F or G) until around the 1920, corresponding to the range of female voice, but it has come down since then to 2 and 3 (D and E) today, which is too low a pitch for many women.

197 The *rasa*, often simplistically translated as mood, emotion, or sentiment, is an extremely complex aesthetic concept which permeates and provides the underlying unity of all artistic expression in India. See Raghavan (1975) for the history of *rasa* concept, and Vatsyayan (1968: 5-22), Prajnanananda (1973: 237-63), and Sambamurthy (1982b: 160-82) for the *rasa* concept as applied in music and dance.

198 See Seetha (1973), Berberich (1974: 168), Chellam Iyengar (1982), Rajam (1986a: 51), and Nijenhuis and Gupta (1987: 203) for the connection between these two *rāgams* and auspiciousness. Although the marriage ceremony takes place in the morning, Kalyani is usually considered an evening *rāgam* (Sambamurthy 1959: 289; Thyagarajan 1968: 23).

199 Muhari *rāgam* is believed to have *sōham* (sorrow) and *koruna* (pity, pathos) *rasas* (Subba Rao 1984: 163-4). Apart from the *rasa* theory, the Muhari has become synonymous with sadness and pessimism even for those who are unaware of what Muhari *rāgam* sounds like. An idiomatic expression in Tamil, '*muharipadade*' which literally means 'Don't sing *Muhari.*', signifies figuratively, 'Don't be pessimistic.' or 'Don't be sad.' (Personal communication with K. Narayanan, 1989). This notion is probably derived from or at least influenced by the association of Muhari *rāgam* with death. Muhari *rāgam* was sung or played at the funeral ritual (*karumādi*). Additionally, Muhari *rāgam* is also prominent in the scenes of the *terukkūttu* dance drama, when a wide range of melancholy and sadness are to be depicted (Frasca 1990: 82).

200 This exclusion of Ahiri *rāgam* is not only because of its association with pathos, but also due to the popular belief that if this *rāgam* is to be played in the morning, the musician will be deprived of his food for the day (Sambamurthy 1952: 10). See also Orr (1986: 31) for an anecdote concerning Ahiri *rāgam*.

201 In recent years, a Telugu composition in Revati *rāgam* by Annamacharya (b. 1424), Nanati Baduku, has been popular at marriage ceremonies. It may serve as a good example of the

weakening sense of the *ragam-rasa* relationship. While Revati *ragam* has *soham rasa*, and the text of this particular composition related to the uncertainty of life, the catchy melody has given the composition its current popularity at marriage ceremonies. Namagiripettai Krishnan, a popular *nagasvaram* player, has included this piece in his commercial cassette (Keerthana 6CA 501) possibly due to its popularity.

202 These *ragams* are known to portray only a single *rasa*, whereas others like Todi, Kalyani and Sankarabharanam have potentials for a variety of *rasas* including *soham rasa*, depending on the way they are rendered. Some musicians, however, claim that no *ragams* should be excluded on the ground that they were all created and given by god (Interview with Sikkal Natarajasundaram Pillai, 1987).

203 Although Sambamurthy reported that the *gettimelam* was also played by a brass band (1959: 186), I have never witnessed the *gettimelam* played by anything but *Periya Melam* ensemble.

204 Naturally, *Pa* is omitted when musicians are playing a *ragam* which does not utilize that *svaram.*

205 The officiating priest always gives a signal first, but he can often not be seen by the musicians because of the people surrounding the marriage dais.

206 For semiotic analyses of noise, see Attali (1985) and Yamaguchi (1988).

207 The *kurai podavai* is a nine-yard *sari* traditionally in red with a gold border.

208 These ritual occasions include *Avaniavittam* (annual changing of sacred thread), *Kartika dipam*, and *Varalakshmi Puja* (Interview with Rajam Raman, 1989).

209 Tying a *tali* around the bride's neck is a very important marriage rite in almost all parts of India except Bengal, although it is not referred to in the Vedas or Sutras (Chatteijee 1978: 243-5, 300-2).

210 Three knots are tied, the first two by the bridegroom, and the last by his sister.

211 See Chatteijee (1978: 179-80) for the different interpretations of this custom.

212 Kaliyaperumal states that Natakurinji *ragam* should be played during the *muhurttam*, so that the guests standing outside

of the hall come inside hearing this *rāgam* as a sign of the commencement of the ritual (1980: 125-6).

213 The *āṇandam* in different *rāgams* were played until the 1960s, especially the one in Bhairavi *rāgam* (Interviews with Kodandaram, 1987, and Sivasubramaniam, 1987; also see Sambamurthy 1952: 149). The reason for the present popularity of the Kapi *rāga māṇandam* is unknown.

214 The *maṇgalam* is a song of salutation, and it is the composition which concludes the performance in *Karnāṭak* music. In *Periya Mēḷam* music, the *maṇgalam* is sometimes omitted. Whether or not the *maṇgalam* is performed, musicians play a short improvisation on Madyamavati *rāgam* to end their performance.

215 When either the bridegroom's or bride's family live at a place far away from where the *muhūrttam* takes place, and thus unable to invite their guests to it, an additional reception is provided at the location of their residence at a later date.

216 *Report on an Enquiry into the Family Budgets of Middle Class Employees of the Central Government* (1949: 97).

217 Although the official ban on the temple dance was implemented in 1947 in Madras Presidency (Madras Devadasi Prevention of Dedication Act of 1947), the effect of the anti-Nautch movement which began in the late nineteenth century started to be felt much earlier. For the details of anti-Nautch movement and the transformation of Nautch into Bharata Natyam, see A. Srinivasan (1983, 1985) and Arudra (1986/87).

218 Well-known *nāgasvaram* musicians expect the interested party to visit them, refusing to make a visit themselves.

219 Summer months are considered best suited for auspicious functions, while the months of Aippasi (October-November) and Margazhi (December-January) are inauspicious, and few marriage ceremonies take place during these two months (K. Subramaniam 1974: 90-1).

220 The almost identical situation is reported concerning the position of *purōhidars* who also depend for the major portion of their income upon the remuneration from domestic rituals (K. Subramaniam 1974: 52-91).

221 When an *Isai Vēḷāḷar* musician sponsors a marriage ceremony for his daughter, fees are often not fixed because musicians regard their participation as a courtesy to the hosts who are often their relatives.

222 Interview with B.M. Sundaram (1987).

223 A similar incident has been reported about a musician who insisted on getting paid one rupee more than his rivals for his radio programmes (Luthra 1986: 300).

224 The reasons for migration vary from assuming an appointment at the Government College of Music as an instructor or at temples in town as *dēvastāṉa vittuvāṉs*, to provide educational opportunities for their offspring.

225 See Figure 4-7 for a caricature of *nāgasvaram* musicians' desire to display many gold coins attached to their instruments.

226 Interview with S.R. Ramamurtti (1986), a Brahman connoisseur of *Periya Mēḷam* music from Tanjavur district.

227 A few examples of such recordings include those by the Madurai Brothers (EMI S/33 ESX 6160), Tiruvalapputtur T.S. Balu (ECHO 6ECI101), and M.K.S. Siva (Shanthi SAC 2001, 1986). Recordings of marriage songs were made as early as the 1930s. For example, a set of four records of *nalaṅgu* and *ūñjal* songs with *nāgasvaram* accompaniment were released in 1936 from Hutchins & Company. However, these early recordings were meant to be gifts to the newlyweds instead of a replacement of the *Periya Mēḷam* ensemble (*The Hindu*, 24 October 1935; 30 April 1936).

228 Brahman women in the past learned a number of these marriage songs from their childhood (Thurston 1909, vol. 1: 290). The number of its practitioners is much smaller today, and the size of the repertoire is diminishing as well with fewer songs actually sung during the ceremony.

229 The use of film songs during the marriage ceremony and the reaction of a *nāgasvaram* musician are depicted even in a short fiction (Saranya 1988).

230 The typical instrumentation of such brass bands is 1 clarinet (leader), 1 to 2 alto saxophones, 1 to 2 trumpets, 1 snare drum, and 1 large drum. The hiring of a Western-style ensemble for weddings and other social occasions is common in other parts of India (Henry 1988: 218; Booth 1990).

231 When a *Periya Mēḷam* ensemble is engaged for Muslim or Christian weddings, it only provides welcoming music prior to the ceremony for arriving guests as a 'Band' does.

232 I was unable to find this author's full name, and the reference is made in this study as it is given in the literature.

233 In *Maha Vaittiyanadaiyar*, published in 1936, the term *viṉihai* was defined as *sangīta kaccēri* (music recital) (Saminadaiyar 1945: 26). This need for definition may indicate that the use of this term had been discontinued for some time.

234 L'Armand and L'Armand report that no *Periya Mēḷam* concert is found before the period of 1938-9 in their statistical samplings of every ten years between 1898 and 1977 (1983: 420). The very first concert-hall recital of *Periya Mēḷam* music I have a record of was performed in 1933 at the Music Academy as part of its music festival by Tiruvidaimarudur Virusami Pillai with Nidamangalam Minakshisundaram Pillai on *tavil*. This concert was held in the middle of the festival as a full-fledged recital, instead of simply fulfilling the ceremonial function at is beginning. In the English medium newspaper advertisement for this concert, the instruments were referred to as *nadhaswaram* and *dowl* respectively.

235 See Mahadevan (1988) and Orr (1990a) for examples.

236 Many *Isai Vēḷāḷars* were actively involved in politics from the early decades of the twentieth century (A. Srinivasan 1983: 81; Irschick 1986: 215).

237 *The Hindu* (12 January 1992).

238 As of 1988, 16 *nāgasvaram* and 14 *tavil* musicians have been awarded this title. *Periya Mēḷam* musicians consider the number of the titles given to them by Brahman-controlled *sabhās* disproportionately low.

239 The names of the featured soloist for the day, who was usually a vocalist, was announced in the newspaper. Judging from a sampling of the newspaper announcements (*The Hindu*) in 1930-6, very few *Periya Mēḷam* musicians performed on the radio during this period. For example, only two out of 348 radio performances I could trace for the year of 1935 were of *Periya Mēḷam* music.

240 This is also true for many years for musicians in Madurai until a separate station opened there in the late 1970s.

241 Although many of his radio programmes were recorded and kept in its Archives, they unfortunately may not be released for uses other than rebroadcasting by AIR.

242 The life of a staff artist at the two AIR stations in North India (Delhi and Lucknow) is cogently described by Neuman (1980: 178-86) and Kippen (1988: 27-31) respectively.

243 The only exception I know of is Tiruvizha Jayasankar who is a staff artist at the Trivandrum station in Kerala. Because of his college education, extremely rare among *Periya Mēḷam* musicians before him, he also works as an announcer.

244 At the Madras station, *nāgasvaram* players with lower grades are sometimes invited individually to perform with a *tavil* player the station selects. In this case, the *nāgasvaram* player is responsible for bringing the players of the other accompanying instruments (*tāḷam* and *srutipeṭṭi*).

245 Also an interview with Tanjore Brinda who served as a MAB member (1986).

246 Referring to the similar situation in North India, Neuman reports the problem in maintaining the objective standard which may be hampered by the gharana affiliations of the committee members (1980: 177). Also see Awasthy (1965: 40-1).

247 In contrast, on AIR Delhi station, the choice of *rāgs* is determined by the station (Personal communication with Daniel Neuman, 1991). This is probably because South Indian music is considerably more composition-oriented than *Hindustani* music, and the large size of the overall compositional repertoire in South Indian music makes it difficult for the station to select compositions which a given performer is able to play.

248 See *The Hindu* (13 December 1956), Isaac (1964: 402), and N. Rajagopalan (1990: 225). V. Gangadaram Pillai (b. 1898) of Kanchipuram insists that he was the very first to play with violin and *mridangam* in the AIR Madras station, accepting a suggestion from the station (Interview with V. Gangadaram Pillai, 1987).

249 *The Hindu* (11 December 1936)

250 *The Hindu* (23 January and 7 August 1935).

251 *Kalki* (11 August 1968); *The Hindu* (10 August 1968).

252 According to B.M. Sundaram, Sembonnarkoyil Ramasami Pillai was the very first *nāgasvaram* musician to make disc recordings (2001: 90)

253 Tanjavur district is still known as a land of temples with the highest concentration of temples per capita in Tamil Nadu. In 1971, the district constituted only 9 per cent of the population but 17 per cent of the temples in Tamil Nadu (Bouton 1985: 78).

254 Tanjore is a corrupted form of Tanjavur used by the British. Others define 'Tanjore Band' as a Western-style brass band first organized by a Maratha king (Seetha 1981: 111; Booth 1990). This interpretation might have been influenced by the existence of a 'Band' (see Chapter 4) named Tanjore Band which was actively performing in Madras around the 1930s.

255 While the term, *Karnāṭak*, to refer to a classical music tradition in South India is often linked by some scholars to the Vijayanagara core territory, which roughly corresponds to the present state of Karnataka (Raghavan 1970; A. Srinivasan 1984: 163), others believe that it is derived from a Tamil word *karnāṭakam* meaning something or someone old-fashioned (Kriya 1992: 257).

256 The concept of *bāṇi* is multi-layered in that it can refer to stylistic features of an individual musician, a group of musicians or a location, and its meaning changes considerably depending upon the context in which it is used. See Wolf for different terms which correspond to the 'style' (1989: 7-9). See Figure 6-1.

257 *Report on the Census of Madras Presidency, 1871* (vol. 2, 1874: 36).

258 *Report of The Backward Classes Commission, Tamil Nadu* (vol. 1, 1974: 175, 179).

259 Bouton divides Tanjavur district into five agro-economic zones. What is referred to here as the northern section corresponds to Bouton's Zone 1, which covers the sub-districts of Mayiladuthurai (western half), Tiruvidaimarudur, Kumbakonam, Nannilam (northern half), Papanasam (northern half), and Tiruvaiyaru (Map 3).

260 C.S. Lakshmi states that the Isai Velalar Sangam's second annual festival was held in 1940, but it is not clear whether the organization was known under that name at that time (1984: 14).

261 *Report of The Backward Classes Commission, Tamil Nadu* (vol. 2, 1975: 22).

262 The *karar* is an honorific form of *kāran* (a masculine termination for 'doer' or 'agent'). As in the case of *walla* in North Indian languages, it is attached as a suffix to various nouns, referring to 'he who does…', as in *vaṇḍikkāran* (vehicle+person, 'driver') and *tōṭṭakkāran* (garden+person, 'gardener').

263 *Report of the Backward Classes Commission, Tamil Nadu* (vol. 1, 1974: 175, 179).

264 *Report of the Backward Classes Commission, Tamil Nadu* (vol. 2, 1975: 49). The usage of the term *Mēḷakkārar* to refer to barber musicians began perhaps in the twentieth century.

265 The prestige of this term has its basis in classical Tamil literature in which the term was used to refer to the music played in the courts (A. Srinivasan 1985: 1876).

266 Many groups created new *jāti* names with the *Vēḷāḷar* suffix to claim a higher social/ritual status (*1901 Census of India, Vol.* 1: 184; Thurston 1909, vol. 7: 376-7). At least two spellings exist for this *jāti*: Vellala and Velalar. Although they appear interchangeably, the agriculturalist Vellalas tend to make the distinction between themselves and *Isai Vēḷāḷars* by consistently using the different spelling.

267 Interview with Radhakrishna Pillai (1989). T.S. Latchappa (b. 1930) also provided the identical information based on what he had heard from his senior relatives. In addition, T. Sankaran also asserts that the traditional occupation of a *jāti* under the same name was to provide music in the temple in the 18th century (n.d.: 7).

268 Govindarajan further equates Nagapasattar with present-day Nagapattinam, an historically important port town since the time of the Chola dynasty.

269 Yet, Dirks uses the term *Mēḷakkārar* exclusively to refer to the players of *Periya Mēḷam* in Pudukkottai district (1987).

270 Personal communication with Nishimura, 1987.

271 The *Report of Backward Classes Commission, Tamil Nadu* states the merger or close identity between *Isai Vēḷāḷar* and *Seṅgundar jātis* in South Arcot, Chingleput, Coimbatore, and Tirunelveli districts and that some *Isai Vēḷāḷar* might have taken to weaving (vol. 2, 1975: 24). Some musicians in Madurai use *Seṅgundar Isai Vēḷāḷar* interchangeably with *Isai Vēḷāḷar* (Interview with M.A. Meera, 1986).

272 A controversy concerning the correct name of the instrument erupted in the mid-1930s *in The Hindu*. This controversy, in which three different names (*nāgasvaram, nādasvaram,* and *nāgachiṉṉam*) were advanced as the correct name of the instrument (Raghavan 1936; Sarma 1936; K. Ramachandran

1937), and the occasional resurgence of this issue since that time serve as a revealing contradiction between theory and practice (Raghavan 1949, 1955; Isaac 1964, 1975; Kuppuswamy and Hariharan 1985). The most striking overall disparity is that, despite scholars' continuous insistence on *nāgasvaram* as the correct term, the mass media, recording industry, and laymen have used *nādasvaram* while musicians call the instrument both *nādasvaram,* and by yet another term, *nāyanam.* Beyond this general tendency, different combinations of contextual variants can affect the actual usage of these terms. For the linguistic connections of each term to the names of aerophones in other areas, see Jairazbhoy (1970, 1980) and Deva (1975).

273 While the most basic meaning of *dār* is wealth, it refers to a substantial person when it is used as an affix as in *jamīndār* (Fabricius 1972: 511).

274 Perhaps because of the different levels of prestige and auspiciousness accorded to the *ottu* and *srutipeṭṭi,* visual representations of the *Periya Mēḷam* ensemble still often include an *ottu* player instead of a *srutipeṭṭi* player, although the *ottu* has been replaced by the *srutipeṭṭi* for at least fifteen years. See Figures 4-5c and 4-6b for example.

275 See Sankaran (1961: 27) and Natarajasundaram Pillai (n.d.). Also interview with Madurai G.S. Mani (1987). Also see Chapter 3 for his role for creating a new category of *tavil* musicians.

276 The prime example is the former movie superstar and Chief Minister of Tamil Nadu, M.G. Ramachandran, who was more frequently than not referred to as M.G.R.

277 See *Tamil Lexicon* (1982: 3361) and Rottler (1834: 123).

278 *Mēḷam* also refers to the parental modal system. Venkatamakhi, a renowned musicologist of the seventeenth century, is credited for the systematization of a *rāgam* classification in which each of the existent *rāgams* belongs to one of 72 *mēḷams.* *Nāgasvaram* musicians sometimes use this term synonymously with *rāgam.*

279 In my survey, the first distinction between *Periya Mēḷam* and *Ciṉṉa Mēḷam* was made by T. Venkasami Row in his The Manual of Tanjore District (1883: 198-9). Sathyanarayana states that the difference between *Periya Mēḷam* and *Ciṉṉa Mēḷam* lies in the size of *nāgasvaram* used in each ensemble (1987: 62),

but this view is not supported by musicians themselves or other scholars. The Kannada equivalent of *Periya Mēḷam* and *Ciṇṇa Mēḷam* are *Dodda Mēḷa* and *Ciṇṇa Mēḷa* or *Cikka Mēḷa* respectively.

280 For example, in the patrilineal lineage of Sembonnarkoyil Ramasami Pillai (1880-1923), fifteen *nāgasvaram* musicians can be identified in the last five generations while there has been no *tavil* player. Similarly, in the lineage of Tirucherai Kalyanasundaram Pillai (1918-89), ten *nāgasvaram* musicians can be identified in the last five generations whereas there was only one *tavil* player.

281 An anecdote which speaks to respectability of the profession of *ottu* playing concerns about a saint *ottu* player who lived during the reign of Tolaja II (1764-87). Because of his intense devotion to god and the art of playing *ottu*, he acquired the skill of producing the drone without actually blowing into the instrument. When Tolaja noticed the *ottu* player's extraordinary skill and his intense devotion, he built a hall for the *ottu* player to meditate at the north entrance of Tanjavur. It is known as the *ottukkāra maṇḍapam* (*ottu* player's hall) or *mauṇasvāmi maṇḍapam* (meditator's hall).

282 Several anecdotes concerning the penalty to *tavil* musicians who violated the custom have been related to me. As recently as around 1970, a *tavil* player who came late was denied the right to perform by the *nāgasvaram* musician who could not tolerate the lack of respect on the part of his accompanist.

283 As Jordan (1989) aptly describes, the shifting concept of the *dēvadāsi*s was a manifestation of the emerging worldview of the Indian elites who, with their Western liberal values influenced by Christianity, sought to define a national culture.

284 Kurainadu Natesa Pillai is said to have decided to switch professions from a *naṭṭuvaṇār* to *nāgasvaram* player when he was treated as a mere panderer to *dēvadāsi*s (Interview with B.M. Sundaram (1987).

285 B.M. Sundaram provides the following episode from the 1920s concerning hierarchy among *Isai Vēḷāḷars* (Interview, 1986). When a well-known *nāgasvaram* musician (A), did not receive customary respect from a *naṭṭuvaṇār* (B), he made a statement offensive to the profession of *naṭṭuvaṇārs*. Greatly insulted, B

asked a *nāgasvaram* musician reputed for his complex *pallavis* (C), to play a *pallavi* in an extremely rare and difficult *tālam* at the temple in Mayiladuthurai where A was scheduled to perform. As mentioned before, the visiting musician was customarily to follow up the *rāgam* and *pallavi* which the local musician had selected/composed and played for a short while. Unable to follow the *pallavi* played by C, A was humiliated and angered especially because his son (D) was married to C's daughter (E). A's indignation was largely derived from C's consent to a 'mere *nattuvanār*' to humiliate him. A expelled E from his house, and told her not to come back until her father (C) apologized him for his inconsiderate behavior to a close relative. C refused A' s request for his apology, maintaining his conviction that competitiveness was an accepted element of the profession. E remained at C's house for the rest of her life, unable either to return to her husband or to remarry.

286 Ramasami's first son, S.R. Govindasami, played the second *nāgasvaram* to Ramasami. After Ramasami's death, Govindasami and his brother, S.R. Dakshinamurthy played together as the Sembonnarkoyil Brothers. They recorded a very abbreviated version of *rakti mēḷam* (labelled as 'rathi mēḷam') in Kamboji *rāgam* for two 78 rpm discs (Columbia GE 823-824).

287 Govindasami's two sons, S.R.G. Rajanna and S.R.G. Sambandam played in 1984 a version of *rakti mēḷam* for Sampradaya, an organization dedicated to preservation of traditional music, which recorded it for archival purpose with the awareness that this form might fall into oblivion in the next generation. Dakshinamurthy's two sons, Muthukumaraswami and Vaidyanathan, are also regarded as contemporary exponents of *rakti mēḷam* (Sankaran 1964), and they were asked to give a lecture-demonstration on this form at the Music Academy in 1984.

288 The other *nāgasvaram* musician conferred the *Saṅgīta Kalānidhi* title was Tiruvidaimarudur Virusami Pillai in 1962. No *tavil* musicians have yet received this title.

289 The *rāgamalika* ('garland of *rāgams*') refers to a successive rendition of several different *rāgams.*

290 Many *Isai Vēḷāḷar* musicians believe that Muttu Tandavar was a *nāgasvaram* musician himself.

291 T.N. Sivasubramania Pillai eventually switched to vocal music, and is known better as a vocalist today.

292 Interview with T.V.S. Sivasubramania Pillai (1987).

293 While this observation is based upon my own interviews and contacts with musicians and *rasikars*, a similar view has been advanced in academic literature and popular journals (Isaac 1964: 384; Rangaramanuja Ayyangar 1977: 34; Mahadevan 1988; Orr 1990a). The glorification of the past in *Periya Mēḷam* music was found as early as 1931 (K. Ramachandran 1931).

294 The unfavourable economic climate and current lack of respect for *Periya Mēḷam* musician was depicted even in a short story in a popular Tamil magazine, *Kungumam* (Saranya 1988: 17-20).

295 One of the earliest attempts to give names and brief descriptions of master musicians was made by Abraham Pandither in his *Karunamirtha Sagaram*, published in 1917, in which the names of ten *nāgasvaram* musicians are included (1984: 151-205).

296 All *soma* and *dohl* players in Afghanistan are reported to be barbers themselves or related closely to barbers (Sakata 1983: 79). Slobin also reports the inseparable connection of barbers and music-making in northern Afghanistan, though he does not mention the instruments they play (1976: 31-3). Although Tsuge mentions barbering as a common avocation for musicians in the Islamic world, he only cites Sakata's work mentioned above (1991: 67-8).

297 The following district gazetteers have references to the connection between barber *jātis* and music-making, types of instruments they play, or names of instruments. For Tamil Nadu, see volumes for South Arcot (1962: 153-4), Coimbatore (1966: 209), Salem (1967: 137, 345-6), Ramanathapuram (1972: 496), and Pudukkottai (1983: 458). For Andhra Pradesh, see volumes for Cuddapah (1967: 693), Anantapur (1970), Nizamabad (1973: 38, 131, 351), Karimnagar (1974: 156), Kurnoor (1974: 150, 423), Adilabad (1976: 120), Mahbubnagar (1976: 123), Medak (1976: 296), Warangal (1976: 137), Guntur (1977: 214), Khammam (1977: 110), Krishna (1977: 149, 411), Nellore (1977: 129), Nalgonda (1978: 125, 327), Chittoor (1979: 120, 401), East Godavari (1979: 144), Srikakulam (1979: 120, 343), Visakhapatnam (1979: 139, 413), West Godavari (1979: 145), Hyderabad (1983: 145). For Karnataka state, see volumes

for Tumkur (1969: 301). Also personal communications with H.L. Nagegowda (1987) and Gayathri Kassebaum (1991).

298 The affiliation of barbers with *Periya Mēḷam* music is also stated in non-academic journals (Mackenzie 1987: 59).

299 Also see Siraj-ul-Hassan (1920: 468) for the association of barbers with *shahnāī* (*sanai*) and drums in the territory of Nizam. However, Dube states the *Madigas* (*dalits*) play drums and pipes while making no mention of the connection between barbers (*Mangali*) and music-making in Shamirpet, a village near Hyderabad (1955: 114).

300 Yet, Day was perhaps the first to provide the morphological description of instruments used in *Periya Mēḷam* (1891: 140, 147-8).

301 The *Paṛaiyars* are mostly agricultural labourers. The folk instrumental ensembles known as *naiyāṇḍi mēḷam* which features *nāgasvaram* are performed today by those belonging to this *jāti*. The street *nāgasvaram* musicians, who go from one house to the next, playing short popular songs on *nāgasvaram* to receive small amounts of money, also belong to the *Paṛaiyar jāti*, but they never play *Karnāṭak* music compositions nor extensive free rhythm improvisation. They are seen most frequently alone, but sometimes with another person accompanying on a drum.

302 Shoberl's observation corresponds to the non-association of barbers with music making in present-day Kerala.

303 Jagadisa Ayyar, however, suggests a more recent origin of barbers playing 'Maṅgaḷa Vādyam' for auspicious rites (1925: 41).

304 The existence of a small number of barber musicians is mentioned by Ananthakrishna Iyer (1912: 366).

305 The use of this term goes back to the time of Chola dynasty, as appeared in inscription from the same period.

306 *Maruttuvar* is the only term used for barbers in a Tamil Nadu Government publication, *Tanjore District Handbook* (1957: 135). The absence of the term *ambaṭṭaṉ* is notable, though this book only includes the people of Tanjavur district. In surveying the Backward Classes, the Kaka Kalelkar Commission (1955) also employs the term *Maruthuvar* for Tamil-speaking barbers.

307 The suffix *ar* is an honorific form of *an*. Non-barbers tend

to use *Ambaṭṭaṉ* to refer to barbers, whereas barbers quite naturally refer to themselves as *Ambaṭṭar*, if they choose to use the term. While *aṉ*-ending is much more frequently used for barbers in common parlance due to their low social status, *ar*-ending is used in this study for consistency.

308 The replacement of traditional doctors with Western-style hospitals in Karnataka state was reported as early as in 1931 (Rao and Ananthakrishna Iyer 1931: 447).

309 According to Thurston, the etymology of the *Pariyāri* is a doctor, and it is a term referring to Tamil barbers (*Ambaṭṭaṉ*) (1909, vol. 6: 158). In contrast, Sherring reported that *Pariāris* (or *Velakatharas*) were barbers for Brahmans and *Nairs* in Travancore (Kerala) and Tirunelveli (1881: 182).

310 In a broader sense, the term *Nāidu* refers to non-Brahmans who migrated from Andhra Pradesh to Tamil Nadu under Nayak rule, and it is not confined to a single *jāti* of barbers (Cf. Thurston 1909, vol. 5: 138; Bouton 1985: 123).

311 The *Isai Vēḷāḷars* and *Nāidus* were described by Thurston as two *jātis* associated with *Periya Mēḷam* music in Tanjavur as Tamil *Mēḷakkār* and Telugu *Mēḷakkār* (1909, vol. 5: 59).

312 This type of ensemble is sometimes referred to as *Karnatak Band* as well, possibly in order to distinguish it from those which play Western compositions. See Chapter 4, Section 2 for the performance context of this type of ensemble.

313 The promotional photograph of *Nadamuni Band* which appeared in *The Hindu* in 1936 showed the following instrumentation: 2 clarinets, 2 trumpets, 2 saxophone, 1 trombone, 2 tuba, 1 snare drum, 1 bass drum, and 1 pair of cymbals, and 1 *tavil*. All the members wore Western-style uniforms including caps. The only exception is the *tavil* player who maintained the traditional attire of *vēṭṭi*, although he had a Western-style shirt on as opposed to having the upper torso bare. Balakrishna Naidu in Tanjavur and Chinnakrishna Naidu in Tiruchirappalli were two other clarinet players who were very popular during this period (Ellarvi 1970: 40).

314 Interviews with G.S. Mani (1987), B.M. Sundaram (1987). Balaraman is widely believed to have belonged to a barber *jāti*, but his exact *jāti* affiliation is unknown.

315 A *nāgasvaram* musician who played for a Muslim social

gathering was fined stiffly by the trustee of the temple to which he was attached (Interview with B.M. Sundaram, 1987).

316 Radhakrishna Naidu was a clarinet player for the internationally known Bharata Natyam dancer T. Balasaraswati (1918-84) (Sankaran 1984a: 64; Knight 2010: 262).

317 See Iyer (1948) for example.

318 Cf. N.M. Narayanan (1973, 1991).

319 Interview with A.V. Narayanappa (1987).

320 A.K.C. Natarajan is Kuppusami Naidu's son-in-law, although the former never studied with the latter. Three *Isai Vēḷāḷar* musicians mentioned are *dēvastāṇa vittuvāṇs* at the Prasanna Venkatesa Perumal Temple, the Meenakshi Sundareswarar Temple, and Alakal Temple respectively. Interviews with Alagusundaram (1989), Ayyasamy (1987, 1989), and G.C. Balaraju (son of Kuppusami Naidu, 1989).

321 The Chennakesava Perumal Temple itself was built by endowments from Nagu Baitan, the powder-maker for the Company (Roche 1975: 395). The present structure was constructed in 1780 by Manali Muttukrishna Mudaliar, a *dubāsh* of Governor Pigot and one of the major patrons of classical music of his time (Krishnaswami Nayudu 1965: 9).

322 The modified version of this article appears in Sambamurthy (1982d: 140-52).

323 Vaidyanatha Bhagavathar recollects that both Tirumarugal Natesa Pillai and Sembonnarkoyil Ramasami Pillai were presented with a gold *nāgasvaram* (*taṅga nāgasvaram*) for their excellent performance one year (1986: 18).

324 Interview with Kottur Rajarattinam Pillai (1987).

325 *Karnataka Backward Classes Commission Report* (vol. 2, 1975: 75). Based on his fieldwork in Mysore district in 1969-71, Bhat suggests that barbers known as *Hajāma* are invited to play music during the weddings (1984: 56, 133). *Hajām*, along with *Naī* and *Naīn*, is the common term to refer to barbers in North India (Bhattacharya 1968: 243).

326 Another senior *nāgasvaram* musician in Bangalore, Damarur Sanjiwappa, studied with Govindarajan's father Darumapuram Abiramasundaram Pillai (1912-62), the *ādīṇa vittuvāṇ* of Darumapuram *Ādīṇa.*

327 Interviews with N.G. Ganesan (1987) and M. Kodandaram (1987).

328 The highest grade given by AIR is A-Top, but no *nāgasvaram* musician holds this grade in either station (See Section 3 for the detail of AIR grading system).

329 For Sarabhoji's predilection to Western music, see Seetha (1981: 111).

330 Interview with V. Subramaniam, a great grandson of Seshanna (1987). Seshanna is usually identified as the founder of modern Mysore school of *vīṇa* playing, one of the four or five major styles recognized in South India (Interview with B.V.K. Sastri, 1987; Wolf 1989: 93-102).

331 Interviews with Shivananda Bekal (1987), programme executive at the All India Radio, Mangalore station, and A.V. Narayanappa (1987).

332 As of 1987, only three saxophone musicians were on the payroll as casual artists at this station, including Gopalnath, Venkatappa Dogra, and Moodabidri M.S. Gopalakrishna.

333 Gopalakrishnan is a Tamil Brahman from Kerala. His brother, N. Gopalkrishna Iyer, has a small private music school, Kalaniketan, in Mangalore, where Gopalnath studied music. Gopalakrishnan is one of the few *Karnāṭak* musicians known for discovering and promoting young talented musicians.

334 The criticism of Gopalnath's music is usually directed to the limitation of the instrument, rather than his musicianship. On the contrary, his skill to compensate the limitations of the instrument is often a point of praise among his listeners.

335 Gopalnath's foreign tours include his participation in Jazz Festival in Prague in 1982 and Berlin Jazz Festival in 1983, where he performed with German jazz musicians.

336 Interviews with Rajasekar Iyer (1987) and Kadri Gopalnath (1987).

337 Based on oral history, Sheik Adam Saheb estimates that the Muslim *nāgasvaram* tradition is about 300 years old (1975: 63-4). Sheik Chinna Moulana provides the identical estimation (n.d.; Chandramouli 1987: 5). Several Muslim *nāgasvaram* musicians such as Madurai Madgani Saheb and Madurai Peeru Saheb were known in the Madurai area in the early decades of the twentieth century, but I have no data concerning their connection with Andhra Muslim musicians.

338 *The Hindu* (14 January 1964).

339 Personal communication with U. Gopalakrishna Sarma (1986). One such example is Sheik Madeena Saheb who has been attached to the Sri Venugopalaswamy Temple in Krishnapuram (Visakhapatnam district) (P. Srinivasan 1988: 5). Even earlier, Chilakaluripet Peddamaula Sahib (1890-1948) was a *dēvastāṉa vittuvāṉ* at the Sri Lakshmi Narasimha Swami Temple in Chilakaluripet (Personal communication with B.M. Sundaram, 1992)

340 Interview with Bismillah Khan (1988).

341 Pavadai gives Moulana's birth year as 1924 (1980: 38).

342 *The Hindu* (26 January 1963).

343 He studied with Nachiyarkoyil K. Rajam and K. Duraikkannu Brothers, *Isai Vēḷāḷar* musicians, while in the Tanjavur area (Pavadai 1980: 38).

344 Chinna Moulana believes and publicly states that Rajarattinam Pillai was the unparalleled *nāgasvaram* musician of all times (*The Hindu*, 14 January 1964; also personal communication with Chinna Moulana, 1987).

345 Chinna Moulana is very popular among younger *Isai Vēḷāḷar* musicians in the Tanjavur area as well. If some senior *Isai Vēḷāḷar* players' appraisal about Moulana's style is to be believed, his popularity would indicate a change in the aesthetic predilection in Tanjavur. The criticism against Chinna Moulana's music tends to centre around his tonguing technique (*tuttukkāram*) and the resulting deviation from correct delineation of the text (See Chapter 3).

346 While Chinna Moulana's school known as Saradha Nadhaswara Sangeetha Ashram, established in 1982 (Malarvizhi n.d.: 68), was open to anyone, as of 1987, most students were Muslims from Andhra Pradesh, many his own relatives.

347 The similarities include the size of the body of instruments, the size of the reed, the material of which the reed is made, and the length of staple.

348 Thurston reports that the title Panicker was used by barbers, *Kammalan, Marar, Panan,* and *Paṟaiyan* in addition to *Nāyar* (1909, vol. 6: 54). This may suggest the potential connection between barbers and the *Periya Mēḷam* music in central Kerala. *The Cochin Tribes and Castes* by Ananthakrishna Iyer includes a photograph of *Marar* musicians, one of whom appears to be

holding an instrument resembling the *kuṟuṅkuḻal* (1912: facing 147), but the degree of participation by the *Marars* in *kuṟuṅkuḻal* playing is unknown.

349 The *kuṟuṅkuḻal* ('short pipe') is between 30 and 45 centimetres long. Apart from the difference in size, a major difference between *kuṟuṅkuḻal* and *nāgasvaram* is that the former has a thumb hole (L.S. Rajagopalan 1975).

350 However, three music schools managed by the temples began offering training on *kuṟuṅkuḻal* recently to prevent the total disappearance of this tradition (L.S. Rajagopalan 1988: 43).

351 By the eighteenth century, Tamil Brahmans had migrated to serve the Rajas of Travancore and Cochin as tutors, temple managers, cooks, and personal servants (Lewandowski 1980: 20).

352 Interview with P. Kuttikrishna Nayar (1987), the *dēvastāna vittuvāṉ* at the Krishna Temple in Guruvayur (Trichur district). Kuttikrishna Nayar studied in the Tanjavur area himself for ten years with Kumbakonam D.G. Natesa Pillai; and his son was also undergoing training in the Tanjavur area at the time of the interview.

353 Also, interviews with M.K.K. Nayar (1987), Nataraja Kambar (1987). An example of Sankaranarayana Panicker's playing was recorded and released by John Levy as part of an anthology of South Indian music (Everyman SRV-73011).

354 As mentioned in Chapter 4 (Section 1), the existence of female 'pipers' in Vijayanagara royal court was reported by Portuguese travelers in the sixteenth century (Sewell 1980), although the instruments described by them cannot be ascertained as *nāgasvaram* or any type of double-reed aerophone.

355 Interviews with B.M. Sundaram (1986) and Muthukumaraswami Pillai (1987). See Trawick for examples of believed consequences caused by menstruating women touching other objects (1990: 51).

356 Because of the strenuous nature of its practice and performance, there is a belief that *nāgasvaram* playing is hazardous to one's health and even causes early death (see Chapter 6, Section 1). Cf. Durga (1979: 82).

357 Tiruvarur Latchappa Pillai also remembers one Kunjudam, a *dēvadāsi*, practising *nāgasvaram* in Tiruvarur in the 1940s.

There is evidence relating to the existence of women playing *nāgasvaram* even earlier in the 1930s (*The Hindu*, 24 October 1935). Sankaran estimates the emergence of women *nāgasvaram* musicians at around 1920s (1987: 61).

358 Her first performance for AIR was in 1946 at the Tiruchirappalli station.

359 *Dinamalar* (21 May 1988).

360 Interview with M. A. Meera (1986). The silk *sari* manufactured in Kanchipuram is famous all over India and is considered classier and more expensive than that produced elsewhere. A young *nāgasvaram* player, Susila, also decided to take up the instrument after seeing Ponnuthayi during the festival procession at Cinnakadai Amman Temple (Interview with Madurai Ponnuthayi, 1989).

361 Some popular female *nāgasvaram* musicians during this period include Tanjavur T.K. Saradambal, Tanjavur T.K. Sarasvati Bai, Tanjavur M.M. Pappa, Parttiyaral M.S. Baby Minakshi, Mannargudi S. Rajalakshmi, and Mayuram T.K. Sarasvati (Interview with Ponnuthayi, 1989).

362 Ponnuthayi is the only female player whose name is recognized all over South India. She is often described as having played like a good male musician. Although this type of judgement may sound bluntly sexist, the intention of the commentators to show respect to Ponnuthayi's achievement is usually genuine.

363 Ponnuthayi reports that there was no resistance from male *tavil* players to perform with her.

364 Tiruvarur Latchappa Pillai recollects that Rajarattinam Pillai used to hit his accompanist during the performance if the latter did not exhibit the competence he expected.

365 A letter Ponnuttayi received from Rajarattinam Pillai in 1945 was treasured in her possession.

366 Interviews with M.A. Meera (1986), Vaidesvarankoyil R. Selvambal (1987), Madurai Ponnuttay (1989), and Mambalam K.R. Premalata and K.R. Sarasvati (1989). Reynolds, in contrast, reports that oil bath is prohibited for menstruating women (1978).

367 This is a reason for the great importance given to a ritual known as *nombu* performed by a wife to promote well-being of her husband. See Harper (1969: 86) and Reynolds (1980: 55-6).

368 Interview with Ponnuthayi (1989). Also see an interview with Ponnuthayi appeared in *Ananda Vikatan,* a popular Tamil weekly magazine (Sauba 1990: 13-4). After many years of public neglect, Ponnuthayi was awarded the prestigious *Kalaimāmaṇi* title toward the end of her life for her achievement by the Tamil Nadu Government in 1990 (*Dinamani,* 15 April 1990).

369 The resistance among orthodox Brahmans against playing *mridangam* in the early 1930s is reported by a renowned *mridangam* player T.K. Murthy (b. 1924). He had to hide his interest and aptitude for playing *mridangam* until his talent was recognized by a famous musician of the time (P.C. Jayaraman 1988: 17).

370 Nevertheless, the polluting quality of the flute was a major hindrance at the initial stage of its introduction, and several players learned to play the flute with their nostrils to avoid the contact with saliva (Sankaran n.d.: 2). Sarabha Sastri (1872-1904), a Tamil Brahman, is said to have been responsible for elevating the flute to a solo concert instrument (Ramachandra Sastri 1986: 35; Ramani 1986: 40). He was encouraged to learn music because he became blind when he was an infant (Sambamurthy 1985a: 69).

371 Several *Isai Vēḷāḷar nāgasvaram* musicians remember that a Brahman named Narasimha Iyengar in Madras played *nāgasvaram* in *sabhā* recitals in the 1940s, having studied with Tiruppamburam Swaminatha Pillai (a famous flute player, see Section 1). Yet, he performed neither for domestic functions nor at temples, and his involvement in performance is regarded as a hobby, probably thus acceptable to other Brahmans (Interview with T.V.S. Sivasubramanya Pillai, 1987).

372 Many *Periya Mēḷam* musicians believe that *nāgasvaram* and *tavil* are not depicted to be played by deities because these instruments were created by gods for humans to play for them. This belief is reiterated by Tumilan (1988: 54).

373 It is often argued that the poverty of his family was the immediate reason for Lakshminarasimhan's decision to become a *nāgasvaram* player, as is said to have often been the case with instrumentalists in *Karnāṭak* music earlier in the twentieth century.

374 Some Brahman students are studying *nāgasvaram* and *tavil* in *gurukulavāsam* at their *guru's* house instead of enrolling at the college (Interview with Tanjavur Godandapani, 1986).

375 *The Hindu* (8 April 1964).

376 Thurston also reported by quoting the 1901 Census that *Vairavi*, a sub-caste of *Paṇḍāram* in Tirunelvelli district, was a *jāti* associated with *Mēlakkārans* (1909 7: 271) who are servants at the temples of *Nattukottai Chettis* in Madurai district.

377 He has left many commercial recordings, as well as played *nāgasvaram* for a popular film, *Koñjum Salaṅgai* (see Chapter 4, Section 3). Surprisingly, very little is known about his life, given his enormous success as a musician.

378 Levinson even relates *Seṅgundam Mudaliyār* directly with temple musicians (1982: 102). This equation may be explained by, as Beck herself points out, the loss of distinctness of this group after the abolition of temple dancing, and by their increasing merging with other *Mudaliyār jātis* (1972: 208).

379 See *Madras District Gazetteers: Coimbatore* (Baliga 1966) and *Salem* (Baliga 1967). Yet, Beck made no mention of barbers (*Nāvidar*) as temple musicians.

380 For example, see M. Narayanan (1987: 7).

381 Also, interview with Nataraja Kambar (1987).

382 *Report of the Backward Classes Commission, Tamil Nadu* provides this figure based upon the memorandum submitted by the caste association (vol. 2, 1975: 104-5). The figure was possibly placed lower than actual amount of earning in order to achieve governmental assistance.

383 The tragic incidents include some gruesome consequences such as a *nāgasvaram* musician in Tiruchendur poisoning his own son due to professional jealousy.

384 Three distinguished *Isai Vēḷāḷar nāgasvaram* musicians, Tiruvidaimarudur Virusami Pillai (1900-73), Injikkudi Pichaikannu Pillai (1904-75), and Kulikkarai Pichaiyappa Pillai (1913-79) all died in the 1970s, while other top-ranked musicians such as Tiruvengadu Subramania Pillai (1906-86) and Tiruvizhimizhalai Brothers retired in the mid-1970s. These *nāgasvaram* musicians helped create the often-discussed 'golden era' of *Periya Mēḷam* music together with Rajarattinam Pillai.

385 The prominence of a musician is measured here by the appearances at prestigious concerts and festivals, the number of commercial recordings, and recognition by popular press. They were the only three *nāgasvaram* musicians who had a top rank in the Music Academy's own rating system to determine the frequency, time slot to be given, and remuneration for the participation in its annual music festival (Interview with T.S. Parthasarathy, 1987). Accordingly, of twenty-two full-fledged *Periya Mēḷam* concerts held during its annual music festivals at the Music Academy between 1964 and 1990, thirteen were given by ensembles led by these three musicians.

386 See Sruti (1987: 41) and Tumilan (1988: 118).

387 This statement is not to be confused with the notion of playing compositions at a fast tempo. Rajarattinam Pillai is known for his fast passages in his *rāgam* elaboration, and in a lesser degree for fast ornamental passages within the framework of compositions.

388 Kulikkarai Pichaiyappa Pillai (1913-79) who played with Rajarattinam Pillai for some time is the *nāgasvaram* musician most frequently mentioned as an expert of this vocal music-based style. Pichaiyappa Pillai was also the *ādīṉa vittuvāṉ* at the Tiruvavadudurai Madam after Rajarattinam Pillai's death (Natarajasundaram Pillai 1980: 102-3). Hearing him on *nāgasvaram* was, as many vocalists recollect, as if listening to vocal music.

389 See Ellarvi (1967: 102-3), Sankaran (1981: 298), Seshagopalan (1983: 35), Narayana (1984), Nilam (1985: 76), Rajam (1986b: 41-2), and N. Rajagopalan (1990: 224, 483) for examples. See Figure 6-1 for the newspaper announcement of these recordings.

390 Rajarattinam Pillai's insistence on the sitting position was interpreted by some patrons, with a slight malice, as deriving from his inability to keep standing during the long procession because of excessive drinking.

391 He is quoted as saying, 'They (Brahmans) are doing this, why not us?'

392 The advance was often not paid back to the sponsor of the event (Interview with Tanjavur Ramasami, 1989).

393 See Srinivas (1952: 30) for example.

394 A belief that the premature deaths were prevalent among

Periya Mēḷam musicians was already common as early as 1931 (K. Ramachandran 1931).

395 Sankaran recollects that Rajarattinam Pillai's car was an eight-seater Buick (1981: 292), while Chidambaram Radhakrishna Pillai remembers it as a Plymouth (Interview, 1989).

396 With few exceptions, *Periya Mēḷam* musicians travel economically, in the second class or sleeper class, regardless of their fame and wealth.

397 The letterhead which Rajarattinam Pillai used in 1945 is shown in Figure 6-2. The picture of Rajarattinam Pillai which appeared in the invitation to his first memorial day celebration in Madras gives us a glimpse of his adornments such as necklaces and earrings (Figure 6-3).

398 Also known as *sādarā*, the *poṉṉāḍai* is a piece of cloth, often containing gold threads, that is wrapped around the waist over the *vēṭṭi* during performances in standing position.

399 At the time of his final collapse, Rajarattinam Pillai did not have enough savings to cover the expenses for hospitalization and subsequent funeral, which some of his close patrons arranged and paid for. See Chapter 2 for details.

400 Interviews with Tiruvizhimizhalai S. Natarajasundaram Pillai (1986), Chidambaram Radhakrishna Pillai (1986), and Sikkal Natarajasundaram Pillai (1987).

401 Interview with S. Balakrishna (1989), son of K. Subramaniyam, who founded the Nagasvaram Artists Association in the late 1940s.

402 See Chapter 5 (Section 3) for the reasons for virtual absence of Brahman *Periya Mēḷam* musicians and its recent exceptions.

403 Muthiah (1987: 147).

404 According to their data, the percentage of Brahman musicians was even higher in the period between 1898/1899 and 1915, but the number of samples during this period is too small to be reliable.

405 Some important exceptions to this tendency include *Isai Vēḷāḷar* musicians actively engaged in professions in *Karnāṭak* music either as soloists or accompanists.

406 Ramaswamy Naicker was the leader of the Self-Respect Movement and the DK (Dravida Kazhagam).

407 For representative descriptions of these composers, see

N.S. Ramachandran (1967), R. Srinivasan (1967), Venkatarama Aiyar (1967, 1968), Sambamurthy (1970, 1985b), Shankar (1970), Raghavan (1975a, 1983), and Rangaccari (1979).

408 With a similar perspective, Srinivasan argues that the elevation of the Tanjore Quartet (four brothers attached to the Tanjore court of the nineteenth century who are believed to have systematized the repertoire for present-day Bharata Natyam) to a similar status in the dance tradition was a non-Brahman cultural answer to the Brahmanical Trinity (1984: 145).

409 Interview with Tiruvarur S. Latchappa Pillai (1987).

410 See Narayanan (1973), T. Viswanathan (1975: 208), Ramanujam (1982: 39), Venkatraman (1984: 27), T.R. Subramaniam (1985: 75), and V.S. Sundararajan (1987: 118). The other two musicians by whom Balasubramaniam was musically influenced included Ariyakudi Ramanuja Iyengar and Maharajapuram Viswanatha Iyer, both Brahman vocalists of the preceding generation.

411 His disciples such as M.L. Vasanthakumari (1928-90) and V. Ramachandran (b. 1940) are considered to have inherited Balasubramaniam's *nāgasvaram* influenced musical style (Narayanan 1973; Ramanujam 1982).

412 Interviews with B. Rajam Iyer (1986) and Madurai G.S. Mani (1986). See also Sankaran (1987: 7) and Pattabhiraman (1989: 46-7). Srinivasa Iyer is a nephew of Rajarattinam Pillai's teacher, Tirukkodikaval Krishna Iyer. Srinivasa Iyer's praise of Rajarattinam Pillai may also be construed as stressing the excellence of his own tradition indirectly.

413 A statement such as 'Rajarattinam Pillai's musical talent was extraordinary, but he could have reached an even higher level of accomplishment if he had a different lifestyle.' is common.

414 See Chapter 3 for detail.

415 For example, Rajarattinam Pillai is quoted to have said, 'I have already accomplished all the things which no *Mēḷakkāra payals* have achieved.' (Sankaran 1961: 45). The use of both the *Mēḷakkāra* and the derogatory term *payal* ('fellow') clearly indicates Rajarattinam Pillai's condescension with regard to other *nāgasvaram* musicians.

416 Personal communications with Sankaran (1988) and B.M. Sundaram (1992). These musicians' perspective is echoed in Arunachalam (1989: 4, 125-7).

417 The best-known incident was a boycott of a procession by
Periya Mēḷam musicians during the Tyagaraja Aradanai Festival
in Tiruvaiyaru in the early 1970s. During the same festival in
1971, handwritten posters protesting against the Brahmans'
predominant position in music were posted in Tiruvaiyaru
(*The Hindu*, 17 January 1971).

418 Anonymity is an important technique universally used by
the members of subordinate groups to avoid retaliation while
protesting against domination (Scott 1990: 140-52).

419 It is generally believed that only two players had been taught
in *gurukulavāsam* by Rajarattinam Pillai. They were Karukurichi
Arunachalam (1921-64) who often played the second
nāgasvaram to Rajarattinam Pillai, and who was considered
the best musician after Rajarattinam Pillai's death, and T.N.R.
Natarajasundaram (d. 1955) who was Rajarattinam Pillai's own
nephew. Kulikkarai Pichaiyappa Pillai is sometimes added as a
third disciple of Rajarattinam Pillai (Sankaran 1981: 294; Nilam
1985: 79).

420 Some musicians state that Rajarattinam Pillai did not have
regular *tavil* musicians because many popular *tavil* musicians
avoided playing with Rajarattinam Pillai due to his harsh and
impolite treatment (Cf. Sankaran 1961).

421 In the past, due to a high degree of professional competitiveness,
nāgasvaram musicians were divided into several important
families of musicians and their followers, and this impeded the
development of a strong professional solidarity or *jāti* identity.

422 See also Yamaguchi (1975, 1990), Tonkin et al. (1989: 17-8), and
Brow (1990: 5) for similar perspectives.

423 This was the year in which the first attempt was made to
encourage the learning of Tamil songs by establishing a cash
prize for the best Tamil manuscript on music at the Raja
Annamalai Music College (Nambi Arooran 1980: 256-7).

424 For example, C. Rajagopalachari, Congress Party leader,
Premier of the Madras Presidency in 1937-9 and Chief Minister
of Madras State in 1952-4, considered this movement non-
communal and encouraged his fellow Brahmans to join the
Tamil Music movement (V. Subramaniam 1969: 1135).

425 Especially, the compositional forms originally adopted from
dance tradition to the concert stage, such as *padam* and *jāvaḷi*
were the virtual monopoly of *dēvadāsis* and their descendants.

426 In fact, there was at least one Brahman enthusiast who practised and played *nāgasvaram* at concert halls in the 1940s, strictly as a hobby. See Chapter 5, Section 3.

427 Apart from the high degree of professional competition, the lack of administrative and political skill, which is often linked to the lack of formal education, impeded them from organizing themselves for achieving their common goals.

428 Interview with Balakrishnan, 1990. Also see Rangarajan (2005: 69). The Association also conducted a felicitous function for the achievement of its members. To give one example, a function was held to celebrate the publication of a book on music (*Saṅgīta Tāḷa Rāga Mālai*) by a *nāgasvaram* musician, M.G. Kuppusami in 1965.

429 See its Inauguration Notice (1981) and Sivaramakrishan (1985).

430 Sri Nagasvaravali ceased to function as an entity when Sivaramakrishnan, its primary organizer, moved to Nagapattinam in 1987. It was then nominally absorbed into a larger organization of musicians.

431 It is believed that his studio was the target of arson for the same reason (Interview with S. Balakrishnan, 1990; see also S. Krishnaswamy 1985: 155).

432 Subbulakshmi acted as Mirabai in a film, *Bhakta Meera*, produced in 1944, which contributed to the emergence of her image as a saint-like figure (Vishwanathan 2003: 58-65; George 2004: 176).

433 For example, a dark blue *sari* she often wore on the stage became popular among Brahman women in the 1950s, and this particular colour was known as M.S. Blue after her initials (Venkataraman 1986: 29).

434 For example, Sulochana Rajendran insists that Sivan be hailed as the twentieth-century Tyagaraja (1990). Similarly, Thirumalai calls Sivan the Tamil Tyagaraja (1975). Also see Sivan (1993).

435 All three taught in the US extensively, and their presence has influenced the direction of scholarship as well as the popular image of *Karnāṭak* music in North America.

436 The abundance of recent scholarly and journalistic studies on nostalgia derives from a conviction that nostalgia is not only prevalent but also increasingly prominent in the contemporary west (Davis 1979; Jacoby 1985; Chase and Shaw

1989; et al.). Nostalgia has also been conceptualized as a key metaphor or paradigm to investigate aspects of modernity and postmodernity (Turner 1987; Stauth and Turner 1988).

437 A player of an instrument such as *vina* (*vinai*, plucked lute), violin, and flute can take the role of the primary soloist who is supported by rhythmic accompanist(s). Although, as Viswanathan points out, a separate instrumental style has developed since the 1930s (Vishwanathan 1975: 5, 208), musical characteristics associated with vocal style continue to serve as a model to emulate among instrumental soloists.

438 The term *Isai Vēḷāḷar* was adopted by the members of the group to discard the derogatory connotation of its previous name, *Mēḷakkārar* (Srinivasan 1985). Other groups associated with the playing of *Periya Mēḷam* music include *Maruttuvar* in northern and western Tamil Nadu, Nayinda in southern Karnataka, Mangala in southern and coastal Andhra Pradesh, and Kambar in southern districts of Kerala and Tamil Nadu, Additionally, *Periya Mēḷam* music has been the monopoly of male musicians. Although female players have existed, their number is minimal.

439 For *Isai Vēḷāḷars*, Brahmans as a group provide a major source of income as well as constitute the most knowledgeable and appreciative patrons of their artistic heritage. Brahmans are not allowed to play *Periya Mēḷam* instruments which are considered ritually polluting. Brahmans depend on *Isai Vēḷāḷars* for *Periya Mēḷam* music at temple and domestic rituals which they consider indispensable. Characterized by the complex combination of rivalry and mutual dependence, the relationship between Brahmans and *Isai Vēḷāḷars* is highly ambivalent. Underneath the tension between these two caste groups are the Brahmans' sense of superiority which is manifest in their manners of speech and behavior on one hand and the *Isai Vēḷāḷars'* frustration that their achievements are not adequately acknowledged by Brahmans on the other. The existence of such a 'love-hate relationship' (Subramaniam 1993: 4) is widely recognized by Brahmans and *Isai Vēḷāḷars* alike, although it is not usually admitted publicly or mentioned directly in the literature (cf. Sankaran 1987).

440 With the recent publication of biographical accounts,

particularly by B.M. Sundaram (1992), more information about past *nāgasvaram* and *tavil* musicians is now being circulated beyond the boundaries of lineages.

441 In 1938, All India Radio opened its Madras station, the first in South India. Although the history of radio programmes in this region goes back to 1924 when the Madras Radio Club began broadcasting with limited facility and air time. The radio performances of *Periya Mēḷam* music prior to 1938 were so infrequent as to be negligible.

442 The continuing popularity of this film may be detected from the repeated reruns on TV, the recent releases of commercial video version and cassette tape sound track of the film, and the publication of the original novel in book form in 1968 (Kalaimani 1968).

443 The dominant and subordinate discourses are not conceived as completely separate entities, since the former persuasively penetrates, and sometimes absorbs or incorporates, the latter.

444 Ani Tirumanjanam and Arudra Darsanam are the two important annual festivals at Nataraja Temple in Chidambaram where Nataraja and his consort Sivakama Sundari are enshrined as the two primary deities. Nadasvaram, the term used in the quotation, is an alternate term for the *nāgasvaram*. The correct name of the instrument has been a subject of continuing controversy at least since the 1930s.

445 The two terms, *bari* and *timiri* are relative to one another, and their approximate meanings are 'higher' and 'lower' instead of 'high' and 'low' respectively. Therefore, the pitch to which each term refers varies from one context to the next. Until the 1920s, the tonic pitch of the commonly used *nāgasvaram* was 5 (g). The pitch was lowered gradually and by the mid-1940s, the majority of musicians were playing *nāgasvarams* in pitch 2, 2½, and 3 (d, *dH*, e). At present, most musicians play the *nāgasvaram* in pitch 2. See Terada (1992: 58) for the discrepant usage of these terms in literature.

446 The lowering of pitch was criticized by many *Periya Mēḷam* musicians themselves (Virusvami Pillai 1962).

447 All the musicians mentioned to be masterful on *nāgasvaram* and *tavil* belonged to the *Isai Vēḷāḷar* caste from the Tanjavur area. The sole exception is Madurai Ponnusami Pillai (1879-1929) who was also an *Isai Vēḷāḷar* but from Madurai.

448 The *Periya Mēḷam* ensemble in the early decades of the century consisted of one *nāgasvaram,* one *tavil,* one *tatam,* and one *ottu* (drone pipe). This instrumentation was suitable for a *nāgasvaram* musician playing extended improvisation, and the standardization of the two *nāgasvaram* format was largely a result of the increasing prominence of composed music in the repertoire of *Periya Mēḷam* music.

449 The Kaveri is a river whose tributaries run through much of northern and eastern Tanjavur district which is credited with the development of classical music and is known for the number of accomplished musicians it has produced. Tiruvaiyaru, a town on the Kaveri River, is famous for its annual festival to commemorate the death of the famed nineteenth century composer Tyagaraja. See Ramnarayan (1987) and Orr (1990) on the influence of *nāgasvaram* music on *Karnāṭak* musicians. For a more lengthy quotation of Srinivasa Iyer on his experience with *nāgasvaram* music, see Pattabhi Raman (1993).

450 Srinivasa Iyer is also quoted as, 'If you want to develop raga nyana (knowledge on *rāgam*), you must listen to *Nāgasvaram* as much as possible' (Mani 1987).

451 Two organizations which sponsor full-fledged concerts of *Periya Mēḷam* music during their respective music festivals are the Tamil Music Association (Tamil Isai Sangam, established in 1943) which aims to propagate Tamil Music, and the Muttamil Peravai, a cultural wing of the caste organization of *Isai Vēḷāḷar* (Isai Velalar Sangam). Both organizations are run outside of mainstream Brahman patronage.

452 The very first full-fledged concert hall recital of *Periya Mēḷam* music of which I have a record was performed in 1933 at the Music Academy as part of a music festival.

453 Nevertheless, many, including ardent patrons of *Periya Mēḷam* music, believe that the music sounds best when it is heard at some distance, and more of the audience is found frequently at the back side of the hall away from the stage in *Periya Mēḷam* recitals.

454 Some trustees fined adventurous *Isai Vēḷāḷar Periya Mēḷam* musicians for breaking the traditional code of behaviour, such as performing with non-Hindu musicians or with Hindu musicians from low castes.

455 The appointment of trustees has been an important strategy for governing political parties to extend networks of power and influence by rewarding faithful party members and other associates (Kennedy 1974: 286-87; Presler 1987: 66-71).

456 The Backward Classes Commission, which was appointed by the Tamil Nadu state government, examined the plea of the caste organizations and made a recommendation that the minimum salary of *Periya Mēḷam* musicians be fixed by the Hindu Religious Endowment Department, the government agency which administers temple affairs (Government of Tamil Nadu 1975: 24).

457 Tyagaraja's ancestor came to the Tanjavur area from what is today the Kurnool district in Andhra Pradesh. Tyagaraja's father, Rama Brahman, was patronized by Tulaja II, a Nayaka king. He was given a house and land, which Tyagaraja is believed to have inherited. The compositions of Tyagaraja have dominated the concert stage of classical music at least since the 1920s.

458 Nine more *Tamiḻ Isai* conferences were held between 1941 and 1945 to raise awareness of the merit of Tamil songs: Tiruchy, Madras (September, 1941), Devakottai (October, 1941), Tiruchy (December, 1941), Madurai (August, 1942), Pudukottai (October, 1942), Kumbakonam (April, 1943), Valampuri (May, 1944), and Ayampettai (August, 1945). At each conference a resolution was passed regarding ways to popularize Tamil songs (Ramanathan Chettiar 1993; Ilankumaran 1993).

459 Even before the 1941 resolution, resentment was expressed toward the *Tamiḻ Isai* movement. For example, in his speech at the All India Oriental Conference in Tirupati, T.V. Subba Rao stated, 'Linguistic considerations ought not [to] be allowed to prevail in the selection of classical items. The highest music transcends the limitation of language.' (Music Academy 1941: 53)

460 Krishnamachari's son, T.T. Vasu (1929-2005), was the president of the Music Academy between 1983 and 2005.

461 The different percentages of Tamil songs requested in the resolution are due to the linguistic constitution of the population. Madras, located in close proximity to Andhra Pradesh, had many Telugu-speaking residents, whereas the

Tiruchirapalli station covered central Tamil Nadu where the vast majority of the population was Tamil.

462 For example, Ariyakudi Ramanuja Iyengar mentioned in his lecture, 'Language in Music,' that '(w)here pieces that came up to approved technical standards were available, there was no reason why Tamil pieces should not be sung. But such pieces were very few in number.' (Music Academy 1942: 19).

463 The compositions of Tyagaraja have dominated the concert stage of classical music at least since the 1920s. William Jackson believes that nationalistic zeal contributed to the promotion of Tyagaraja as the national composer (1991: 106).

464 Popularly known as Rajaji, he was a powerful leader of the Congress party and Premier of Madras Presidency in 1937-9 and chief minister of Madras state in 1952-4. See Muttaiya for a sample of his pro-*Tamiḻ Isai* speech (1996: 24-9). Despite his professed pro-Tamil stance, his intentions were questioned by some non-Brahmans (Ramaswamy 1997: 199).

465 Kalki Krishnamurthy was an influential journalist and publisher who frequently wrote articles in favour of the *Tamiḻ Isai* movement in a popular Tamil weekly, *Kalki,* which he had established in 1941. A sample of his writing is provided in Muttaiya (1996: 83-7).

466 *Periya Mēḻam* refers to a tradition of instrumental ensemble that provides music at both temple and life-cycle rituals in South India. It features *nāgasvaram* (double-reed aerophone), *tavil* (barrel-shaped double-headed drum), *tālam* (a pair of small hand cymbals) and *sruti* box (free reed instrument to provide drone).

467 For example, in the 1960s and 1970s, an average of five *Periya Mēḻam* concerts were sponsored by the Sangam during its annual music festival in December, whereas only one was given at the Academy.

468 Some non-Brahmans regard these acts as representing Brahmans' cunning tendency in pursuit of money.

469 The figures given here are based on the list of compositions in the concert souvenir programme. Musicians occasionally makes changes in their performance and the figures for the songs actually performed may be slightly different. But for my analysis, the musicians' intentions are just as significant as what they actually played.

470 For its first twenty-five years of existence (1949-74), it was
    called the Central College of Carnatic Music (*Mattiya Karnāṭaka
    Isai Kallūri*).

471 Some opine that his motivation to appear frequently at *Tamiḻ
    Isai*-related events was more for monetary rewards than from
    his commitment to the movement. Even so, his participation
    should be read, regardless of his real intentions, in the context
    that performance opportunities for non-Brahman musicians
    were limited and that the sense of being discriminated against
    by Brahmans was shared by virtually all non-Brahman
    musicians.

472 Interview with T.S. Latchappa Pillai, director of the programme
    (Chennai, 2001). Bharata Nāṭyam traces its origin to the ritual
    dance offered at Hindu temples, and its practitioners (known
    as *dēvadāsi*) belonged invariably to non-Brahman castes. As the
    institution of temple dance was banned due to its suspected
    connection to prostitution, it was 'revived' in the 1930s as a
    respectable and national (*bharat* meaning India) art form for
    the emerging urban middle class. Brahmans were instrumental
    in sanitizing the tainted dance tradition by changing its name
    (from *Sadir* to Bharata Natyam) and practitioners (*dēvadāsis* to
    Brahmans) and by reformulating the repertoire to eliminate
    excessive eroticism (Allen 1997; Natarajan 1997).

473 Interviews with P. Kodandaraman, Vice-Chancellor of Madras
    University, and N. Ramanathan, Head of the Department of
    Indian Music (Chennai, 2000).

474 The *āradhana* refers to a ritual of worship in memory of saints.

475 According to *The Hindu*, the disruption occurred three times,
    and a total of eighteen persons were arrested (29 January 1997).

476 Written communication with T. Sankaran (1991).

477 The original Tamil texts read as follows:

> *kaḷavāṭiya isaiyē karnāṭaka isai*
> *tamiḻil pāḍu! illaiyēl pāḍavaippōm*
> *tamiḻisai mēḍai daṇḍapāṇi dēsikar*
> *tamiḻil pāḍiyatarku tīṭṭukkaḷittu*
> *avamāṉappaḍuttiya tiyākayyar*
> *viḷākkuḻu kumpalē*
> *pagiraṅga maṉṉippukkēḷ!*

The theme of Brahman (Aryan) appropriation of non-Brahman (Dravidian) culture and their claim of it as their own is by no means new. For examples, see Ramaswamy (1997: 44)

478 He served as dean of the Music Department at Annamalai University in the 1950s-60s, and supported the *Tamiḻ Isai* movement by giving all-Tamil performances, giving speeches at conferences and appearing on radio programmes.

478 Somasundara Desikar, a disciple of Dandapani Desikar who accompanied him in Tiruvaiyaru, remembers that some Brahman musicians requested the stage to be purified because it had been polluted by Desikar's singing of Tamil songs (interview, Chennai, 2000). Desikar never performed for the *Āradhana* again. This anecdote has been exaggerated to the extent that many believe Desikar was physically removed from the stage by angry Brahmans when he was singing a Tamil song.

480 A similar incident is also frequently mentioned regarding T.N. Rajarattinam Pillai (1898-1956) who was one of the top-ranking musicians during the first half of the twentieth century. He was best-known as an extraordinary player of *nāgasvaram*, but he was also a fine vocalist. When he sang Tamil songs in a temple in Koraccal (near Tiruvaiyaru), the place he had been sitting was washed with cow-dung for purification after he left the site, allegedly because Tamil songs were sung (interview with Periya Dasan, Chennai, 1999). While this anecdote is told mostly to illustrate Brahman discrimination against non-Brahman musicians, even those musicians whose ability is highly appreciated by Brahmans, this provocative action was possibly a display of their criticism of the *Tamiḻ Isai* movement as Rajarattinam Pillai was considered one of its ardent supporters (Sadasivam 1992: 34; Soranadan 1998: 53).

481 At the *Āradhana* function held at the Music Academy in 1999, the *pañcatantira kīrttaṇa* (a set of five compositions by Tyagaraja) were performed according to custom by about fifty musicians on the stage who were invited for the occasion. Semmangudi Srinivasa Iyer, the senior vocalist, was seen directing the group, while B. Rajam Iyer, the principal of the music college attached to the Music Academy, was the host of the gathering, sitting prominently in the centre. The

musicians on the stage were virtually all Brahmans, as were the vast majority of the audience. None of the surviving non-Brahman *Sangīta Kalānidhis* were present. Many non-Brahmans mentioned to me that non-Brahman recipients of the coveted title stay away from the Music Academy because of the overtly Brahmanical orientation with which most of the Academy's activities are perceived. For most non-Brahmans, it was an exclusively Brahman affair. Non-Brahmans were not prohibited from entering the site, but many have stated that the atmosphere was so overtly Brahmanical as to make it prohibitive for them to participate. The deification of the 'saint-composer' was evident in this event. Prominent on the left side of the stage was a portrait of Tyagaraja to which worship (*puja*) was conducted after the performance in a manner identical to that for a deity. The songs were sung with outwardly visible devotion, emulating, consciously or not, the spiritualism that Tyagaraja was supposed to represent.

482 Periyar served as the president of the Second *Tamil Isai* Conference in Tiruchirapalli in 1941 (Ramanathan Chettiar 1993: 4-5).

483 Interview with N. Arunachalam (Chennai, 1998).

484 The portion of the original poem translated in the main text is given below (Anandan 1998: 142-3).

> *Tamilā! nīpēsuvadutamilā?*
> *Annaiyait tamilvāyāl*
> *'Mammi' enralaittāy...*
> *Alaguk kulandaiyai*
> *'Bēbi' enralaittāy...*
> *Ennadā tandaiyai*
> *'Dādi' enralaittāy...*
> *Innuyirt tamilai*
> *Konrut tolaittāy...*
> *Tamilānīpēsuvadutamilā?*

485 *Tamizhisai Paadalgal* [*Tamil Isai* Songs] by Pushpavanam Kuppusami (Vijay Musicals, VMC 556-557).

486 During the festival in 1999, the composition written in Mohanam *rāgam* (C-D-E-G-A) was reset in another pentatonic *rāgam*, Hamsadvani (C-D-E-G-B).

487 Interview with B.M. Sundaram (Tanjavur, 1999). Sundaram also questions the validity of the widely believed notion that Tyagaraja was born in Tiruvaiyaru, challenging the rare coincidence of their birth places (also see Gurukrupa 1985).

488 Also interview with Muttukumarasami, a disciple of Dandapani Desikar (Chennai, 2000).

489 Other related terms such as Sirkari Muvar (Chelladurai 1996) and Tamil Isai Muvar (TPTIM 1999) have been used to refer to these three non-Brahman composers of Tamil songs. They comprise Muttutandavar (1525-1625), Arunachala Kavirayar (1711-79), and Marimutta Pillai (1712-87). The Sirkari in the appellation is taken from the name of the town where Muttutandavar was born. Also see Selvaganapati (1996) for a similar argument.

490 Music and dance are the only remaining cultural spheres of Brahmans; their dominance in other spheres such as politics, administration, and education has been taken away as the result of the non-Brahman movement (interview with S.V. Rajadurai and V. Geetha, Chennai, 1999).

491 Shanmugasundaram Pillai is frustrated over the internalization of the dominant discourse by foreign scholars and students who already have a preconceived notion of South Indian music, drawn from the dominant Brahmanical narrative on history and present practice (interview, Chennai, 1999).

492 The circular nature of the flow has also been pointed out by other writers (Eckstein and Najam 2013) but the emphasis has so far been on economic and social domains.

493 Interview with Amirthalingam Baheerathan (27 September 2009, in London).

494 The news media outside of India tend to focus on this aspect, frequently to the exclusion of other examples of economic success such as medical and pharmaceutical industries.

495 There is no hard evidence, but individuals involved in classical music traditions in both North and South varieties seem to agree that the latter has gained much more in popularity and exposure in recent years.

496 From an interview with V.V. Sundaram (5 March 2011, in Chennai).

497 While this is a virtually unanimous opinion in Indian Tamil and Sri Lankan Tamil communities alike, no concrete statistics are available because in the UK census, people are counted based on the country of their origin, and no differentiation is made between different ethnic groups.

498 Nagarajan reports that there are twenty-three Tamil schools in the UK, most of which teach music and dance, at the time of his writing (1995: 362-70). Incidentally, there are many Tamil language schools (often called Tamil Sangam) in the USA, but no school provides classes on music and dance.

499 Its parental organization, Kalasagara, Academy of Fine Arts, was established in Chennai in 1972 by Usha's parents.

500 Interviews with Usha Raghavan (28 September 2009, in London) and Tiruvarur L. Kothandapani (25 September 2009 in London).

501 Some parents even take out loans to conduct an *arangētram*, and in one extreme case, the father of a dancer in Toronto, Canada died of heart attack during the *arangētram*, presumably due to the stress of organizing it. Having lost face, his family disconnected themselves from the community (Interview with Sel Aathavan, 27 August 2013, in Toronto).

502 The common custom is to arrange a few *arangētrams* during the same time period so that the cost of inviting musicians from India can be shared by several families.

503 Interviews with Tiruvarur L. Kothandapani (25 September 2009, in London).

504 Interview with V.V. Sundaram (5 March 2011, in Chennai).

505 Interview with Sivasakthi Sivanesan, a teacher of *vīṇa*, at the Bharatiya Vidya Bhavan (26 September 2009, in London). Also, an interview with Rasika Kumar, who runs Abhinaya Dance Company, an American-born Bharata Natyam dancer, with her mother and its founder, Mythili Kumar in San Jose, California (21 August 2011, in San Jose).

506 Interview with V.V. Sundaram (5 March 2011, in Chennai).

507 Interview with Lata Pada, director of Sampradaya Dance Academy in Toronto (19 August 2013, in Toronto).

References Cited and Consulted

Abbreviations

JMA   The Journal of Music Academy
JSNA   Journal of the Sangeet Natak Akademi
MAS   Music Academy Conference Souvenir
TTVM   *Tamiḷ Isai* Viḷa Malar

Abraham Pandither, M.
1984(1917)   *Karuṇāmirta Cākaram on Srutis.* New Delhi: Asian Educational Services.

Adam Saheb, Sheik
1975   'Nādasvaram.' In *Telugvani*, 63-4. Hyderabad: Raknaugadi. In Telugu.

Adamson, Walter L.
1980   *Hegemony and Revolution: A Study of Antonio Gramsci's Political and Cultural Theory.* Berkeley: University of California Press.

Ajnani, Sangeetha
1997   'Musical Tributes to Tyagaraja.' *Sruti* 151: 7-8

Alavandar, R.
1981   *Tamiḷar Tōr̲ Karuvigaḷ* [Tamil Percussion instruments]. Chennai: Ulaha Tamilaraycci Niruvanam.

Allen, Mathew Harp
1997   'Rewriting the Script for South Indian Dance.' *The Dance Review* 41(3): 63-100.

Allison, Charlene Jones
1980   'Belief and Symbolic Action: A Cultural Analysis of a Non-Brahmin Marriage Ritual Cycle.' Ph.D. dissertation, University of Washington.

Alonso, Ana Maria
1988a   'The Effects of Truth: Re-Presentation of the Past and the Imagining of Community.' *Journal of Historical Sociology* 1/1: 33-57.

1988b   '"Progress" as Disorder and Dishonor: Discourses of Serrano Resistance.' *Critique of Anthropology* 8/1: 13-33.

Anand, S.

1998   'TNR and Self-respect.' *Indian Express* (October).

Anandan, Kasi

1998   *Kāsi Āṉandaṉ Kavidaigaḷ* [Poems of Kasi Anandan]. Chennai: Mannavar Puttahappannai.

Ananthakrishna Iyer, K.

1912   *The Cochin Tribes and Castes, Vol. 2*. Madras: Higginbotham. Annamalai University

1955   *The Annamalai University Silver Jubilee Souvenir, 1929-1954.* Annamalainagar: Annamalai University

1979   *The Annamalai University Golden Jubilee Souvenir, 1929-1979.* Annamalainagar: Annamalai University

Anonymous

1961   '35-vatu Māṉāṭṭut Talaivar Nāgasvara Vittuvāṉ Srī Vīrusvāmi Piḷḷai' [The President of the 35th Conference, Nagasvaram Musician Virusvami Pillai]. MAS: 4-5. In Tamil.

1980   'Vittuvāṉ Poṉṉusāmi Piḷḷai Avarhaḷ: Vāḻkkai Kuṟippu' [A Biographical Note of the Musician, Ponnusami Pillai]. In *Madurai Poṉṉusāmi Piḷḷai Avarhaḷ Nūṟṟāṇḍu Viḻā Malar*, 1-3. In Tamil.

Appaji Rao, T.

1937   'Maharashtra Influence on South Indian Music.' In *South Indian Maharashtrians*, 163-4. Madras: The Mahratta Education Fund.

Arnold, Edwin

1886   *India Revisited*. Boston: Roberts Brothers.

Arudra

1986/87   'The Transfiguration of a Traditional Dance.' *Sruti* 27-28: 17-36.

Arumuhan Pillai, M.

1980   'Uṟaiyūr Muttuvīrusvāmi Piḷḷai (1828-72): Biographical Notes.' Unpublished manuscript. 8pp. In Tamil.

Arunachalam, M.

1980   'The Brahmotsava Festival.' *Bulletin of the Institute of Traditional Cultures* 46: 29-58.

1989   *Musical Tradition of Tamilnadu*. Madras: International Society for the Investigation of Ancient Civilization.

Aside (biweekly magazine, Madras)
1986   'Truant Genius.' 10/12: 18-9.

Attali, Jacques
1984   *Noise: The Political Economy of Music.* Minneapolis: University of Minnesota Press.

Awasthy, G.C.
1965   *Broadcasting in India.* Bombay: Allied Publishers.

Awaya, Toshie
1988   'Indo Kindaishikenkyu ni mirareru Shinchoryu' [New Research Trends in Indian Modern History]. *Shigakuzasshi* 97/9: 81-99. In Japanese.

Baily, John
2010   'The Circulation of Music between Afghanistan and the Afghan Disapora.' In *Beyond the 'Wild Tribes': Understanding Modern Afghanistan and Its Diaspora,* eds., Ceri Oeppen and Angela Schlenkhoff, 157-71. London: Hurst & Co.

Baker, C.J.
1975   *The Politics of South India, 1920-1937.* Cambridge: Cambridge University Press.

Bakhtin, Mikhail M.
1981   *The Dialogic Imagination,* tr. Michael Holquist and Caryl Emerson. Austin: University of Texas Press.

Balakrishnan, P.
1986   *Isai Nūl: Isai Kalai Valarcci* [The Book of Music: The Development of Musical Art]. Madras: Brindahana Vityalaya. In Tamil.

Balasubramaniyan, Kudavayil
1988   *Tiruvārūrt Tirukkōvil* [The Holy Temple of Tiruvarur]. Tiruvarur: Arulmihu Tiyaharaja Suvami Tirukkoyil. In Tamil.
1991   'Nāgasvaram—Tavil Apūrva Siṟpam' [The Rare Sculpture of Nagasvaram and Tavil]. *Dinamani* (17 March). In Tamil.

Balasubramanyam, S.R.
1966   *Early Chola Art, Part 1.* Bombay: Asian Publishing House.

Baliga, B.S.
1957   *Tanjore District Handbook.* Madras: Government Press.
1960   *Madras District Gazetteers: Madurai.* Madras: Government of Madras.
1962   *Madras District Gazetteers: South Arcot.* Madras: Government of Madras.

1966   *Madras District Gazetteers: Coimbatore*. Madras: Government
                of Madras.

1967   *Madras District Gazetteers: Salem*. Madras: Government of
                Madras.

Barnett, Marguerite Ross

1976a   *The Politics of Cultural Nationalism in South India*. Princeton:
                Princeton University Press.

1976b   'Competition, Control and Dependency: Urban Politics in
                Madras City.' In *The City in Indian Politics*, ed., Donald B.
                Rosenthal, 94-116. Faridabad: Thomson Press.

Barnouw, Erik, and S. Krishnaswamy

1980   *Indian Film*. New York: Oxford University Press.

Barth, Fredrik

1969   'Introduction.' In *Ethnic Groups and Boundaries*, ed. F. Barth,
                9-38. Boston: Little Brown.

Baruah, U.L.

1983   *This Is* All India Radio: *A Handbook of Radio Broadcasting
                in India*. New Delhi: Ministry of Information and
                Broadcasting.

Basavaraja, K.R.

1984   *History and Culture of Karnataka*. Dharwad: Chalukya
                Publications.

Baskaran, S. Theodore

1976   'Tamil Cinema and the Intelligentsia: The Gap.' In *Indian
                Films and Film World*. Madras: JWALA.

1981   *The Message Bearers: The Nationalist Politics and the
                Entertainment Media in South India, 1880-1945*. Madras:
                Cre-A.

1996   *The Eye of the Serpent: An Introduction to Tamil Cinema*.
                Madras: East West Books.

Beck, Brenda E.F.

1972   *Peasant Society in Konku: A Study of Right and Left Subcastes in
                South India*. Vancouver: University of British Columbia
                Press.

Berberich, Frank

1974   'The Tavil: Construction, Technique and Context in
                Present-day Jaffna.' MA thesis, University of Hawaii.

Beteille, Andre

1965a   *Caste, Class, and Power: Changing Patterns of Stratification in a
                Tanjore Village*. Berkeley: University of California Press.

1965b   'Social Organization of Temples in a Tanjore Village.'
            History of Religions 5/1: 74-92.
1969   *Castes Old and New: Essays in Social Structure and Social
            Stratification.* London: Asia Publishing House.
1974   *Studies in Agrarian Social Structure.* Delhi: Oxford University
            Press.

Bharati, Srirama
1984   'Reviving Temple Music.' *Indian Music Journal* 13: 49-59.

Bhat, Chandrashekhar
1984   *Ethnicity and Mobility: Emerging Ethnic Identity and Social
            Mobility among the Waddars of South India.* New Delhi:
            Concept Publishing Company.

Bhattacharya, Jogendranath
1968(1896) *Hindu Castes and Sects.* Calcutta: Editions Indian.

Bhuvarahan, N.R.
1984   'Nādasvara Isai Mēdaikaḷ: Srī Tī. Eṉ. Rājarattiṉam Piḷḷai.'
            Saṉmuka 13/1: 57-60. Originally published in the Tamil
            Weekly, *Hanuman* (19 April 1942). In Tamil.

Blackburn, Stuart H.
1988   *Singing of Birth and Death: Texts in Performance.* Philadelphia:
            University of Pennsylvania Press.

Blackburn, Stuart H., and A.K. Ramanujan, eds.
1986   *Another Harmony: New Essays on the Folklore of India.*
            Berkeley: University of California Press.

Bommes, Michael and Patrick Wright
1982   'Charms of Residence: The Public and the Past.' In *Making
            Histories: Studies in History-Writing and Politics*, eds. Richard
            Johnson et al., 253-301. London: Hutchinson.

Booth, Gregory
1990   'Brass Bands: Tradition, Change, and the Mass Media in
            Indian Wedding Music.' *Ethnomusicology* 34/2: 245-62.

Bor, Joep
1988   'The Rise of Ethnomusicology: Sources on Indian Music
            c.1789-c.1890.' *Yearbook for Traditional Music* 20: 51-73.

Bourdieu, Pierre
1977   *Outline of A Theory of Practice.* Cambridge: Cambridge
            University Press.
1984   *Distinction: A Social Critique of the Judgement of Taste.*
            Cambridge: Harvard University Press.

Bouton, Marshall M.
1985   *Agrarian Radicalism in South India.* Princeton: Princeton
                 University Press.
Bowrey, Thomas
1905(1650)   *A Geographical Account of Countries Round the Bay of Bengal,
                 1669-1679.* Cambridge: Hakluyt Society.
Braudel, Fernand
1980   *On History.* Chicago: University of Chicago Press.
Briggs, Sheila
1989   'The Politics of Identity and the Politics of Interpretation.'
                 Union Seminary Quarterly Review 43/1-4: 163-80.
Brow, James
1990   'Notes on Community, Hegemony, and Uses of the Past.'
                 Anthropological Quarterly 63/1: 1-6.
Brown, Robert E.
1965   'The Mrdanga: A Study of Drumming in South India.' Ph.D.
                 dissertation, University of California, Los Angeles.
Brunton, Paul
1949   *A Search in Secret India.* London: Rider and Company.
Bryant, Wanda
1990   'The Keyless Double Reed Aerophone: Its Usage,
                 Construction, and Worldwide Distribution.' *Journal of the
                 American Musical Instrument Society* 14: 132-76.
Buchanan, Francis
1988(1807)   *A Journey from Madras through the Countries of Mysore,
                 Canara, and Malabar.* New Delhi: Asian Educational Service.
                 Bulletin of the Institute of Traditional Cultures
1980   'Reports of Seminars.' 46: 115-66.
Bynum, Caroline Walker
1986   'Introduction: The Complexity of Symbols.' In *Gender and
                 Religion: On the Complexity of Symbols*, eds., C.W. Bynum
                 et al., 1-20. Boston: Beacon Press.
Capwell, Charles
1991   'Marginality and Musicology in Nineteenth-Century
                 Culcutta: The Case of Sourindro Mohun Tagore.' In
                 *Comparative Musicology and Anthropology of Music: Essays
                 on the History of Ethnomusicology*, eds., Bruno Nettl and
                 Philip Bohlman, 228-43. Chicago: University of Chicago
                 Press.

Catlin, Amy R.

1980   'Variability and Change in Three Karnataka Kriti-s: A Study
             of South Indian Classical Music.' Ph.D. dissertation, Brown
             University.

1985   'Pallavi and Kriti of Karnatak Music: Evolutionary
             Processes and Survival Strategies.' *Journal of National
             Centre for the Performing Arts* 14/1: 26-44

Chandramouli (Candiramouli), S.

1986   '8 Varuḍaṅgaḷāy oru Pōrāṭṭam' [The Eight-year Struggle].
             Kalki (21 September): 12-3. In Tamil.

1987   'Maṭaṅkaḷaikkaṭanta Maṅgalak Kalaiñar' [An Auspicious
             Artist Who Crossed Over Religions]. *Kalki* (20 December):
             5-6. In Tamil.

Chandra Shekar

1987a   'Obituary: Pallavi Chandrappa.' *Sruti* 30: 11.

1987b   'Kadri Gopalnath: Musician with Sax Appeal.' *Sruti* 36:
             27-9.

Chandra Shekar, and Kadri Gopalnath

1985   'East Meets West.' *Sruti* 36: 30-1.

Chandrasekhar, S.

1964   'Growth of Population in Madras City 1639-1961.'
             Population Review 8/1: 3-45.

Charukesi

1989(1990)   'Kunnakudi Vaidyanathan & His Violin: Magical Music for
             the Masses.' *Sruti* 63-64: 47-53.

Chase, Malcolm and Christopher Shaw

1989   The Dimensions of Nostalgia. In *The Imagined Past:
             History and Nostalgia*, eds., M. Chase and C. Shaw, 1-17.
             Manchester: Manchester University Press.

Chelladurai, P.T.

1996   'The Great Services Rendered by Doctor Rajah Sir
             Annamalai Chettiar to the Cause of Tamil Culture
             and Tamil Community.' In Tamil Isai Sangam 1995-6,
             unpaged. Chennai: *Tamiḻ Isai* Sangam.

Chellam Iyengar, Salem

1982   'Saṅgīta Sāhitya Lakṣaṇa Mahāvittuvāṉ Rāmanādapuram
             Srīmaṉ Srīnivāsa Aiyaṅgār: Vāḻkkai Varalāṟu (1860-1919)'
             [The Biography of the Great Musician, Ramanadapuram
             Srinivasa Iyengar]. In *Compositions of Ramanathapuram*

Asthana Vidwan Sriman 'Poochi' Srinivasa Iyengar, ed., Salem Chellam Iyengar, unpaged. Madras: Higginbothams. In Tamil.

Chidambaram, M.A.
1993   'Tamiḻ Isai Saṅgattiṇ Varalāṟu' [The Development of Tamil Music Association]. In *Tamiḻ Isai Saṅgam Poṇ Viḻā Sirappu Malar 1943-1993*, 7-10. Chennai: Tamil Isai Sangam.

Chinna Moulana, Sheik
n.d.   'Our Forefathers.' Unpublished manuscript.

Chuyen, Gilles
2004   *Who is a Brahmin?: The Politics of Identity in India.* New Delhi: Manohar.

'Civilian', The
1921   *The Civilian's South India: Some Places and People in Madras.* London: John Lake, the Bodley Head, Limited.

Clark, Katerina, and Michael Holquist
1984   *Mikhail Bakhtin.* Cambridge: Harvard University Press.

Clothey, Fred W.
1983   *Rhythm and Intent: Ritual Studies from South India.* Madras: Blackie and Son Publishers.
1984   *Quiescence and Passion: The Vision of Arunakiri, Tamil Mystic.* Madurai: Madurai Kamaraj University.

Coaldrake, A. Kimi
1989   'Female Tayu in Gidayu Narrative Tradition of Japan.' In *Women and Music in Cross-Cultural Perspective*, ed., Ellen Koskoff, 151-61. Urbana: University of Illinois Press.

Cohen, Abner
1973   *Two-Dimensional Man.* Berkeley: University of California Press.

Conway, Moncure Daniel
1906   *My Pilgrimage to the Wise Men of the East.* Boston: Houghton, Mifflin and Company.

Corner, Caroline
1890   *Ceylon: The Paradise of Adam.* London: John Lane, The Bodley Head.

Dandapani Desikar, Ca.
1948   *Tiruvārūrt Tala Varalāṟu* [The History of Tiruvarur Temple]. In Tamil.

Das, R.K.
1964   *Temples of Tamil Nadu.* Bombay: Bharatiya Vidya Bhavan.

Datcanamurtti Pillai (Dakshinamurthy), Sembonnarkoyil R.
n.d.   'Pallavi: Eṉ Aṉupavam' [Pallavi: My experience]. *TIVM:* 43-4. In Tamil.

Day, Charles Russel
1890   *The Music and Musical Instruments of Southern India and the Deccan.* New Delhi: B.R. Publishing Corporation.

de Certeau, Michel
1969   *L'étranger ou l'union dans la différence.* Desclee de Brouwer.
1984   *The Practice of Everyday Life.* Berkeley: University of California Press.
1988   *The Writing of History.* New York: Columbia University Press.

della Valle, Sig Pietro
1665   *The Travels of Sig. Pietro della Valle.* London: J. Macock.

Deva, B. Chaintanya
1974   *Indian Music.* New Delhi: Indian Council for Cultural Relations.
1975   'The Double-Reed Aerophone in India.' *International Folk Music Council Yearbook* 7: 77-84.
1977   *Musical Instruments.* New Delhi: National Book Trust.

Devadoss, T.S.
1979   *Hindu Family and Marriage: A Study of Social Institutions in India.* Madras: University of Madras.

Davis, Fred
1979   *Yearning for Yesterday: A Sociology of Nostalgia.* New York: Free Press.

Dick, Alastair
1984a   'The Earlier History of the Shawm in India.' *Galpin Society Journal* 37: 80-98.
1984b   'Kulal.' In *The New Grove Dictionary of Musical Instruments,* Vol. 2: 479.
1984c   'Tavil.' In *The New Grove Dictionary of Musical Instruments,* Vol. 3: 534-5.

Diehl, Carl Gustav
1956   *Instrument and Purpose: Studies on Rites and Rituals in South India.* Lund: C.W.K. Gleerup.

Dinamalar (Tamil daily newspaper)
1989   'Nāgasvara Kalaiñariṉ Sōkam' (21 May).

Dinamani (Tamil daily newspaper)
1956a 'Nādasvara Mēdai Srī Rājarattiṇam Kālamāṇār' (13 December).
1956b 'Nādasvarak Kalaiyaip Pōṟrattakka ēṟpāḍu Vēṇḍum.' (23 December).
1990 'Ponnuttay' (15 April).

Dinattandi (Tamil daily newspaper)
1986 'Amerikkāvil Vināyakar Cadurtti!: Nāmagiripēṭṭai Krishṇan Nādasura Kaccēri' (6 September).

Dirks, Nicholas B.
1987 *The Hollow Crown: Ethno-history of an Indian Kingdom.* Cambridge: Cambridge University Press.

Dirlik, Arif
1987 'Culturalism as Hegemonic Ideology and Liberating Practice.' *Cultural Critique* 6: 13-50.

Doane, Janice and Devon Hodges
1987 *Nostalgia and Sexual Difference: The Resistance to Contemporary Feminism.* New York: Methuen.

Dorai Rangaswamy, M.A.
1958 *The Religion and Philosophy of the Tevaram.* Madras: University of Madras.

Douglas, Mary
1966 *Purity and Danger.* London: Routledge & Kegan Paul.

Dube, S. C.
1955 *Indian Village.* London: Routledge & Kegan Paul.

Dubois, Abbe J.A.
1986(1906) *Hindu Manners, Customs and Ceremonies.* New Delhi: Asian Educational Services.

Dumont, Louis
1970 *Homo Hierarchies: The Caste System and Its Implications.* Chicago: University of Chicago Press.
1986 *A South Indian Sub-caste: Social Organization and Religion of the Pramalai Kallar,* tr. M. Moffat and A. Morton. Delhi: Oxford University Press.

Durga, S.A.K.
1979 'Women as Agents of Change in the Aspects of Music and Other Fine Arts.' *Bulletin of the Institute of Traditional Cultures*: 81-5.

Eagleton, Terry
1985/86 'Marxism and the Past.' *Salmagundi* 68-69: 271-90.

Eckstein, Susan and Najam Adil, eds.

2013   *How Immigrants Impact Their Homelands.* Durham and London: Duke University Press.

Ellarvi (L.R. Viswanatha Sarma)

1965   *Kalai Maṇigaḷ.* Madras: Amuda Nilaiyam. In Tamil.

1967   *Isai Maṇigaḷ.* Madras: Amuda Nilaiyam. In Tamil.

1970   *Kalaippūṅgā.* Madras: Vairam Padippaham. In Tamil.

Fabricius, J.P.

1972   *Tamil and English Dictionary.* Tranquebar: Evangelical Lutheran Mission Publishing House.

Fanon, Franz

1967   *Black Skin, White Masks: The Experiences of A Black Man in a White World.* New York: Grove Press.

Femia, Joseph V.

1981   *Gramsci's Political Thought: Hegemony, Consciousness, and the Revolutionary Process.* Oxford: Clarenden Press.

Firth, Raymond

1973   *Symbols: Public and Private.* Ithaca: Cornell University Press.

Fisher, Alfred Hugh

1911   *Through India and Burmah with Pen and Brush.* London: T. Werner Laurie.

Flora, Reis

1983   'Double-Reed Aerophones in India to A.D. 1400.' Ph.D. dissertation, University of California, Los Angeles.

1984   'Nāgasvaram.' In *The New Grove Dictionary of Musical Instruments, Vol.* 2: 741-2.

1986   'Spiralled-leaf Reedpipes and Shawms of Indian Ocean Littoral: Two Related Regional Traditions.' *Musicology Australia* 9: 39-52.

Foucault, Michel

1972   'History, Discourse, and Discontinuity.' *Salmagundi* 20: 225-48.

1980   *Knowledge/Power: Selected Interviews and Other Writings, 1972-1977.* New York: Pantheon.

Frasca, Richard Armand

1990   *The Theatre of the Mahabharata: Terukkūttu Performances in South India.* Honolulu: University of Hawaii Press.

Freire, Paulo

1970   *Pedagogy of the Oppressed.* New York: Seabury Press.

1985   *The Politics of Education: Culture, Power, and Liberation.* South
               Hadley: Bergin and Garvey Publishers.

Friedson, Elliot
1986   *Professional Powers: A Study of the Institutionalization of
               Formal Knowledge.* Chicago: University of Chicago Press.

Frykenburg, R.E.
1984   'The Socio-Political Morphology of Madras: An Historical
               Interpretation.' In *Changing South Asia: City and Culture,*
               eds., Kenneth Ballhatchet and David Taylor, 21-41. Hong
               Kong: Asian Research Service.

Fukui, Norihiko
1987   *Atarashii Rekishigaku towaNanika* (Quest-ce que la nouvelle
               histoire ?). Tokyo: Nihon Editor School. In Japanese.

Fuller, C.J.
1988   'The Hindu Temple and Indian Society.' *Temple in Society,*
               ed., Michael V. Fox, 49-66.

Fuller, C.J. and Haripriya Narasimhan
2007   'From Landlords to Software Engineers: Migration and
               Urbanisation among Tamil Brahmins.' *Comparative Studies
               in Society and History* 50/1: 170-96

G.R.
1986   'Concert? Cutcheri?' *Kalakshetra Quarterly* 8/1-2: 26-7.

1989   'Pivotal Role in Preserving Music.' *The Hindu* (1
               December).

Gaisberg, Fred W.
1942   *The Music Goes Around.* New York: The Macmillan Co.

Ganapati, R.
1990   'Sivan's Life and Career.' *Sruti* 69-70: 21-6.

Ganesh, A.V.M.
1982   'Kaḍaisi Sandippu' [The Last Meeting]. *Kalki* (3 October):
               64. In Tamil.

Gangadhar, V.
2002   *M.S. Subbulakshmi: The Voice Divine.* New Delhi: Rupa &
               Co.

Gaston, Anne-Marie
1997   *Bharata Natyam: From Temple to Theatre.* New Delhi:
               Manohar.

Geekie, Gordon
1980   'The Study of Individual Carnatic Musicians.' *Yearbook of
               the International Folk Music Council* 12: 84-9.

Geertz, Clifford
1968   *Islam Observed: Religious Development in Morocco and Indonesia.* Chicago: University of Chicago Press.

Geetha, V. and S.V. Rajadurai
1998   *Towards a Non-Brahmin Millennium: From Iyothee Das to Periyar.* Calcutta: Samya.

Gennep, Arnold van
1960   *The Rites of Passage.* Chicago: University of Chicago Press.

George, T.J.S.
2004   *MS: A Life in Music.* New Delhi: HarperCollins.

Ginzburg, Carlo
1980   *The Cheese and the Worms: The Cosmos of a Sixteenth Century Miller.* Baltimore: Johns Hopkins University Press.

Goffman, Erving
1951   'Symbols of Class Status.' *British Journal of Sociology* 2/2: 294-304.

Gomadisankara Aiyar, V.S.
1970   *Isaikkalai Vallunarkaḷ* [Music Experts]. Madras: publisher unknown. In Tamil.

Gore, M.S.
1989   *Non-Brahman Movement in Maharashtra.* New Delhi: Segment Book Distributors.

Gorringe, Magdalen.
2005   'Arangetram and Manufacturing Identity: The Changing Role of a Bharata Natyam Dancer's Solo Debut in the Context of the Diaspora.' In *Diasporas and Interculturalism in Asian Performing Arts: Translating Traditions,* ed., Hae Kyungun, 91-103. London and New York: Routeledge and Curzon.

Gough, E. Kathleen
1955   'The Social Structure of a Tanjore Village.' In *Village India: Studies in the Little Community,* ed., McKim Marriott, 36-52. Chicago: University of Chicago Press.
1962   'Caste in a Tanjore Village.' In *Aspects of Caste in South India, Ceylon and North-West Pakistan,* ed., E.R. Leach, 11-60. Cambridge: Cambridge University Press.
1981   *Rural Society in Southeast India.* Cambridge: Cambridge University Press.

Government of Madras

1962   *Administration Report of the Hindu Religious and Charitable*
                Endowments (Administration) Department.

Government of Tamil Nadu

1972   *Tamil Nadu District Gazetteers: Ramanathapuram*, ed., A.
                Ramaswami.

1975   *Report of the Backward Classes Commission, Tamil Nadu,*
                1970, Volume II.

1983   *Tamil   Nadu   District   Gazetteers: Pudukkottai,   ed.,*
                Gopalkrishna Gandhi.

Govindarajan, Darumai (Darumapuram) A.

1987   'Nāgasuram.' Unpublished manuscript. In Tamil. 8pp.

Gramsci, Antonio

1971   *Selections from Prison Notebooks of Antonio Gramsci.* New
                York: International Publishers.

1981   *Selections from Cultural Writings*, eds., David Forgacs and
                Geoffrey Nowell-Smith. Cambridge: Harvard University
                Press.

Granow, Pekka

1981   'The Record Industry Comes to the Orient.' *Ethnomusicology*
                25/2: 251-84.

Gurukrupa

1985   *The Birth Place of Sri Tyagaraja.* Karaikal: Sapthaswaram
                Music Academy.

Guy, Randor

1985   'Tamil Cinema.' In *70 Years of Indian Cinema (1913-1983)*, ed.,
                T.M. Ramachandran, 462-75. Bombay: CINEMA India-
                International.

1988/89   'Carnatic Musicians and The Cinema: A Cavalcade of Fifty-Five
                Years.' *Sruti* 51-52: 67-77.

1990   'Motherly Love.' *Aside* 14/21-22: 42-3.

1991   'The Stars Shine On.' *Aside* 15/10: 36-7.

Hall, Basil

1931   *Travels in India, Ceylon and Borneo*, ed., H. G. Rawlingson.
                London: George Routledge and Sons.

Hall, Stuart

1977   'Culture, the Media and the 'Ideological Effect'.' In *Mass*
                Communication and Society, eds., James Curran, Michael
                Gurevitch, and Janet Woollacott, 315-48. Beverly Hills: Sage
                Publications.

1986   'Gramsci's Relevance for the Study of Race and Ethnicity.' *Journal of Communication Inquiry* 10/2: 5-27.

Hanchett, Suzanne
1988   *Coloured Rice: Symbolic Structure in Hindu Family Festivals.* Delhi: Hindustan Pub. Corp.

Hansen, Kathryn
1996   'Performing Identities: Tyagaraja Music Festival in North America.' *South Asia Research* 16: 155-74

Hardgrave, Robert
1965   *The Dravidian Movement.* Bombay: Popular Prakashan.
1969   *The Nadars of Tamilnad: The Political Culture of a Community in Change.* Berkeley: University of California Press.

Harper, Edward B.
1969   'Fear and the Status of Women.' *Southwestern Journal of Anthropology* 25: 81-95.

Hayavadana Rao, C., ed.
1927   *Mysore Gazetteer, Volume I: Descriptive.* Bangalore: The Government Press
1930   *Mysore Gazetteer, Volume II: Historical.* Bangalore: The Government Press

Hebdige, Dick
1979   *Subculture: The Meaning of Style.* New York: Methuen and Co.

Hemingway, F.R.
1906   *Madras District Gazetteers: Tanjore,* ed., W. Francis. Madras: Government of Madras.

Henry, Edward O.
1988   *Chant the Names of God: Music and Culture in Bhojpuri-Speaking India.* San Diego: San Diego State University Press.

Hiebert, Paul G.
1971   *Konduru: Structure and Integration in a South Indian Village.* Minneapolis: University of Minnesota Press.

Higgins, Jon B.
1973   'The Music of Bharata Natyam.' Ph.D. dissertation, Wesleyan University.
1976   'From Prince to Populace: Patronage as a Determinant of Change in South Indian (*Karnatak*) Music.' *Asian Music* 7: 20-6.

Hindu, The
1956a   'T.N. Rajaratnam Pillai Dead: Eminent Nagaswara Vidwan' (13 December).
1956b   'Late Rajaratnam Pillai' (19 December).
1956c   'Late Rajaratnam Pillai' (22 December).
1963   'Akshavani: From Tiruvaiyaru' (26 January).
1964a   'K. Arunachalam Dead: Noted Nagaswara Vidwan' (8 April).
1964b   'Raghava Pillai: Noted Tavil Vidwan' (11 April).
1968a   'City Cinema Fare: *Tillana Mohanambal*' (10 August).
1968b   'Thillana Mohanambal'. (August 10).
1986   'Thavil, the Main Instrument in Laya' (8 August).
1989   'Artistic Brilliance on Temple Walls' (1 January).
1992   'Rajarathna Award' (12 January).

Hobsbawm, Eric, and Terence Ranger, eds.
1983   *The Invention of Tradition.* Cambridge: Cambridge University Press.

hooks, bell
1989   *Talking Back: Thinking Feminist, Thinking Black.* Boston: South End Press.

Ilankumaran, R.
1990   *Tamilisai Iyakkam* [Tamil Music Movement]. Chennai: Manivasakar Padippaham.

Inden, Ronald
1988   *Imagining India.* Cambridge: Basil Blackwell.

Indian Express
1970   'Woman Shows Mettle on Nadaswaram.' (22 September, Bombay Edition).

Irschick, Eugene F
1969   *Politics and Social Conflict in South India: The Non-Brahman Movement and Tamil Separatism, 1916-1929.* Berkeley and Los Angeles: University of California Press.
1971   'Dravidianism in South Indian Politics.' In *Symposium on Dravidian Civilization*, ed., Andree F. Sjoberg, 147-69. Austin: Jenkins Publishing Company.
1986   *Tamil Revivalism in the 1930s.* Madras: Cre-A.

Isaac, L
1964   'Wind Instruments of India.' Ph.D. dissertation, University of Madras.

1972 'The Nagasvara: Its Origin and Evolution.' *Journal of the Madras University* 44/1-2: 167-82.

1975 'Musical Compositions: Source for the Study of Music and Musicians.' *Journal of the Madras University* 47/1: 145-61.

1990 'Ganakala Niyama or The Time Theory of Ragas.' In *Studies in India. Music and Allied Arts, Volume V*, eds., Leela Omchary and Deepti Omchary Bhalla, 25-32. Delhi: Sundeep Prakashan.

Ismail, K.

1984 *Karnataka Temples: Their Role in Socio-Economic Life*. Delhi: Sundeep Prakashan.

Iyalisai (Tamil newspaper)

1983 'Teṉṉindiya Vāṉoli Nilaiyaṅkaḷil Nādasvarak Kalaiñarkaḷ Niyamaṉam' [Appointment of Nadasvara Artists in South Indian Radio Stations]. (15 September).

Iyer, C.S.

1948 'The Clarinet and Classical Carnatic Music.' *JMA* 19: 51-7.

Jackson, William J.

1988 'The Nuances of 'Ra': Tyagaraja's Songs Yearning for Rama's Presence.' *Shanmukha* 14/2: 25-8.

1991 *Tyagaraja: Life and Lyrics*. Madras: Oxford University Press.

1994 *Tyagaraja and the Renewal of Tradition and Reflections*. Delhi: Motilal Banarsidass.

Jacoby, Mario

1985 *The Longing for Paradise: Psychological Perspectives on a Archetype*. Boston: Sigo Press.

Jagadisa Ayyar, P.V.

1925 *South Indian Customs*. Madras: Diocesan Press.

1982 *South Indian Shrines*. New Delhi: Asian Educational Services.

Jairazbhoy, Nazir A.

1970 'A Preliminary Survey of the Oboe in India.' *Ethnomusicology* 14: 375-88.

1980 'The South Asian Double-Reed Aerophone Reconsidered.' *Ethnomusicology* 24/1: 147-56.

Janaki, S.S., ed.

1988 *Siva Temple and Temple Rituals*. Madras: The Kuppuswami Sastri Research Institute.

Jayaraman
1986   'Vettikkavala Shashikumar: Nagaswaram Not Given Its
               Due.' *Indian Express* (Cochin Edition, 16 December).
Jayaraman, Lalgudi G.
1986   'The Violin in Carnatic Music.' *Kalakshetra Quarterly* 8/1-
               2: 28-34.
Jayaraman, P.C.
1988   'The Greening of a Mridangam Maestro: A Tani by T.K.
               Murthy.' *Sruti* 44: 17-21.
Jeyechandran, A.V.
1985   *The Madurai Temple Complex.* Madurai: Madurai Kamaraj
               University.
Johnson, Richard, Gregor McLennan, Bill Schwarz, and David Sutton, eds.
1982   *Making Histories: Studies in History-Writing and Politics.*
               London: Hutchinson.
Jordan, Kay Kirkpatrick
1989   'From Sacred Servant to Profane Prostitute: A Study of the
               Changing Legal Status of the Devadasis, 1857-1949.' Ph.D.
               dissertation, University of Ohio.
Joshi, O.P.
1982   'The Changing Social Structure of Music in India.'
               International Social Science Journal 34/4: 625-37.
Kajiwara, Kageaki
1984   'Rekishi to Shocho' [History and Symbolism]. In
               Shochojinruigaku [Symbolic Anthropology], ed. Aoki
               Tamotsu, 28-41. Tokyo: Shibundo. In Japanese.
Kalaimani (Kottamangalam Suppu)
1968   *Tillāṉā Mōhaṉāmbāḷ.* Madras: Palaniyappa Brothers. In
               Tamil.
Kalidas, K.S.
1986   'Evolution of Mridangam Styles: Thanjavur & Pudukottai
               Schools.' *Sruti* 35: 42.
Kaliyappan, K.
1999   'Tamiḻil Pāḍuvatu Takudi Kuṟaivāṉadā?' [Is Singing in
               Tamil less worthy?]. *Sarigamapadani* 3/4: 38-47.
Kaliyaperumal, K.
1980   *Tamiḻar Tirumaṇa Muṟaikal* [Tamil Marriage Patterns].
               Madras: Ulahat Tamil Eruttalar Padippaham. In Tamil.

Kalki (Tamil weekly magazine)
1968   'Tillānā Mōhanāmbāḷ.' (11 August).
Kamat, Jyotsna K.
1980   *Social Life in Medieval Karnataka.* New Delhi: Abhinav
            Publications.
Kane, P.V.
1968   *History of Dharmasastra.* Revised and enlarged edition.
            Poona: Bhandarkar Oriental Research Institute.
Kanya
1987   'Ēṉ Karnāṭakam?' [Why Karnataka (Isai)?]. *Kalki* (20
            December): 66-7. In Tamil.
Karashima, Noboru
1988   'Minzoku to Kasuto' [Ethnicity and Caste]. In *Minzokutowa
            Nanika* [What is Ethnicity?], eds., Kawada Junzo and
            Fukui Katsuyoshi, 149-69. Tokyo: Iwanamishoten. In
            Japanese.
Karnataka Backward Classes Commision Report
1974   Bangalore: Government of Karnataka. In four volumes.
Karunakaran, K., and C. Shanmugam Pillai
1975   *Saiva Vellala Tamil Dialect.* Annamalainagar: Annamalai
            University.
Kassebaum, Gayathri
2004   'The Saxophone in Karnataka: A 21st Century Cultural
            Adaptation of a Foreign Instrument in Traditional South
            Indian Concert and Ritual Contexts.' A paper presented
            at the 8th International Conference of the Asia Pacific
            Society for Ethnomusicology (Phnom Penh, Cambodia),
            24-27 August.
Kaul, H.K., ed.
1979   *Travellers' India: An Anthology.* Delhi: Oxford University
            Press.
Kavlekar, Kasinath K.
1979   *Non-Brahmin Movement in Southern India 1873-1949.*
            Kolhapur: Shivaji University Press.
Keil, Charles
1979   *Tiv Song: The Sociology of Art in a Classless Society.* Chicago:
            University of Chicago Press.
Kennedy, Richard
1974   'Status and Control of Temples in Tamil Nadu.' *The
            Indian Economic and Social History Review* 11: 260-90.

Kersenboom-Story, Saskia C.

1987　　　*Nityasumangali: Devadasi Tradition in South India.* Delhi: Motilal Banarsidass.

Khagram, S., M. Desai and J. Varughese

2001　　　'Seen, Rich but Unheard? The Politics of Asian Indians in the United States.' In *Asian-Americans and Politics: Perspectives, Experiences, Prospects,* ed., G.H. Chang. Washington: Woodrow Wilson Press.

Kippen, James

1985　　　*The Tabla of Lacknow: A Cultural Analysis of a Musical Tradition.* Cambridge: Cambridge University Press.

Knight, Douglas M. Jr.

2010　　　*Balasaraswati: Her Art and Life.* Chennai: Tranquebar.

Koizumi, Fumio

1985　　　*Minzokuongaku no Sekai* [The World of Ethnic Music]. Tokyo: Nihon Hososhuppan Kyokai. In Japanese.

Krishna, R. Gopal

1984　　　'How Indian Are We?' *The Illustrated Weekly of India* (19 October), 32-5.

Krishna Iyer, E.

1933　　　*Personalities in Present Day Music. Madras: Rochouse & Sons.*

Krishnan, Namagiripettai and Tiruvarur Latchappa Pillai

1985　　　'Apūrva Nādasvaram' [Rare Nadasvaram]. *Kungumam* (22 January): 72-7. In Tamil.

Krishnan, T.N.

1985　　　'G.N. Sir...' In *G.N.B. 75th Birthday Celebrations Souvenior,* 31-3. Madras: G.N.B. Trust.

Krishnamurti, R.

n.d.　　　'Karnatic Music: Impact of Political, Socio-economic and Technological Factors on its Evolution.' Unpublished manuscript.

Krishnaswami Nayudu, W.S.

1965　　　*Old Madras.* Madras: author.

Krishnaswamy, S.

1985　　　'K. Subramanyam: Pioneer of Tamil Cinema.' In *70 Years of Indian Cinema (1913-1983),* ed., T.M. Ramachandran, 153-7.Bombay: Cinema India-International.

Krishnaswamy, S.Y.
1986   'A Genius Self-Taught.' *The Hindu* (June 8).
Kriya (Cre-A)
1992   *Kriyāviṉ Taṟkālat Tamiḻ Aharādi* [Cre-A's Comtemporary Tamil Dictionary]. Madras: Cre-A.
Kuppusami, M.G.
1965   *Saṅgīta Tāḷa Rāga Mālai* [Garland of Musical Rhythm and Melody]. Madras: K. Subramaniyam. In Tamil.
Kuppuswamy, M. Gowri, and M. Hariharan
1984   *Royal Patronage to Indian Music.* Delhi: Sundeep Prakashan.
1985   *Music in Indian Art.* Delhi: Sundeep Prakashan.
1989   'Pallavi in Karnataka Music.' *Shanmukha* 15/3: 9-13.
LaCapra, Dominick
1983   *Rethinking Intellectual History: Text, Contexts, Language.* Ithaca: Cornell University Press.
Laclau, Ernesto, and Chantal Mouffe
1982   'Recasting Marxism: Hegemony and New Political Movements.' *Socialist Review* 66: 91-113.
Lakshmanan, A. Radha.
1997   'Desecretion of Tyagaraja's Memory: A Retort.' *Sruti* 152: 22-3
Lakshmi, C.S.
1984   *The Face Behind the Mask: Women in Tamil Literature.* New Delhi: Vikas Publishing House.
L'Armand, Kathleen and Adrian L'Armand
1978   'Music in Madras: The Urbanization of a Cultural Tradition.' In *Eight Urban Musical Cultures*, ed., Bruno Nettl, 115-45. Chicago: University of Illinois Press.
1983   'One Hundred Years of Music in Madras: A Case Study in Secondary Urbanization.' *Ethnomusicology* 27/3: 411-38.
Lawrence, Lady
1920   *Indian Embers.* Oxford: George Ronald.
Leach, Edmund
1986   'Aryan Invasions over Four Millennia.' In *Culture Through Time: Anthropological Approaches*, ed., Emiko Ohnuki-Tiemey, 227-45. Stanford: Stanford University Press.
Lears, T.J. Jackson
1981   'The Concept of Cultural Hegemony: Problems and Possibilities.' *American Historical Review* 90: 567-93.

Leonard, Karen
1997   'Changing South Asian identities in the United States.' In
              Beyond Black and White: New Facesand Voices in U.S. Schools,
              eds., Maxine Seller and Lois Weis, 165-79. Albany: State
              University of New York Press.

Levinson, Stephen C.
1982   'Caste Rank and Verbal Interaction in Western Tamilnadu.'
              In *Caste Ideology and Interaction*, ed., Dennis B. McGilvray,
              98-203. Cambridge: Cambridge University Press.

Levi-Strauss, Claude
1969   *The Raw and the Cooked: Introduction to a Science of
              Mythology I.* New York: Harper and Row Publishers.

Lewandowski, Susan J.
1975   'Urban Growth and Municipal Development in the
              Colonial City of Madras, 1860-1900.' *Journal of Asian
              Studies* 34/2: 341-60.
1977   'Changing Form and Function in the Ceremonial and
              the Colonial Port City in India: An Historical Analysis
              of Madurai and Madras.' *Modern Asian Studies* 11/2: 183-
              212.
1980   *Migration and Ethnicity in Urban India: Kerala Migrants in
              the City of Madras, 1870-1970.* New Delhi: Manohar.

Loti, Pierre
1906   *India.* London: T. Werner Laurie Ltd.

Luthra, H.R.
1986   *Indian Broadcasting.* Ministry of Information and
              Broadcasting, Government of India.

Mackenzie, Caroline
1987   'Melkote: A Temple Town.' *The India Magazine* (March):
              57-63.

Maclean, C.D.
1982(1893)   *Glossary of the Madras Presidency.* New Delhi: Asian
              Educational Services.

Madan, T.N.
1987   *Non-Renunciation: Themes and Interpretations of Hindu
              Culture.* Delhi: Oxford University Press.

Mahadevan, K.S.
1988   'The Decline of Nagaswara Art.' *Shanmukha* 14/2: 33-5.
1990   'Cultural Decadence: The Villain.' *Shanmukha* 16/4: 31-32.

Maharam

1966   '*Kalyāṇa Virundu*' [Wedding Feast]. *Kalki* (31 July). In Tamil.

Malarvizhi, K.

n.d.   'Nagaswaram.' MA thesis, Madurai Kamaraj University.

Malhotra, Inder

1969   'Corruption in the Houses of God: Hindu, Muslim, Sikh.' *The Illustrated Weekly of India* (3 September), 8-17.

Mandelbaum, David G.

1968   *Society in India, Volume Two: Change and Continuity.* Berkeley: University of California Press.

Mangalamurugesan, N.K.

1979   *Self-Respect Movement in Tamil Nadu 1920-1940.* Madurai: Koodal Publishers.

Manucci, Niccolao

1965-66(1907-8) *Storia Do Mogor, or Mogul India 1653-1708*, trans. William Irvine. Calcutta: Editions Indian.

Manuel, Peter

1984   *Popular Musics of the Non-Western World.* New York: Oxford University Press.

Matejka, Ladislav, and I.R. Titunik

1991   'Translators' Preface, 1986.' In *Marxism and the Philosophy of Language* by V.N. Volosinov, vii-xii. Cambridge: Harvard University Press.

Mathur, J.C.

1970   'The Impact of A.I.R. on Indian Music.' In *Aspects of Indian Music*, ed., Ministry of Information and Broadcasting, 97-103. Original edition in 1957.

Matter, Samuel

1883   *Native Life in Travancore.* London: W.H. Allen.

McDonald, Maryon

1986   'Celtic Ethnic Kinship and the Problem of Being English.' *Current Anthropology* 27/4: 333-41.

Memmi, Albert

1965   *The Colonizer and the Colonized.* New York: Orion Press.

1984   *Dependence: A Sketch for a Portrait of the Dependent.* Boston: Beacon Press.

Mencher, Joan P.

1970   'A Tamil Village: Changing Socioeconomic Structure in Madras State.' In *Change and Continuity in India's Villages*, ed., K. Ishwaran, 197-218. New York: Columbia University Press.

Menon, K. Sankara
1989   'Sri Semmangudi Srinivasa Iyer.' *In Semmangudi 80*, 34-37. Madras: Sri Semmangudi Srinivasier Sathabhishekam Celebrations Committee.

Mitchell, Frank
1978   *Navajo Blessingway Singer: The Autobiography of Frank Mitchell 1881-1967*, edited by Charlotte J. Frisbie and David P. McAllester. Tucson: The University of Arizona Press.

Mitchell, Mrs Murry
1885   *In Southern India: A Visit to Some of the Chief Mission Stations in the Madras Presidency.* Piccadilly: The Religious Tract Society.

Moffatt, Michael
1975   *An Untouchable Community in South India.* Princeton: Princeton University Press.

Monier-Williams, M.
1974(1883)   *Religious Thought and Life in India: Vedism, Brahmanism and Hinduism.* New Delhi: Oriental Books Reprint Corp.

Morson, Gary Saul, and Caryl Emerson
1985   'Introduction: Rethinking Bakhtin.' In *Rethinking Bakhtin: Extensions and Challenges*, eds., Gary Saul Morson and Caryl Emerson, 1-60. Evanson: Northwestern University Press.

Mouffe, Chantal, ed.
1979   *Gramsci and Marxist Theory.* London: Routledge and Kegan Paul.

Mousset, Louis Marie, and M. Depuis
1981(1895)   *Dictionaire Tamoul-Francais.* New Delhi: Asian Educational Services.

Mudaliar, Chandra Y.
1976   *State and Religious Endowments in Madras.* Madras: University of Madras.
1978   'Non-Brahmin Movement in Kolhapur.' *The Indian Economic and Social History Review* 15/1: 1-19.

Murray-Aynsley, J.C.
1883   *Our Tour in Southern India.* London: F.V. White and Co.
Music Academy
n.d.   *Report of the All-India Music Conference* (1927, Madras).
              Journal of the Music Academy, Vols. XII-XIX.
1988   *Music Academy Diary 1988-9.*
1997   *Sangita Kalanidhi Sangita Kalanidhi Mudicondan Venkatrama*
              Iyer Birth Centenary (1897-1997) Souvenir. Chennai: Music
              Academy.
1997   *E. Krishna Iyer Centenary Issue.* Chennai: Music Academy.
Muthiah, S.
1987   *Madras Discovered: A Historical Guide to Looking Around,*
              Supplemented with Tales of 'Once Upon a City'. New Delhi:
              East-West Press.
1989   *Tales of Old and New Madras.* New Delhi: Affiliated East-
              West Press.
Muttaiya, Mullai Piel.
1996   *Tamiḻ Isai Muḻakkam* [Speech on Tamil Music]. Chennai:
              Mullai Padippaham.
Nadar, A.C. Paul
1959   'A Pioneer Research Worker in Tamil Music.' *Tamil*
              Culture 8/3: 110-20.
Nagam Aiya, V.
1906   *The Travancore State Manual.* Trivandrum: The Travancore
              Government Press.
Nagarajan, K.
1989   *Dr. Rajah Sir Muthiah Chettiar: A Biography.* Chidambaram:
              Annamalai University
Nagarajan, S.
1995   *Tamils Abroad: Non-Asian Countries.* Tanjavur: Tamil
              University.
Nagaswamy, R.
1965   'South Indian Temple as an Employer.' *Indian Economic*
              and Social History Review 2/4: 367-72.
1987   'Thanjavur Natya on Canvas.' *The Hindu* (4 January).
Nambi Arooran, K.
1980   *Tamil Renaissance and Dravidian Nationalism: 1905-1944.*
              Madurai: Koodal Publications.
1981   'The Origin of Three Saiva Mathas in Thanjavur District.'

In *Proceedings of the Fifth International Conference-Seminar of Tamil Studies*, Vol. II, ed., M. Arunachalam, 12/77-85. Madras: International Association of Tamil Research.

1984   'The Changing Role of Three Saiva Maths in Tanjore District from the Beginning of the 20th Century.' In *Changing South Asia: Religion and Society*, eds., Kenneth Ballhatchet and David Taylor, 51-8. Hong Kong: Asian Research Service.

Nandakumar, R.

1993   'Sociology of Listening: Case of the Nagaswaram.' *Sangeet Natak* 108-109: 23-9.

Nandy, Ashis

1983   *The Intimate Enemy: Loss and Recovery of Self under Colonialism*. Delhi: Oxford University Press.

Nanjundayya, H.V., and Anantha Krishna Iyer

1928-35   *The Mysore Tribes and Castes*. Mysore: Mysore University. In four volumes.

Narasimhachar, T.B.

1978   'Vainika Sikhamani Seshanna of Mysore.' *Shanmukha* 4/3: 3-10.

Narasimhan, V.M.

1950   'Some Temple Curiosities.' *The Hindu* (12 November).

1979(1954)   'Temple Curiosities: Some Strange Musical Objects.' In *Readings on Music and Dance*, eds., Gowri Kuppuswamy and M. Hariharan, 189-92. Delhi: B.R. Publishing Corporation.

Narayana Murthy, Surya J.

2005   *Devadasis and Bharatha Natyam in Tamilnadu*. Chennai: Ulaga Thamizhar Pathippakam.

Narayana Panicker, Kavalam

1968   'Ambalapuzha Sankaranarayana Panicker.' *Keli* (January issue): 3-4. In Malayalam.

Narayanan, Mohan

1987   'Record Review: Enchanting Nadhaswaram Recital: Namagiripettai Krishnan.' *Aside* 11: 7-8.

Narayanan (N.), N.M.

1973   'High Ideal of Instrumental Style.' *The Hindu* (13 April).

1991   'Art of Missing the Music.' *The Hindu* (3 May).

Narayanaswami, H.
1987   *Saint Tyagaraja.* Cochin: Diwakar Deo.
Narayanaswami, R.S.
1969   'A Thanjavur Tradition: R.S. Narayanaswami Listens to Tiruvegadu Subramania Pillai.' *Indian Express* (14 August).
Natarajan, B.
1970   *The City of Cosmic Dance.* New Delhi: Orient Longman.
Natarajan, Srividya
1997   'Another Stage in the Life of the Nation: Sadir, Bharata Natyam, Feminist Theory.' Ph.D. thesis, University of Hyderabad.
Natarajasundaram Pillai, Tiruvizhimizhalai S.
n.d.   'Tavil Mēdai Nīḍamaṅgalam Mīṇāṭcisundaram Piḷḷai.' *TIVM:* 37-42. In Tamil.
1980   'Nādasvara Kalai Mēdaikaḷ' [Geniuses in the Art of Nadasvaram]. In *Tamilnadu Eyal Isai Nataka Mandram-Madras, Silver Jubilee Souvenir,* 99-105. In Tamil.
Navinson, Henry Wood
1975(1906)   *The New Spirit in India.* Delhi: Metropolitan Book Company.
Nayar, R.B.
1990a   'Why Trinity?' *Sruti* 67: 34-5.
1990b   'Tradition in Indian Classical Music.' *Sruti* 73: 35-7.
Needham, Rodney
1967   'Percussion and Transition.' *Man* 2/4: 606-14.
Neelkant, K.
1986   'Matchless Flutist.' *Frontline* (28 June-11 July issue): 110-2.
Nettl, Bruno
1985   *The Western Impact on World Music: Change, Adaptation, and Survival.* New York: Schirmer Books.
Nettl, Bruno, and Philip V. Bohlman, eds.
1987   *Comparative Musicology and Anthropology of Music: Essays on the History of Ethnomusicology.* Chicago: University of Chicago Press.
Neuman, Daniel M.
1980   *The Life of Music in North India: The Organization of an Artistic Tradition.* Detroit: Wayne State University Press.
1985   'Indian Music as a Cultural System.' *Asian Music* 17/1: 98-113.

Nietzsche, Friedrich
1949   *The Use and Abuse of History.* New York: The Liberal Arts Press.

Nijenhuis, Emmie te, and Sanjukta Gupta
1987   *Sacred Songs of India: Diksitar's Cycle of Hymns to the Goddess Kamala, Part I: Musicological and Religious Analysis, Text and Translation.* Winterthur, Schweiz: Amadeus.

Nilakanta Sastri, K.A.
1963   *Development of Religion in South India.* Bombay: Orient Longmans.
1966   *A History of South India from Prehistoric Times to the Fall of Vijayanagar.* Madras: Oxford University Press.

Nilam, S.
1985   *Saṅgīta Kalaimaṇigaḷ* [Gems in Music]. Madras: Vanadi Padippakam. In Tamil.

Nishimura, Yuko
1987   *A Study on Mariyamman Worship in South India: A Preliminary Study on Modern South Indian Village Hinduism.* Tokyo: Institute for the Study of Languages and Cultures of Asia and Africa.

Nixon, Michael J.
1988   'Nantanar Carittiram in Performance: An Item in the Tamil Musical-Dramatic Repertoire.' MA thesis, Wesleyan University.

O'Brien, Jay, and William Roseberry, eds.
1991   *Golden Ages, Dark Ages: Imagining the Past in Anthropology and History.* Berkeley: University of California Press.

Oddie, G.A.
1979   *Social Protest in India: British Protestant Missionaries and Social Reforms 1850-1900.* New Delhi: Manohar.
1984   'The Character, Role and Significance of Non-Brahman Saivite Maths in Tanjore District in the Nineteenth Century.' In *Changing South Asia: Religion and Society*, eds., Kenneth Ballhatchet and David Taylor, 37-50. Hong Kong: Asian Research Service.
1985   'Recent Writings on the Social and Cultural Aspects of Modern South Indian History.' In *Studies of South India: An Anthology of Recent Research and Scholarship*, eds., Robert Frykenburg and Pauline Kolenda, 171-93. Madras: New Era Publications.

Orr, P.

1986   'The Many-Sided Mali: Personali-Tales.' *Sruti* 24/24-S: 29-36.

1990a   'Neglect of Nagaswaram.' *Sruti* 65: 56-7.

1990b   'Birth Centenary of Ariyakudi: Commemoration Society Starts Celebrations.' *Sruti* 69-70: 7-8.

O'Shea, Janet

2007   *At Home in the World: Bharata Natyam on the Global Stage.* Middletown: Wesleyan University Press.

Padfield, J.E.

1975(1908)   *The Hindu at Home.* Delhi: B.R. Publishing Corporation.

Padmavadi, S.

1965   'Kalyāṇa Vīḍu.' *Kalla* (21 March). In Tamil.

Panan

1986   'Mirudaṅgattiṟkum Tavilukkum Eṉṉa Vēṟupāṭu?' [What is the Difference between a Mridangam and a Tavil?]. *Kungumam* (12 September). In Tamil.

Pandey, Rajbali

1969   *Hindu Samskaras: Socio-Religious Study of the Hindu Sacraments.* Delhi: Motilal Banarsidass.

Pandian, J.

1987   *Caste, Nationalism and Ethnicity: An Interpretation of Tamil Cultural History and Social Order.* Bombay: Popular Prakashan.

Papa (K. Sundar Rajan)

1998(1953)   'Peerless Rajaratnam Pillai.' In *Nādasvara Cakravartti Tiruvāvaḍuturai Ti. En. Rājarattiṉam Piḷḷai Nūṟṟāṇḍu Viḻā Siṟappu Malar* [100th Anniversary Festival Special Issue of Nagasvaram Emperor Tiruvavadudurai T.N. Rajarattinam Pillai]. Chennai: Hamsadhvani.

Parameswaran, Sarojini

1971   'The Twain Meet Again.' *Sruti* 1: 7-8.

Parasher, Alka, and Usha Naik

1987   'Temple Girls of Medieval Karnataka.' *The Indian Economic and Social History Review* 23/1: 63-91.

Park, Robert E.

1928   'Human Migration and the Marginal Man.' *The American Journal of Sociology* 33/6: 881-93.

Parthasarathy, T.S.
1981   'Nāgasvaram.' *MAS*, unpaged.
1986a   'Changing Concert Patterns.' *Kalakshetra Quarterly* 8/1-2: 69-73.
1986b   'Doyen among Composers: Papanasam Sivan.' *Indian Express* (3 October).
1989   'The "Seenu" I Have Known.' In *Semmangudi 80*, 15-16. Madras: Sri Semmangudi Srinivasier Sathabhishekam Celebrations Committee.

Pattabhiraman, N.
1983   'Gone Down the Pipe.' *Sruti* 2: 21-3.
1986a   'The Passage of a Prodigy.' *Sruti* 24-24S: 12-8.
1986b   'The Perversities of Mali.' *Sruti* 24-24S: 25-7.
1989   'Semmangudi and His Contemporaries.'*Sruti* 60-61: 43-7.
1993   'Music His Heartbeat.' *In Semmangudi: A Mosaic-Portrait*, ed., N. Pattabhi Raman, 3-16. Madras: The Sruti Foundation.

Pattabhiraman, N., and T.T. Nadendran
1983   'Carnatic Music Today: Making Sense of the Cross-Talk, Part I.' *Sruti* 3: 4-8.

Pattabhiraman, N., and Gowri Ramnarayan
1983   'Point-Counterpoint.' *Sruti* 3: 35.

Pattabhiraman, N., and T. Sankaran
1976   'Endaro Mahanubhavulu: Carnatic Musicians of Kerala, Part II.' *Sruti* 30: 33-7.

Pattammal, D.K.
1983   'On Pallavi Singing.' *Sruti* 1: 38-9.

Pavadai, V.S.V.
1988   'Nāṉ Aṟinda Nādasvara Mēdaikaḷum Tavil Mēdaikaḷum' [Nadasvaram and Tavil Geniuses I Knew]. In *Madurai Poṉṉusāmi Piḷḷai Avarkaḷ Nūrrāṇṭu Viḻā Malar*, 32-43. In Tamil.

Perkins, John F., Alan Kelly, and John Ward
1976   'On Gramophone Company Matrix Numbers, 1898 to 1921.' *The Record Collector* 23/3-4: 51-90.

Presler, Franklin
1987   *Religion Under Bureaucracy: Policy and Administration for Hindu Temples in South India*. Cambridge: Cambridge University Press.

Peterson, Indira V.

1980   'Singing of a Place: Pilgrimage as Metaphor and Motif in the Tevaram Songs of the Tamil Saivite Saints.' An unpublished paper delivered at the University Seminar on Tradition and Change in South and Southeast Asia, Columbia University.

1989   *Poems to Siva: The Hymns of the Tamil Saints.* Princeton: Princeton University Press.

Pillay, Kulappa Kanakasabhapathi

1969   *A Social History of the Tamils.* Madras: University of Madras.

Ponnammal, G.K.

1966   'Iraṭṭai Nāyaṉam' [Double Nayanam]. *Kalki* (July 31): 74-9. In Tamil.

Ponnusami Pillai, M.K.M.

1930   *Pūrvīka Saṅgīta Uṇmai* [The Truth about Native Music]. Madurai: Minalosani Acciyandirasalai.

Ponnusamy, S.

1972   *Sri Tyagaraja Temple.* Madras: The State Department of Archaeology, Government of Tamil Nadu.

Popular Memory Group

1982   'Popular Memory: Theory, Politics, Method.' In *Making Histones: Studies in History-Writing and Politics*, eds., Richard Johnson et al., 205-52. London: Hutchinson.

Poster, Mark

1980   'Foucault and History.' *Social Research* 49: 116-42.

Powell, E. Alexander

1929   *The Last Home of Mystery.* New York: Garden City Publishing Company.

Powers, Harold

1980   'India (Sections I-II).' In *Grove's Dictionary of Music (7th edition), Vol. 9:* 69-141.

Prabhu, K.M.

1937   'Nagaswara and Nagachinna.' *The Hindu* (17 January).

Prajnanananda, Swami

1973   *The Historical Development of Indian Music: A Critical Study.* Calcutta: Firma K.L. Mukhopadhyay.

Premeela, M.

1984   'Kathakalakshepa: A Study.' Ph.D. dissertation, University of Madras.

Presler, Franklin A.
1988   *Religion under Bureaucracy: Policy and Administration for Hindu Temples in South India.* Cambridge: Cambridge University Press.

Pudiya Kalaccaram, ed.
2002   *Isai: Pōtai, Poḷudupōkku, Pōrāṭṭam* [Music: Intoxification, Entertainment, and Struggle]. Chennai: Pudiya Kalaccaram.

Qureshi, Regula Burckardt
1991   'Whose Music?: Sources and Contexts in Indie Musicology.' In *Comparative Musicology and Anthropology of Music: Essays on the History of Ethnomusicology,* eds., Bruno Nettl and Philip Bohlman, 152-68. Chicago: University of Chicago Press.

Radhakrishna Pillai, Chidambaram
1985   'Rakti Mēḷam.' A Lecture-Demonstration at the Music Academy, Madras (31 December). In Tamil.

Raghavan, V.
1936   'Nagasvara or Nadaswara?: The Case for the Former.' *The Hindu* (6 December).
1937   'Nagaswara and Nagachinna.' *The Hindu* (17 January).
1945   'Some Musicians and Their Patrons about 1800 A.D. in Madras City.' *JMA* 16: 127-36.
1949   'Nagasvara.' *JMA* 20: 155-9.
1955   'Nagasvara.' *JMA* 26: 149.
1958   *Sarva-Deva-Vilasa.* Madras: Adyar Library and Research Centre.
1970   'Karnataka and Karnataka Music.' *MAS,* unpaged.
1975a   'Muttuswami Dikshitar.' In *Muttuswami Dikshitar,* 1-26. Bombay: National Centre for the Performing Arts.
1975b   'Dikshitar's Shishya Parampara.' In *Muttuswami Dikshitar,* 34-7. Bombay: National Centre for the Performing Arts.
1977   *Nōṭṭu Svara Sahityas of Sri Muttusvami Dikshitar.* Madras: Music Academy.
1978   'An Inseparable Adjunct of Life.' *The Hindu* (5 February).
1983   *Tyagaraja.* New Delhi: Sahitya Akademi.

Rajadurai, S.V.
1997   'Tamiḻ Isaik Kiḻarcciyum Pārppaṇarallādār Iyakkamum' [Tamiḻ Isai Agitation and Non-Brahmin Movement]. Unpublished manuscript. 80pp. In Tamil.

Rajagopal, Indhu
1985   *The Tyranny of Caste: The Non-Brahman Movement and Political Development in South India.* New Delhi: Vikas Publishing House.

Rajagopalan, K.R., and T. Sankaran
1987   'Tirukodikaval Krishna Iyer (1857-1913): A Great Violinist, Possibly the First Soloist.' *Sruti* 31: 31-2.

Rajagopalan, L.S.
1975   'The Kurum Kuzhal of Kerala.' *JMA* 46: 144-57.
1988   'The Kurum Kuzhal of Kerala.' *JSNA* 88: 39-43.

Rajagopalan, N.
1965   'Influence of Western Music and Hindustani Music on Karnatic Music.' *JMA* 36: 88-90.
1990   *Garland: Biographical Dictionary of Carnatic Composers and Musicians, Book I.* Bombay: Bharatiya Vidya Bhavan.

Rajam, S.
1986a   'Kalyani Raga.'*Sruti* 21: 51-3.
1986b   'Todi Raga.' *Sruti* 22: 41-2.
1988   'Anandabhairavi Raga.' *Sruti* 47: 41-3.

Rajan, Savithri, and Michael Nixon, eds.
1982   *Shobhillu Saptasvara.* Madras: Cre-A.

Rajendran, Sulochana
1990   'The Twentieth Century Tyagaraja.' *Shanmukha* 16/1: 7-11.

Raju, T.S.
1983   *In the Foot Step of Thiagaraja.* Madras: Amudha Nilayam.

Rama Rau, Santha
1954   *This Is India.* New York: Harper & Brothers.

Ramachandra Dikshitar, V.R.
1939   'Around the City Pagodas.' In *The Madras Tercentenary Commemoration Volume,* 355-69. London: Oxford University Press.

Ramachandran, Anandhi
1983   'The *Tamil Isai* Movement: A Battle of Words.' *Sruti* 2: 4-7, 9.

Ramachandran, Kumbakonam S.
1931   'South Indian Wind Instruments: The Nadhaswaram.' *The Hindu* (4 October).
1937   'Nagasvaram or Nadaswaram: The Case for a Third One.' *The Hindu* (10 January).

Ramachandran, N.S.

1966		'Classical Music and the Mass-Media (With Special Reference to South India).' In *Music East and West*, ed., Indian Council for Cultural Relations, 166-70. Bombay: Bhatkal Books International.

1967		'Musical Image of Tyagaraja in Tradition and Practice.' *JSNA* 6: 25-35.

1973		'Venkatamakhi and the Raga System: Some Basic Aspects of His Contribution to Indian Music.' *JSNA* 28: 24-9.

Ramachandran, S.

1985		'G.N.B.'s Music: An Appreciation.' In *G.N.B. 75th Birthday Celebrations Souvenir*, 23-9. Madras: G.N.B. Trust.

1989		'Lasting Impact of Two Styles.' *Shanmukha* 15/4: 7-11.

Ramachandran, T.M., ed.

1985		*70 Years of Indian Cinema (1913-1983)*. Bombay: CINEMA India-International.

Ramachandra Sastri, H.

1986		'Winds of Change.' *Kalakshetra Quarterly* 8/1-2: 35-6.

Ramakrishnan, K.

1930		'South Indian Wind Instruments: the Nagaswara.' *The Hindu* (4 October).

Ramakrishnan, K.P.

1985		'Mali & His Musical Contemporaries.' *Sruti* 24-24/S: 37-40.

1986		'Mali & Mani Iyer.' *Sruti* 35: 29-32.

Ramanathan Chettiar, L.P.K.

1967		'Tamil Isai Sangam: Veḷḷi Viḻā Malar 1943-1968.' *Kalki* (24 December): 13-6

1992		'The History of the Tamil Isai Sangam, Madras.' *The Hindu* (21 December).

Ramanathan, S.

1984		*Srī Tiyāgarāja Svāmikaḷiṉ Utcava Sampradāya Kīrttaṉaikaḷ*. Madras: Kalaimahal Isaik Kalluri. In Tamil.

1986		'The 'Cutcheri Paddhati' in Carnatic Music.' *Kalakshetra Quarterly* 8/1-2: 10-8.

Ramani, N.

1986		'When Breath Becomes Music.' *Kalakshetra Quarterly* 8/1-2: 37-42.

Ramanujachari
1966   *The Spiritual Heritage of Tyagaraja.* Madras: Sri Ramakrishna
               Math.
Ramanujam, T.V.
1982   'M.L.V.' *Kalla* (August 22): 39. In Tamil.
Ramaswami, M.S.
1987   *The Ambrosia of Muthuswamy Dikshitar.* Madras: Karnatik
               Music Book Centre.
Ramaswami Aiyar, M.S.
1936   'Nadasvara or Nagasvara.' *The Hindu* (13 December).
Ramaswamy, Sumathi
1997   *Passions of the Tongue: Language Devotion in Tamil Nadu,
               1891-1970.* New Delhi: Munshiram Manoharlal Publishers.
Ramnarayan, Gowri
1987   'The Musical Genius of M.S.' *Indian Express* (29 July).
Rangaccari, K.S.
1979   *Srī Tiyāgarāja Svāmigaḷ: Vāḻkkai Carittiram* [Sri Tyagaraja
               Swamy: A Biography]. Kumbakonam: Svadi Padippaham.
Rangacharya, V.
1985(1919)   *A Topographical List of the Inscriptions of the Madras
               Presidency, Collected till 1915: With Notes and References.*
               In three volumes. New Delhi: Asian Educational Services.
Rangarajan, M.R.
2005   *Director K. Subrahmanyam: A Biography.* Chennai: East
               West Books.
Rangaramanuja Ayyangar, R.
1972   *History of South Indian (Carnatic) Music: From Vedic Times
               to the Present.* Madras: by the author.
1977   *Musings of a Musician: Recent Trends in Carnatic Music.*
               Bombay: Wilco Publishing House.
Rao, Bahadur, and L.K. Ananthakrishna Iyer
1931   *The Mysore Tribes and Castes, Vol. IV.* Mysore: Mysore
               University.
Rao, S.T. and Shankar Ramachandran.
2007   'The Cleveland Aradhana Festival Sustaining Sampradaya
               in North America.' *Sruti* 272: 12-3.
Ravi, N. ed.
1999   *The Hindu Speaks on Music.* Chennai: Kasthuri and Sons.

Reck, David

1984   'India/South India.' In *Worlds of Music: An Introduction to the Music of the World's Peoples*, eds. Jeff Todd Titon et al., 208-58. New York: Schirmer.

Reiniche, Marie-Louise

1979   *Les Dieux et les Hommes: Etude des cultes d'un Village du Tirunelveli Inde du Sud*. Paris: Mouton Editeur.

Reynolds, Holly Baker

1978   'To Keep the Tali Strong': Women's Rituals in Tamilnad, India.' Ph.D. dissertation, University of Wisconsin-Madison.

1980   'The Auspicious Married Woman.' In *The Power of Tamil Women*, ed., Susan Wadley, 35-60. Syracuse: Syracuse University.

Ries, Reymond E.

1969   'The Cultural Setting of South Indian Music.' *Asian Music* 1/2: 22-31.

1971   'Traditional Society and Kamatic Music.' In *Proceedings of the Second International Conference Seminar of Tamil Studies 1968, Vol. II*, ed., R.E. Asher, 466-73. Madras: International Association of Tamil Research.

Roche, Patrick A.

1975   'Caste and the British Merchant Government in Madras, 1639-1749.' *Indian Economic and Social History Review* 12/4: 381-407.

Rosaldo, Renato

1989   'Imperialist Nostalgia.' *Representations* 26: 107-22.

Rottler, J.P.

1834   *Dictionary of the Tamil and English Languages*. Madras: The Vepery Mission Press.

Row, T. Venkasami

1883   *A Manual of the District of Tanjore in the Madras Presidency*. Madras: Lawrence Asylum Press.

Ryan, Michael

1988   'The Politics of Film: Discourse, Psychoanalysis, Ideology.' In *Marxism and the Interpretation of Culture*, eds., Cary Nelson and Lawrence Grossberg, 477-86. Urbana: University of Illinois Press.

Ryerson, Charles A.
1988   *Regionalism and Religion: The Tamil Renaissance and Popular Hinduism.* Madras: The Christian Literature Society.

Sadasivam, M.S.
1992   'Tiruvāvaḍuduṟai Em. Rājarattiṉam Piḷḷai.' *Panan* 1/5: 31-4.

Said, Edward W.
1978   *Orientalism.* New York: Vintage Books.

Sakata, Hiromi Lorraine
1983   *Music in the Mind: The Concepts of Music and Musicians in Afghanistan.* Kent: Kent State University Press.

Sambamurthy (Sambamoorthy), P.
1939   'Madras as a Seat of Musical Learning.' In *Madras Tercentenary Commemoration Volume*, 429-37. London: Oxford University Press.

1952   *A Dictionary of South Indian Music and Musicians, Volume I (A-F).*Madras: Indian Music Publishing House.

1959   *A Dictionary of South Indian Music and Musicians, Volume II (G-K).* Madras: Indian Music Publishing House.

1968   *The Flute.* Madras: Indian Music Publishing House.

1970   *Great Composers II: Tyagaraja (2nd edition).* Madras: Indian Music Publishing House.

1971a   *A Dictionary of South Indian Music and Musicians, Volume III (L-N).* Madras: Indian Music Publishing House.

1971b   'Chidambaram and Its Musical Importance.'*MAS*, unpaged.

1976   *Catalogue of Musical Instruments Exhibited in the Government Museum.* Madras: Government of Tamil Nadu.

1982a   *South Indian Music, Book TV (5th edition).* Madras: Indian Music Publishing House.

1982b   *South Indian Music, Book V (4th edition).* Madras: Indian Music Publishing House.

1982c   *South Indian Music, Book VI (2nd edition).* Madras: Indian Music Publishing House.

1982d   *History of Indian Music.* Madras: Indian Music Publishing House.

1983   *South Indian Music, Book III (8th edition).* Madras: Indian Music Publishing House.

1985a   *Great Musicians (2nd edition).* Madras: Indian Music Publishing House.

1985b   *Great Composers, Book I (4th edition)*. Madras: Indian Music
               Publishing House.
1986   *The Melakarta Janya-Raga Scheme*. Madras: The Indian
               Music Publishing House.

Saminadaiya, U.V.
1945(1936)   *Mahā Vaittiyanādaiyar*. Madras: Kaliyanasundara Aiyar
               (Author's son). In Tamil.

Sangeeta Vimarsaka
1931   'South Indian Music To-Day: Technical Compositions.'
               The Hindu (1 February).

Sankaran, T.
n.d.   'Nagaswaram: The Periya Mēḷam.' Unpublished
               manuscript. 23pp.
1961   *Isai Mēdaikaḷ*. Madras: Tamil Isai Sangam. In Tamil.
1964   'Sembonnārkōyil Rāmasvāmi Piḷḷai.' *MAS*, unpaged. In
               Tamil.
1974   'Nādasura Vittuvān Padmasrī Tiruvīḷimiḷalai E.S.
               Subbaramaṇiya Piḷḷai Avarh aḷin Vāḷkkai Varalāṟu.' In
               Paṉ Ārāycci Veḷḷi Viḻā Siṟappu Malar, 108-9. Madras: Tamil
               Isai Sangam. In Tamil.
1976   'The Nagaswaram Tradition Systematized by Ramasami
               Dikshitar.' *Indian Musicological Society*, 16-21.
1981(1967)   'T.N. Rajaratnam Pillai.' In *Sangeet Natak Silver Jubilee
               Volume*, 290-8.
1983   'The (Old) Boys of Tiruveezhimizhalai.' *Sruti* 2: 18-20.
1984a   'Bala's Musicians.' *Journal of the Sangeet Natak Akademi*
               72-73: 61-5.
1984b   'A Few Music Dynasties of South India.' *Vivekananda
               Kendra Patrika* 13/2: 181-6.
1986a   'Nāgasvaram.' In *Seminar Papers on Performing Arts of the
               Southern Region-Dance Styles, and on Nāgasvaram, Tavil and
               Bhajana Sampradayas in Southern Region*, 65-73. Madras:
               The Institute of Traditional Cultures.
1986b   'Women Singers.' *Kalakshetra Quarterly* 8/1-2: 58-65.
1987   *The Life of Music in South India*. Unpublished manuscript.
               96pp.
1988   'Ariyakudi: Seniority, A Magnificent Obsession.' *Sruti* 42:
               26.
1990a   'Obituary: Madurai Somasundaram.' *Sruti* 65: 16-7.

1990b   'The Nagaswara Tradition.' In *Studies in Indian Music and Allied Arts, Volume V*, eds., Leela Omchary and Deepti Omchary Bhalla, 33-40. Delhi: Sundeep Prakashan.

Saranya, Arun

1988   'Idaṉāldāṉāappā?' [This is Why, Isn't It, Father?] *Kungumam* (28 October): 17-20. In Tamil.

Saraswathi, S.

1974   *Minorities in Madras State: Group Interests in Modern Politics.* Delhi: Impex India.

Sarma, S.S.

1936   'Nadaswaram or Nagaswaram: A Reply to Dr. Raghavan.' *The Hindu* (27 December).

Sasivalli, S.

1985   *Tamiḻar Tirumaṇam* [Tamil Marriage]. Madras: International Institute of Tamil Studies. In Tamil.

Satish, Rajeshwari

2007   'Difficulties of NRI Artists.' *Sruti* 269: 39

Sathyanarayana, R.

1987   'Karnataka Music: A Synoptic Survey.' In *Aspects of Indian Music: A Collection of Essays*, ed., Sumati Mutalkar, 29-75. New Delhi: Sangeet Natak Akademi.

Sauba

1990   'Oru Kalaimāmaṇiyiṉ Kaṇṇīr' [The Tears of an Artist]. *Ananda Vikatan* (25 February), 10-4. In Tamil.

Scott, James C.

1985   *Weapons of the Weak: Everyday Forms of Peasant Resistance.* New Haven: Yale University Press.

1990   *Domination and the Arts of Resistance: Hidden Transcripts.* New Haven: Yale University Press.

Seetha (Sita), S.

1973   'History of Anandabhairavi Raga.' *Journal of the Madras University* 45/2: 21-8.

1981   *Tanjore as a Seat of Music.* Madras: University of Madras.

Selvaganapati, Sanmuka

1996   *Tamiḻisai Ādimūmmurtti Sīkāḻi Aruṇācalak Kavirāyar.* [The Original Trinity of *Tamiḻ Isai*, Seerkazhi Arunachala Kavirayar]. Tanjavur: Karpakam Padippaham.

Seshagopalan, Madurai

1983   'Point-Counterpoint.' *Sruti* 3: 35.

Sewell, Robert
1980(1900)   *A Forgotten Empire (Vijayanagar): A Contribution to the History of India.* New Delhi: Asian Educational Service.

Shanmukasundaram Pillai, Valangaiman A.
1980   'Tavil Kalai.' In *Tamilnadu Eyal Isai Nataka Mandram-Madras, Silver Jubilee Souvenir,* 109-10. In Tamil.

Shankar, Vidya
1970   *Shyama Sastri.* New Delhi: National Book Trust.
1985   *The Art and Science of Carnatic Music.* Madras: The Music Academy, Madras.

Shankari, Uma
1984   'Brahman, King and Bhakta in a Temple in Tamil Nadu.' *Contributions to Indian Sociology* 18/2: 169-87.

Shelvankar, R.S.
1937   'Literature and the Arts in Maratha Tanjore.' In *South Indian Maharashtrians,* 160-2. Madras: The Mahratta Education Fund.

Sherring, M.A.
1881   *Hindu Tribes and Castes, Vol. III.* Calcutta: Thacker, Spink, and Co.

Shils, Edward A.
1975   *Center and Periphery: Essays in Macrosociology.* Chicago: University of Chicago Press.

Shiva Kumar, S.
1985   'Mali, the Man.' *Frontline* (28 June-11 July): 117.

Shoberl, Frederic, ed.
1822   *The World in Miniature: Hindoostan.* London: Ackerman.

Simmel, Georg
1971   *On Individuality and Social Forms: Selected Writings.* Chicago: University of Chicago Press.

Simon, Robert Leopord
1983   *Spiritual Aspects of Indian Music.* Delhi: Sundeep Prakashan.

Singer, Milton
1972   *When A Great Tradition Modernizes: An Anthropological Approach to Indian Civilization.* New York: Praeger Publishers.

Sinnathamby, S.
1985   'G.N.B.: Some Reflections.' In *G.N.B. 75th Birthday Celebrations Souvenir,* 37-9. Madras: G.N.B. Trust.

Siraj al-Hassan, Syed
1920   *The Castes and Tribes of H.E.H. The Nizam's Dominions.*
            Bombay: The Times Press.
Sitaramiah, V.
1971   *Prandaradasa.* New Delhi: National Book Trust.
Sittart
1983   'Kriṣṇn Nādam.' *Kalki* (18 December): 5. In Tamil.
Sivan, Papanasam
1993   'Interview by N.S. Ramachandran and S. Sethraman.'
            Sangeet Natak 108-109: 3-9.
Sivaramakrishnan, N.
n.d.   'Traditional Nagaswaram Music at Thiruvarur Temple.'
            Unpublished manuscript. Pp.3.
1985   'Nathaswaram and Thavil: Give Them a Place in the Sun!'
            Tamil Information 1/6: 19.
Sivasubramaniya Pillai, Tiruppamburam S.
1979   'Tiruppāmburam Naṭarājasundaram Piḷḷai.' *TIVM* 78-79.
            In Tamil.
Sivavadivel, G.
1992   'Nāgasvara Cakravartti T.N. Rājarattiṉam Piḷḷai.' In *Isai
            Vēḷāḷar Māanāḍu Siṟappu Malar.* Unpaged.
Skelton, William
1971   'The Nagaswaram and the South Indian Hindu Festival.'
            Asian Music 2: 18-23.
Slawek, Stephen M.
1991   'Ravi Shankar as Mediator between a Traditional Music
            and Modernity.' In *Ethnomusicology and Modern Music
            History*, eds., Stephen Blum, Philip V. Bohlman, and
            Daniel M. Neuman, 161-80. Urbana: University of Illinois
            Press.
Slobin, Mark
1976   *Music in the Culture of Northern Afghanistan.* Tucson:
            University of Arizona Press.
Soranadan, P.
1998   *Nāgasura Cakravartti Tiruvāḍuduṟai Ti. Eṉ. Rājarattiṉam
            Piḷḷai Varalāṟu.*
            [A Biography of T.N. Rajarattinam Pillai, the Emperor of
            Nagasuram]. Chennai: Risabam Padippaham.

South Indian Inscriptions
1982-86   New Delhi: Navarang. In twelve volumes. Originally
               published by Archaeological Survey of India, Madras in
               1885-1913.

Srinivas, M.N.
1952   *Religion and Society among the Coorgs of South India.* Oxford:
               Oxford University Press.
1971   *Social Change in Modern India.* Berkeley: University of
               California Press.

Srinivasa Iyer (Srinivasier), Semmangudi
1978   'My Gurukula Days.' *Kalakshetra Quarterly* 1/1: 40-4.
1986a   'Those Were the Days.' *Kalakshetra Quarterly* 8/1-2: 19-25.
1986b   *Maharaja Swathi Thimnal.* New Delhi: National Book
               Trust.

Srinivasachari, C.S.
1939   *History of the City of Madras.* Madras: P. Varadachary.

Srinivasan, Amrit
1983   'The Hindu Temple-Dancer: Prostitute or Nun?' *Cambridge
               Anthropology* 8/1: 73-99.
1984   'Temple "Prostitution" and Community Reform: An
               Examination and Textual Context of the Devadasi of
               Tamil Nadu.' Ph.D. dissertation, Cambridge University.
1985   'Reform and Revival: The Devadasi and her Dance.'
               Economic and Political Weekly 20/44: 1869-76.

Srinivasan, Manna
1991   'Valayapatti A.R. Subramaniam: New Dimensions to the
               Tavil.' *Sruti* 77: 43-4.
1993   'A History of Nagaswara and Tavil Vidwans.' *Sruti* 102:
               39-42.

Srinivasan, N.
1999   'Tyagaraja Mahotsavam in Tiruvaiyuru.' *Sruti* 173: 3-5

Srinivasan, N.S.
n.d.   'Origin and Development of Wind Instruments.' In *Vadya
               Kala,* 13-5. Madras: Development Centre for Musical
               Instruments.

Srinivasan, P.
1988   'Madeena Sastry.' *Sruti* 42: 5.

Srinivasan, R.
1962   *Facets of Indian Culture.* Mumbai: Bhartiya Vidya Bhavan.

1967　　　　　'Sri Tyagaraja: Musician Saint and Mystic.' *Bulletin of the Institute of Traditional Cultures*: 1-6.

Srinivasan, T.R.

1987　　　　　'Max Factor.' *Sruti* 33-34: 45

1990　　　　　'H. Ramachandra Sastri: Bringing Up the Rear.' *Sruti* 67: 27-8.

1991　　　　　'Maṟakka Muṭiyāda Maṇidar Ti. Ki. Jeyarāmaṉ' [The Unforgettable Man, D.K. Jayaraman] *Dinamani* (1 February).

Sruti

1983　　　　　'A Sruti Critique: Mandolin U. Srinivas.' 1: 42-3.

1984　　　　　'Famous Nagaswara Vidwan Passes Away.' 9: 4.

1987　　　　　'Sounds of Music: T.N. Seshagopalan.' 31: 41-2.

1988　　　　　'Notes on the Nagaswaram.' 42: 9.

Stam, Robert

1986　　　　　*Subversive Pleasures: Bakhtin, Cultural Criticism, and Film.* Baltimore: Johns Hopkins University Press.

Stauth, Georg and Bryan S. Turner

1988　　　　　'Nostalgia, Postmodernism and the Critique of Mass Culture.' *Theory, Culture & Society* 5: 509-26.

Stevenson, Sinclair

1971(1920)　　*The Rites of the Twice-Born.* New Delhi: Oriental Books Reprint Corp.

Subba Rao, B.

1984　　　　　*Raganidhi: A Comparative Study of Hindustani and Karnatak Ragas, Volume III.* Madras: The Music Academy, Madras.

Subbudu

1991　　　　　'Nādasvarappēṭṭaiyā, Nāmakiripēṭṭaiyā?' *Dinamani* (20 December). In Tamil.

Subotnik, Rose Rosengard

1991　　　　　*Developing Variations: Style and Ideology in Western Music.* Minneapolis: University of Minnesota Press.

Subrahmanian, N.

1983　　　　　*History of Tamil Nadu (A.D. 1565-1984).* Madurai: Ennes Publications.

Subramania Pillai, Palani

1954　　　　　'Vittuvāṉ Māṉpūṇṭiyā Piḷḷai.' *JMA* 25: 73-5. In Tamil.

Subramania Pillai, Tiruvizhimizhalai S.

n.d.　　　　　'Pallaviyiṉ Vaḷarcci' [The Development of Pallavi]. *TIVM:* 45-6. In Tamil.

1958   'Presidential Address.' *JMA* 28: 8-11.
Subramaniam, K.
1974   *Brahmin Priest of Tamil Nadu.* New York: John Wiley &
                  Sons.
Subramaniam, T.R.
1984   'The Pallavi of the Future, the Future of the Pallavi.' *Sruti*
                  6: 5-10.
1985   'GNB, The Complete Musician.' In *G.N.B. 75th Birthday
                  Celebrations Souvenir*, 75-9. Madras: G.N.B. Trust.
Subramaniam, V.
1969   'Emergence and Eclipse of Tamil Brahmins: Some
                  Guidelines to Research.' *Economic and Political Weekly*
                  4/28-30: 1133-6.
1988   'Muthutandavar: A Landmark Composer.' *Sruti* 87/88:
                  51-3.
1993   'The Historical Dialectic between Classical Music and
                  Dance in India.' *Sangeet Natak* 110: 22-30.
Subramanian, Lakshmi
1999   'The Invention of a Tradition: Nationalism, Carnatic
                  Music and the Madras Music Academy, 1900-1947.'
                  Indian Economic and Social History Review 36/2: 131-63
Subrahmanya Aiyar (Subramania Iyer), Musiri
1962   'Presidential Address.' *JMA* 33: 68-71.
1966   'Classical Music under the Impact of Industrial Change.'
                  In *Music East and West*, ed., Indian Council for Cultural
                  Relations, 143-5.
Suckling, Horatio John
1876   *Ceylon: A General Description of the Island, Historical,
                  Physical, Statistical.* London: Chapman & Hall.
Sugarman, Jance C.
2004   'Diasporic Dialogues: Mediated Musics and the Albanian
                  Transnation.' In *Identity and the Arts in Diaspora
                  Communities*, eds., Thomas Turino and James Lea, 21-38.
                  Warren, Michigan: Harmonic Park Press.
Sugimoto, Yoshio
1991   'Anchi-Burahuman: Tamirunadu no kasutosei to
                  kenryoku' [Anti-Brahman: Caste System and Power in
                  Tamil Nadu]. In *Dento Shukyo to Chishiki* [Traditional
                  Religion and Knowledge], ed., Sugimoto Yoshio, 65-120.
                  Nagoya: Manzam University.

2009   'Kanryusuruindo: Kaigaizariryuindojin no inpakuto' [Indian Circular Flow: The Impact of Non-resident Indians]. Programme note for the public talk at Oval Hall (Osaka, Japan).

Sujatha, G.

1987   'Socio-Religious Implications of Marriage Ceremonies.' In *Religion and Society in South India*, eds., V. Sudarsen, G. Prakash Reddy, and M. Suryanarayana, 107-1. Delhi: B.R. Publishing Corporation.

Sundaram, B.M.

n.d.   *Great Layavaadyakaaraas of Karnatak Music.* Bangalore: Percussive Art Centre.

1973   'Nāgappaṭṭiṉam Vēṉugōpalā Nāyaṉakkārar (1861-1917).' *TIVM* 72/73. In Tamil.

1975   'Dīkṣitariṉ Citaṟil Cilar.' *MAS*, unpaged. In Tamil.

1977   'Nāgasvara Isaiyulakil Sila Pallavik Kalaiñarkaḷ.' *MAS*, unpaged. In Tamil.

1979   'Tavilukku Oru Kurupīṭam.' *TIVM* 78/79. In Tamil.

1980   'Mirutaṅga Vittuvāṉ Tañjai Aṅgaṇṇa Nāyakkar.' *MAS*, unpaged. In Tamil.

1981   'Tirumarugaḷ Naṭēsa Nāyaṉakkārar (1874-1903).' *TIVM* 80/81. In Tamil.

1986   'Tavil.' In *Seminar Papers on Performing Arts of the Southern Region-Dance Styles, and on Nāgasvaram, Tavil and Bhajana Sampradayas in Southern Region*, 75-89. Madras: The Institute of Traditional Cultures.

1987/88   'Kottur Rajarathnam: A Musicians' Musician.' *Sruti* 39/40: 13.

1988   'Obituary: Injikudi E.P. Kandaswami.' *Sruti* 50: 8.

1990   *Ālayavaḻipāṭṭil Isai* [Music in Temple Worship]. Tanjavur: Tamil Palkalaikkalaham.

1992   *Mangala Isai Mannargal.* Madras: INTACH. In Tamil.

1998   *Nagaswara Chakravarthy T.N. Rajarathnam Pillai.* Bangalore: Percussive Arts Centre.

2001   *Maṅgala Isai Maṉṉargaḷ* [The Kings of Auspicious Music]. Chidambaram: Meyyappan Tamilayvaham.

Sundaram, S.P.

1996   'Please Don't Desecrate Tyagaraja's Memory.' *Sruti* 145: 17-8.

Sundaram, V.P.K.
1985   *Tamiḻisai Vaḷam* [The Resources of *Tamiḻ Isai*]. Madurai:
        Madurai Kamaraj University. In Tamil.
1992-97   *Tamiḻisai Kalaikkaḷañciyam* [The Encyclopedia of *Tamiḻ Isai*]
        Vols 1-3, Tiruccirappalli: Baratidasan Palkalaikkalaham.
        In Tamil.

Sundararajan, Saroja
1989   *March to Freedom in Madras Presidency 1916-1947*. Madras:
        Lalitha Publications.

Sundararajan (Su. Ra.), V.S.
1987   *Irupadām Nūṟṟāṇḍin Saṅgīta Mēdaihaḷ* [*Musical Geniuses of
        the Twentieth Century*]. Madras: The Alliance Company.
        In Tamil.

Surya Prasad, M.
1988   'The Rich Tradition of Nagaswara.' *The Hindu* (5
        February).

Suttananda Baradiyar
1965   'Innūlāsiriyar Tiru Em. Ji. Kuppusāmi Avarkaḷin
        Vāḻkkai Varalāṟu.' [The Biography of the Author,
        M.G. Kuppusami]. In *Saṅgīta Taḷa Rāga Mālai* by M.G.
        Kuppusami, 171-8. Madras: K. Subramaniyam. In Tamil.

Suvaminadan, Ariyamangalam
1965   'Nī Oru Maṇucaṉā?' *Kalki* (3 January): 36-40. In Tamil.

Suvaminadan, Gomadi
1964   'Ippadiyum Aḷaikkalām.' [You Can Also Call It Like
        This]. *Kalki* (27 November): 77. In Tamil.

Svami, N.V.R.
1988   'Nāgasvaram Eppaḍi Vāsikka Vēṇḍum?' [How Should
        Nāgasvaram Be Played?] *Dinamani* (25 December). In
        Tamil.

Swamy, B.G.L.
1979   *Chidambaram and Nataraja: Problems and Rationalization*.
        Mysore: Geetha Book House.

Swedenburg, Ted
1991   'Popular Memory and the Palestinian National Past.' In
        *Golden Ages, Dark Ages: Imagining the Past in Anthropology
        and History*, eds., Jay O'Brien and William Roseberry, 152-
        79. Berkeley: University of California Press.

Takimura, Ryuichi

1988   'Ryukono "Shakaishi" towananika: Sono Hohotekikaitai' [What is the Prevailing 'Social History': An Analysis of its Methodology]. *Shicho* 24: 27-44. In Japanese.

Tamayandi

1983   'Sikāmaṇi Sōmu.' *Kalki* (18 December): 31. In Tamil.

Tamil Isai Saṅgam

1967   *Tamiḻ Isai Sangam Veḷḷi Viḻa Siṟappu Malar 1943-1968* [The Special Issue of Tamil Isai Sangam's Silver Year, 1943-68]. Chennai: Tamil Isai Sangam.

1992   *Tamiḻ Isai Sangam Poṉ Viḻa Siṟappu Malar 1943-1993* [The Special Issue of Tamil Isai Sangam's Golden Year, 1943-93]. Chennai: Tamil Isai Sangam.

Tandai Periyar *Tamiḻ Isai* Manram (TPTIM)

1999   *Ēḻām Āṇḍu Isai Viḻa Isai Malar* [Souvenir Issue of the 7th Music Festival]. Chennai: Tandai Periyar Tamiḻ Isai Manram.

Tamiḻ Isai Vira Malar (TIVM)

1974   'Isai Pēraṟiñar Vīrusāmi Piḷḷai.' 65-66. In Tamil.

Tanihai, R.

1990   'Mudalil Kōvil Piṟakudāṉ Kaccēri!' [The Temple First, Then a Concert!]. *Ananda Vikatan* (16 December). In Tamil.

Tarabout, Gilles

1996   *Sacrifier et Donner a Voiren Pays Malabar: Les Fetes de Temple au Kerala (Inde du Sud)*. Paris: Ecole Francaised'Extreme-Orient.

Tarlekar, G.H., and Nalini Tarlekar

1972   *Musical Instruments in Indian Sculpture*. Poona: Pune Vidyarthi Griha Prakashan.

Terada, Yoshitaka

1996   'Effects of Nostalgia: The Discourse of Decline in Periya Melam Music of South Indian Culture.' *Bulletin of the National Museum of Ethnology* 21/4: 921-39

1999   'Book Review of William Jackson, Tyagaraja and the Renewal of Tradition: Translations and Reflections.' *Journal of the Japanese Society of Musicology* 44/2: 131-5

2000   'T.N. Rajarattinam Pillai and Caste Rivalry in South Indian Classical Music.' *Ethnomusicology* 44/3: 460-89

2008   '*Tamiḻ Isai* as a Challenge to Brahmanical Music Culture in South India.' *Music and Society in South Asia: Perspectives from Japan*, ed. Yoshitaka Terada, 203-26. Osaka: National Museum of Ethnology.

Thani Nayagam, Xavier S., ed.
1966   *Antao de Proenca'e Tamil-Portuguese Dictionary, A.D. 1679.* Kuala Lumpur: University of Malaya.

Thirumalai
1974   'Papanasam Sivan: The Tamil Tyagaraja.' *The Illustrated Weekly of India* 96 (28 December), 43-5.

Thurston, Edgar
1909   *Castes and Tribes of Southern India.* In seven volumes. Madras: Government Press.

Thyagarajan, S.K.
1967   *Nadhopasana.* Palni: Sarada Publishing House.

Tiyagarajan, K.C.
1968   *Isaippaṇbu* [Musicality]. Madras: Amudasurabi Accaham. In Tamil.

Tonkin, Elizabeth, Maryon McDonald, and Malcolm Chapman.
1989   'Introduction.' In *History and Ethnicity*, eds., Elizabeth Tonkin et al., 1-21. London: Routledge.

Trawick, Margaret
1990   'The Ideology of Love in a Tamil Family.' In *Divine Passions: The Social Constitution of Emotion in India*, ed., Owen Lynch, 37-63. Berkeley: University of California Press.

Tsuge, Gen'ichi
1991   *Sekai Ongaku eno Shotai: Minzokuongakugaku Nyumon* [Invitation to World Music: Introduction to Ethnomusicology]. Tokyo: Ongakunotomosha. In Japanese.

Tumilan (N. Ramasami)
1988   *Nādasura Cakkaravartti Rājarattiṇam Piḷḷai.* Madras: Vanadi Padippaham. In Tamil.

Turino, Thomas
1984   'Structure, Context, and Strategy in Musical Ethnography.' *Ethnomusicology* 34/3: 399-412.

Turner, Bryan S.
1987   'A Note on Nostalgia.' *Theory, Culture & Society* 4: 147-56.

Turton, Andrew, and Shigeharu Tanabe, eds.

1984   'Introduction.' In *History and Peasant Consciousness in South East Asia* (*Senri Ethnological Studies* 13), eds., Andrew Turton and Tanabe Shigeharu, 1-8. Osaka: National Museum of Ethnology.

Uma, K.

1987   'Music in Some of the Leading Temples of Kerala and Tamilnad.' In *Studies in Indian Music and Allied Arts, Volume III*, eds., Leela Omchery and Deepti Omchery Bhalla, 171-237. Delhi: Sundeep Prakashan.

University of Madras

1924-36   *Tamil Lexicon.* In seven volumes.

Vaidyanatha Bhagavathar, Sulamangalam (Soolamangalam)

1946   'Nadaswaram Vidwans,' trans. R. Ramanuja Iyenger. *The Hindu* (11 October).

1986   'Great Nagaswara Vidwans: Tirumarugal Natesan.' *Shanmukha* 12/4: 17-8.

Vander, Judith

1988   *Songprints: The Musical Experience of Five Shoshone Women.* Urbana: University of Illinois Press.

Varadaccari, K.

1977   'Eṉṉuḍaiya Saṅgīta Niṉaivuhaḷ' [My Thoughts on Music]. In *Tiger Varadachariar Birth Centenary Commemoration Volume*, ed., T.S. Parthasarathy, 32-8. Madras: Tiger Varadachariar Birth Centenary Celebration Committee. In Tamil.

Vasudevan, D.V.

1965   'Able Exponent of the Clarionet.' *The Hindu* (14 January).

1989   'Judicious Change in Format.' *The Hindu* (29 December).

Vatsyayan, Kapila

1968   *Classical Indian Dance in Literature and the Arts.* New Delhi: Sangeet Natak Akademi.

Vayuputra

1984   'Different Strokes.' *Sruti* 10: 42.

Vedagiri, T.S., K.S. Muthuraman, and K.S. Mahadevan

1985   *G.N.B.: A Biography.* Madras: G.B. Duraiswamy.

Venkatarama Iyer, T.L.

1967   'Sri Tyagaraja: An Appreciation.' *JSNA* 6: 5-10.

1968   *Muthuswami Dikshitar.* New Delhi: National Book Trust.

1979   'Muthuswami Dikshitar.' In *Cultural Leaders of India: Composers*, ed., V. Raghavan 55-65. New Delhi: Ministry of Information and Broadcasting.

Venkataraman, Janaki

1986   'Singer as Saint.' *Aside* 10/12-13: 18-22.

1989   'Warning!' *Aside* 13/23: 11-9.

1990   'A Riot in Madras.' *Aside* 14/18: 10-8.

1991   'Temples of Neglect.' *Aside* 15/17: 8-16.

Venkataramayyar, Mudikondan

1956   'Nāgasvara Vitvāṉ Tiruvīḷimiḷalai Subbiramaṇiya Piḷḷai.' *MAS*, 32-4. In Tamil.

1970   'Mahāvittuvāṉ Kōṉērirājapuram Vaittinādayyar.' *MAS*, unpaged. In Tamil.

1971   'Saṅgītam Aṉṟum Iṉṟum' [Music Then and Today] *MAS*, unpaged. In Tamil.

1989   'Pallavi Māmēdaihaḷ' [The Experts in Pallavi]. *Shanmukha* 15/4: 44-8. In Tamil.

Venkatraman, P.N.

1984   'GNB and His Great New Bani.' *Sruti* 7: 22-31.

Venkatramani, S.H.

1984   'Ruining the Temples.' *India Today* (31 May): 70-5.

Vijayaraghavacharya, V. ed.

1933   *Tirumalai-Tirupati Devasthanam Epigraphical Series Vol. II: Inscriptions of Saluva Narasimha's Time (from AD 1445 to A.D. 1504)*. Tirupati: Devasthanam Committee.

1937   *Tirumalai-Tirupati Devasthanam Epigraphical Series Vol. V: Inscriptions of Sadasivaraya's Time (from A.D. 1541 to A.D. 1574)*. Tirupati: Devasthanam Committee.

Virusvami Pillai, Tiruvidaimarudur

1949   'Nāgasvaram.' *JMA* 20: 110-3. In Tamil.

1962   'Presidential Address.' *JMA* 33: 14-20.

Viswanathan, E. Sa.

1982   'The Emergence of Brahmans in South India: With Special Reference to Tamil Nadu.' In *India: History of Thought*, ed., S.N. Mukheijee, 282-325. Calcutta: Subamarekha.

1983   *The Political Career of E.V. Ramasami Naicker: A Study in the Politics of Tamilnadu 1920-1949*. Madras: Ravi & Vasanth Publishers.

Visuvanadayyar, Maharajapuram
1980 'Kōṉērirājapuram Vaittinādayyar.' *MAS*, unpaged. In Tamil.
Viswanathan, Gomati
1981 'The Temple Music of South India.' *JMA* 52: 217-27.
Vishwanathan, Lakshmi
2003 *M.S. Subblakshmi.* New Delhi: Roli Books.
Viswanathan, T.
1966 'Traditional Music in South India: A Dynamic Force.' In *Music East and West,* ed., Indian Council for Cultural Relations, 186-91.
1975 'Raga Alapana in South Indian Music.' Ph.D. dissertation, Wesleyan University.
Volosinov, V.N.
1973 *Marxism and the Philosophy of Language.* Cambridge: Harvard University Press.
Washbrook, David A.
1975 'Political Change in a Stable Society: Tanjore District 1880 to 1920.' In *South India: Political Institutions and Political Change 1880-1940,* eds., Christopher Baker and David Washbrook, 20-68. Delhi: Macmillan.
1989 'Caste, Class and Dominance in Modern Tamil Nadu: Non-Brahmanism, Dravidianism and Tamil Nationalism.' In *Dominance and State Power in Modern India: Decline of a Social Order,* eds., Francine R. Frankel and M.S.A. Rao, 204-64. Delhi: Oxford University Press.
Weber, Max
1947 *The Theory of Social and Economic Organization.* New York: Oxford University Press.
1968 *On Charisma and Institution Building.* Chicago: University of Chicago Press.
Weinstein, Fred
1988 *History and Theory after the Fall: An Essay on Interpretation.* Chicago: University of Chicago Press.
Welbon, Guy R., and Glenn E. Yocum, eds.
1977 *Religious Festivals in South India and Sri Lanka.* New Delhi: Manohar.
Wheeler, James Talboys, and Michael Macmillan
1861-62 *Madras in the Olden Time: Being a History of the Presidency from the First Foundation.* Madras: Higginbotham.
1956 *European Travellers in India.* Culcutta: Susil Gupta.

White, Hayden
1973   *Metahistory: The Historical Imagination in Nineteenth-Century Europe.* Baltimore: Johns Hopkins University Press.

Williams, Raymond
1977   *Marxism and Literature.* Oxford: Oxford University Press.
1980   *Problems in Materialism and Culture: Selected Essays.* London: Verso.

Winslow, M.
1987(1862)   *A Comprehensive Tamil and English Dictionary.* Delhi: Asian Educational Services.

Wolf, Eric R.
1982   *Europe and The People without History.* Berkeley: University of California Press.

Wolf, Richard Kent
1989   'Innovation, Interpretation, and The Maintenance of Tradition in the Karaikkudi Style of Vina Playing.' MA thesis, University of Illinois at Urbana-Champaign.

Yamaguchi, Masao
1975   *Bunka to Ryogisei* [Culture and Duality]. Tokyo: Iwanamishoten. In Japanese.
1988   'Soon no Kigogaku' [Semiotics of Noise]. In *Nihon no Ongaku, Ajia no Ongaku, Vol. 4,* 313-27. Tokyo: Iwanamishoten. In Japanese.
1990(1978)   *Chi no Enkinho* [Perspectives on Knowledge]. Tokyo: Iwanamishoten. In Japanese.

Ziegenbalg, Bartholomaeus
1926   *Ziegenbalg's Malabarisches Heidenthum.* Amsterdam: Koninklijke Akademie van Wetenschaappen.